STOP!

This is the back of the book. You wouldn't want to spoil a great ending!

This book is printed "manga-style," in the authentic Japanese right-to-left format. Since none of the artwork has been flipped or altered, readers get to experience the story just as the creator intended. You've been asking for it, so TOKYOPOP® delivered: authentic, hot-off-the-press, and far more fun!

1
2
3
4
5
6
7
8
9
10

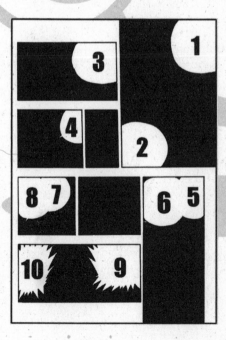

DIRECTIONS

If this is your first time reading manga-style, here's a quick guide to help you understand how it works.

It's easy... just start in the top right panel and follow the numbers. Have fun, and look for more 100% authentic manga from TOKYOPOP®!

THE MANGA REVOLUTION • LEADING THE MANGA REVOLUTION • LEADING

漫画革命

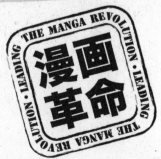

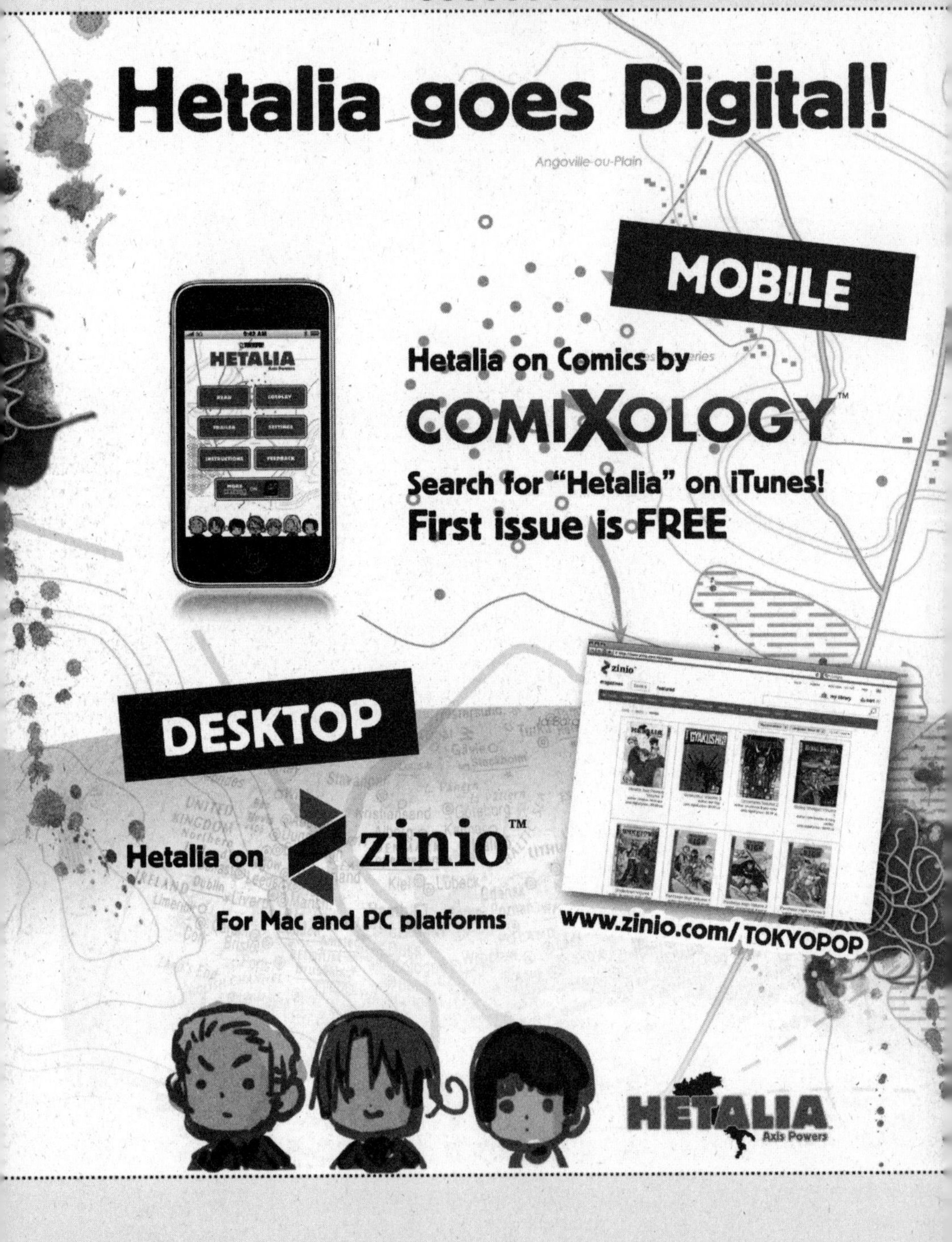
Hetalia goes Digital!
MOBILE
Hetalia on Comics by
COMIXOLOGY™
Search for "Hetalia" on iTunes!
First issue is FREE
DESKTOP
Hetalia on zinio™
For Mac and PC platforms
www.zinio.com/TOKYOPOP
HETALIA
Axis Powers

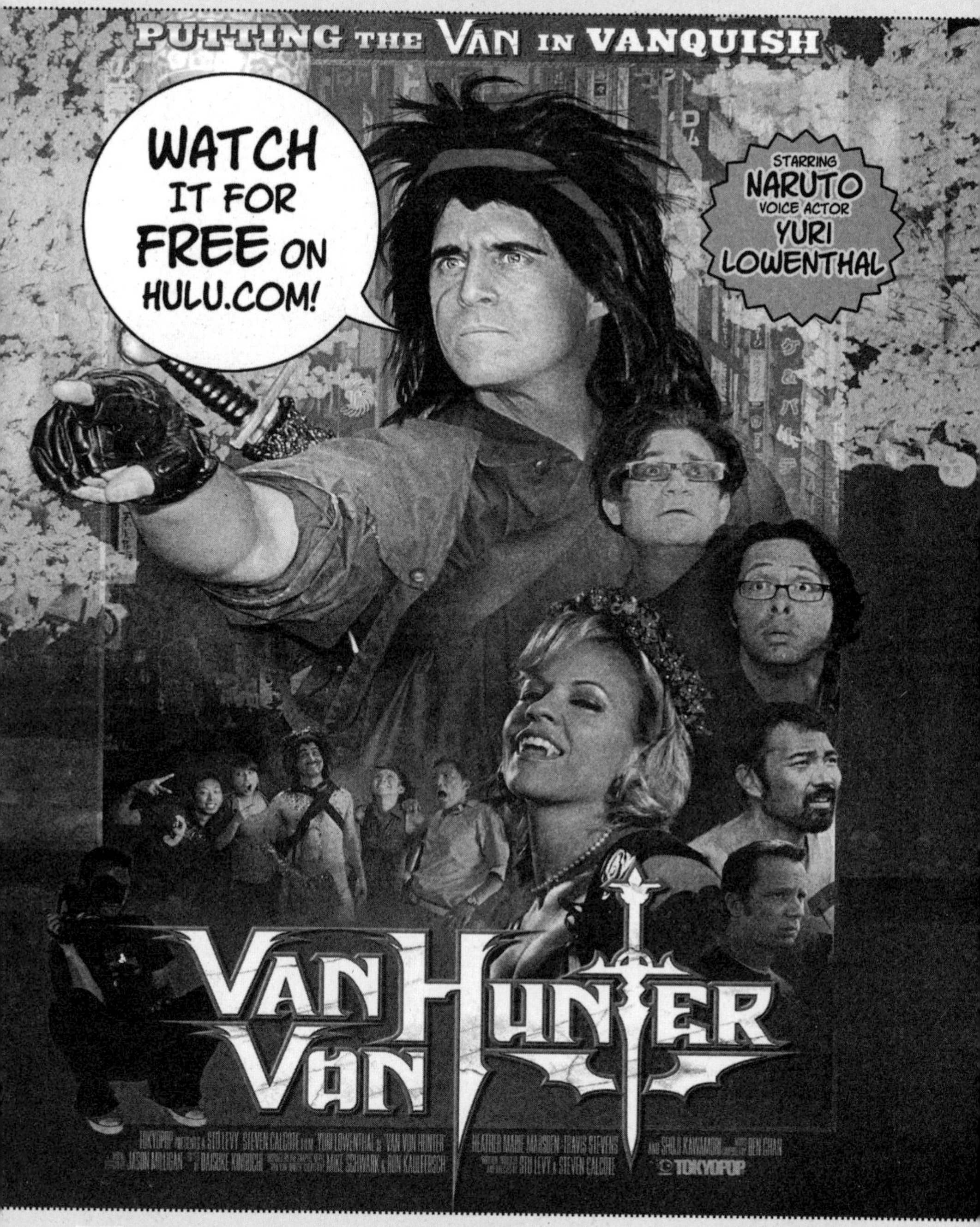
PUTTING THE VAN IN VANQUISH
WATCH IT FOR FREE ON HULU.COM!
STARRING NARUTO VOICE ACTOR YURI LOWENTHAL
VAN VON HUNTER
STU LEVY · STEVEN CALCOTE · YURI LOWENTHAL · "VAN VON HUNTER"
HEATHER MARIE MARSDEN · TRAVIS STEVENS
MIKE SCHWARK & RON KAUFERSCH
STU LEVY & STEVEN CALCOTE
BEN CHAN
TOKYOPOP

CHIBISAN DATE

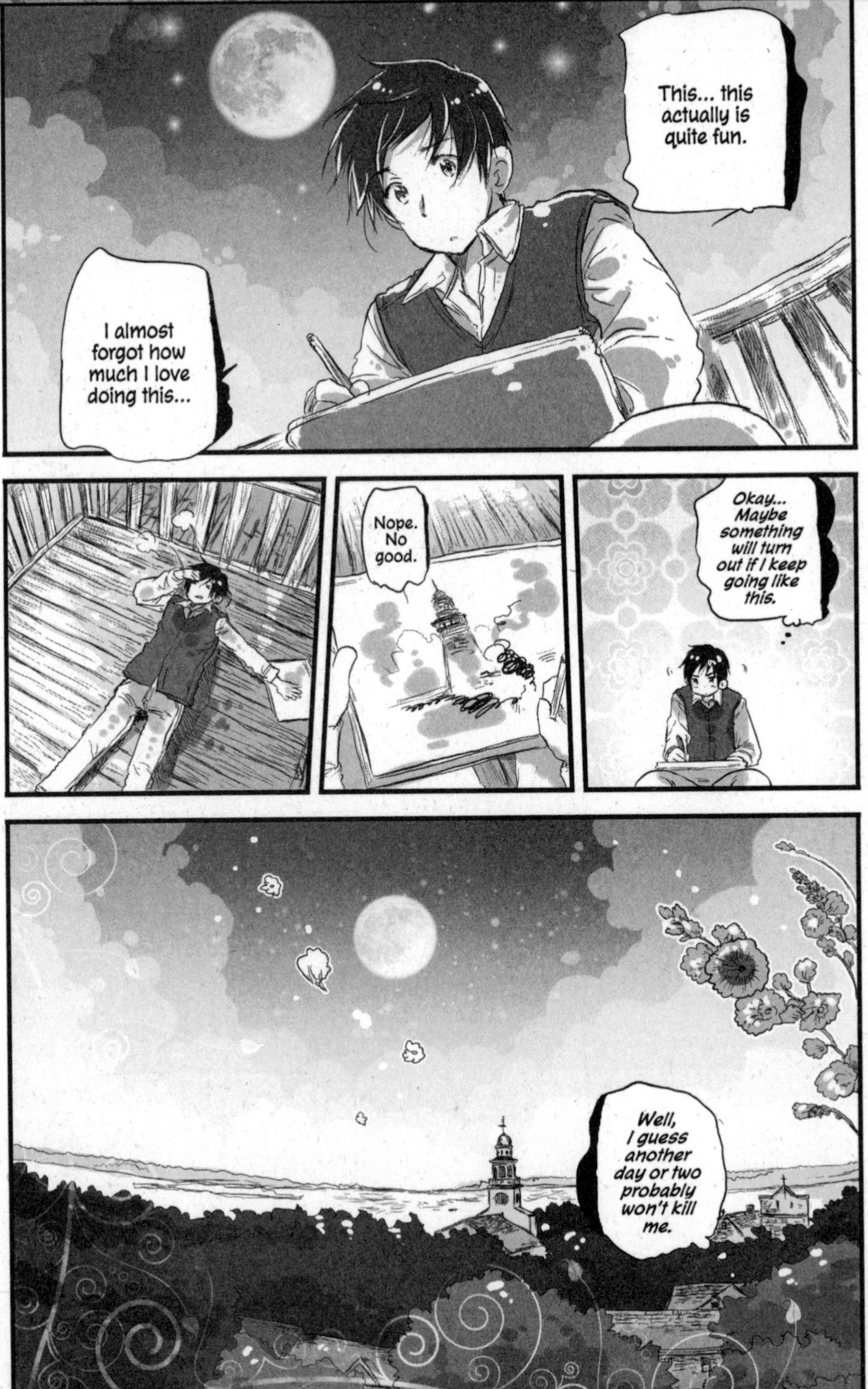
This... this actually is quite fun.
I almost forgot how much I love doing this...
Okay... Maybe something will turn out if I keep going like this.
Nope. No good.
Well, I guess another day or two probably won't kill me.

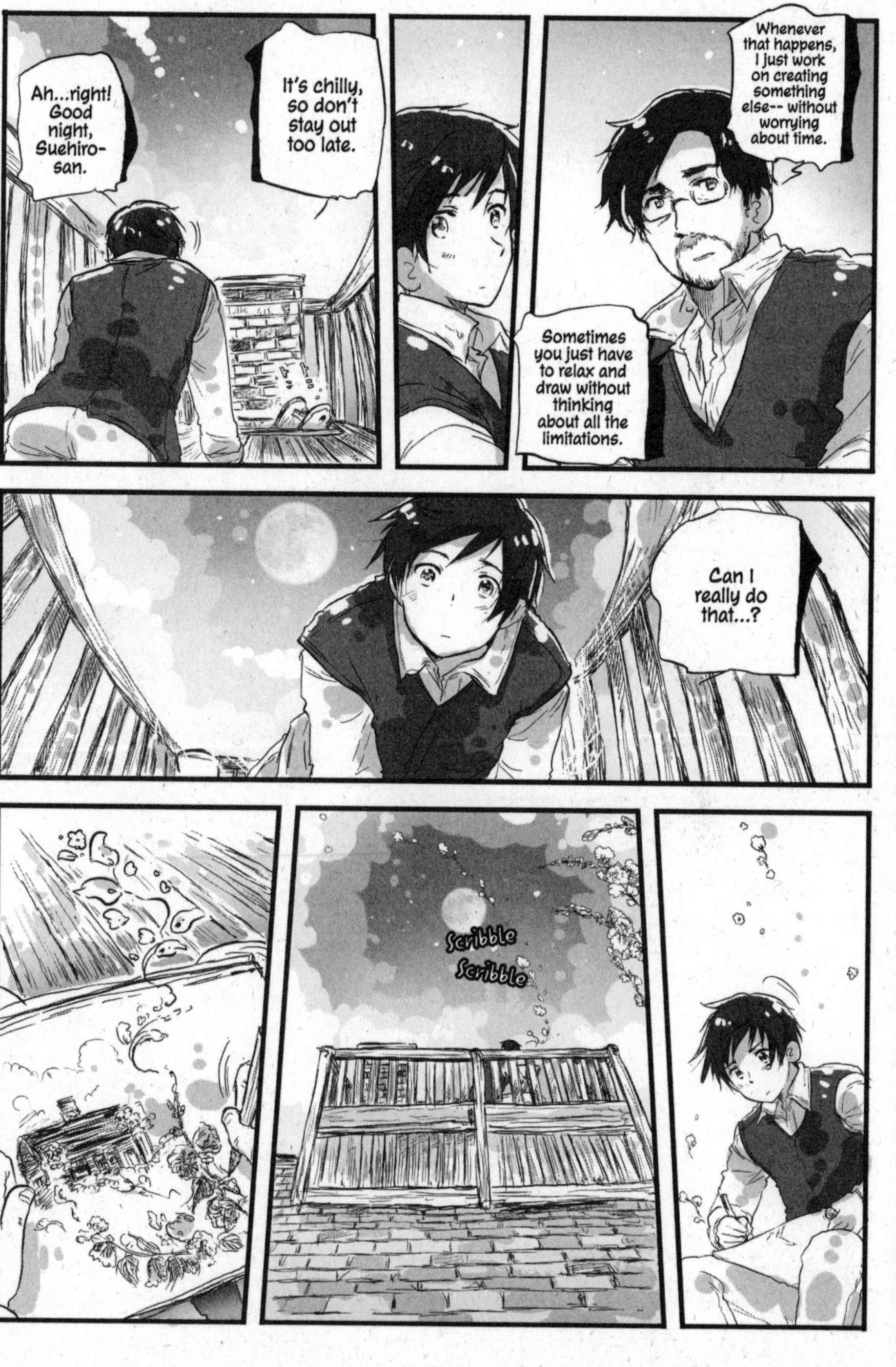
Whenever that happens, I just work on creating something else-- without worrying about time.
Sometimes you just have to relax and draw without thinking about all the limitations.
It's chilly, so don't stay out too late.
Ah...right! Good night, Suehiro-san.
Can I really do that...?
Scribble
Scribble

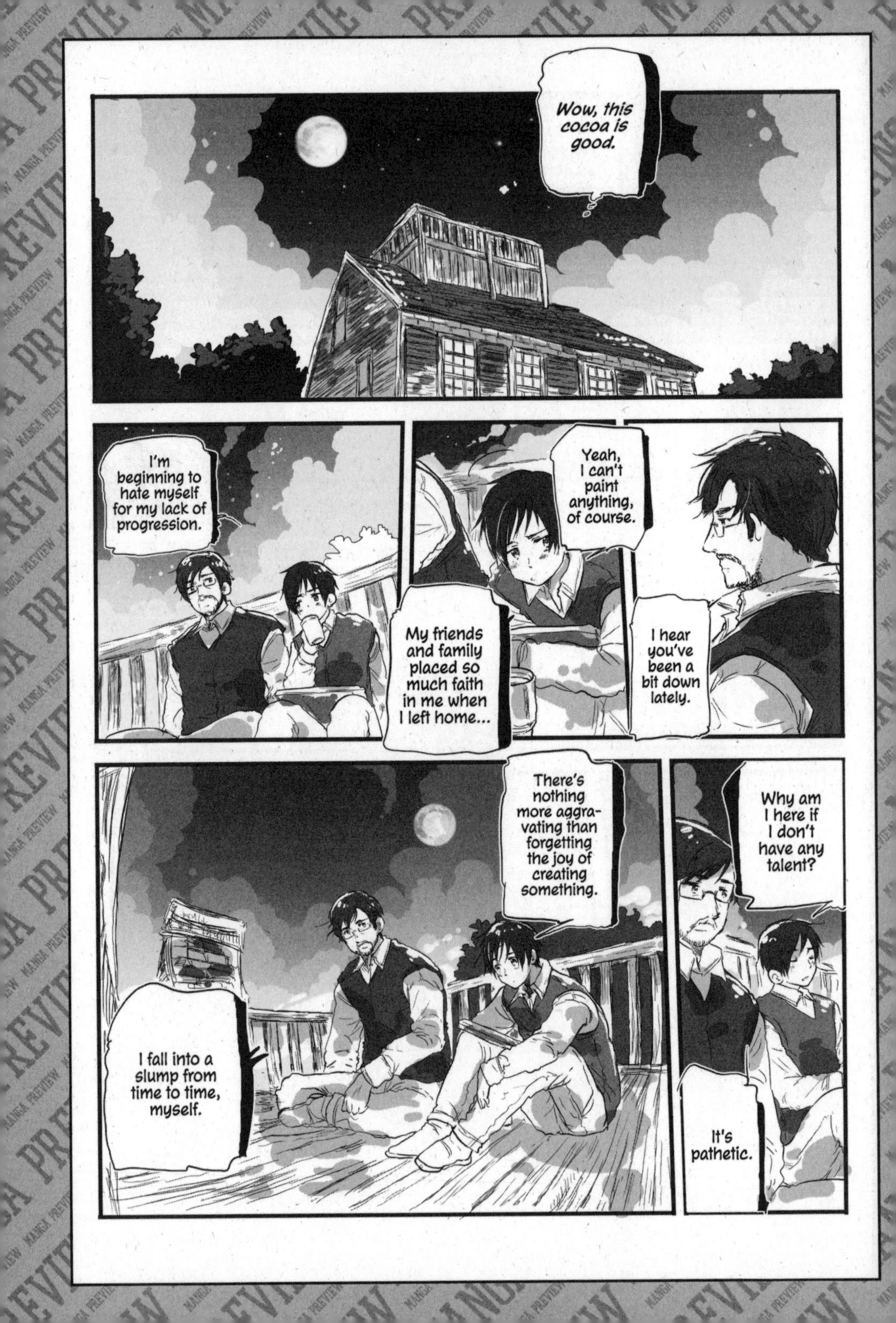
Wow, this cocoa is good.
I hear you've been a bit down lately.
Yeah, I can't paint anything, of course.
My friends and family placed so much faith in me when I left home...
I'm beginning to hate myself for my lack of progression.
Why am I here if I don't have any talent?
It's pathetic.
There's nothing more aggravating than forgetting the joy of creating something.
I fall into a slump from time to time, myself.

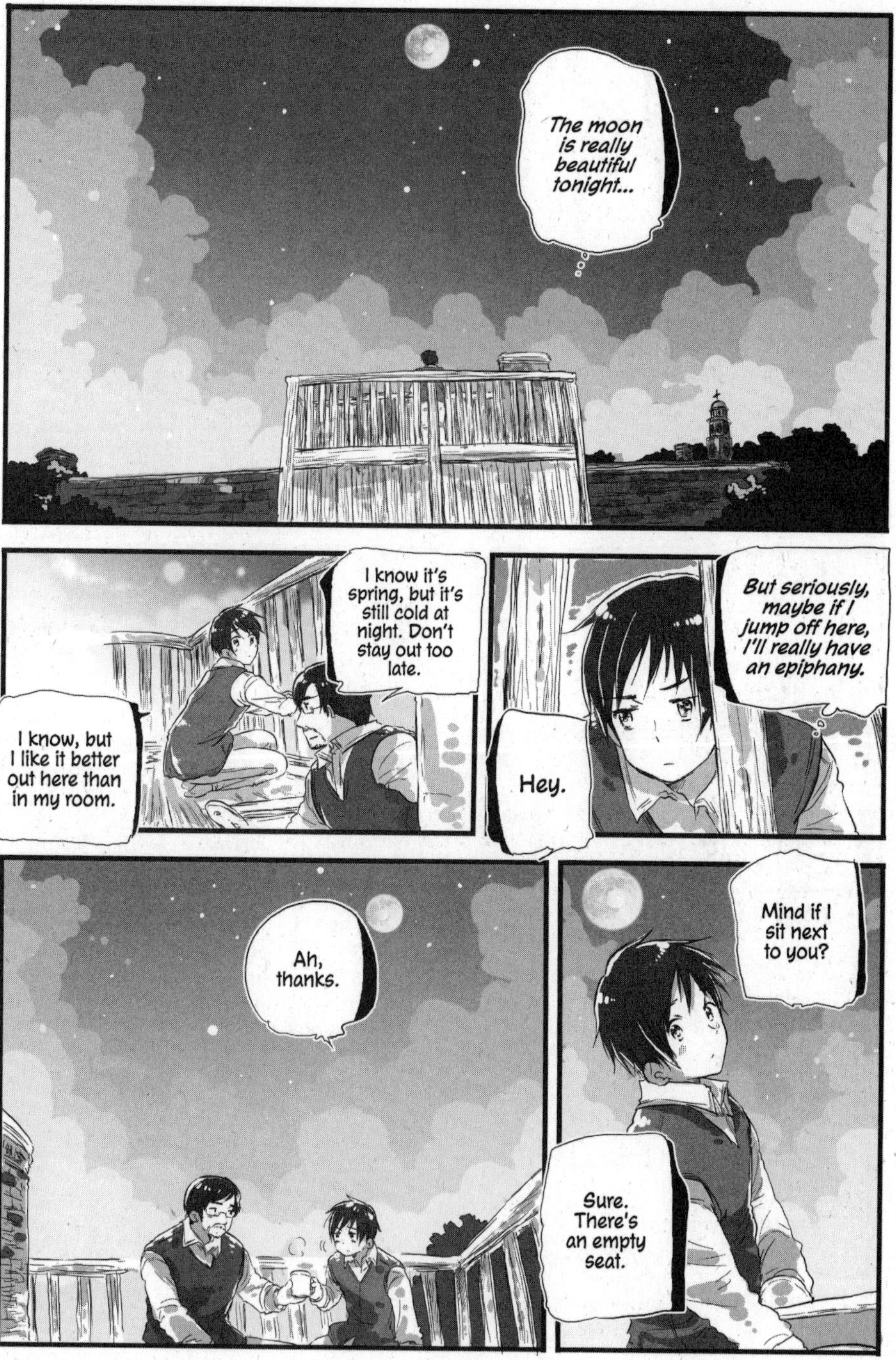
The moon is really beautiful tonight...
But seriously, maybe if I jump off here, I'll really have an epiphany.
Hey.
I know it's spring, but it's still cold at night. Don't stay out too late.
I know, but I like it better out here than in my room.
Mind if I sit next to you?
Sure. There's an empty seat.
Ah, thanks.

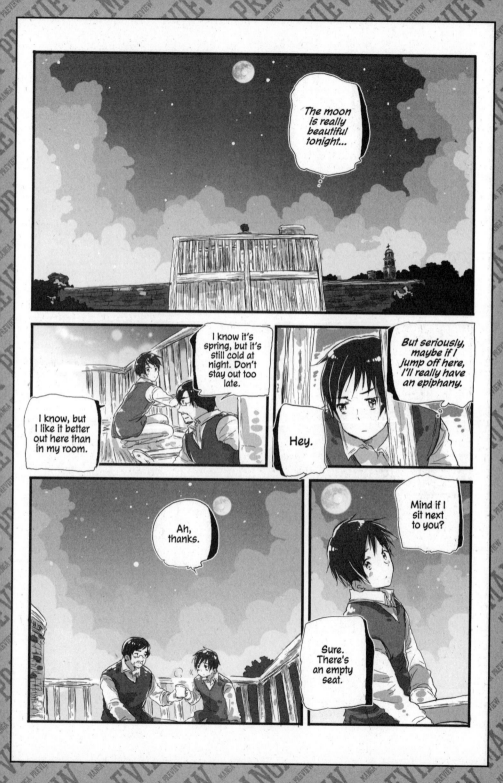

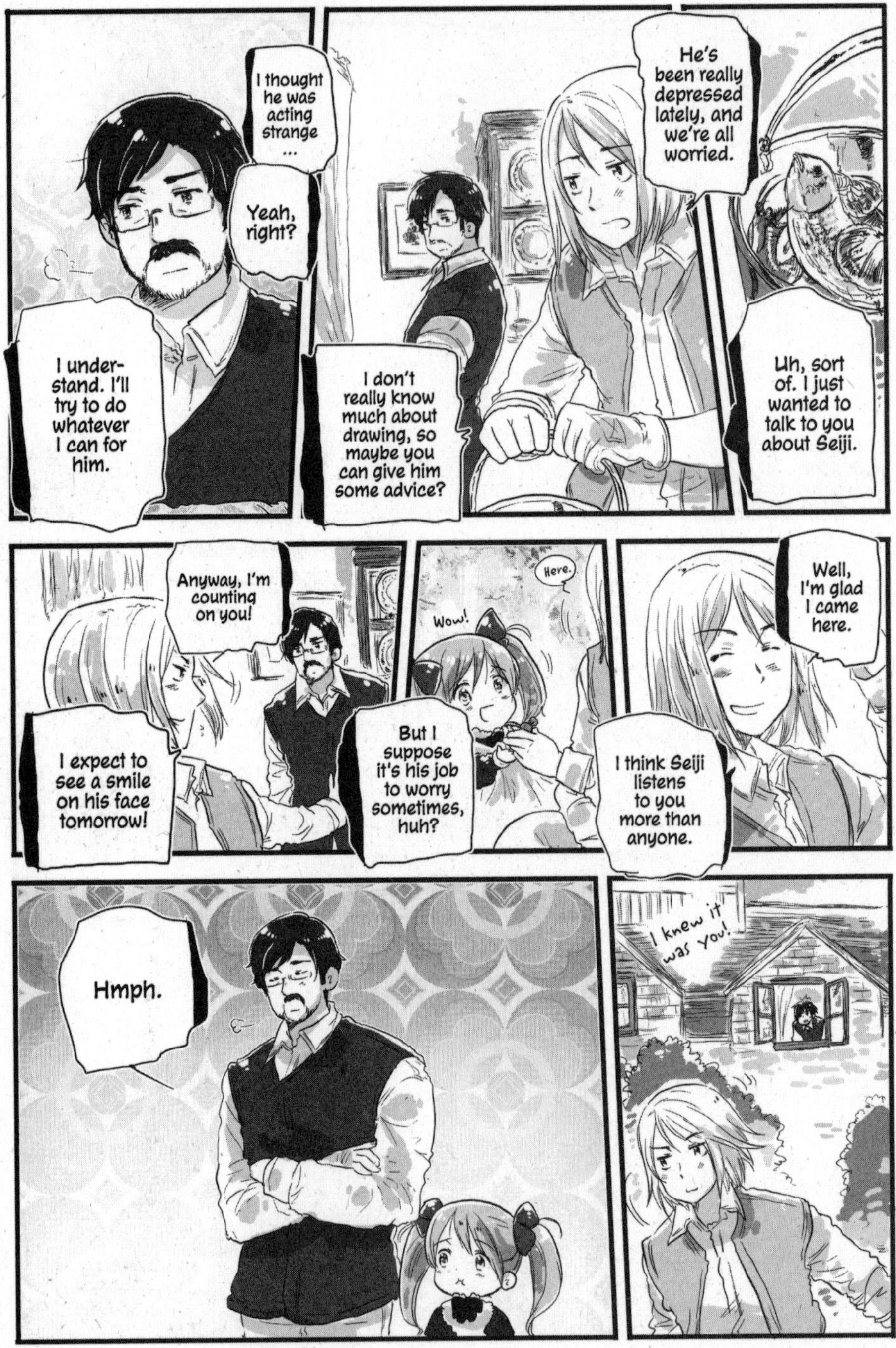
Uh, sort of. I just wanted to talk to you about Seiji.
He's been really depressed lately, and we're all worried.
I don't really know much about drawing, so maybe you can give him some advice?
I thought he was acting strange ...
Yeah, right?
I understand. I'll try to do whatever I can for him.
Well, I'm glad I came here.
I think Seiji listens to you more than anyone.
Here.
Wow!
But I suppose it's his job to worry sometimes, huh?
Anyway, I'm counting on you!
I expect to see a smile on his face tomorrow!
I knew it was you!
Hmph.

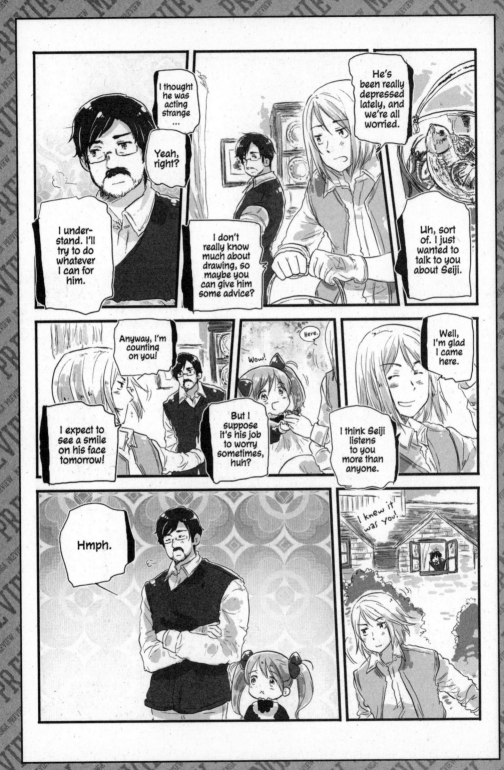

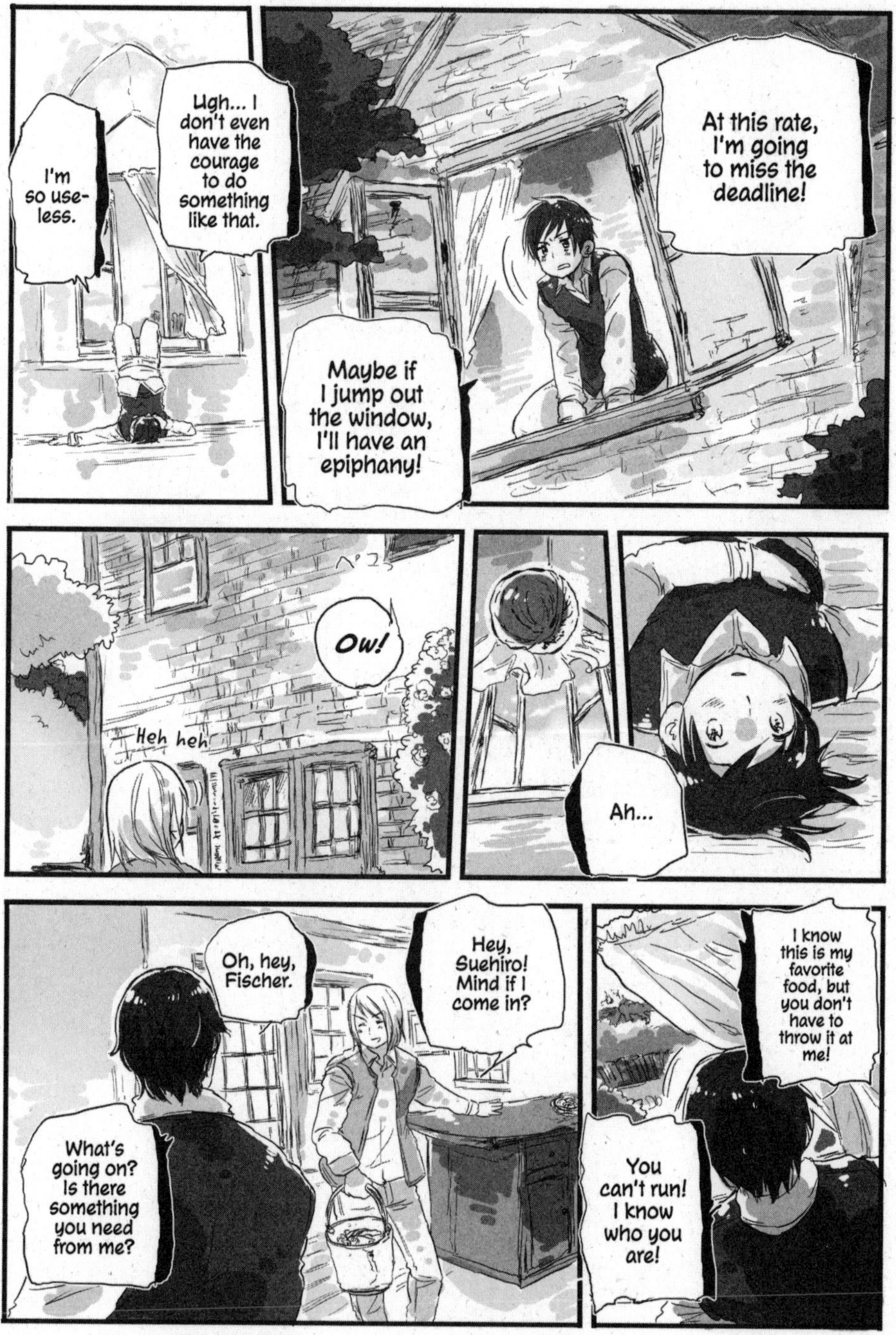
At this rate, I'm going to miss the deadline!
Maybe if I jump out the window, I'll have an epiphany!
Ugh... I don't even have the courage to do something like that.
I'm so useless.
Ah...
Ow!
Heh heh
I know this is my favorite food, but you don't have to throw it at me!
You can't run! I know who you are!
Hey, Suehiro! Mind if I come in?
Oh, hey, Fischer.
What's going on? Is there something you need from me?

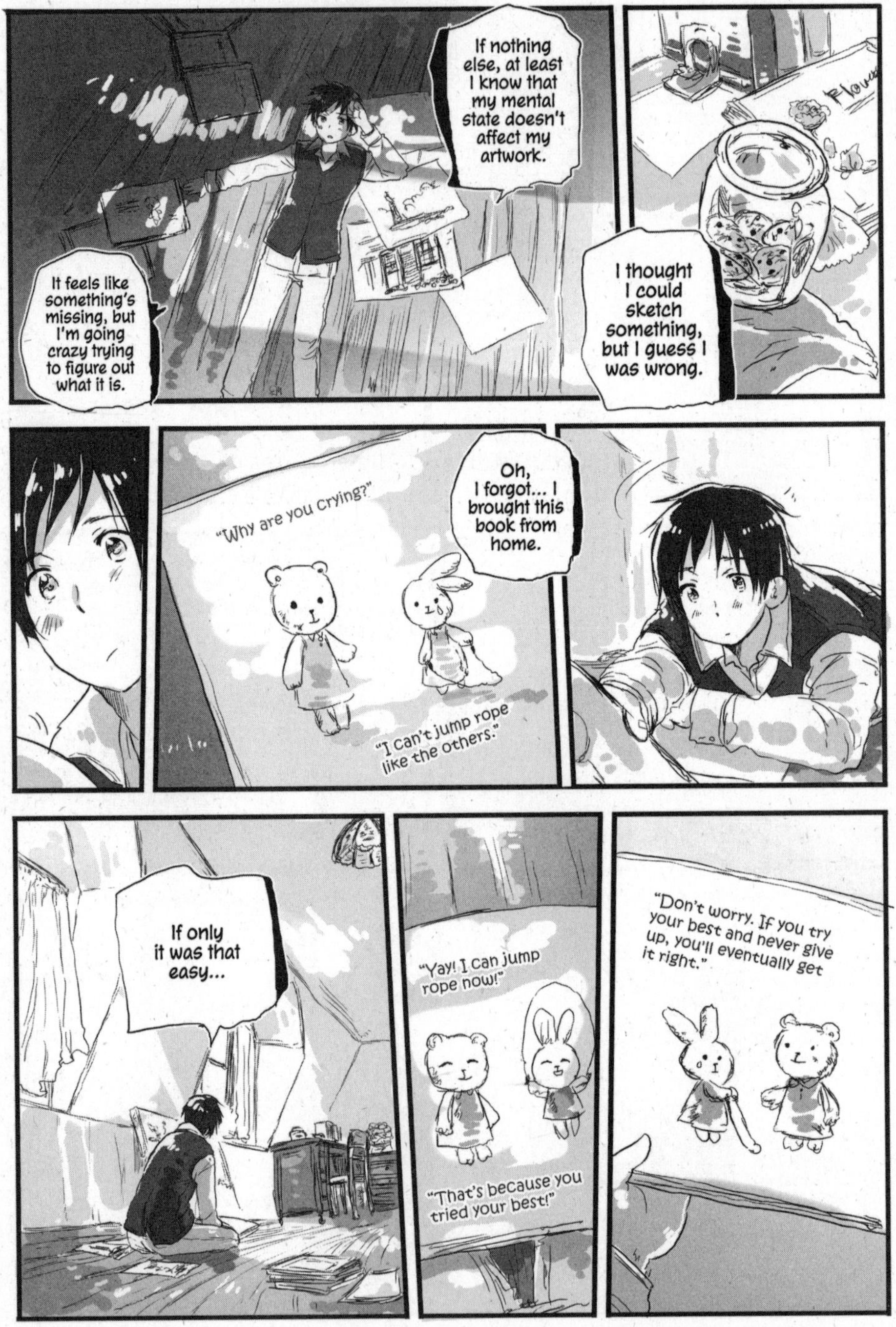
I thought I could sketch something, but I guess I was wrong.
If nothing else, at least I know that my mental state doesn't affect my artwork.
It feels like something's missing, but I'm going crazy trying to figure out what it is.
Oh, I forgot... I brought this book from home.
"Why are you crying?"
"I can't jump rope like the others."
"Don't worry. If you try your best and never give up, you'll eventually get it right."
"Yay! I can jump rope now!"
"That's because you tried your best!"
If only it was that easy...

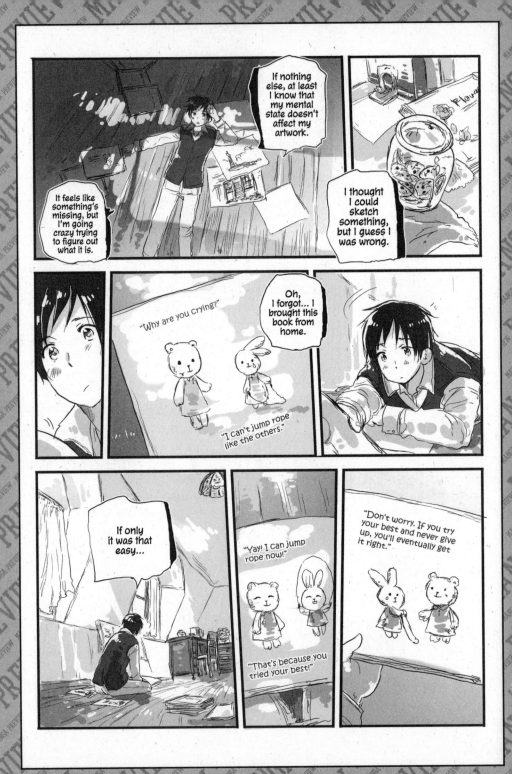

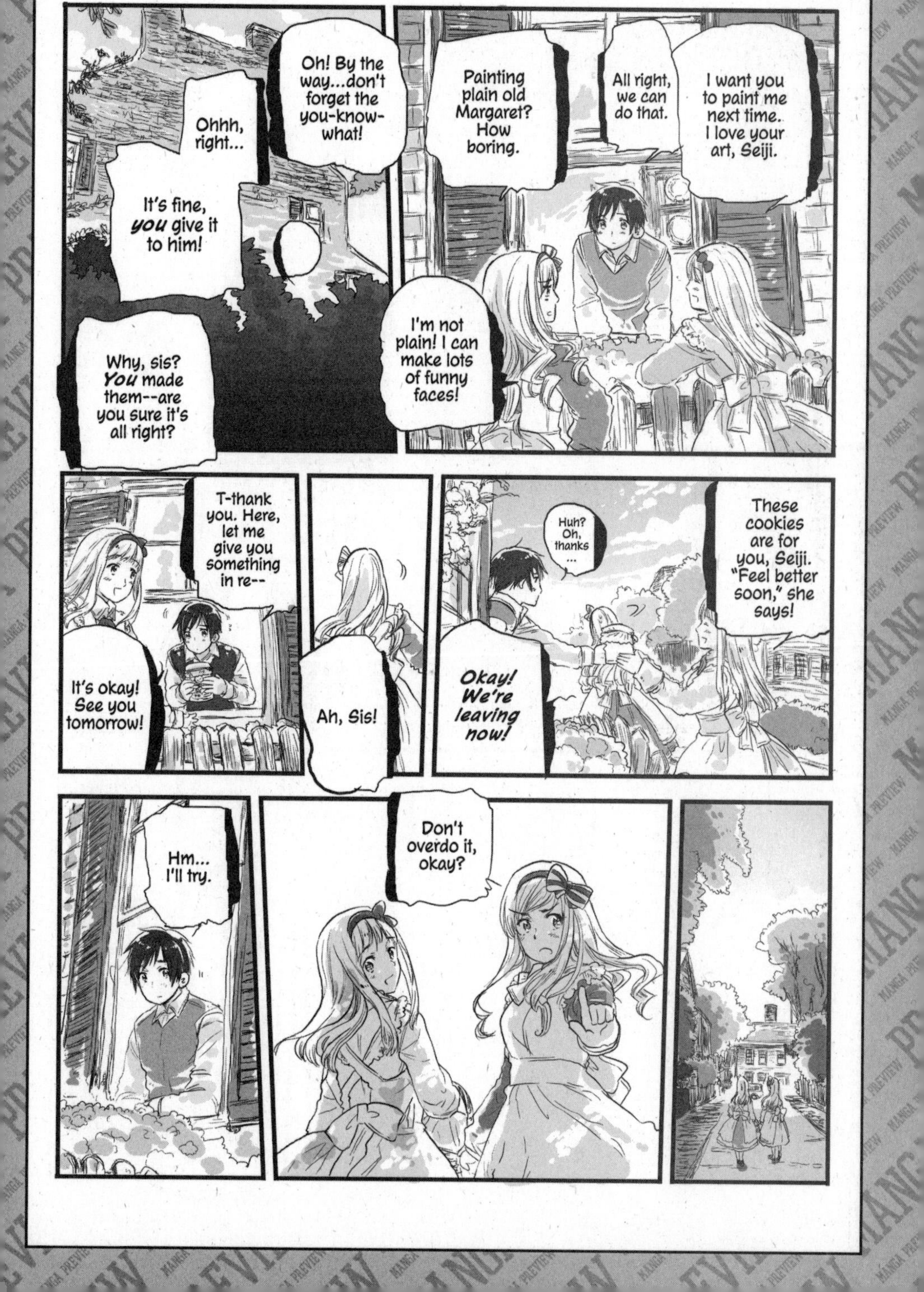
I want you to paint me next time. I love your art, Seiji.
All right, we can do that.
Painting plain old Margaret? How boring.
I'm not plain! I can make lots of funny faces!
Oh! By the way...don't forget the you-know-what!
Ohhh, right...
It's fine, *you* give it to him!
Why, sis? *You* made them--are you sure it's all right?
These cookies are for you, Seiji. "Feel better soon," she says!
Huh? Oh, thanks ...
Okay! We're leaving now!
Ah, Sis!
T-thank you. Here, let me give you something in re--
It's okay! See you tomorrow!
Don't overdo it, okay?
Hm... I'll try.

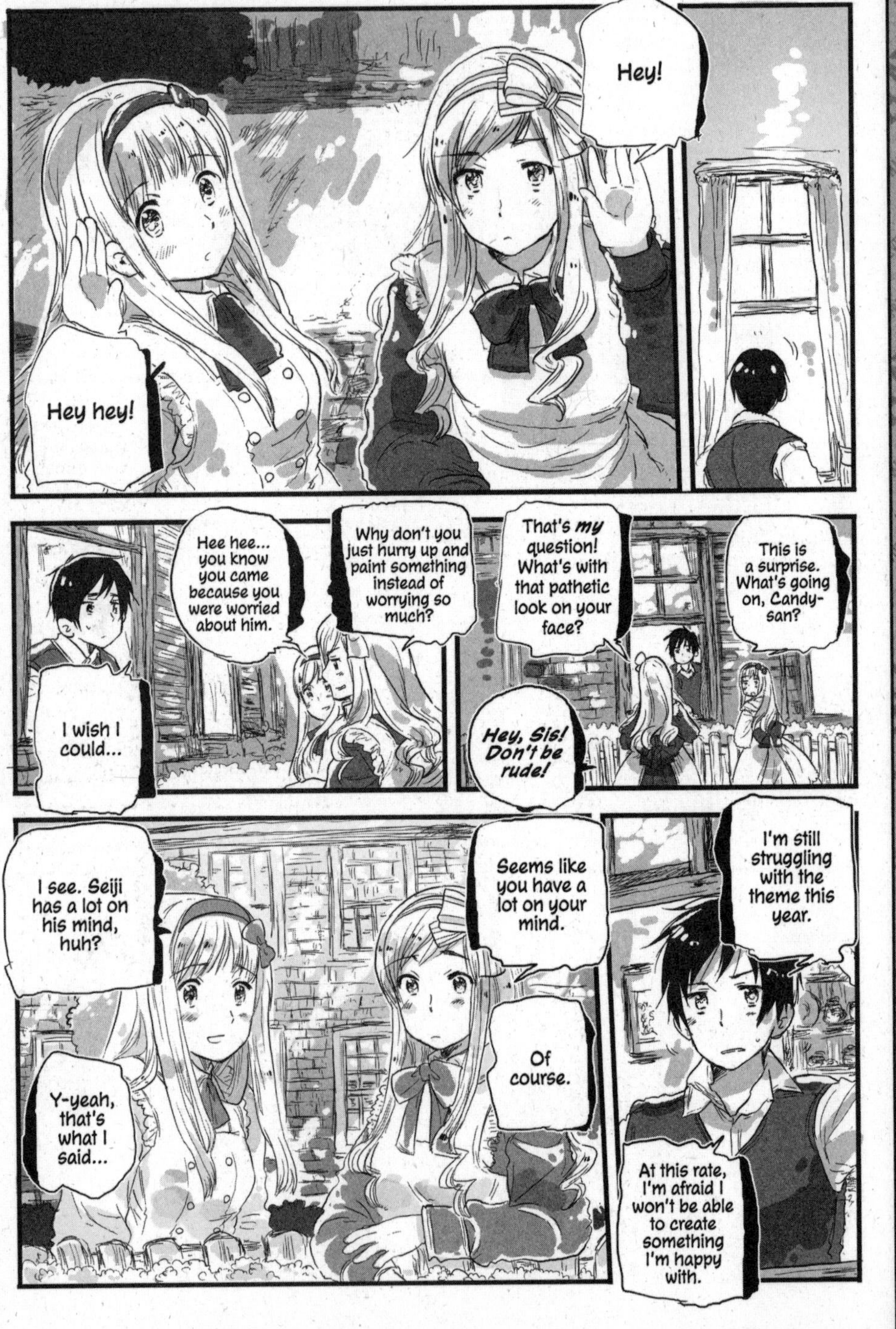
Hey!
Hey hey!
This is a surprise. What's going on, Candy-san?
That's *my* question! What's with that pathetic look on your face?
Hey, Sis! Don't be rude!
Why don't you just hurry up and paint something instead of worrying so much?
Hee hee... you know you came because you were worried about him.
I wish I could...
I'm still struggling with the theme this year.
At this rate, I'm afraid I won't be able to create something I'm happy with.
Seems like you have a lot on your mind.
I see. Seiji has a lot on his mind, huh?
Of course.
Y-yeah, that's what I said...

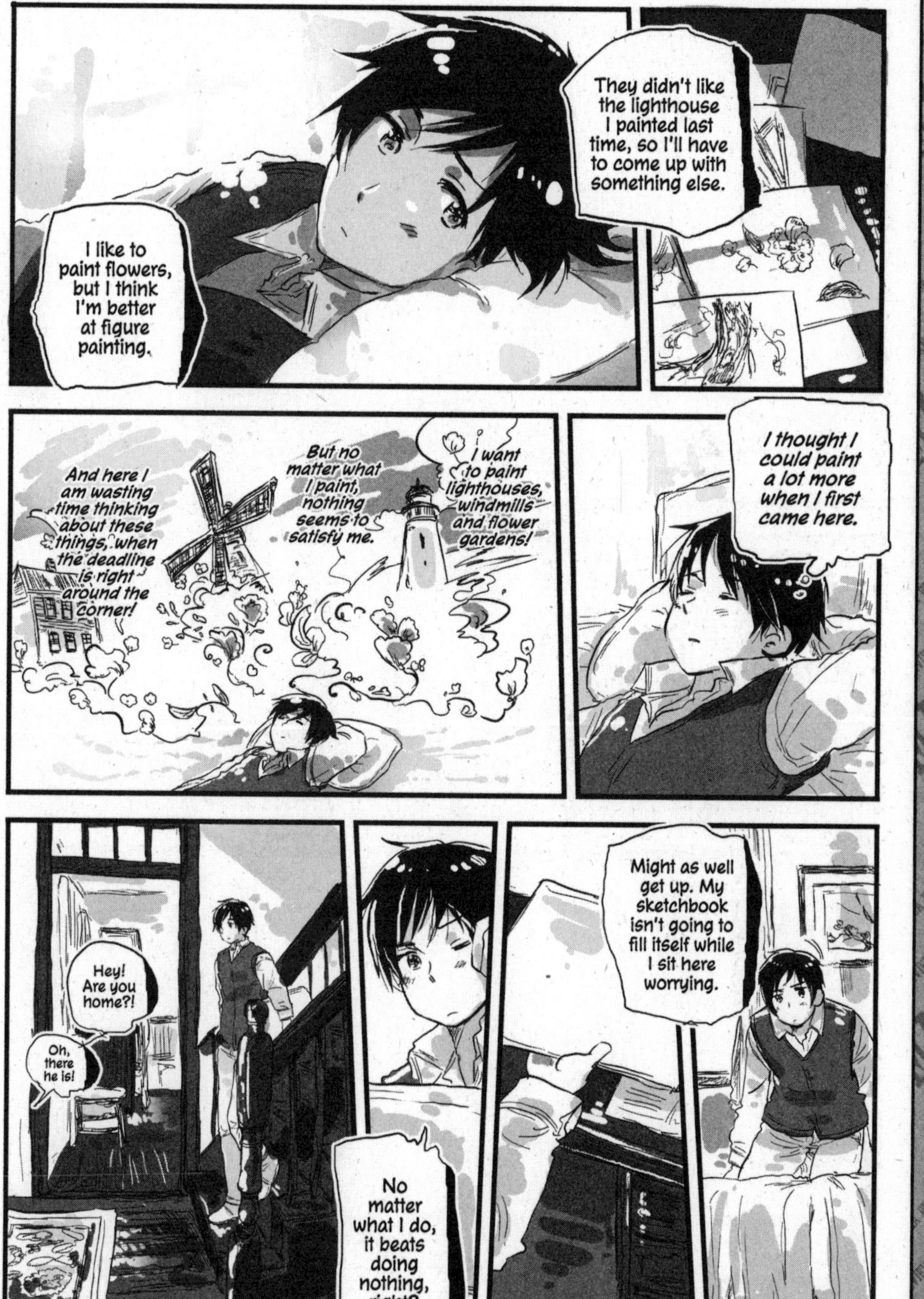
They didn't like the lighthouse I painted last time, so I'll have to come up with something else.
I like to paint flowers, but I think I'm better at figure painting.
I thought I could paint a lot more when I first came here.
I want to paint lighthouses, windmills and flower gardens!
But no matter what I paint, nothing seems to satisfy me.
And here I am wasting time thinking about these things, when the deadline is right around the corner!
Might as well get up. My sketchbook isn't going to fill itself while I sit here worrying.
No matter what I do, it beats doing nothing, right?
Hey! Are you home?!
Oh, there he is!

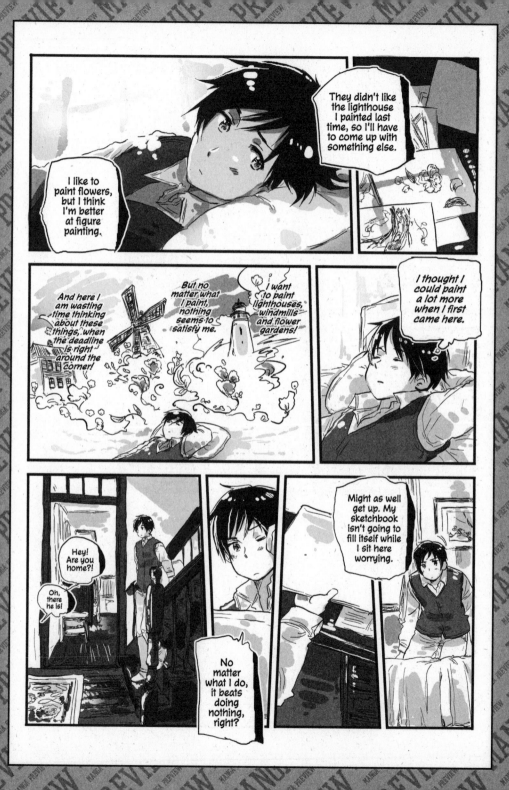

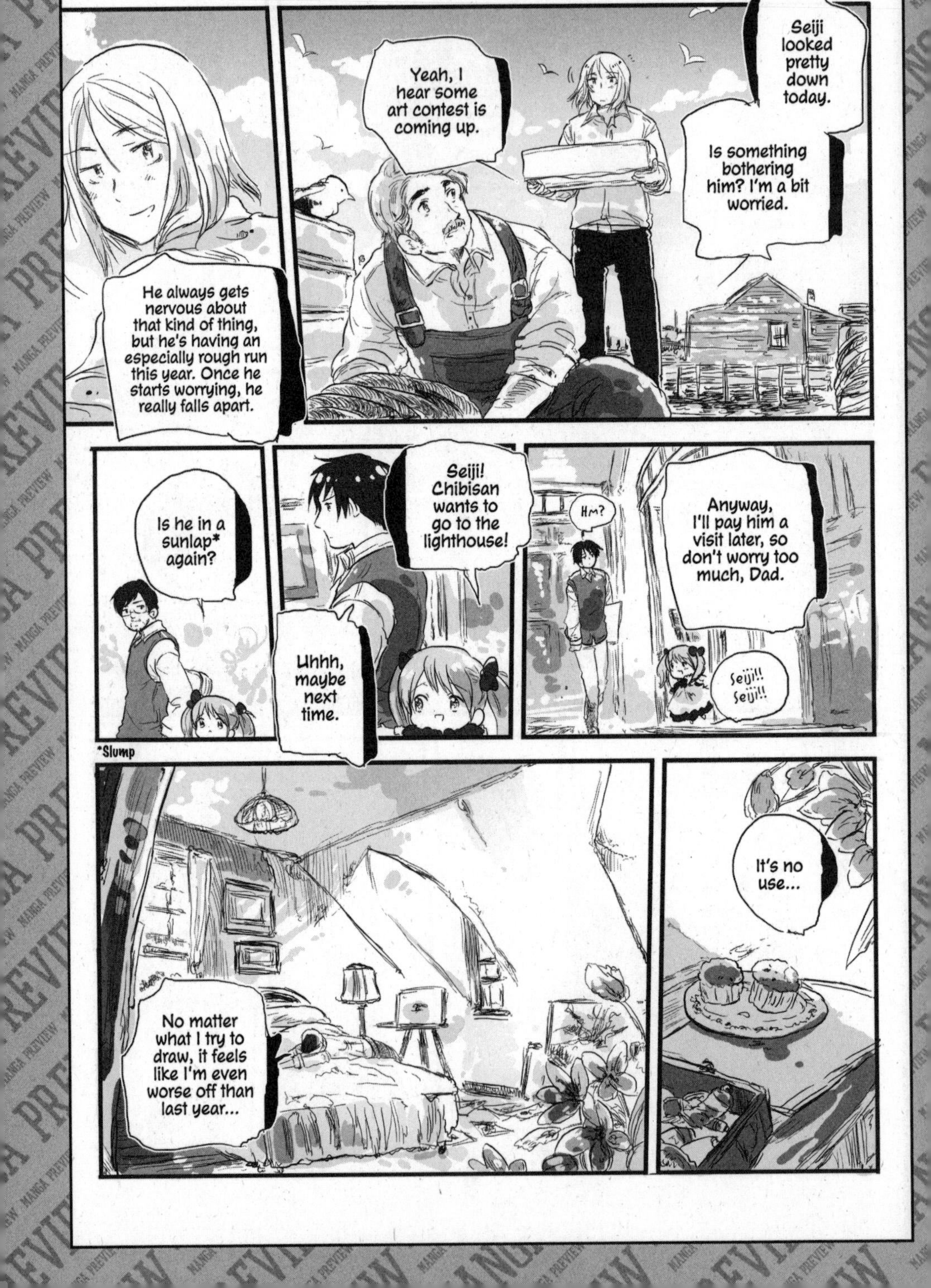
Seiji looked pretty down today.
Is something bothering him? I'm a bit worried.
Yeah, I hear some art contest is coming up.
He always gets nervous about that kind of thing, but he's having an especially rough run this year. Once he starts worrying, he really falls apart.
Anyway, I'll pay him a visit later, so don't worry too much, Dad.
Hm?
Seiji!! Seiji!!
Seiji! Chibisan wants to go to the lighthouse!
Uhhh, maybe next time.
Is he in a sunlap* again?
It's no use...
No matter what I try to draw, it feels like I'm even worse off than last year...

*Slump

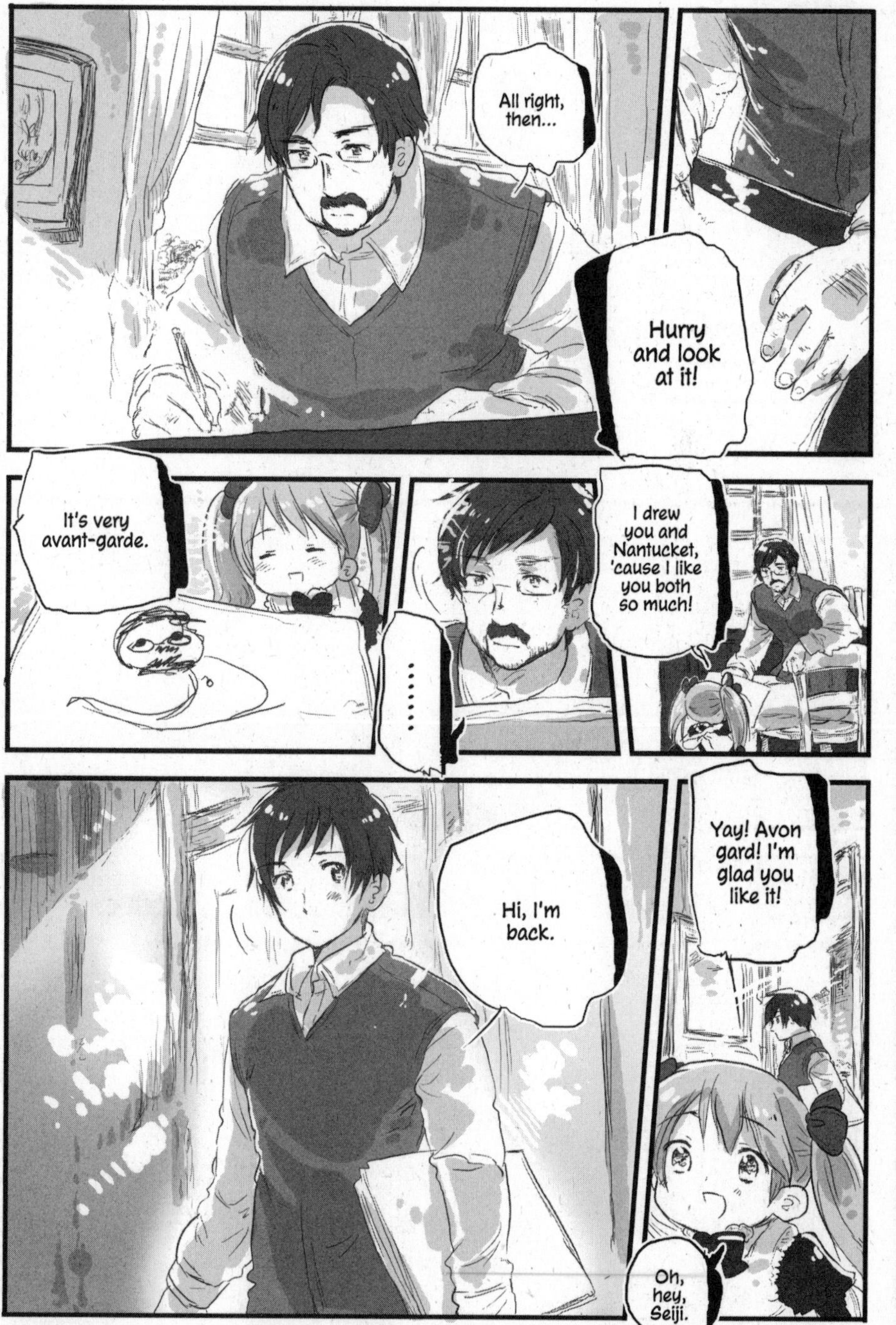
Hurry and look at it!
All right, then...
I drew you and Nantucket, 'cause I like you both so much!
......
It's very avant-garde.
Yay! Avon gard! I'm glad you like it!
Oh, hey, Seiji.
Hi, I'm back.

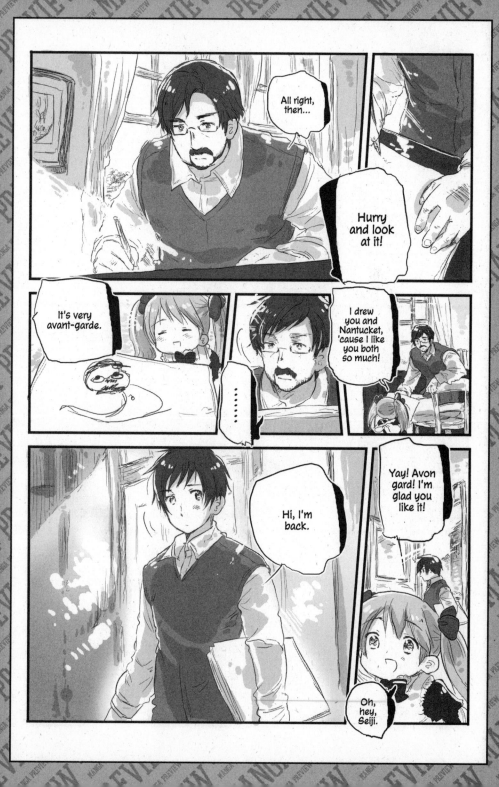

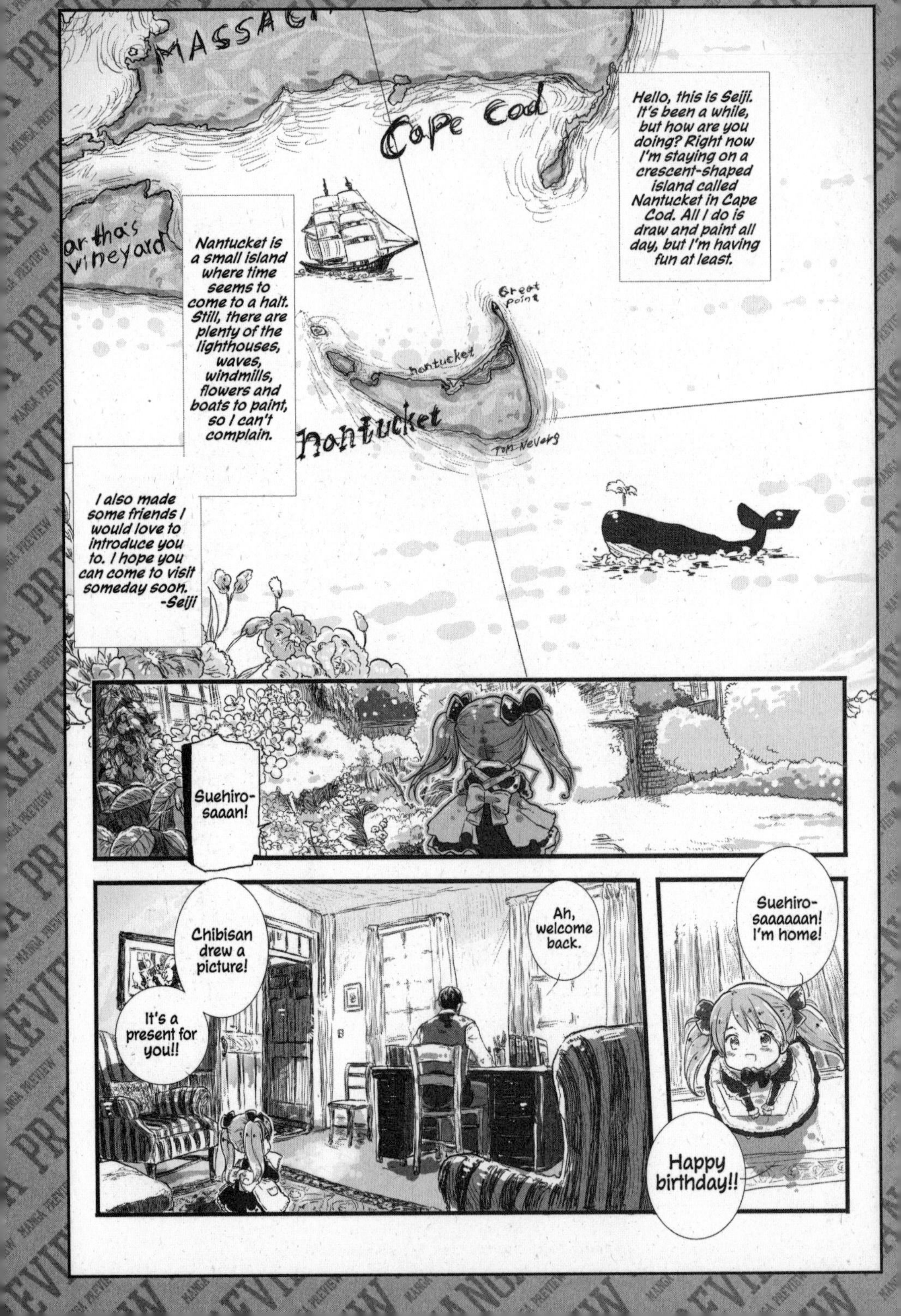
MASSACH
Cape Cod
Hello, this is Seiji. It's been a while, but how are you doing? Right now I'm staying on a crescent-shaped island called Nantucket in Cape Cod. All I do is draw and paint all day, but I'm having fun at least.
Nantucket is a small island where time seems to come to a halt. Still, there are plenty of the lighthouses, waves, windmills, flowers and boats to paint, so I can't complain.
ar tha's vineyard
Great Point
Nantucket
Nantucket
Tom-Nevers
I also made some friends I would love to introduce you to. I hope you can come to visit someday soon. -Seiji
Suehiro-saaan!
Suehiro-saaaaaan! I'm home!
Happy birthday!!
Ah, welcome back.
Chibisan drew a picture!
It's a present for you!!

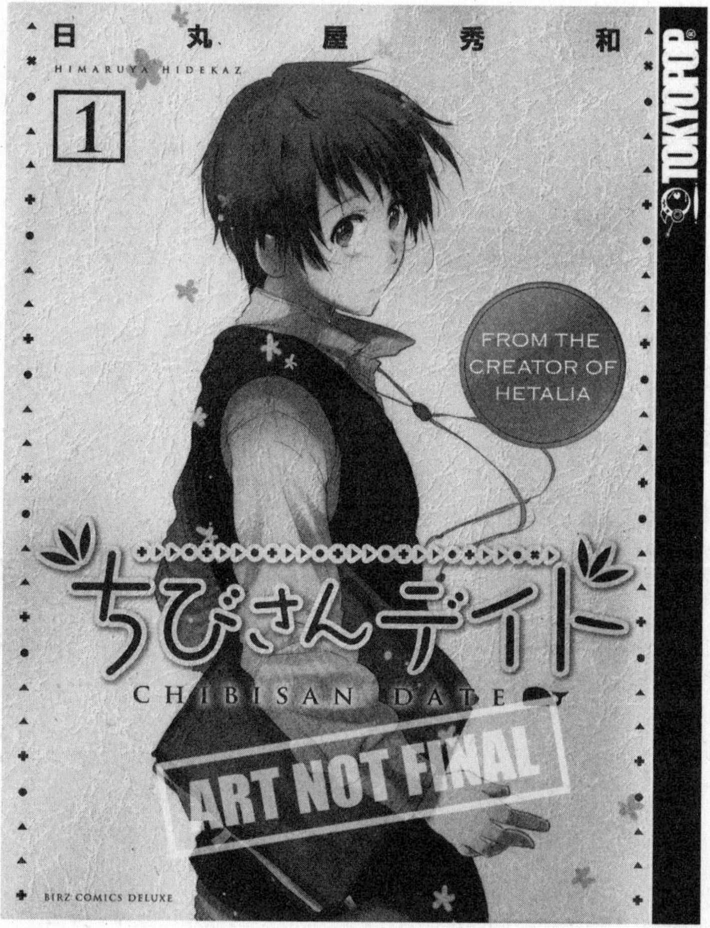
日丸屋秀和
HIMARUYA HIDEKAZ
1
TOKYOPOP
FROM THE CREATOR OF HETALIA
ちびさんデイト
CHIBISAN DATE
ART NOT FINAL
BIRZ COMICS DELUXE

Hello Hetalia Fans!

Thank you so much for your support for this property. The first volume was a huge success! As you may know, Hetalia Volume 1 hit the number one spot on the New York Times Manga Bestseller list the week of its release, and it's all thanks to you! One thing we've noticed about the Hetalia fans is that you are one loyal bunch. We genuinely thank every single one of you who purchased a copy.

The Hetalia project has been a whirlwind of fun and new initiatives for TOKYOPOP. For those unaware, we launched a Hetalia App on the iPhone, iPad and iPod Touch this past September that features a free first chapter, fan photos and the Hetalia manga trailer and can be downloaded for free from iTunes. The rest of the issues can be downloaded on the comiXology app for $0.99 per issue*. Make sure to watch out for special promotions!

These mobile and online initiatives with Hetalia are very important to TOKYOPOP as it places us on the forefront of the digital space. Digital publishing in manga is like the Wild West right now so it's extremely exciting to initiate these digital projects and see all of your responses. Thanks to everyone who downloaded the app as well as all those who purchased a digital copy at Zinio.com. Let us know on our Facebook wall if you have any suggestions for us!

Speaking of Facebook, we had a lot of Hetalia action on our wall! We love the excited interaction and enthusiasm, and we encourage you all to continue. We have more exciting plans for Facebook so stay tuned.

Again, thanks to everyone for your Hetalia love and support!

Cindy Suzuki, Editor

*Issues: Hetalia chapters are referred to as "issues." Volume 1 consists of issues 1-6. Volume 2 is issues 7-12 and so on.

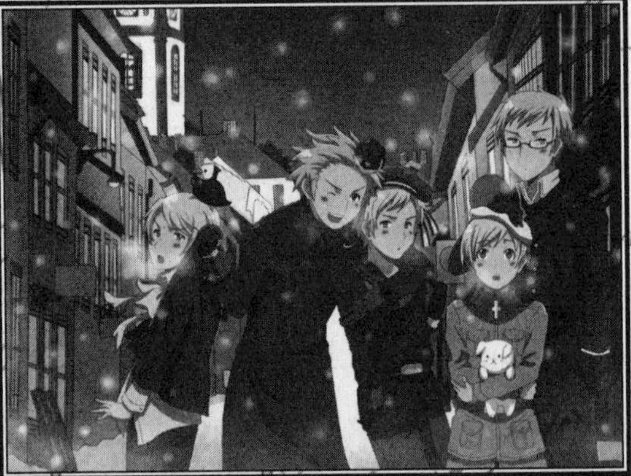

Paloma Otarola

Salt Lake City, UT, USA

"I LOVE the NORDICS!!! I just had to draw them because I really like their personalities especially Denmark's and Iceland's XD" Plus they all made their anime debut just recently! "

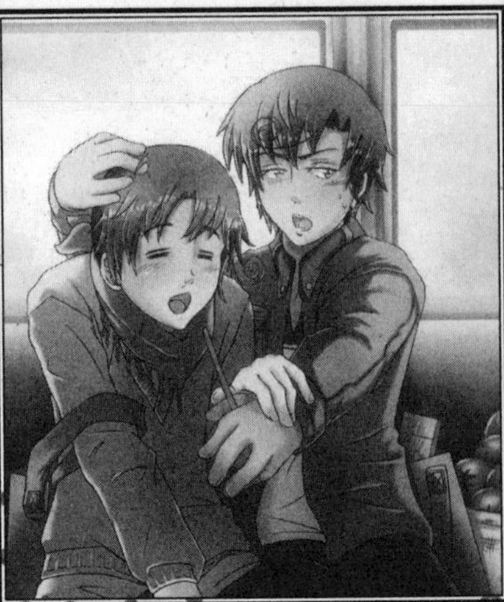

Bridgette Wilhelmi

Chicago, IL, USA

Veneziano and Romano

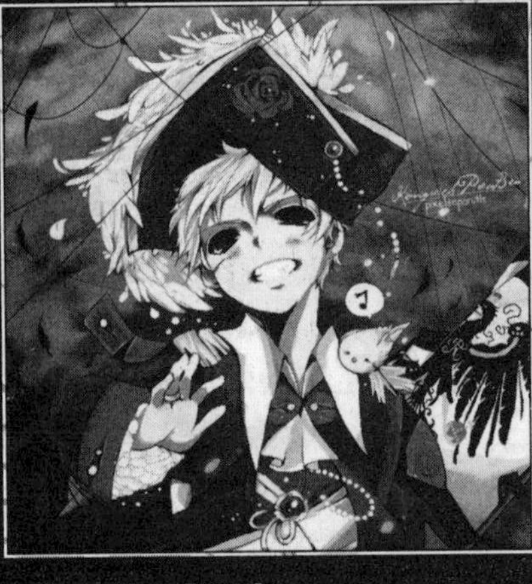

Angelica Acacio

Rio de Janeiro, Brazil

"I really LOVE Prussia...even though he's a nation, he has one of the most human, realistic personalities in the series. He makes lots of mistakes and is terribly impulsive..."

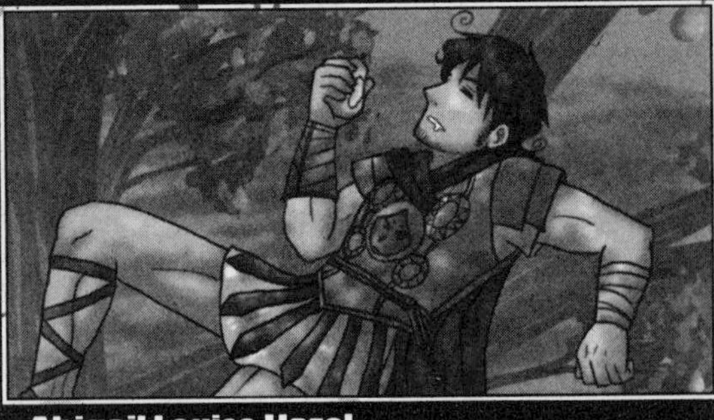

Abigail Louise Hazel

Twinsburg, OH, USA

"Grandpa Rome doesn't get enough love! "

All the Hetalia fan submissions are still on our Facebook page so be sure to check it out.

www.facebook.com/TOKYOPOP

Leslie Roldan
Lancaster, CA,USA

"My favorite Hetalia pairing. HRE & Chibitalia."

Shaina Kumar
Reisterstown, MD, USA

"This is a picture of Liechtenstein that I drew using Paint Tool SAI and Adobe Photoshop CS...in chibi form."

Alice Yuraq Carhuallanqui Zelada
Clifton, NJ, USA

"...this took so long to make I thought I wouldn't be able to finish before the deadline...I'm a first timer on my tablet and photoshop coloring... Well, anyways, here are the Allies and Axis as their popular national food."

Camus Lin
Seattle, WA, USA

"One of my one-hour sketches of Alfred and Arthur. All done in SAI."

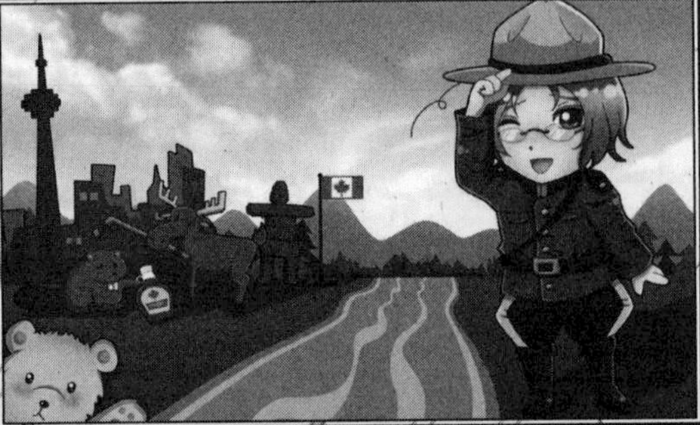

Laura Russell

Vancouver, BC, Canada

"I tried to pack in as much Canadiana as possible."

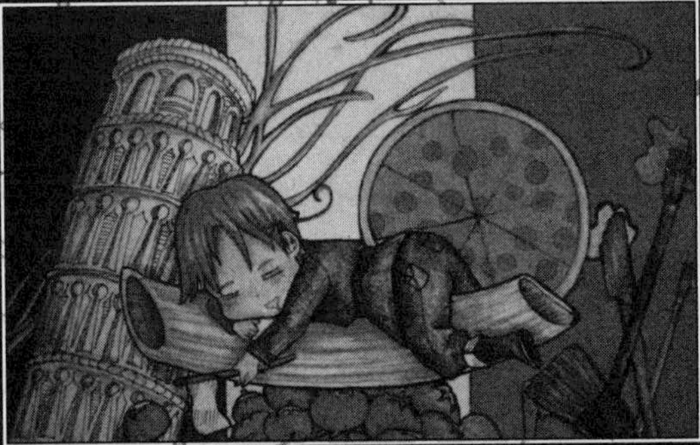

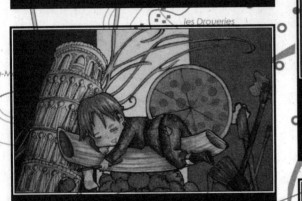

Elysia Shae

Phialdelphia, PA, USA

"I'm half Italian, and Italy's too cute, so :P"

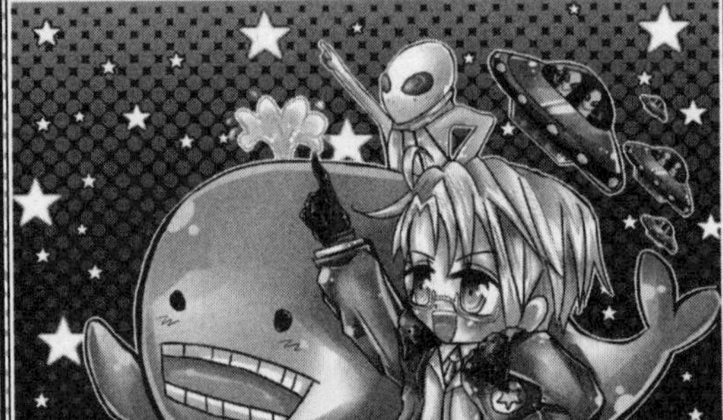

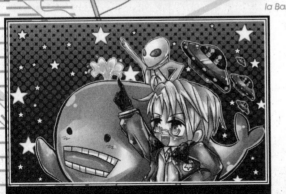

Ashlee Topete

Hayward, CA, USA

"I LOVE America. And I LOVE his crazy friends! I just had to draw a really strange group pic. Plus I think Tony the Alien needs more love. ♥"

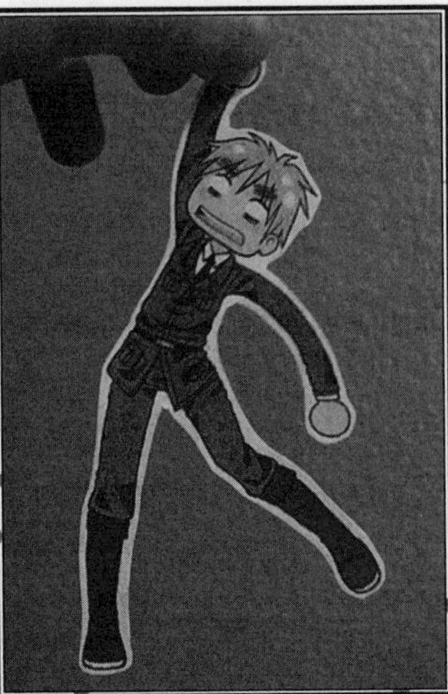

Kestin Larsen

Phoenix, AZ, USA

"I love England, he's such a jerk. Now I get to take him everywhere with me."

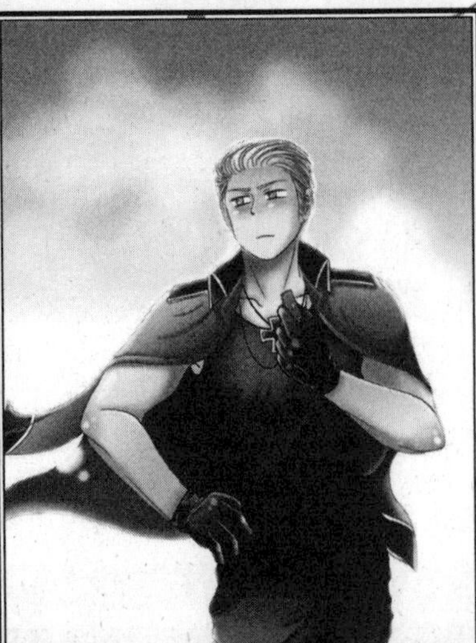

Astari Bratahalim

Bogor, West Java, Indonesia

"I thought I'd draw Germany. He's one of my fave characters in Hetalia (along with Italy as well ^^) made in Photoshop =)"

Shelly Vo
San Jose, CA, USA

"I absolutely adored baby America when I first saw him, and since I'm in AP U.S. History, I was like, 'Hey, why not?' A month ago, we learned in class that Britain neglected America, and an image of little America waiting at the door for Iggy popped in my head."

HETALIA
Fantastic Fan Art!

Angoville-ou-Plain

Yay for Hetalia Fan Art!!

Thanks to everyone who posted your Hetalia Fan Art to the TOKYOPOP Facebook page! Just like the cosplay photos from the first volume, it was truly a treat for us to see such a talented bunch of fans showing off their Hetalia love. We really enjoyed the chibis, all the pasta and burgers, and some of the pairings just made us laugh. It was a lot of fun!

We know that drawing is not a simple task. It takes a lot of time, thought, and dedication, and we really appreciate all the effort that went into your creations. We received well over 300 submissions to show once again how much heart you all have.

To show our appreciation, we have decided to choose 16 pieces of fan art instead of the original 12. Let's take this time to congratulate and admire

Celia Rose
Coeur d'Alene, ID, USA

"Fan art of Kiku Honda (Japan). Pochi (Japan's Shiba hybrid) was the most difficult part of this piece to draw, since he looks more feline than Shiba."

Meghan Williams
Tolland, CT, USA

"I had sketched this other picture of the axis for the contest...I fooled around in shop a bit, and it became something like a stencil."

See you!
Ciao!

To be continued in Hetalia 3 ...maybe...

POSTSCRIPT

Hello. This is Hidekaz Himaruya. Thank you very much for picking up volume 2!! Heh heh...hope it was worth the wait. I really enjoyed drawing my beloved Italy and his friends!! This volume is chock-full of some of my best material. I hope I've improved since the first book. I feel very fortunate to have met so many people from around the world during the time I spent in America! I used a lot of what I learned in this book. I'd be happy if people from around the world would use this book as an inspiration to learn more about other countries.

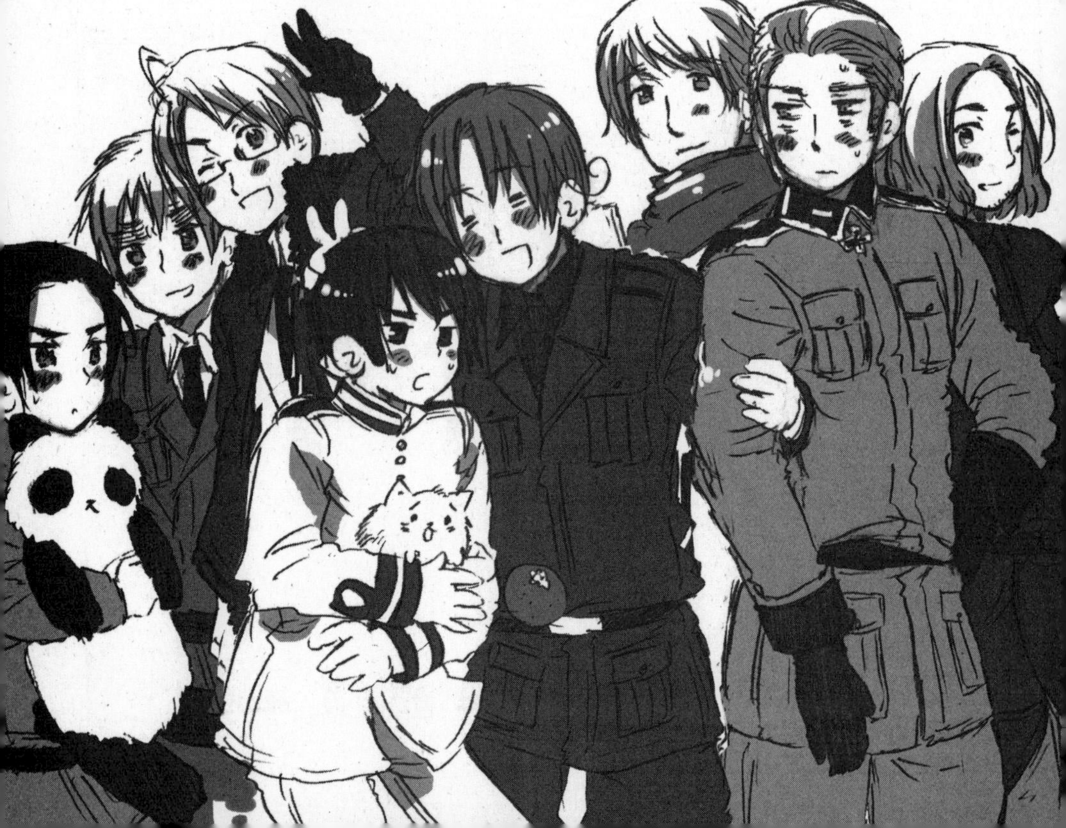

Bonus
Specialty=Cuteness. Occupation=Cuteness.

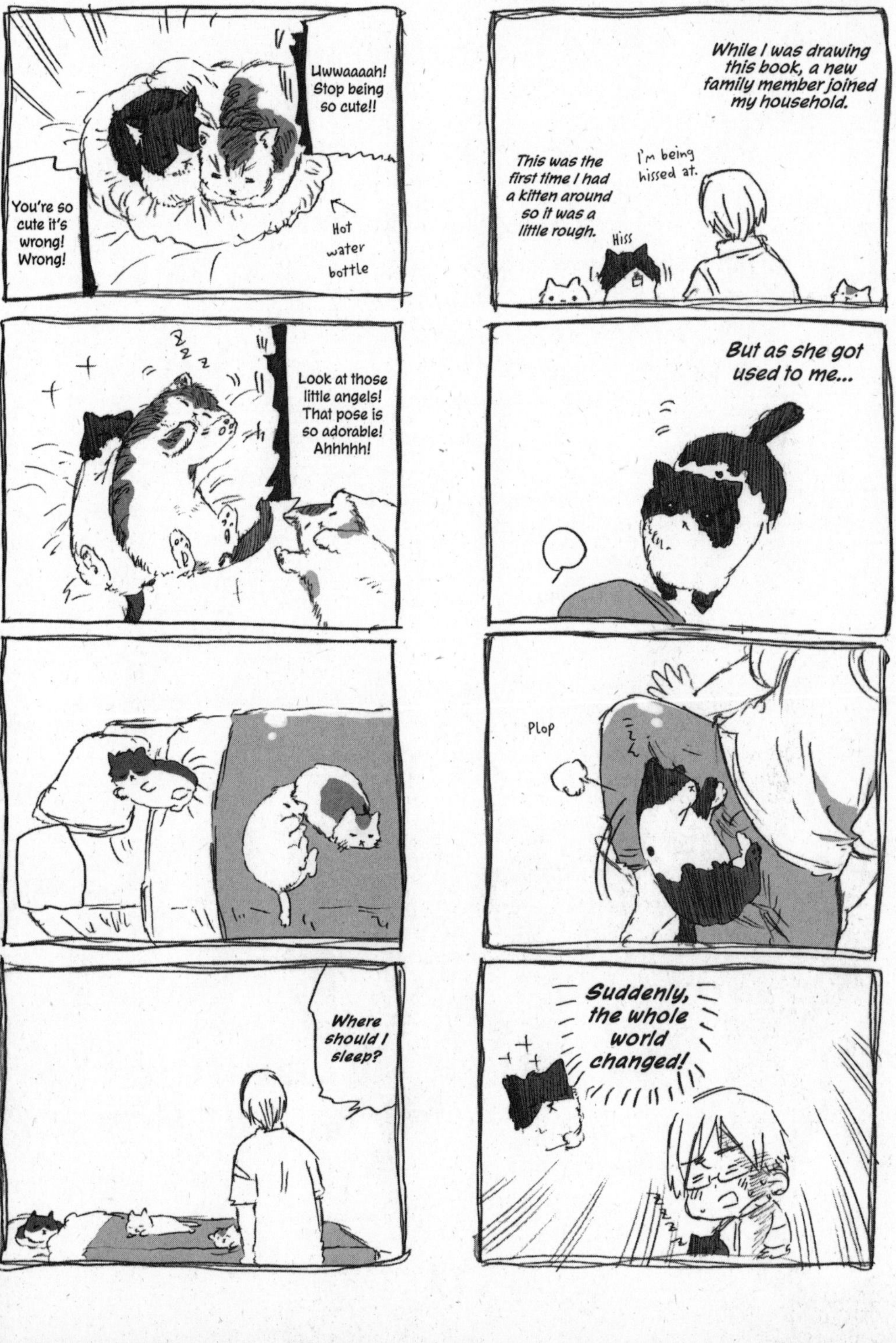
While I was drawing this book, a new family member joined my household.
I'm being hissed at.
This was the first time I had a kitten around so it was a little rough.
Hiss
But as she got used to me...
Plop
Suddenly, the whole world changed!
Uwwaaaah! Stop being so cute!!
You're so cute it's wrong! Wrong!
Hot water bottle
Look at those little angels! That pose is so adorable! Ahhhhh!
Where should I sleep?

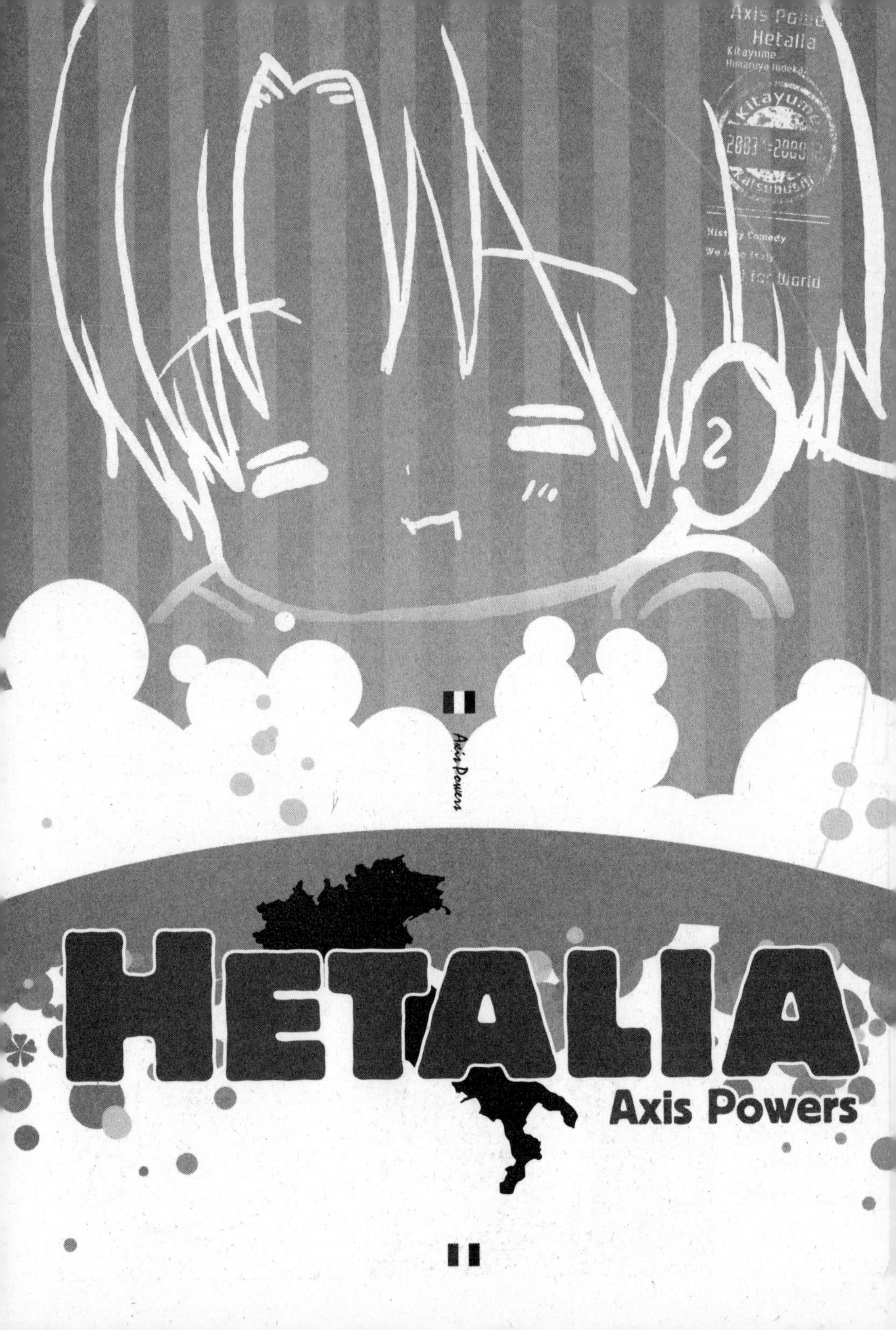
Hetalia
Kitayume
Kitayume
Katsubushi
History Comedy
for World
Axis Powers
HETALIA
Axis Powers

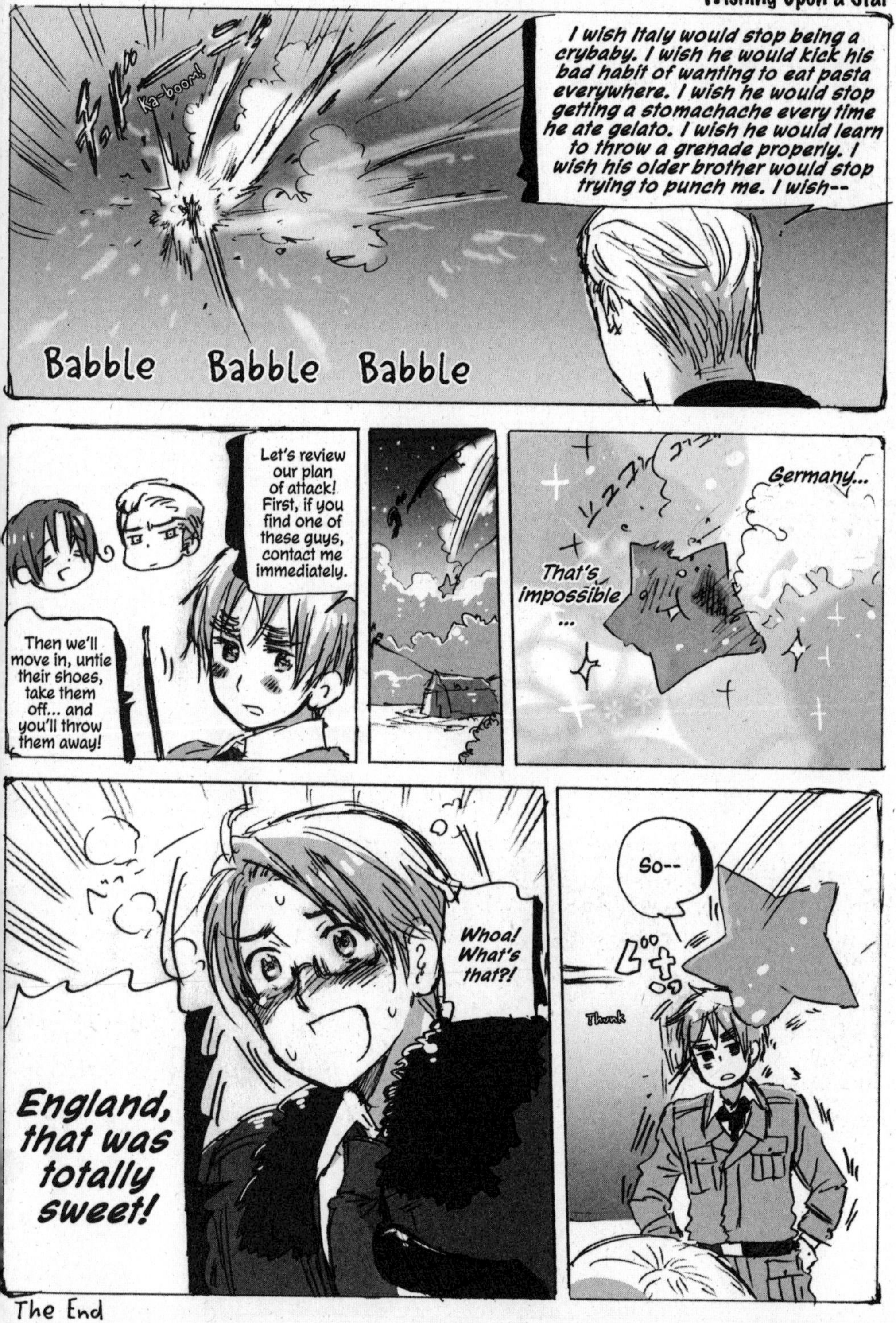
I wish Italy would stop being a crybaby. I wish he would kick his bad habit of wanting to eat pasta everywhere. I wish he would stop getting a stomachache every time he ate gelato. I wish he would learn to throw a grenade properly. I wish his older brother would stop trying to punch me. I wish--
Ka-boom!
Babble Babble Babble
Germany...
That's impossible...
Let's review our plan of attack! First, if you find one of these guys, contact me immediately.
Then we'll move in, untie their shoes, take them off... and you'll throw them away!
So--
Thunk
Whoa! What's that?!
England, that was totally sweet!

The End

Wishing Upon a Star

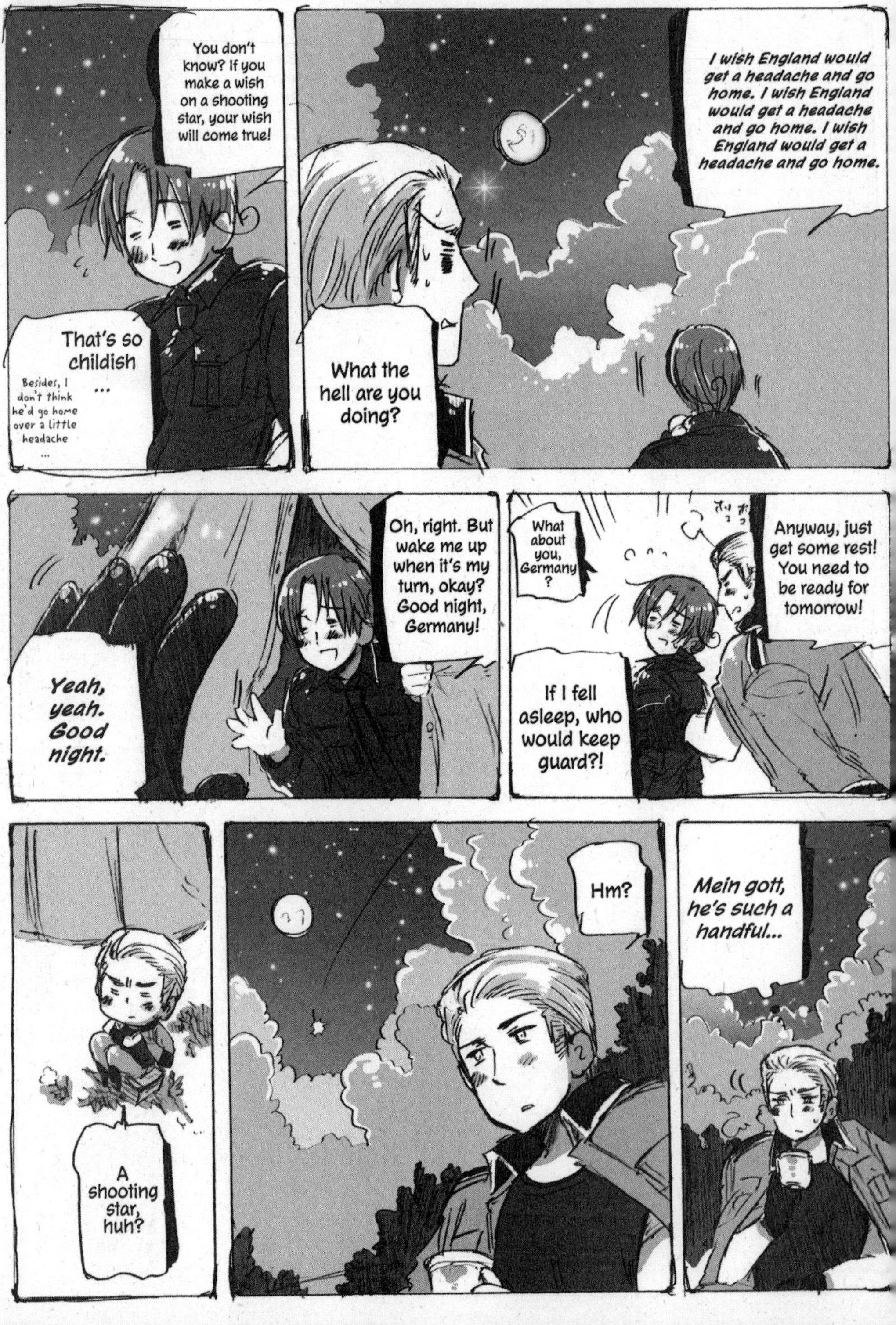
I wish England would get a headache and go home. I wish England would get a headache and go home. I wish England would get a headache and go home.
What the hell are you doing?
You don't know? If you make a wish on a shooting star, your wish will come true!
That's so childish ...
Besides, I don't think he'd go home over a little headache ...
Anyway, just get some rest! You need to be ready for tomorrow!
What about you, Germany?
If I fell asleep, who would keep guard?!
Oh, right. But wake me up when it's my turn, okay? Good night, Germany!
Yeah, yeah. Good night.
Mein gott, he's such a handful...
Hm?
A shooting star, huh?

Right now, Germany and I are in the middle of a war in Africa. Big Brother started the fight but left us behind. Worst of all, whenever I run into England, he has the urge to shoot me. –Italy

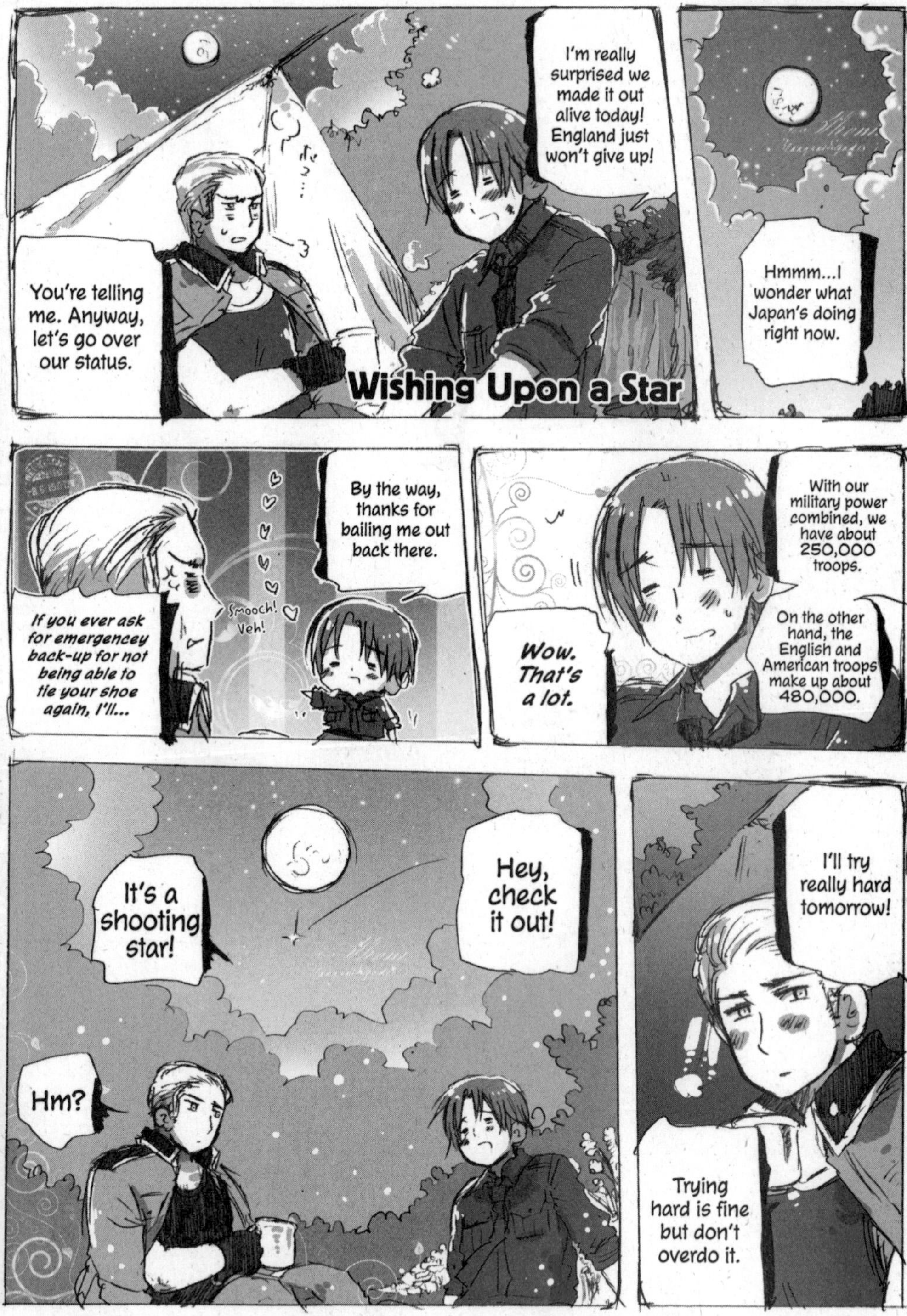
Hmmm...I wonder what Japan's doing right now.
I'm really surprised we made it out alive today! England just won't give up!
You're telling me. Anyway, let's go over our status.
Wishing Upon a Star
With our military power combined, we have about 250,000 troops.
On the other hand, the English and American troops make up about 480,000.
Wow. That's a lot.
By the way, thanks for bailing me out back there.
Smooch! Veh!
If you ever ask for emergencey back-up for not being able to tie your shoe again, I'll...
I'll try really hard tomorrow!
Trying hard is fine but don't overdo it.
Hey, check it out!
It's a shooting star!
Hm?

Japan-kun and America-kun 10

Americans really like thrills. There's even a roller coaster on top of a skyscraper in Las Vegas!

AXIS POWERS HETALIA 2

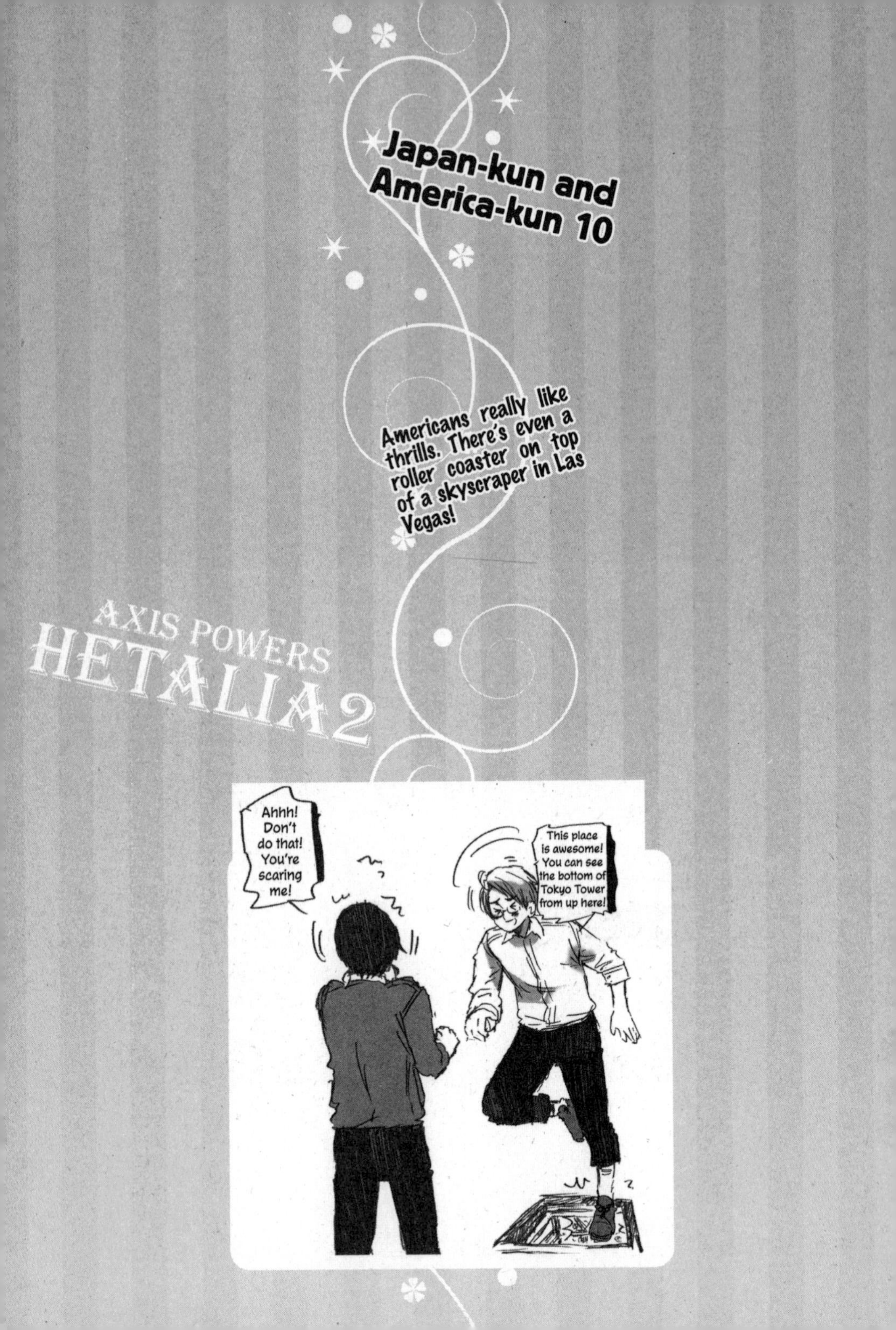
This place is awesome! You can see the bottom of Tokyo Tower from up here!
Ahhh! Don't do that! You're scaring me!

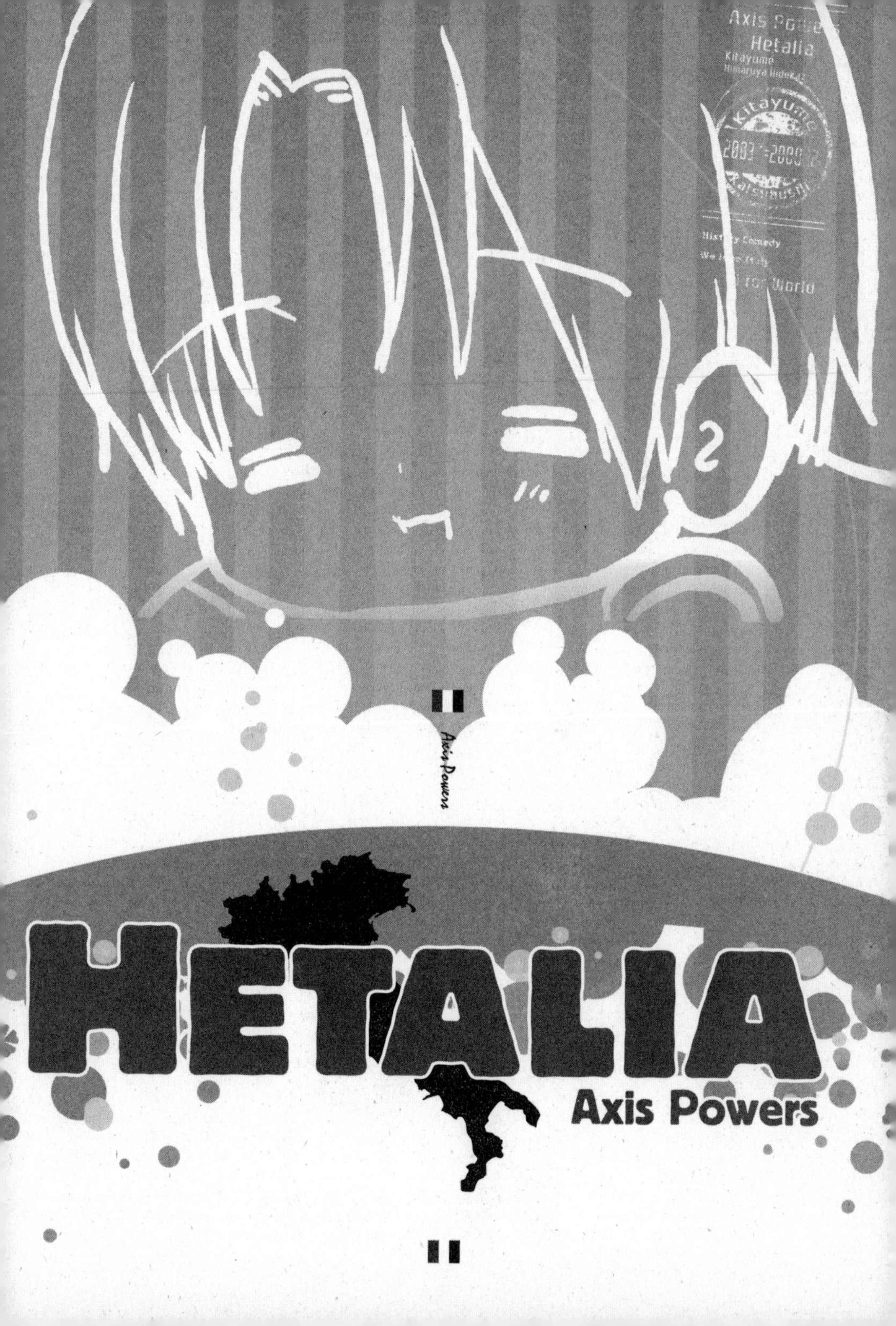
Axis Powers
Hetalia
Kitayume
Himaruya Hidekaz
Kitayume
Katsubushi
History Comedy
World
Axis Powers
HETALIA
Axis Powers

America's Convenience Stores

Unlike Japan, In America, there are not many convenience stores that are open 24 hours. If you go into rural areas, many of the local businesses tend to close early. So if you happen to need food or light bulbs in the dead of night, you might be in for a long drive. In short, if you're out of the city with no car and out of light bulbs, you're out of luck.

AXIS POWERS HETALIA 2

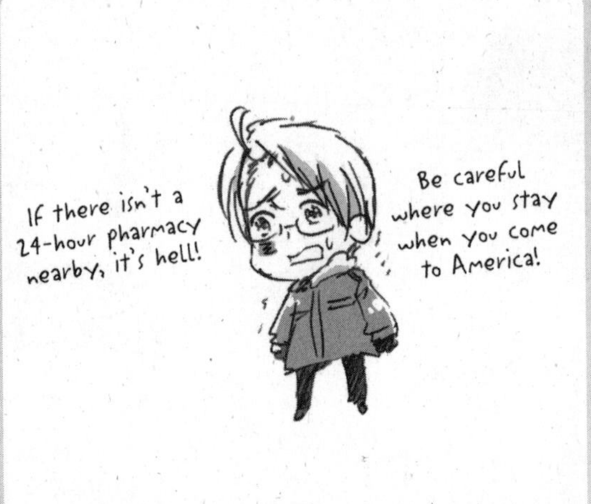
Be careful where you stay when you come to America!
If there isn't a 24-hour pharmacy nearby, it's hell!

Why Americans Love Spring

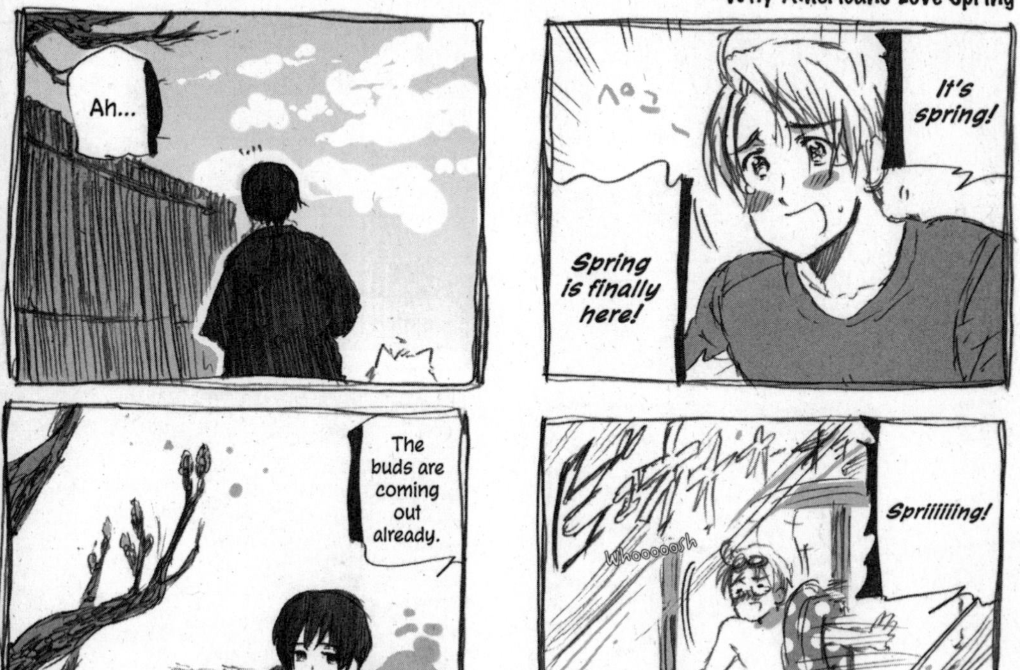
It's spring!
Spring is finally here!
Spriiiiiing!
Whoooooosh
Oh, wait...
False alarm. It's just morning.
Ah...
The buds are coming out already.
I suppose we should get ingredients for sweet dango.
Woof!

Japan enjoys the changing of seasons a bit too much.

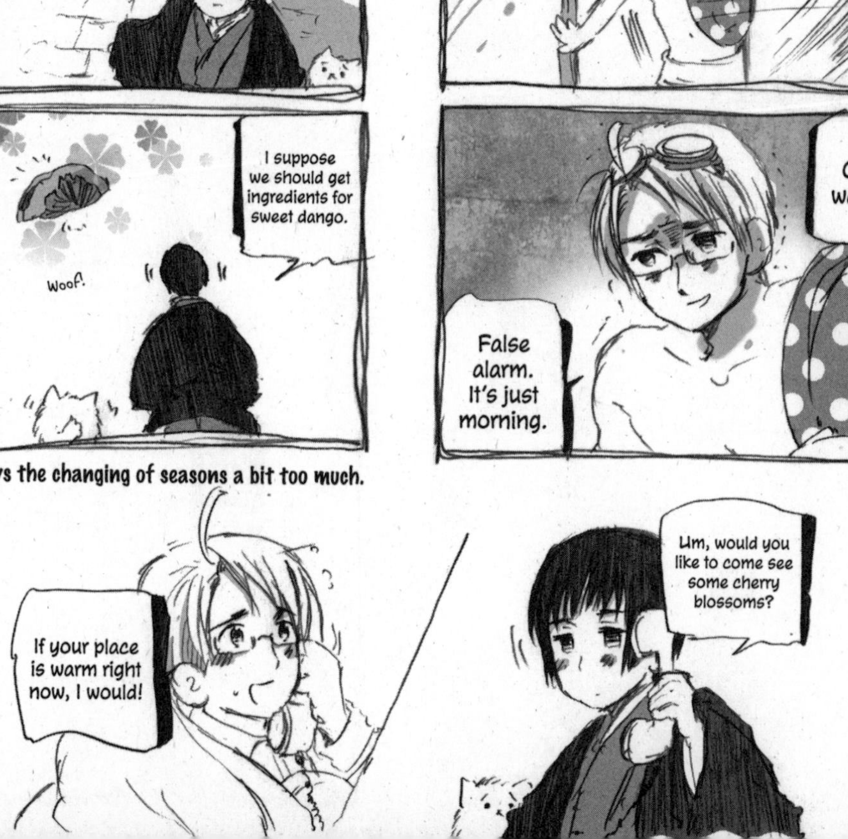
Um, would you like to come see some cherry blossoms?
If your place is warm right now, I would!

Why Americans Love Spring

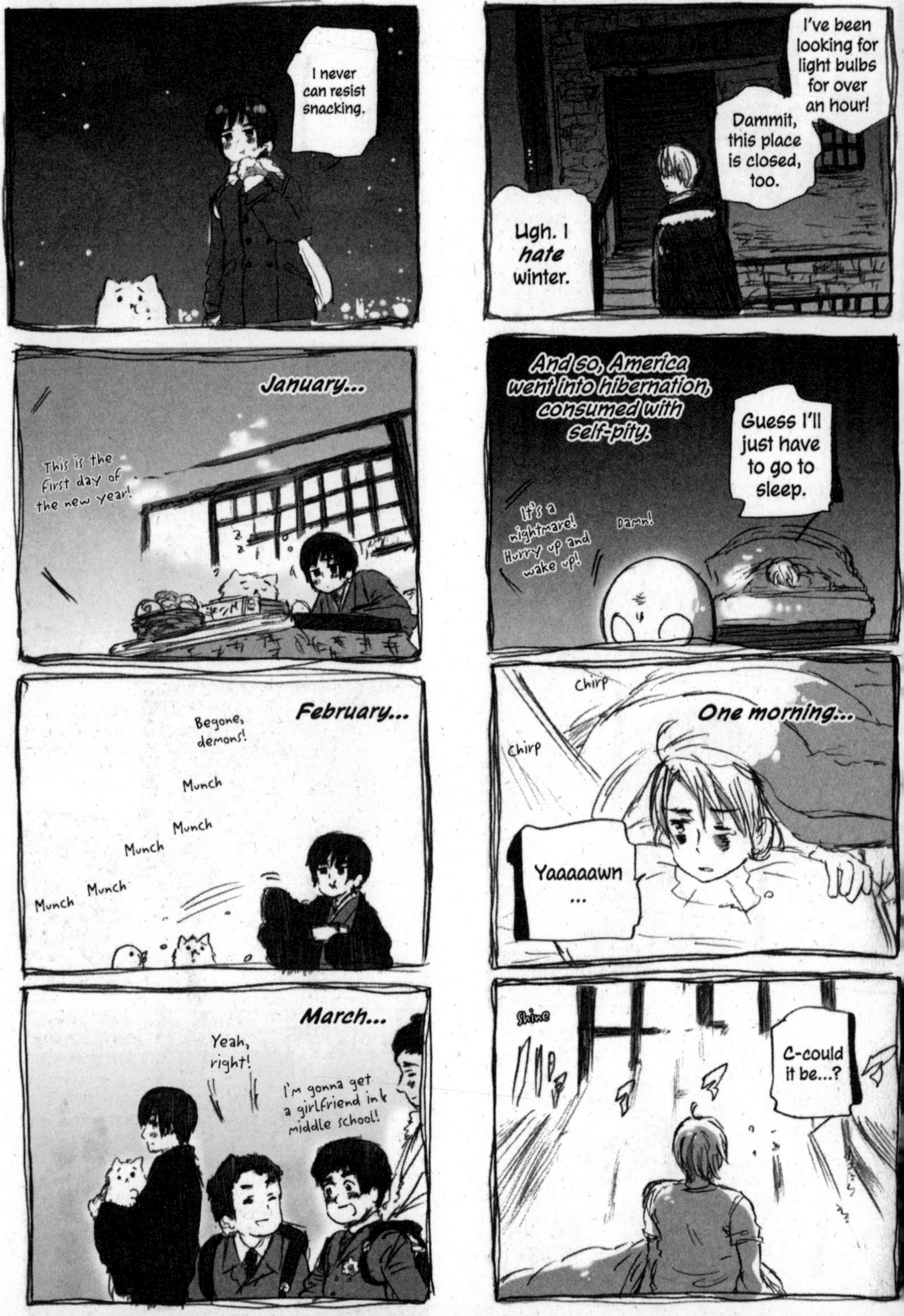

I've been looking for light bulbs for over an hour!
Dammit, this place is closed, too.
Ugh. I *hate* winter.
And so, America went into hibernation, consumed with self-pity.
Guess I'll just have to go to sleep.
Damn!
It's a nightmare! Hurry up and wake up!
One morning...
Chirp
Chirp
Yaaaaawn ...
C-could it be...?
Shine
I never can resist snacking.
January...
This is the first day of the new year!
February...
Begone, demons!
Munch
Munch
Munch
Munch
Munch
March...
I'm gonna get a girlfriend in middle school!
Yeah, right!

Why Americans Love Spring

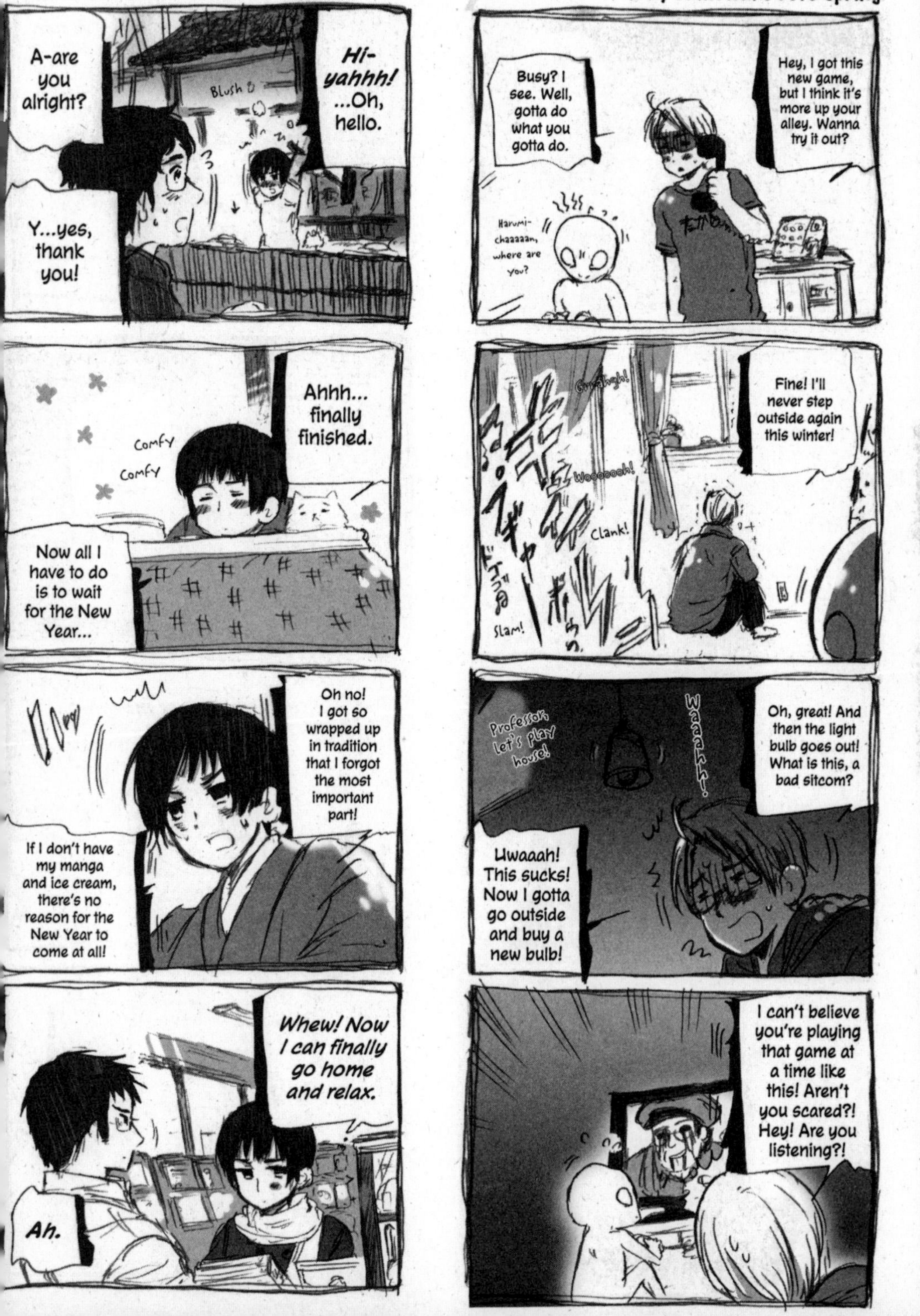
Hey, I got this new game, but I think it's more up your alley. Wanna try it out?
Busy? I see. Well, gotta do what you gotta do.
Harumi-chaaaaan, where are you?
Fine! I'll never step outside again this winter!
Wooooooh!
Clank!
Slam!
Oh, great! And then the light bulb goes out! What is this, a bad sitcom?
Waaaahh!
Professor, let's play house!
Uwaaah! This sucks! Now I gotta go outside and buy a new bulb!
I can't believe you're playing that game at a time like this! Aren't you scared?! Hey! Are you listening?!
Hi-yahhh! ...Oh, hello.
A-are you alright?
Blush
Y...yes, thank you!
Ahhh... finally finished.
Comfy
Comfy
Now all I have to do is to wait for the New Year...
Oh no! I got so wrapped up in tradition that I forgot the most important part!
If I don't have my manga and ice cream, there's no reason for the New Year to come at all!
Whew! Now I can finally go home and relax.
Ah.

Why Americans Love Spring

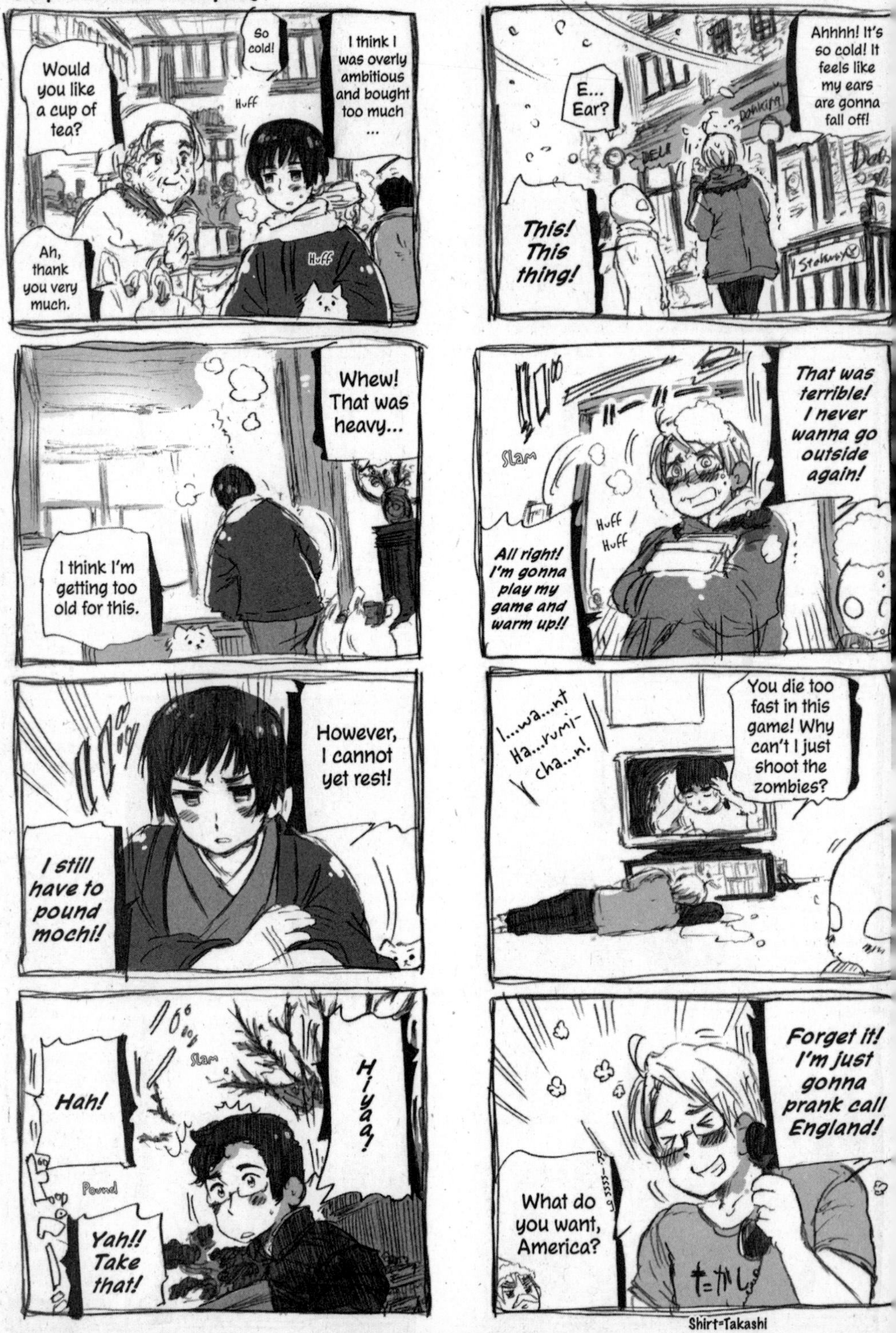

Ahhhh! It's so cold! It feels like my ears are gonna fall off!
E... Ear?
This! This thing!
That was terrible! I never wanna go outside again!
Slam
Huff Huff
All right! I'm gonna play my game and warm up!!
You die too fast in this game! Why can't I just shoot the zombies?
I...wa...nt Ha...rumi-cha...n!
Forget it! I'm just gonna prank call England!
What do you want, America?
たかし
I think I was overly ambitious and bought too much ...
So cold!
Huff
Would you like a cup of tea?
Huff
Ah, thank you very much.
Whew! That was heavy...
I think I'm getting too old for this.
However, I cannot yet rest!
I still have to pound mochi!
Hiyaa!
Slam
Hah!
Pound
Yah!! Take that!

Shirt=Takashi

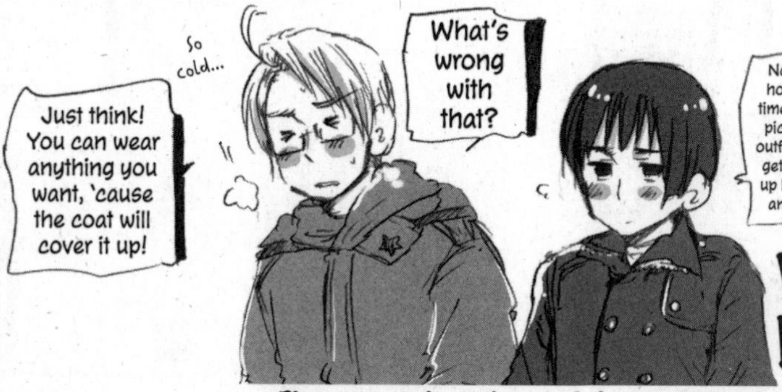
No matter how much time I take to pick out an outfit, it'll just get covered up by a coat anyway...
What's wrong with that?
So cold...
Just think! You can wear anything you want, 'cause the coat will cover it up!

Why Americans Love Spring

↓ Please read the right and left panels simultaneously ↓

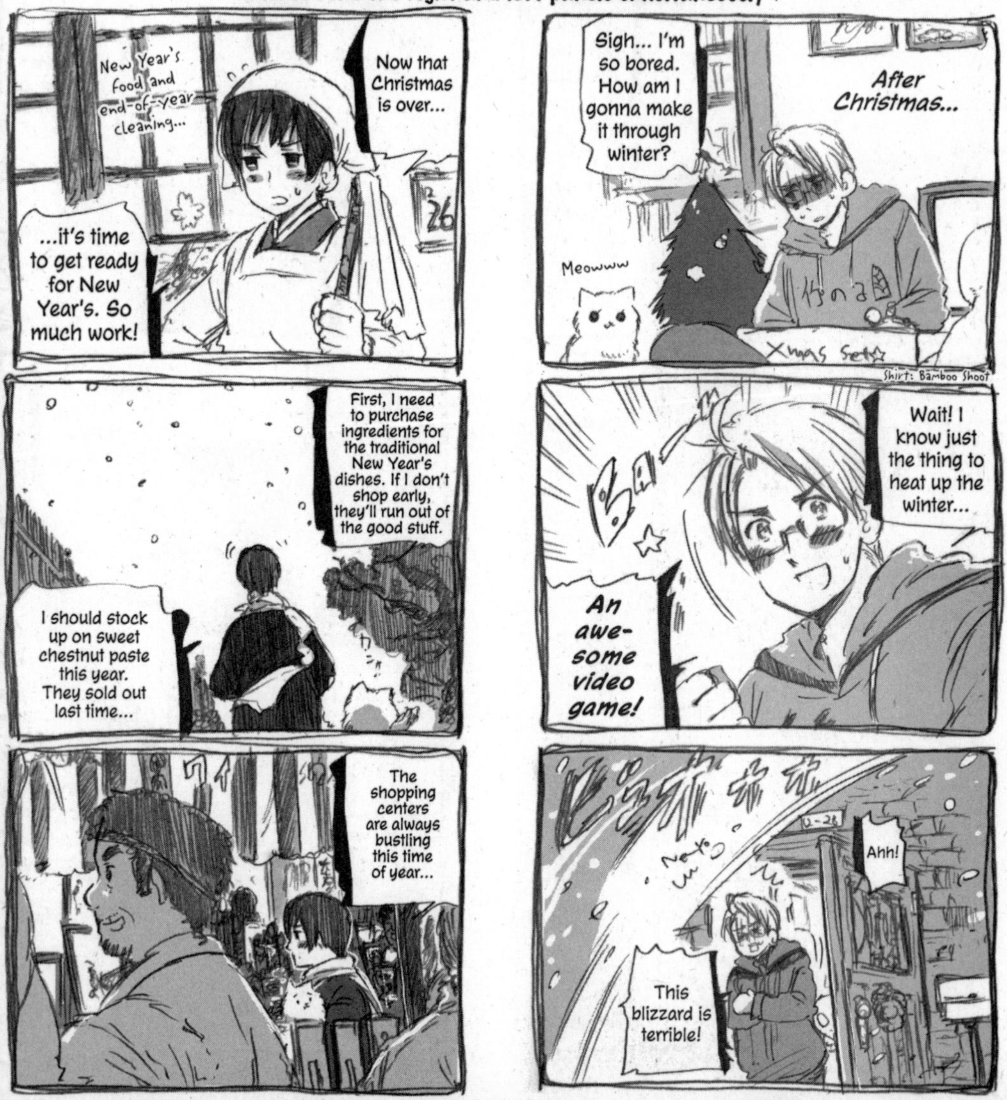
After Christmas...
Sigh... I'm so bored. How am I gonna make it through winter?
Meowww
Xmas Set☆
Shirt: Bamboo Shoot
Now that Christmas is over...
New Year's food and end-of-year cleaning...
...it's time to get ready for New Year's. So much work!
Wait! I know just the thing to heat up the winter...
An awe-some video game!
First, I need to purchase ingredients for the traditional New Year's dishes. If I don't shop early, they'll run out of the good stuff.
I should stock up on sweet chestnut paste this year. They sold out last time...
Ahh!
This blizzard is terrible!
The shopping centers are always bustling this time of year...

Japan-kun and America-kun 9

Find out why America needs a Japanese convenience store in the next chapter!

AXIS POWERS HETALIA 2

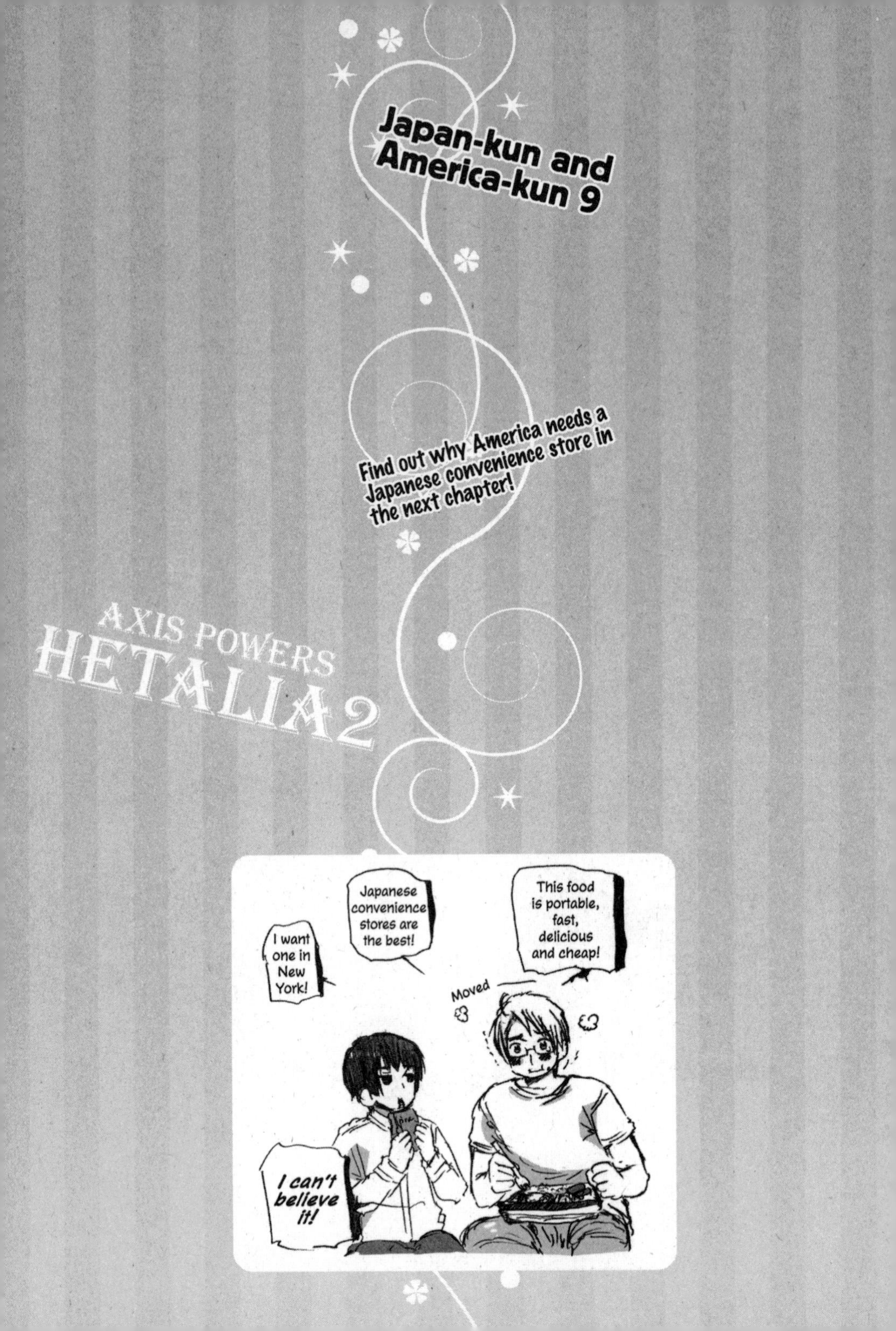

This food is portable, fast, delicious and cheap!
Japanese convenience stores are the best!
I want one in New York!
Moved
I can't believe it!

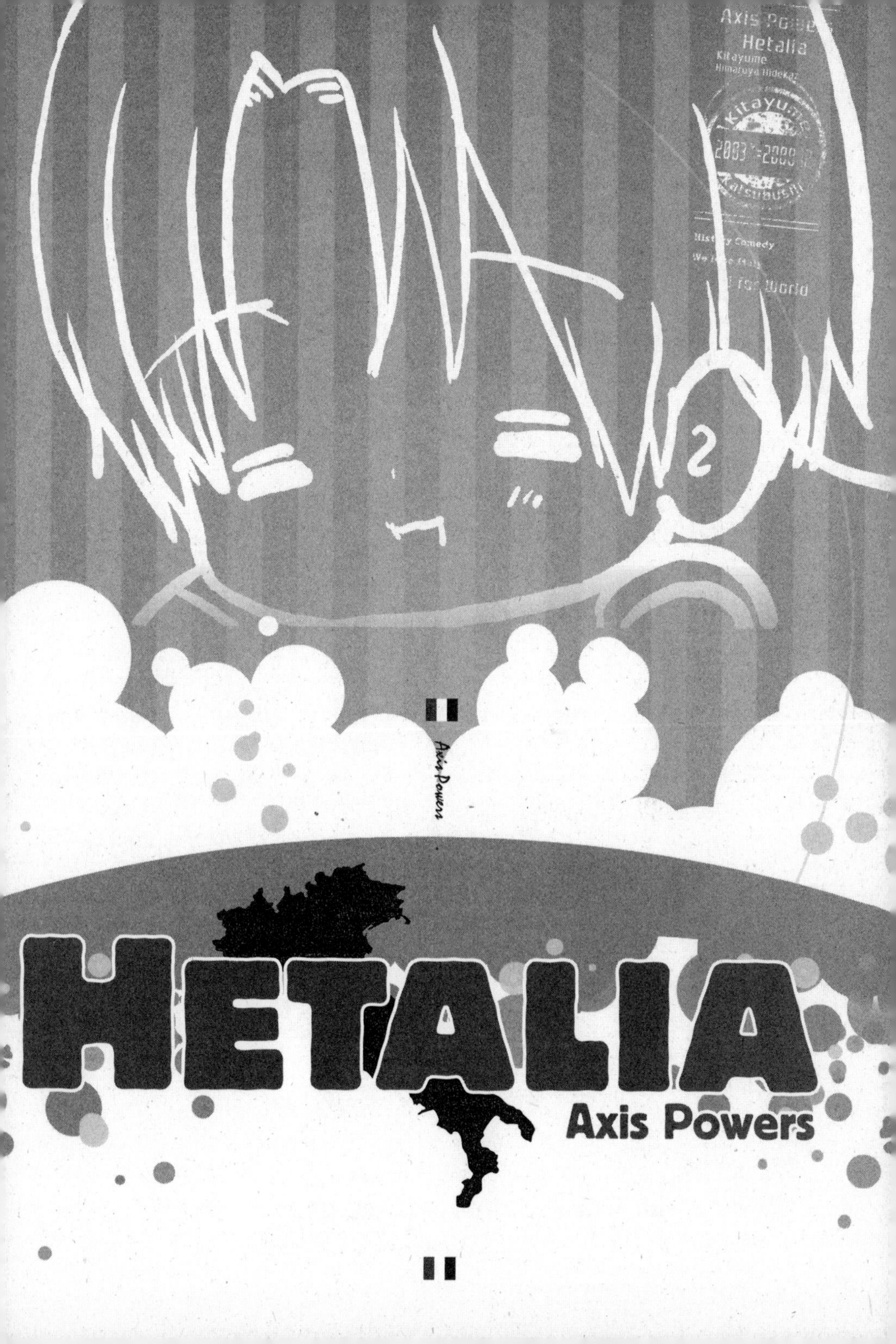

Hetalia
Kitayume
HETALIA
Axis Powers

English and Japanese Monster Culture

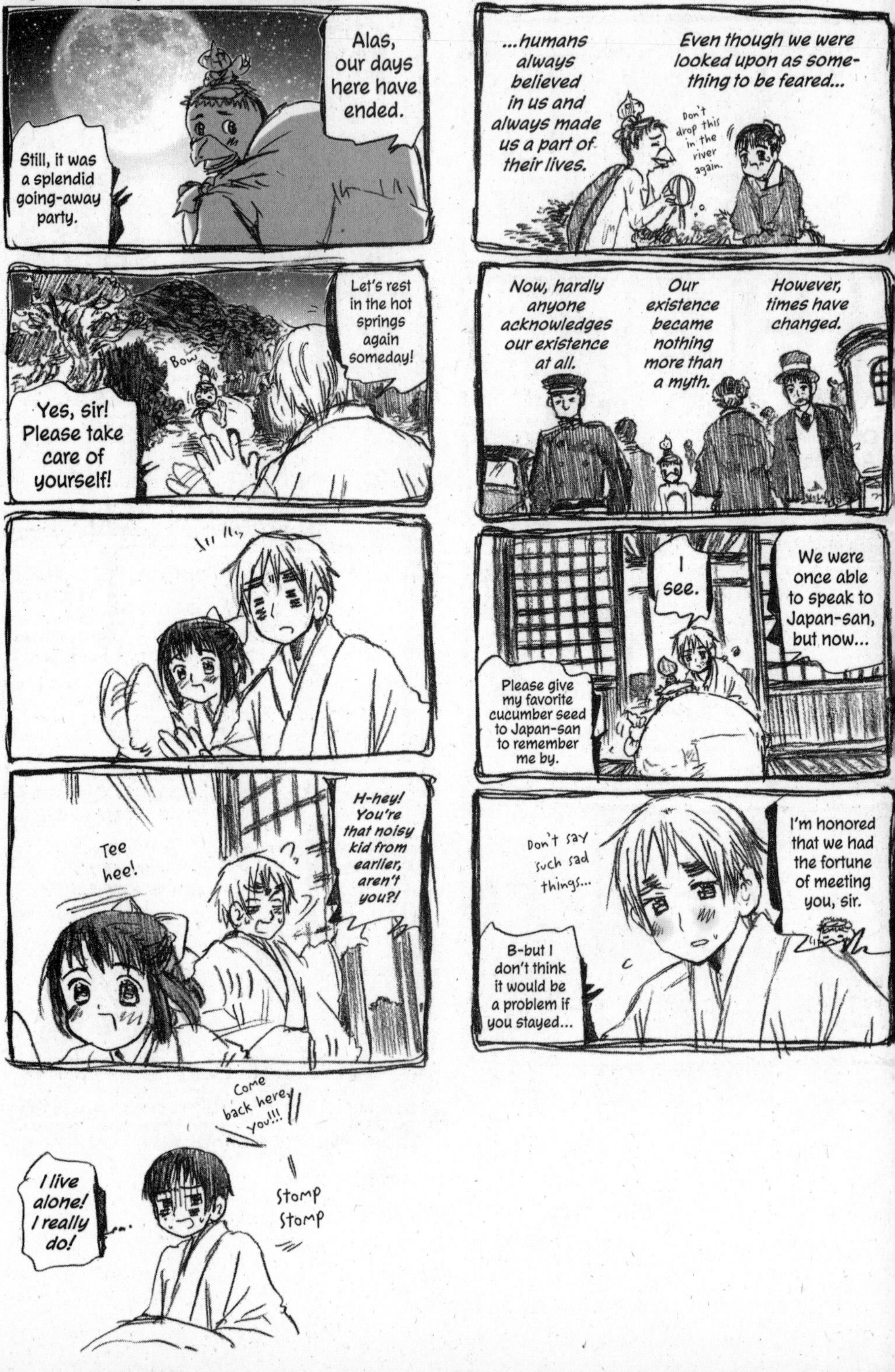

Even though we were looked upon as some-thing to be feared...
...humans always believed in us and always made us a part of their lives.
Don't drop this in the river again.
However, times have changed.
Our existence became nothing more than a myth.
Now, hardly anyone acknowledges our existence at all.
We were once able to speak to Japan-san, but now...
I see.
Please give my favorite cucumber seed to Japan-san to remember me by.
I'm honored that we had the fortune of meeting you, sir.
Don't say such sad things...
B-but I don't think it would be a problem if you stayed...
Alas, our days here have ended.
Still, it was a splendid going-away party.
Let's rest in the hot springs again someday!
Bow
Yes, sir! Please take care of yourself!
H-hey! You're that noisy kid from earlier, aren't you?!
Tee hee!
Come back here, you!!!
Stomp Stomp
I live alone! I really do!

English and Japanese Monster Culture

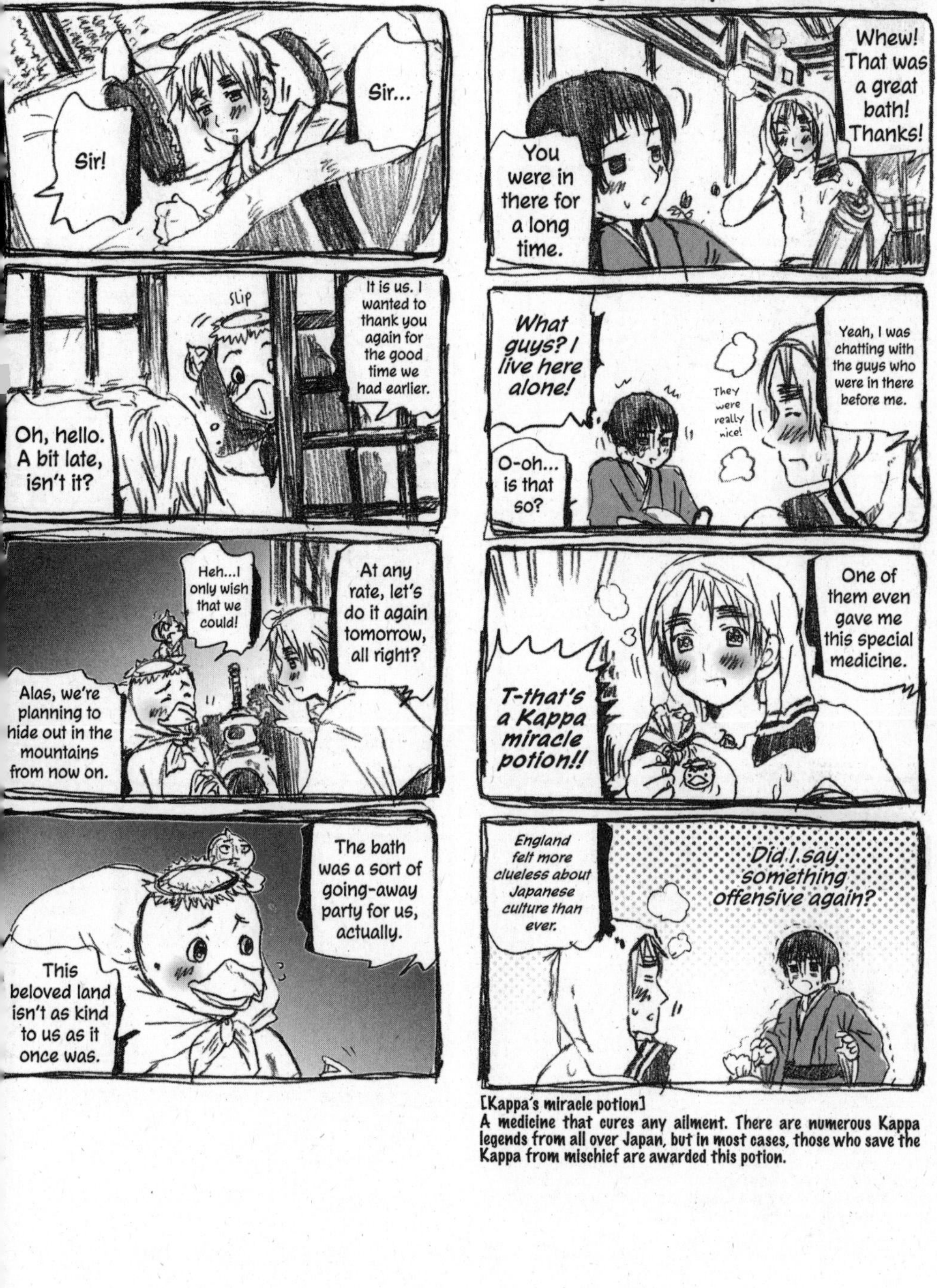
Whew! That was a great bath! Thanks!
You were in there for a long time.
Yeah, I was chatting with the guys who were in there before me.
They were really nice!
What guys? I live here alone!
O-oh... is that so?
One of them even gave me this special medicine.
T-that's a Kappa miracle potion!!
Did I say something offensive again?
England felt more clueless about Japanese culture than ever.
Sir...
Sir!
Slip
It is us. I wanted to thank you again for the good time we had earlier.
Oh, hello. A bit late, isn't it?
At any rate, let's do it again tomorrow, all right?
Heh...I only wish that we could!
Alas, we're planning to hide out in the mountains from now on.
The bath was a sort of going-away party for us, actually.
This beloved land isn't as kind to us as it once was.

[Kappa's miracle potion]
A medicine that cures any ailment. There are numerous Kappa legends from all over Japan, but in most cases, those who save the Kappa from mischief are awarded this potion.

English and Japanese Monster Culture

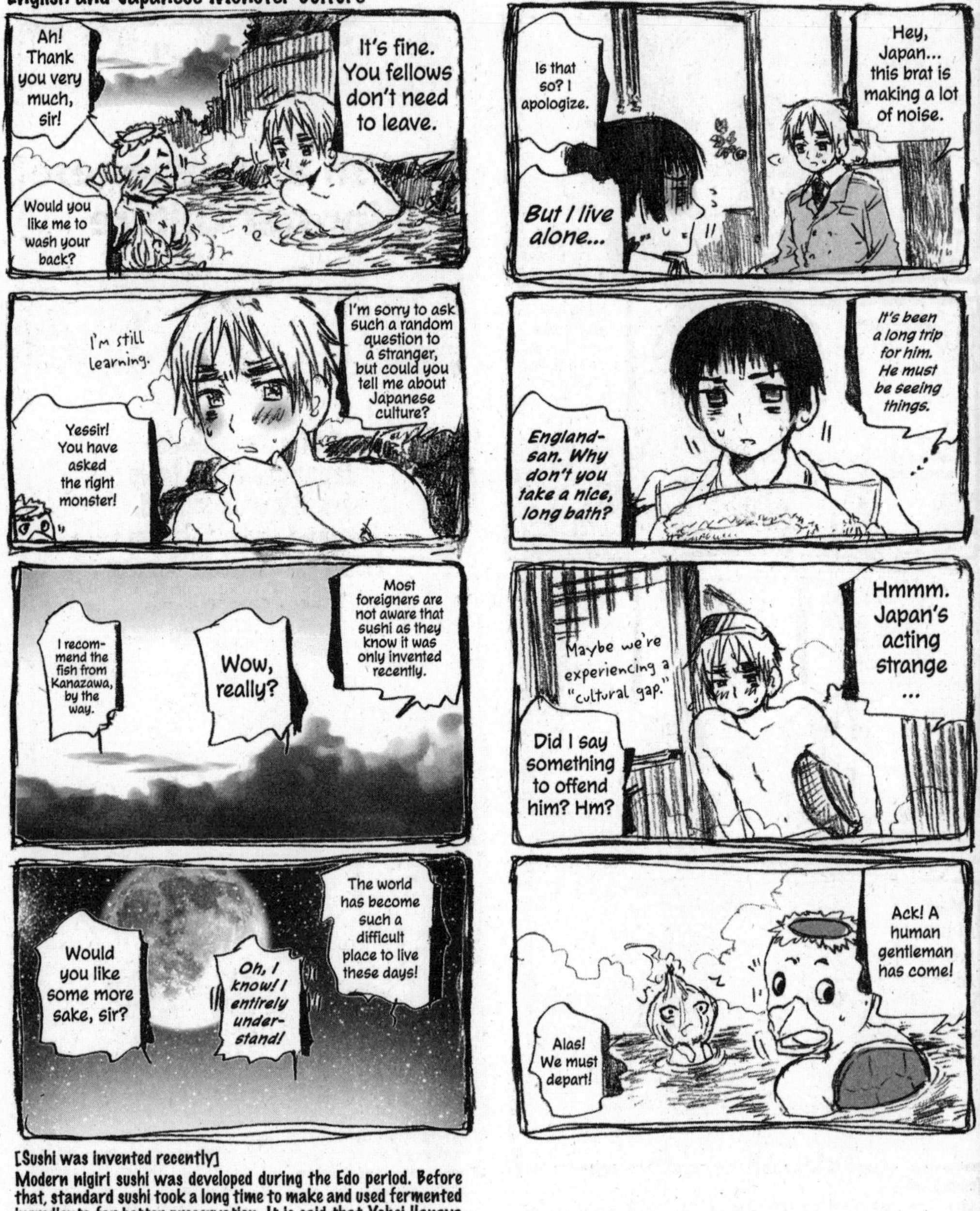
Hey, Japan... this brat is making a lot of noise.
Is that so? I apologize.
But I live alone...
It's been a long trip for him. He must be seeing things.
England-san. Why don't you take a nice, long bath?
Hmmm. Japan's acting strange ...
Maybe we're experiencing a "cultural gap."
Did I say something to offend him? Hm?
Ack! A human gentleman has come!
Alas! We must depart!
It's fine. You fellows don't need to leave.
Ah! Thank you very much, sir!
Would you like me to wash your back?
I'm sorry to ask such a random question to a stranger, but could you tell me about Japanese culture?
I'm still learning.
Yessir! You have asked the right monster!
Most foreigners are not aware that sushi as they know it was only invented recently.
Wow, really?
I recommend the fish from Kanazawa, by the way.
The world has become such a difficult place to live these days!
Oh, I know! I entirely understand!
Would you like some more sake, sir?

[Sushi was invented recently]
Modern nigiri sushi was developed during the Edo period. Before that, standard sushi took a long time to make and used fermented ingredients for better preservation. It is said that Yohei Hanaya invented the present day sushi shape, which was a big hit with the impatient people of Edo.

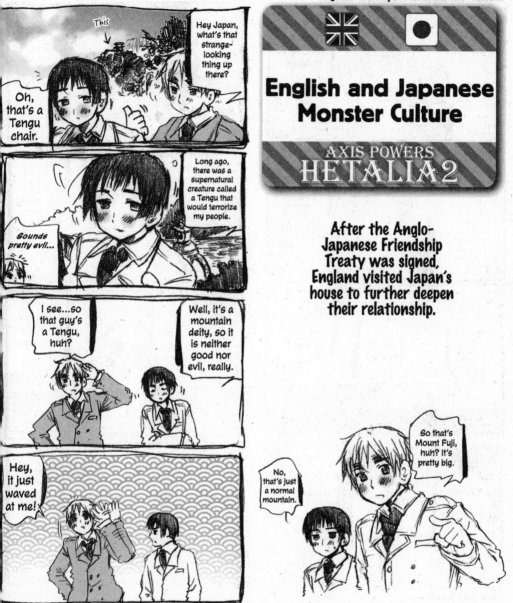

English and Japanese Monster Culture

AXIS POWERS HETALIA 2

After the Anglo-Japanese Friendship Treaty was signed, England visited Japan's house to further deepen their relationship.

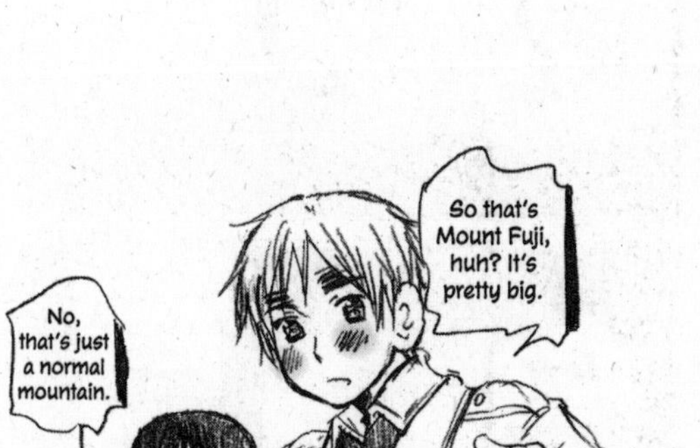
So that's Mount Fuji, huh? It's pretty big.
No, that's just a normal mountain.

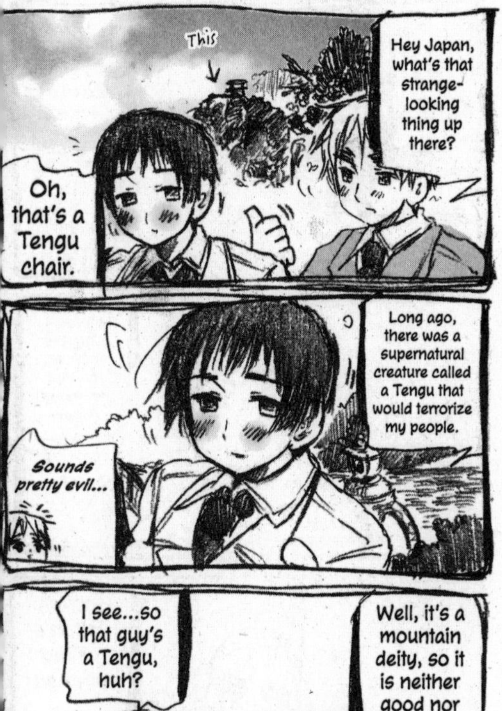
Hey Japan, what's that strange-looking thing up there?
This
Oh, that's a Tengu chair.
Long ago, there was a supernatural creature called a Tengu that would terrorize my people.
Sounds pretty evil...
Well, it's a mountain deity, so it is neither good nor evil, really.
I see...so that guy's a Tengu, huh?
Hey, it just waved at me!

Tengu chair]

structure that Tengu, or crow demons, supposedly rested on. They ncluded pine trees, cedar trees and stones. Tengu chairs also warned eople not to climb the mountain any higher, lest they step into Tengu erritory.

Japan-kun and America-kun 8

Maybe yours are too big.

AXIS POWERS HETALIA 2

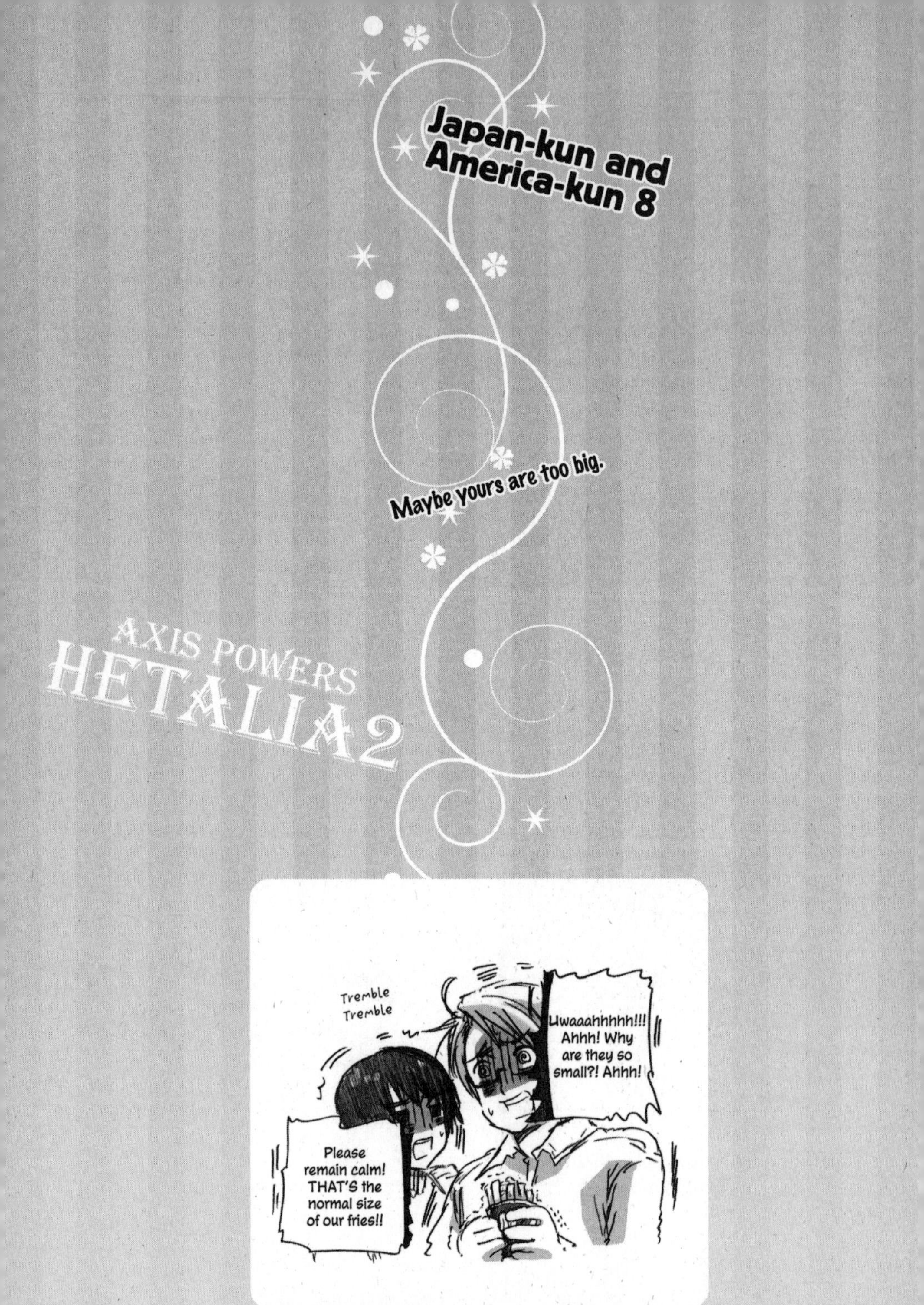
Uwaaahhhhh!!! Ahhh! Why are they so small?! Ahhh!
Tremble Tremble
Please remain calm! THAT'S the normal size of our fries!!

Don't Give Up, Canada!
And Then There Were Eight...Again

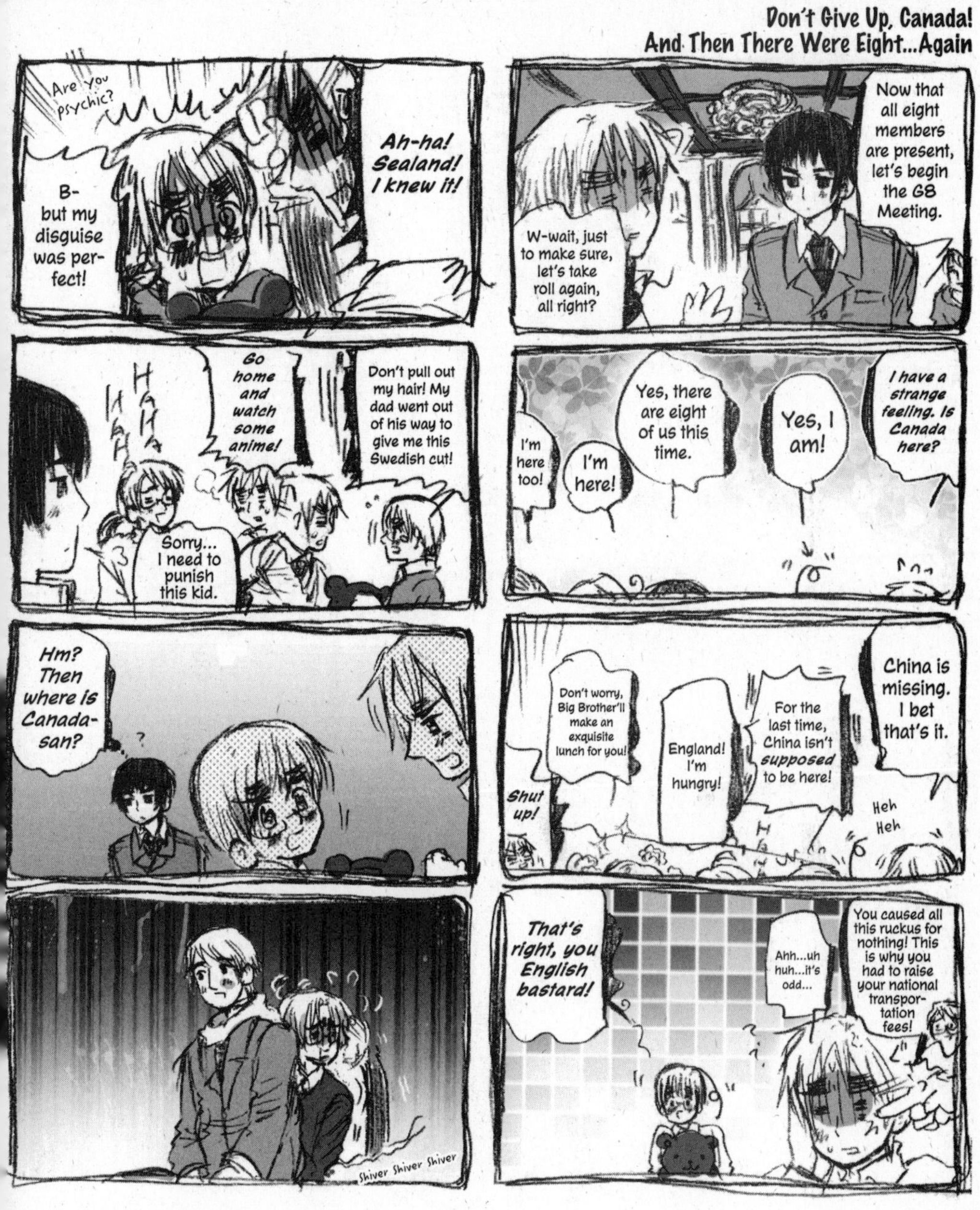
Now that all eight members are present, let's begin the G8 Meeting.
W-wait, just to make sure, let's take roll again, all right?
Ah-ha! Sealand! I knew it!
Are you psychic?
B- but my disguise was perfect!
I have a strange feeling. Is Canada here?
Yes, I am!
Yes, there are eight of us this time.
I'm here!
I'm here too!
Don't pull out my hair! My dad went out of his way to give me this Swedish cut!
Go home and watch some anime!
Sorry... I need to punish this kid.
China is missing. I bet that's it.
For the last time, China isn't *supposed* to be here!
England! I'm hungry!
Don't worry, Big Brother'll make an exquisite lunch for you!
Shut up!
Heh Heh
Hm? Then where is Canada-san?
You caused all this ruckus for nothing! This is why you had to raise your national transportation fees!
Ahh...uh huh...it's odd...
That's right, you English bastard!
Shiver Shiver Shiver

Don't Give Up, Canada!
A Common Bond

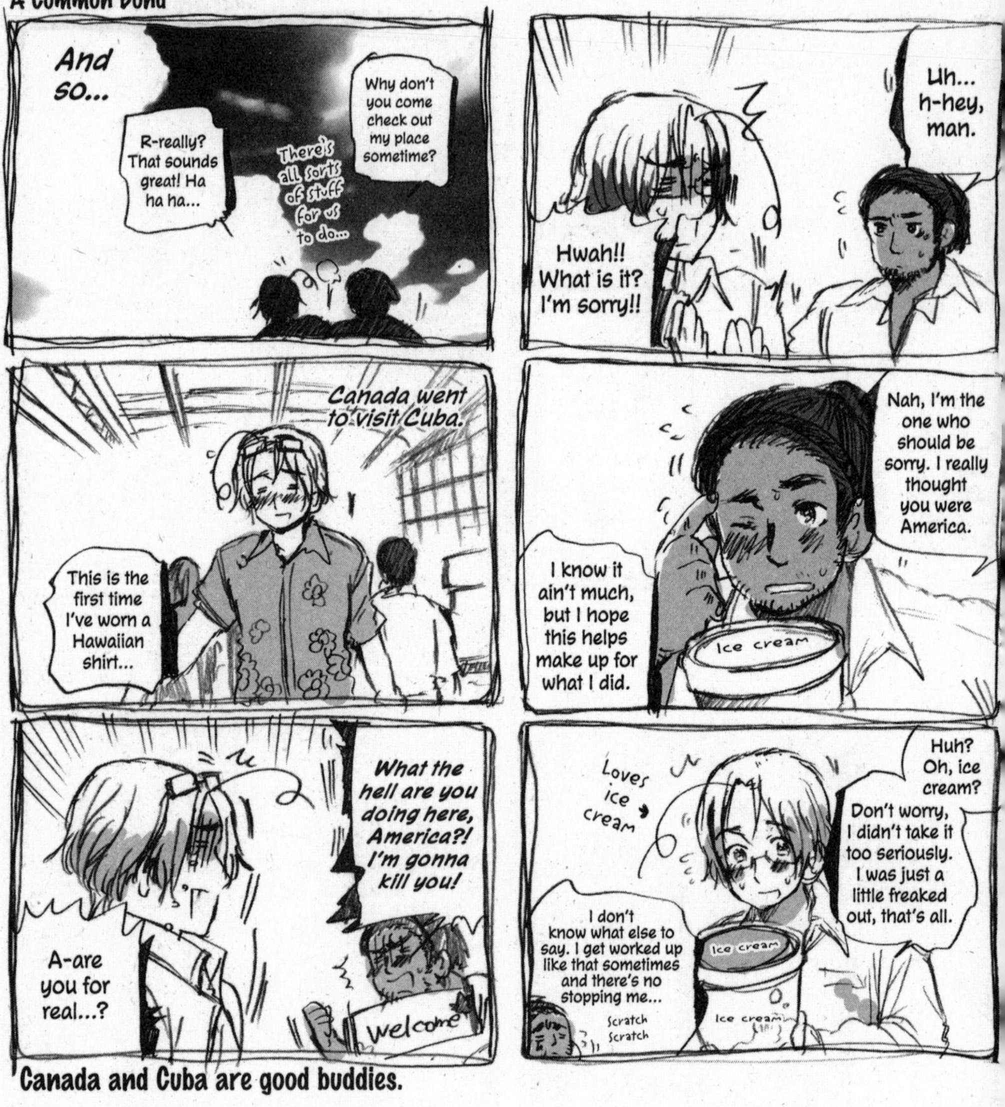
And so...
Why don't you come check out my place sometime?
There's all sorts of stuff for us to do...
R-really? That sounds great! Ha ha ha...
Canada went to visit Cuba.
This is the first time I've worn a Hawaiian shirt...
What the hell are you doing here, America?! I'm gonna kill you!
A-are you for real...?
welcome
Uh... h-hey, man.
Hwah!! What is it? I'm sorry!!
Nah, I'm the one who should be sorry. I really thought you were America.
I know it ain't much, but I hope this helps make up for what I did.
Ice cream
Huh? Oh, ice cream?
Loves ice cream
Don't worry, I didn't take it too seriously. I was just a little freaked out, that's all.
I don't know what else to say. I get worked up like that sometimes and there's no stopping me...
Ice cream
Ice cream
Scratch Scratch

Canada and Cuba are good buddies.

Don't Give Up, Canada! Just Put Your Mind to It!

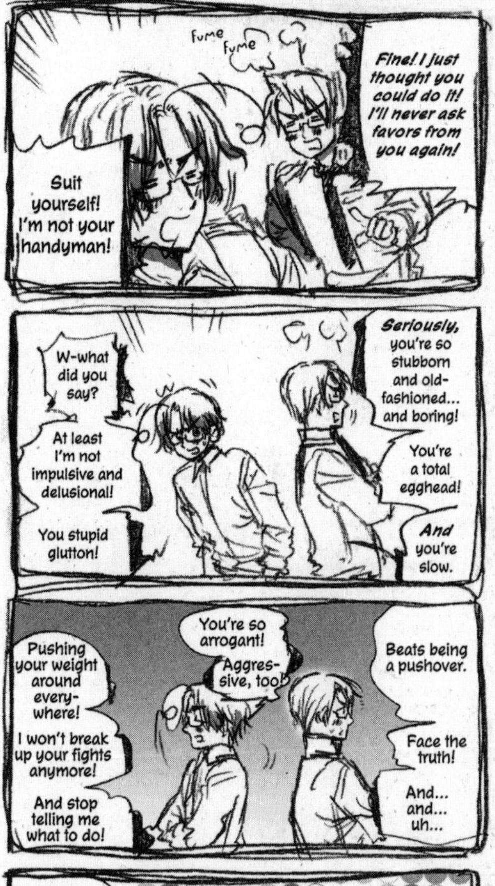
Fume Fume
Fine! I just thought you could do it! I'll never ask favors from you again!
Suit yourself! I'm not your handyman!
Seriously, you're so stubborn and old-fashioned... and boring!
You're a total egghead!
And you're slow.
W-what did you say?
At least I'm not impulsive and delusional!
You stupid glutton!
Beats being a pushover.
Face the truth!
And... and... uh...
You're so arrogant!
Aggres-sive, too!
Pushing your weight around every-where!
I won't break up your fights anymore!
And stop telling me what to do!
You eat hamburgers all the time...
You buy useless crap over the internet...
...then you try to pawn it off to me!
What, am I your underling or something?

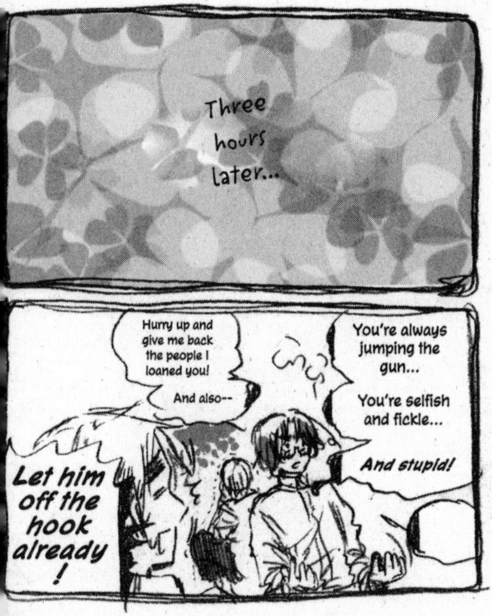
Three hours later...
You're always jumping the gun...
You're selfish and fickle...
And stupid!
Hurry up and give me back the people I loaned you!
And also--
Let him off the hook already!

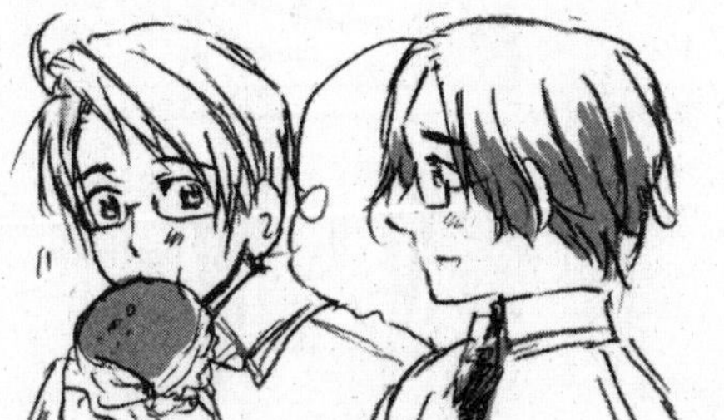

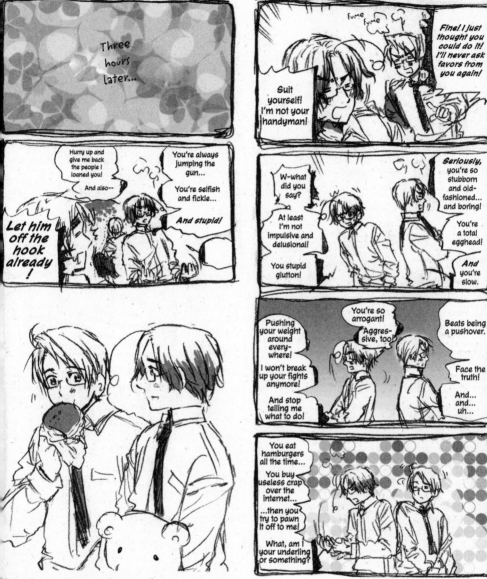

Useless fact about Japan and Canada-san]
here was a song titled "Mr. Roboto" that was a big hit in Canada ome time ago. In the chorus, peculiar Japanese words are used: Domo arigato,♪ domo domo♪" As a result, Canadians thought the ong was popular in Japan as well.

Don't Give Up, Canada!
Once Canada, Always Canada

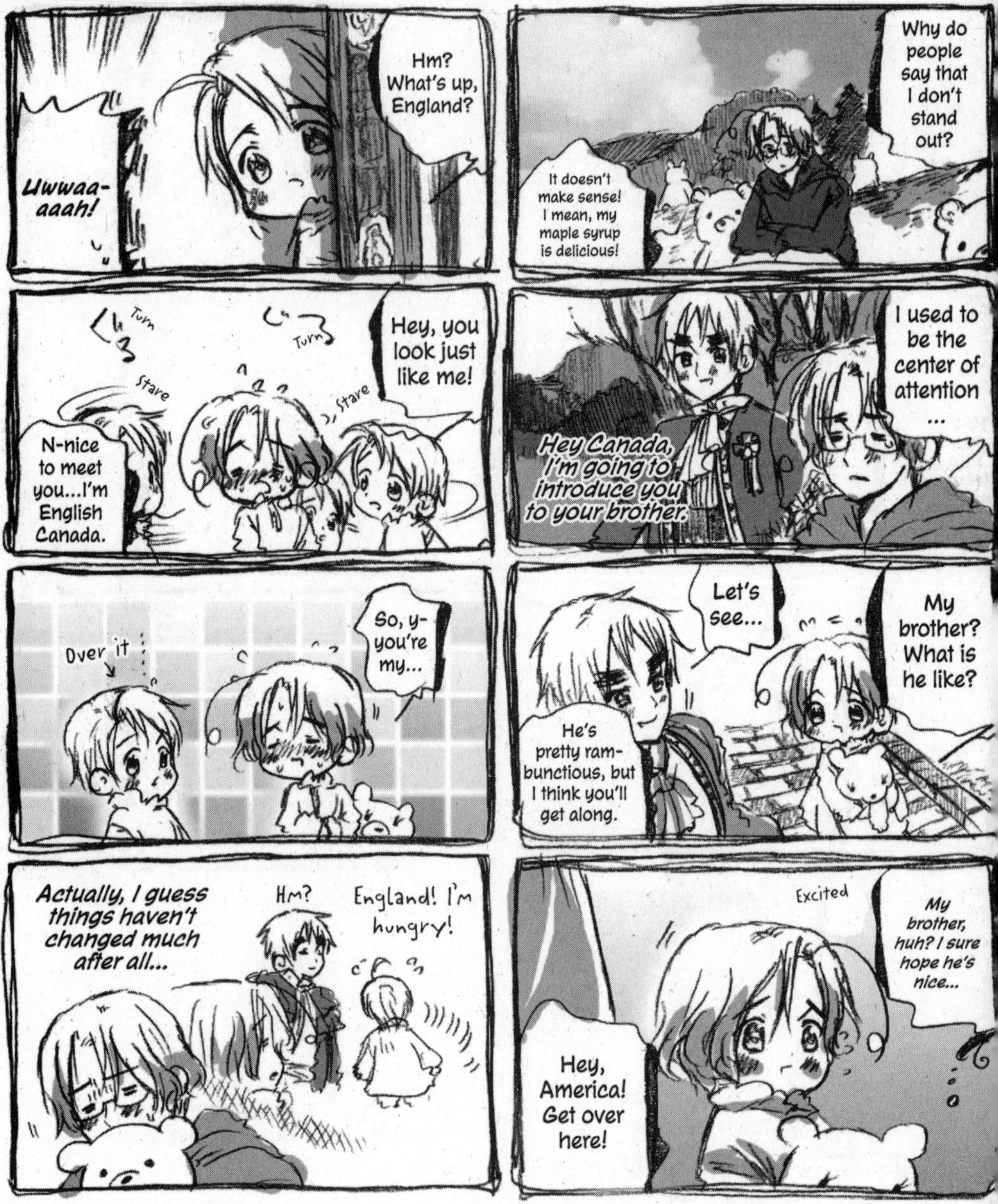
Why do people say that I don't stand out?
It doesn't make sense! I mean, my maple syrup is delicious!
Hm? What's up, England?
Uwwaa-aaah!
I used to be the center of attention ...
Hey Canada, I'm going to introduce you to your brother.
Hey, you look just like me!
Turn
Turn
Stare
Stare
N-nice to meet you...I'm English Canada.
My brother? What is he like?
Let's see...
He's pretty ram-bunctious, but I think you'll get along.
So, y-you're my...
Over it
My brother, huh? I sure hope he's nice...
Excited
Hey, America! Get over here!
England! I'm hungry!
Hm?
Actually, I guess things haven't changed much after all...

Canadian Time

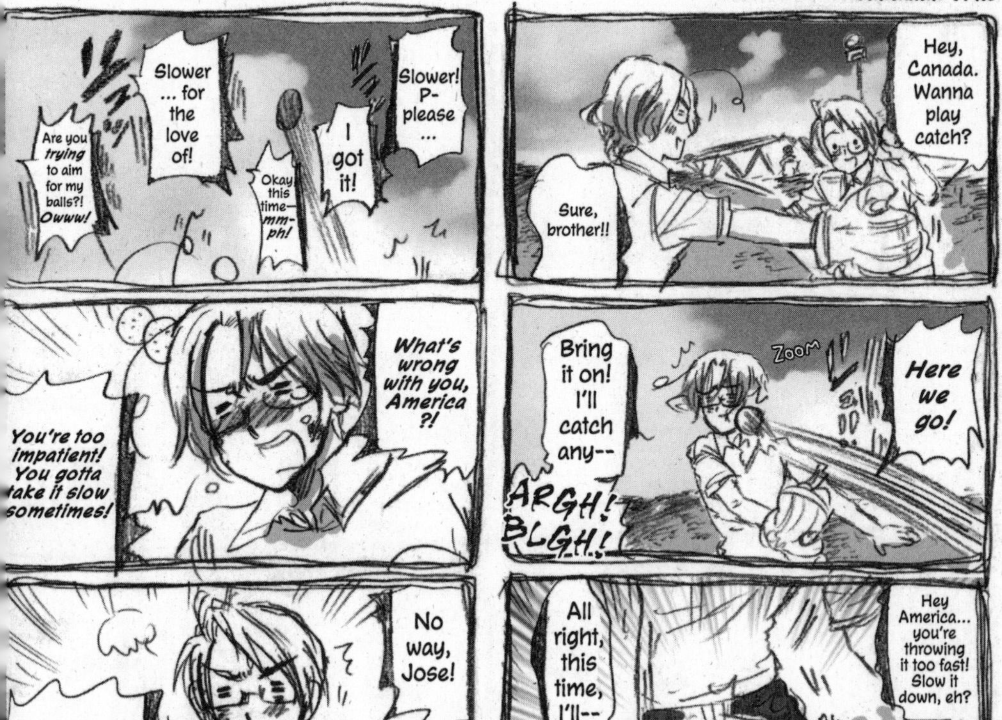
Hey, Canada. Wanna play catch?
Sure, brother!!
Here we go!
Zoom
Bring it on! I'll catch any--
ARGH! BLGH!
Hey America... you're throwing it too fast! Slow it down, eh?
All right, this time, I'll--
OK! Go for it!!
ARGH!
Slower! P-please ...
I got it!
Slower ... for the love of!
Okay this time—mmph!
Are you trying to aim for my balls?! Owww!
What's wrong with you, America ?!
You're too impatient! You gotta take it slow sometimes!
No way, Jose!
The problem is, you're too slow!
What did you say? Take this!
Punch
Punch
Ha ha ha! Slow poke!
Another peaceful day in Canada.

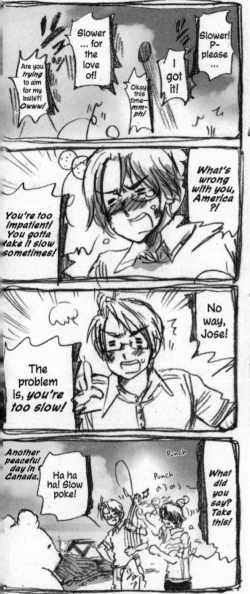

[Canadian Time]
Beware of Canada's laid-back attitude. Even entering the country can take forever. No matter how busy a place is, Canadians will always take their lunch and coffee breaks. Be prepared...bring a book!

[No way Jose]
Who is Jose? Nobody knows, but that doesn't stop Americans from saying this.

Don't Give Up, Canada!
We're Cheering for You, Canada!

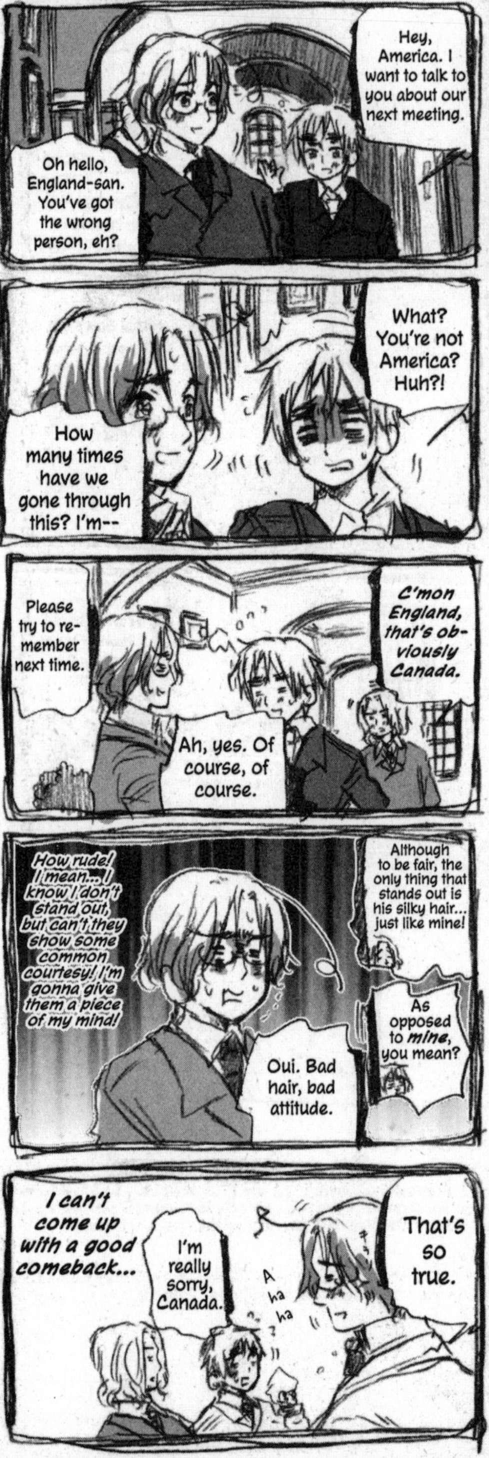
Hey, America. I want to talk to you about our next meeting.
Oh hello, England-san. You've got the wrong person, eh?
What? You're not America? Huh?!
How many times have we gone through this? I'm--
Please try to remember next time.
C'mon England, that's obviously Canada.
Ah, yes. Of course, of course.
How rude! I mean... I know I don't stand out, but can't they show some common courtesy! I'm gonna give them a piece of my mind!
Although to be fair, the only thing that stands out is his silky hair... just like mine!
As opposed to mine, you mean?
Oui. Bad hair, bad attitude.
I can't come up with a good comeback...
I'm really sorry, Canada.
That's so true.
A ha ha

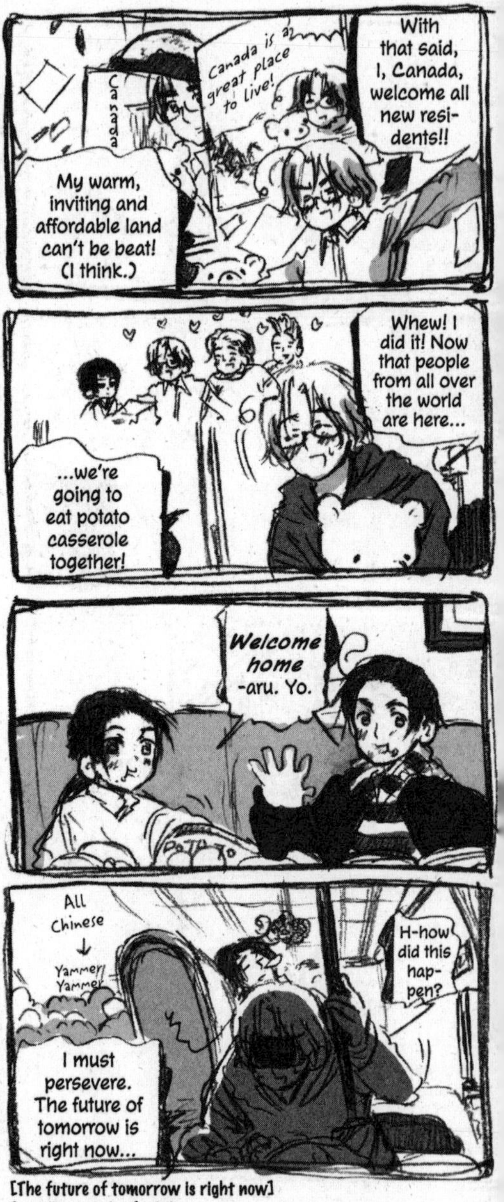
Canada
Canada is a great place to live!
With that said, I, Canada, welcome all new residents!!
My warm, inviting and affordable land can't be beat! (I think.)
Whew! I did it! Now that people from all over the world are here...
...we're going to eat potato casserole together!
Welcome home -aru. Yo.
All Chinese
↓
Yammer Yammer
H-how did this happen?
I must persevere. The future of tomorrow is right now...

[The future of tomorrow is right now]
Canadian words of wisdom.

[Very ethnic]
Canada's open door policy led to a heavy influx of immigrants and exchange students from Korea and China. It's not uncommon to see Korean signs and shops in numerous Canadian cities like Toronto and Vancouver. Apparently it's a sort of status symbol for Koreans to go to English-speaking nations as foreign exchange students.

Don't Give Up, Canada!
The Proud People of Canada

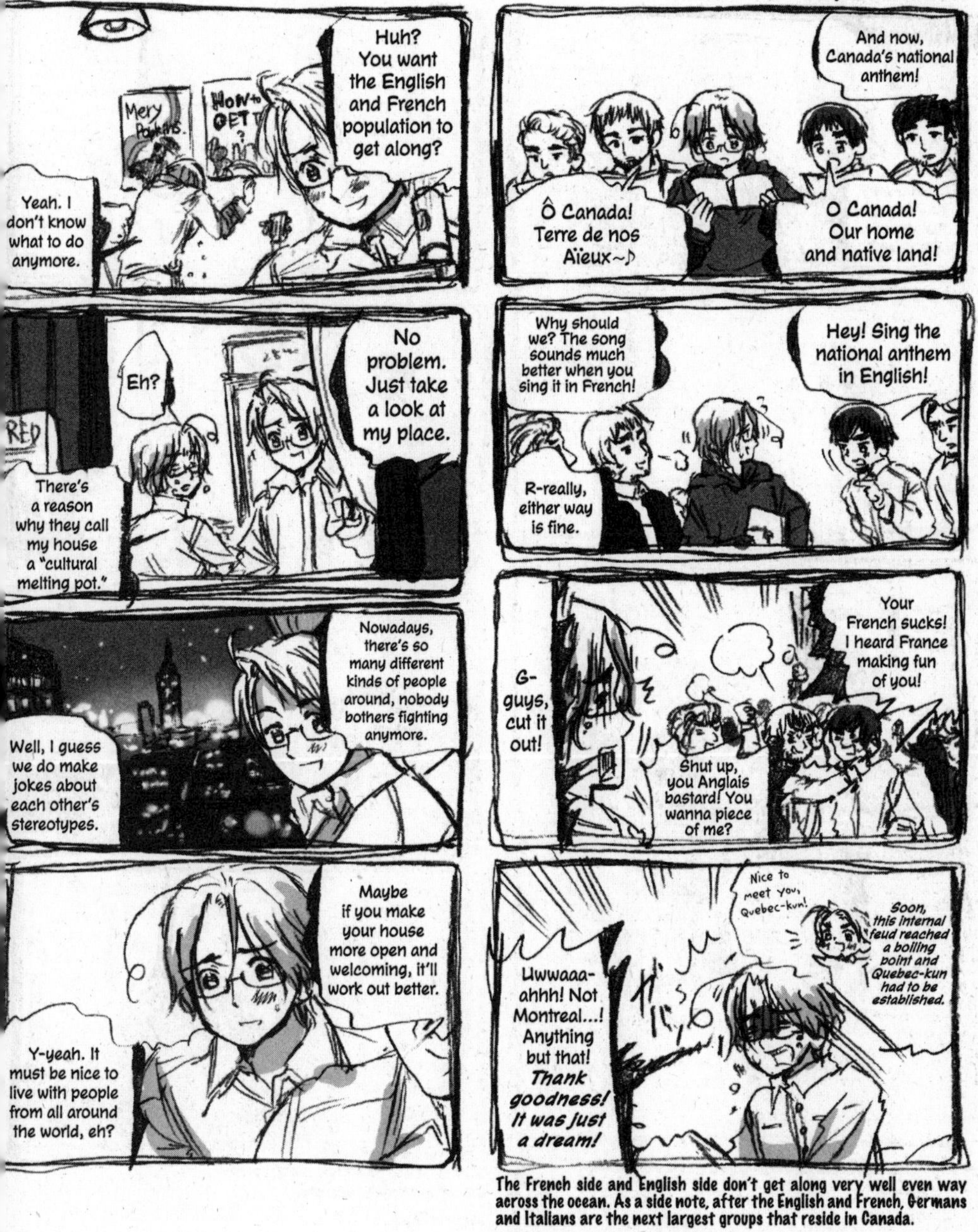

And now, Canada's national anthem!
O Canada! Our home and native land!
Ô Canada! Terre de nos Aïeux~♪
Hey! Sing the national anthem in English!
Why should we? The song sounds much better when you sing it in French!
R-really, either way is fine.
Your French sucks! I heard France making fun of you!
G-guys, cut it out!
Shut up, you Anglais bastard! You wanna piece of me?
Soon, this internal feud reached a boiling point and Quebec-kun had to be established.
Nice to meet you, Quebec-kun!
Uwwaaa-ahhh! Not Montreal...! Anything but that!
Thank goodness! It was just a dream!
Huh? You want the English and French population to get along?
Yeah. I don't know what to do anymore.
No problem. Just take a look at my place.
Eh?
There's a reason why they call my house a "cultural melting pot."
Nowadays, there's so many different kinds of people around, nobody bothers fighting anymore.
Well, I guess we do make jokes about each other's stereotypes.
Maybe if you make your house more open and welcoming, it'll work out better.
Y-yeah. It must be nice to live with people from all around the world, eh?

The French side and English side don't get along very well even way across the ocean. As a side note, after the English and French, Germans and Italians are the next largest groups that reside in Canada.

[Quebec]
A predominantly French province in Canada. In 1995, they pushed for independence but failed when 50.6% voted against it.

Don't Give Up, Canada!
I'm Going To Assert Myself!

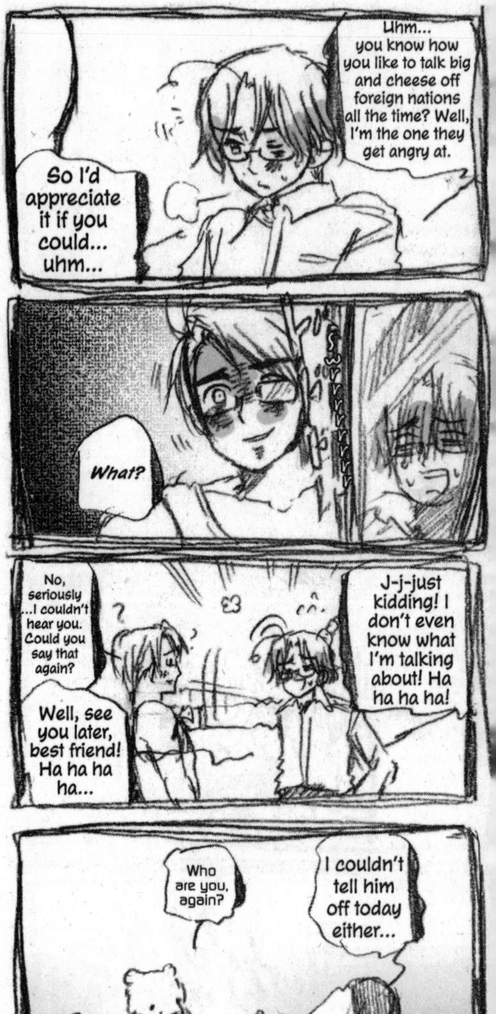
Uhm... you know how you like to talk big and cheese off foreign nations all the time? Well, I'm the one they get angry at.
So I'd appreciate it if you could... uhm...
What?
J-j-just kidding! I don't even know what I'm talking about! Ha ha ha ha!
No, seriously ...I couldn't hear you. Could you say that again?
Well, see you later, best friend! Ha ha ha ha...
I couldn't tell him off today either...
Who are you, again?
CANADA!!

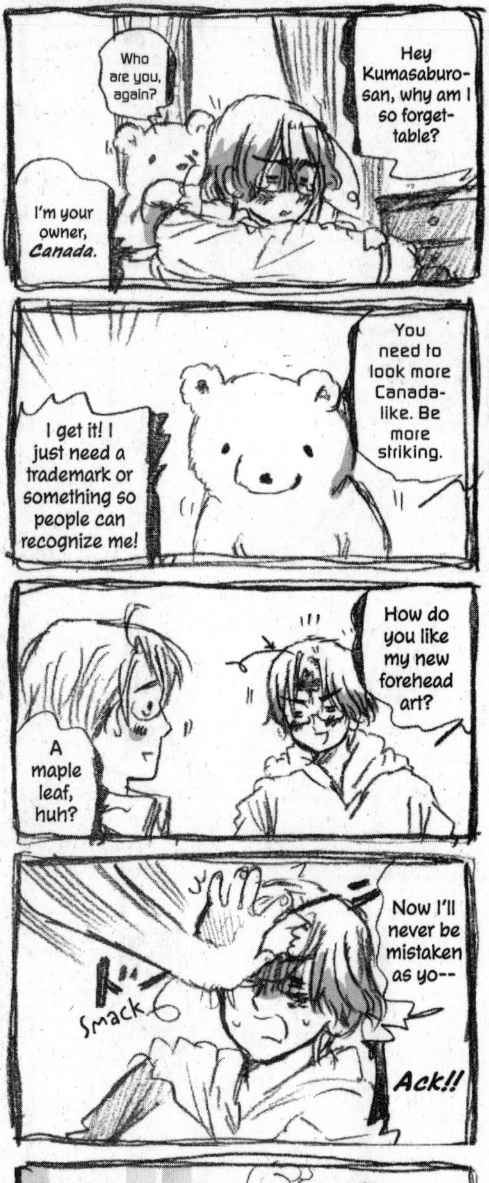
Hey Kumasaburo-san, why am I so forget-table?
Who are you, again?
I'm your owner, *Canada*.
You need to look more Canada-like. Be more striking.
I get it! I just need a trademark or something so people can recognize me!
How do you like my new forehead art?
A maple leaf, huh?
Now I'll never be mistaken as yo--
Smack
Ack!!
Huh? What was that?
Ouch
I like you better this way.

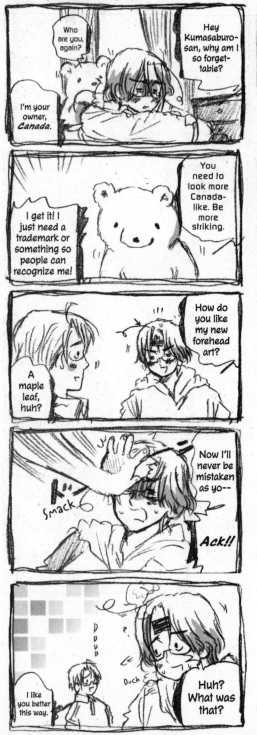

[Maple]

A common Canadian plant that is also the nation flower. Its future is in danger due to global warmin If Canada didn't have maple, then... no, I don't eve want to think about that.

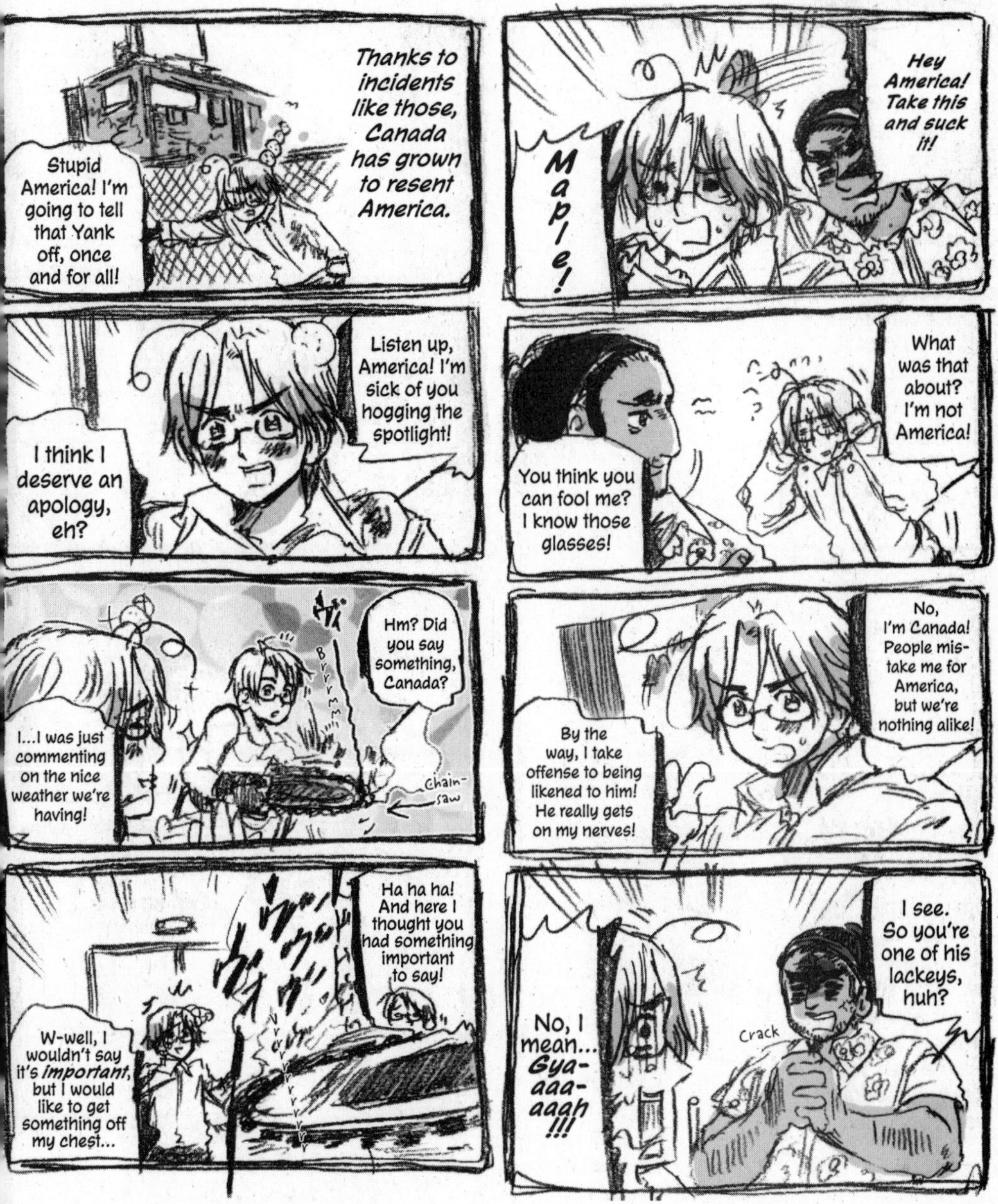
Hey America! Take this and suck it!
Maple!
What was that about? I'm not America!
You think you can fool me? I know those glasses!
No, I'm Canada! People mistake me for America, but we're nothing alike!
By the way, I take offense to being likened to him! He really gets on my nerves!
I see. So you're one of his lackeys, huh?
Crack
No, I mean... Gyaaaaaaah!!!
Thanks to incidents like those, Canada has grown to resent America.
Stupid America! I'm going to tell that Yank off, once and for all!
Listen up, America! I'm sick of you hogging the spotlight!
I think I deserve an apology, eh?
Hm? Did you say something, Canada?
Brrrrmm
Chain-saw
I...I was just commenting on the nice weather we're having!
Ha ha ha! And here I thought you had something important to say!
W-well, I wouldn't say it's *important*, but I would like to get something off my chest...

Don't Give Up, Canada!
The Eight Are Here!!

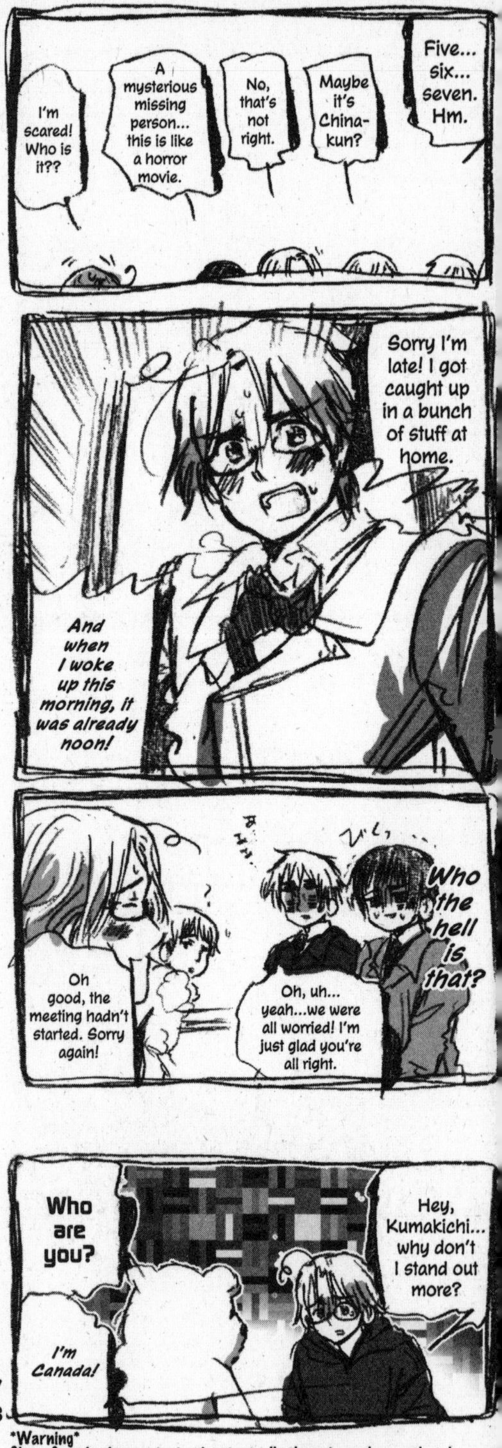

Five... six... seven. Hm.
Maybe it's China-kun?
No, that's not right.
A mysterious missing person... this is like a horror movie.
I'm scared! Who is it??
Sorry I'm late! I got caught up in a bunch of stuff at home.
And when I woke up this morning, it was already noon!
Who the hell is that?
Oh, uh... yeah...we were all worried! I'm just glad you're all right.
Oh good, the meeting hadn't started. Sorry again!
Hey, Kumakichi... why don't I stand out more?
Who are you?
I'm Canada!

Warning
Since Canada does not stand out at all, there is a chance that he may disappear without notice.

Canada

An unfortunate nation who is constantly in America's shadow. Canada is laid-back, kind and honest, but easily forgotten all the same. Many of the Europeans perceive Canada as "a nation to retire in."

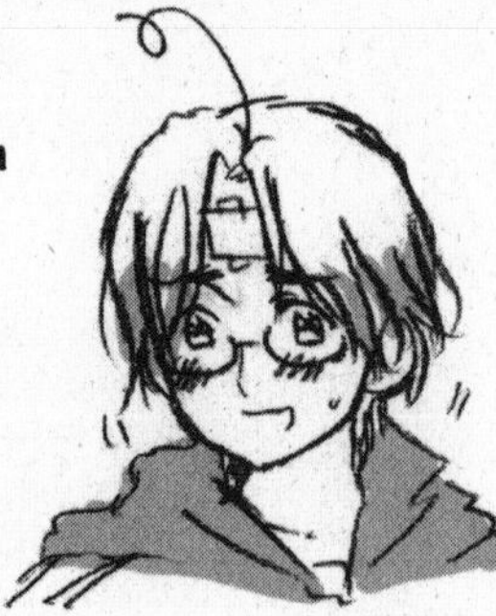

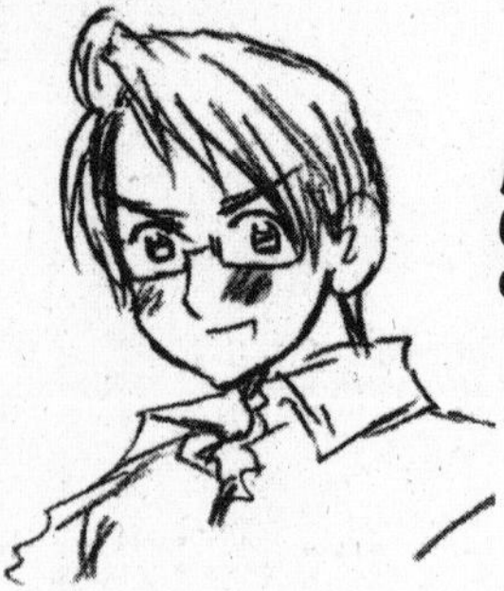

America

Canada's cause of misfortune.

Cuba

Cuba is a brave and energetic bro who loves ice cream. Unfortunately, that love has caused him to pack on a few extra pounds. He and America hate each other so much that they aren't on speaking terms anymore.

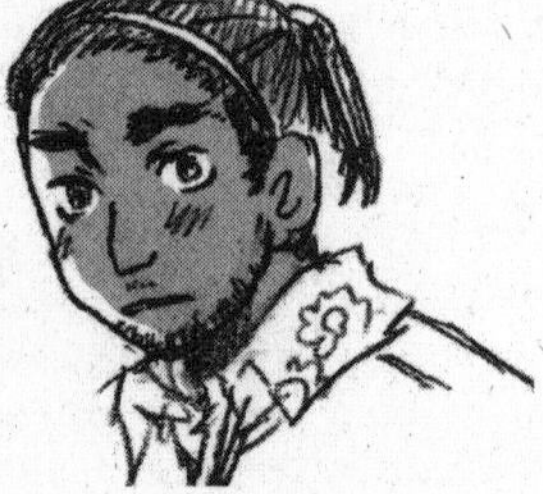

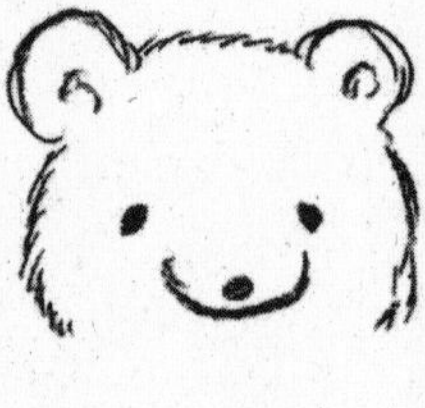

Kumajiro-san

A cute bear. Even though he's always hanging around Canada, he has a tough time remembering him. This is only fair since Canada always gets Kumajiro's name wrong.

Don't Give Up, Canada!

AXIS POWERS HETALIA 2

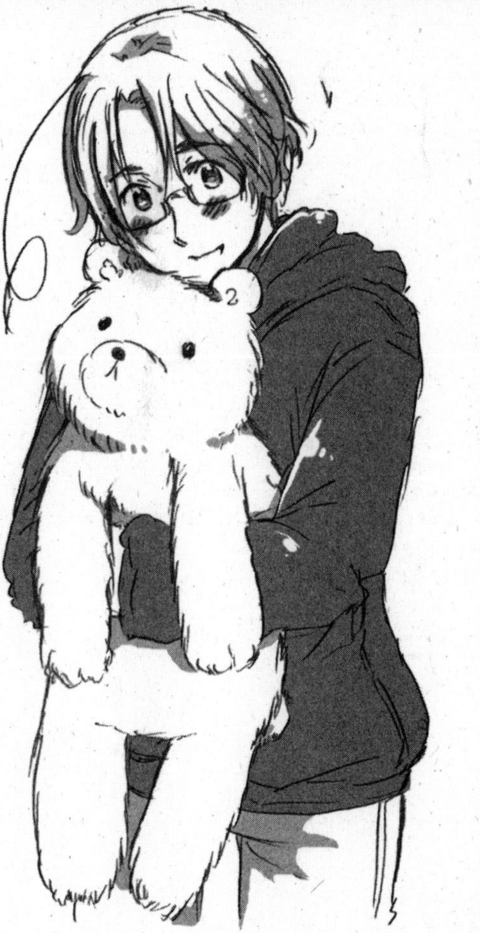

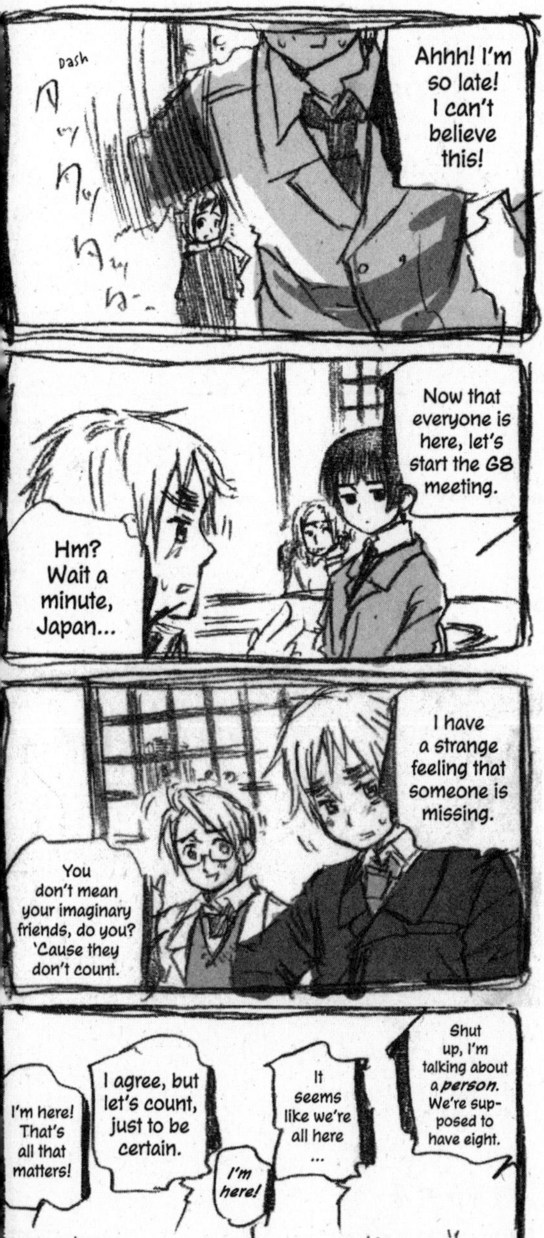
Ahhh! I'm so late! I can't believe this!
Dash
Now that everyone is here, let's start the G8 meeting.
Hm? Wait a minute, Japan...
I have a strange feeling that someone is missing.
You don't mean your imaginary friends, do you? 'Cause they don't count.
Shut up, I'm talking about a *person.* We're supposed to have eight.
It seems like we're all here ...
I'm here!
I agree, but let's count, just to be certain.
I'm here! That's all that matters!

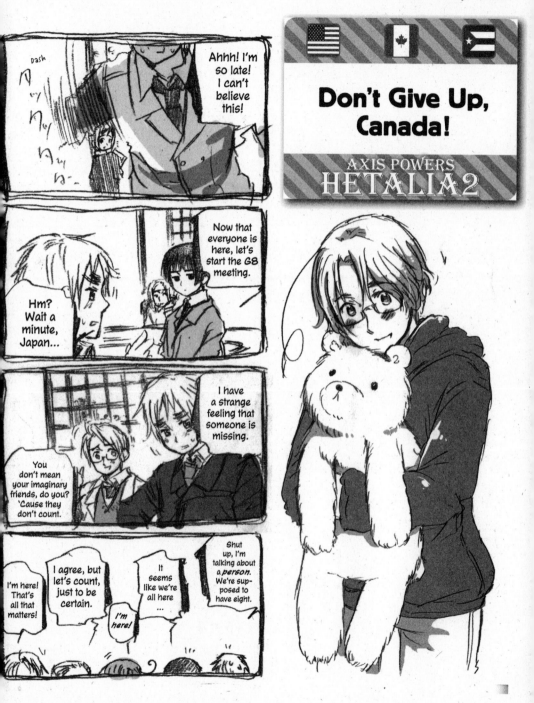

Japan-kun and America-kun 7

In America, people sometimes say: "I just saw your wife running over to Nevada." It's intended as a burn, as it's infamously easy to get a divorce in Nevada.

AXIS POWERS
HETALIA 2

Ah... r-right.

Nevada? Sounds like that type of person'll be in a bar in L.A.

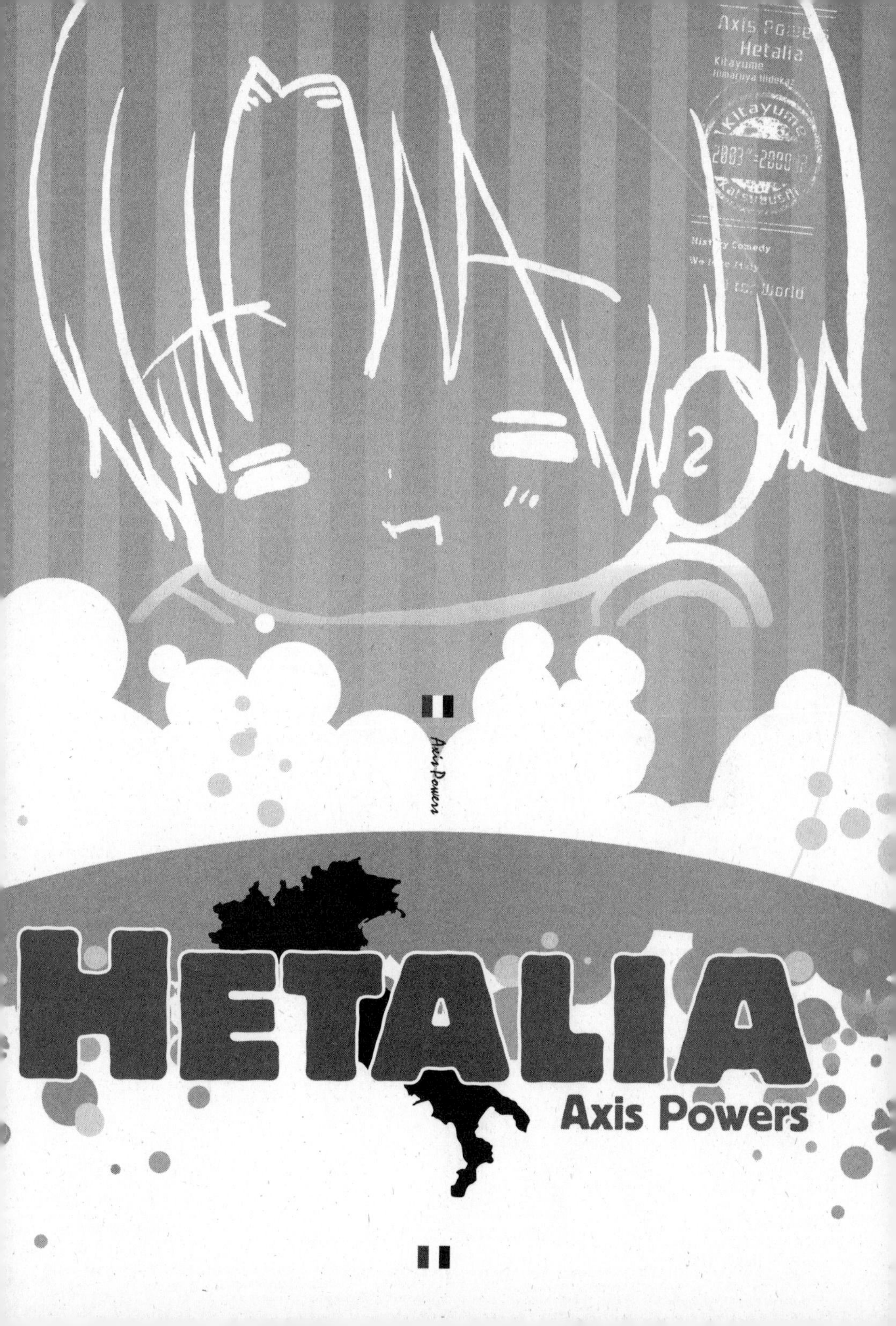
Hetalia
Kitayume
Kitayume
Axis Powers
HETALIA
Axis Powers

Battle for the New World
They Grow Up So Fast!

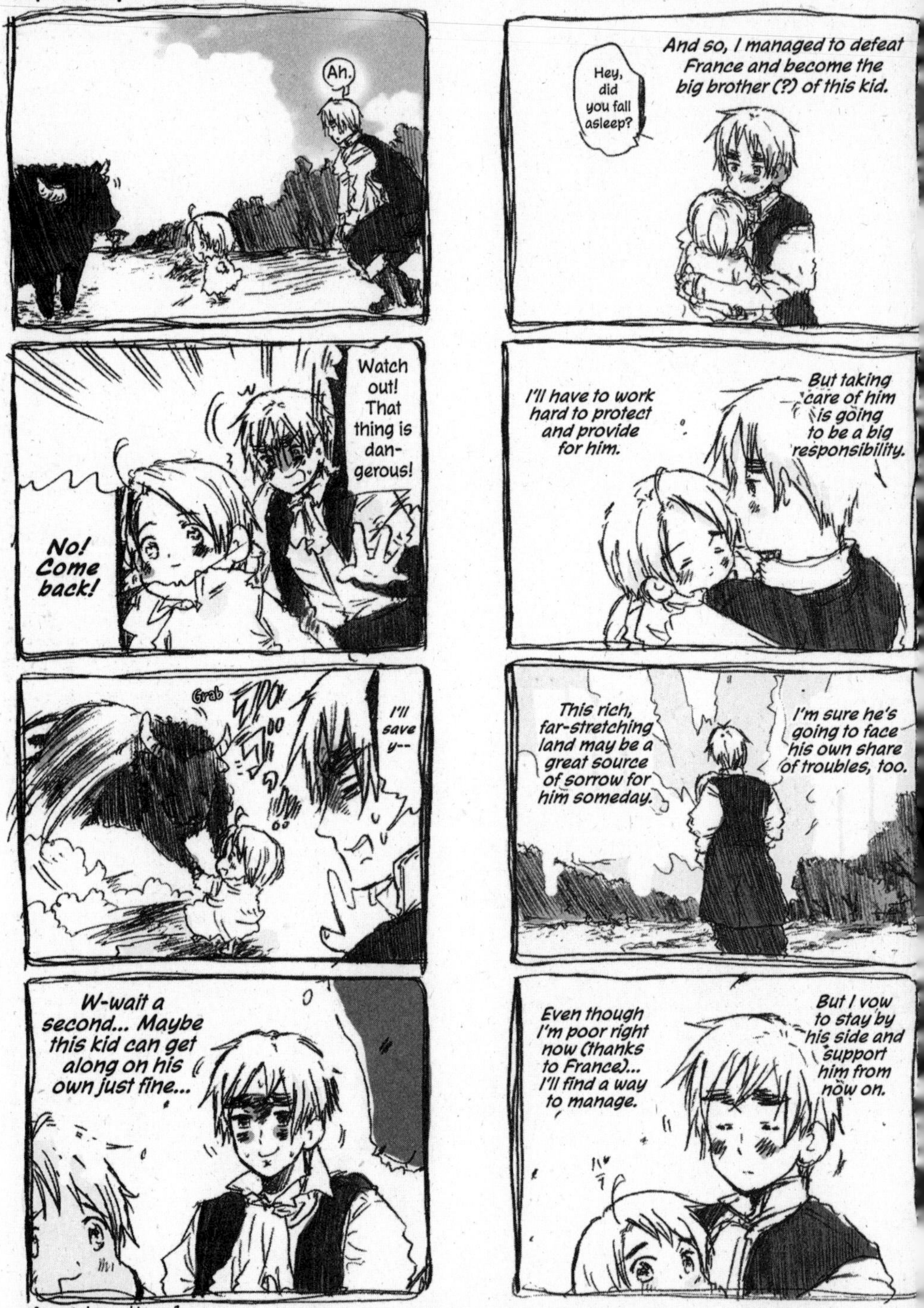

And so, I managed to defeat France and become the big brother (?) of this kid.
Hey, did you fall asleep?
But taking care of him is going to be a big responsibility.
I'll have to work hard to protect and provide for him.
I'm sure he's going to face his own share of troubles, too.
This rich, far-stretching land may be a great source of sorrow for him someday.
But I vow to stay by his side and support him from now on.
Even though I'm poor right now (thanks to France)... I'll find a way to manage.
Ah.
Watch out! That thing is dangerous!
No! Come back!
I'll save y--
Grab
W-wait a second... Maybe this kid can get along on his own just fine...

[Can get along on his own]
England gave Americans exemption from taxes, religious freedom and free trade. This is one of the reasons why America developed a reputation as "the la[...] of the free." As different countries came together and left their mark on America, it developed its own unique culture and economy. It was not long befo[...] America's industrial power rivaled that of England. As an added note, England only had control over America for about 10 to 20 years in total.

Battle for the New World
His Taste Buds Were Ruined for Life

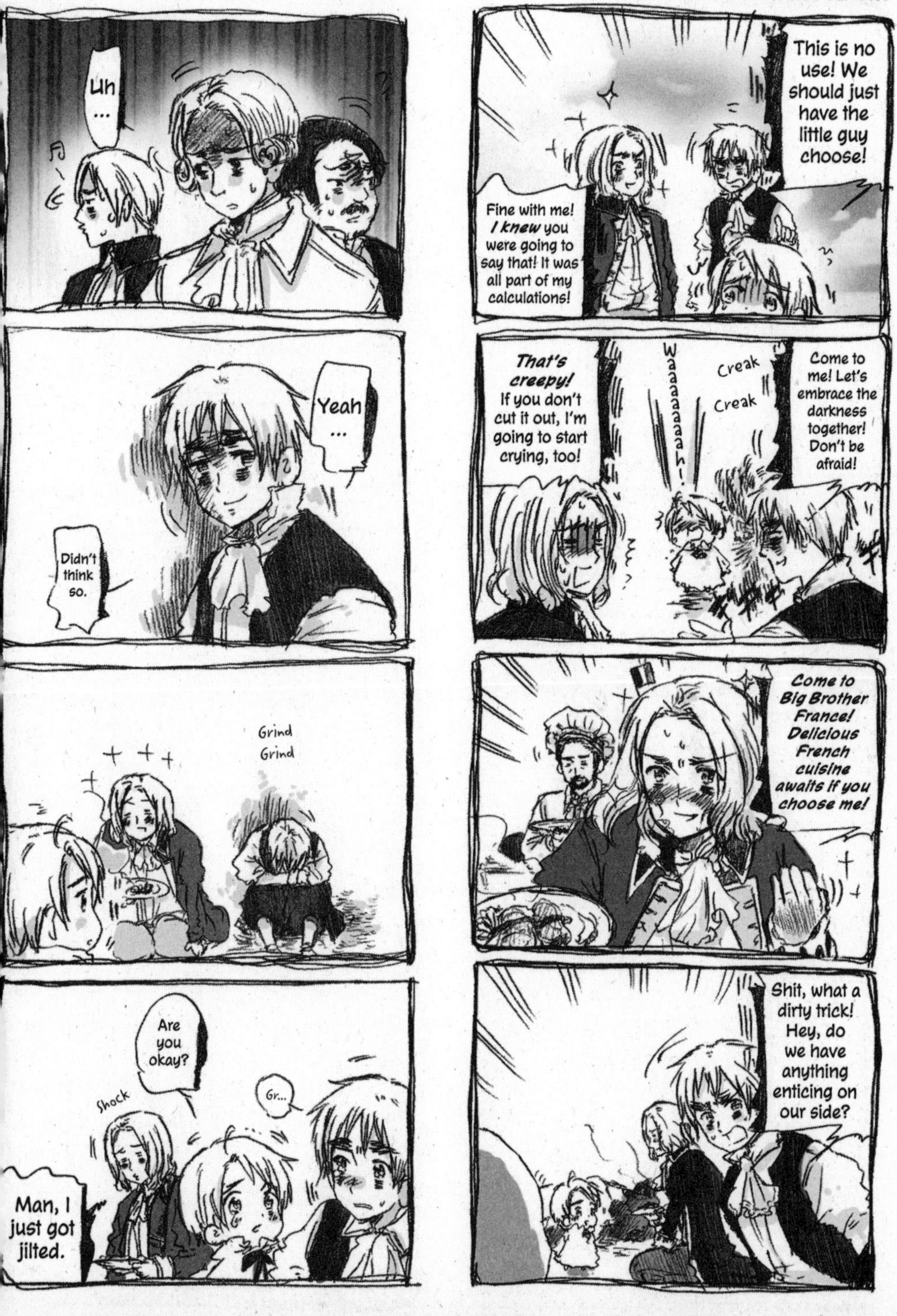

This is no use! We should just have the little guy choose!
Fine with me! *I knew* you were going to say that! It was all part of my calculations!
Come to me! Let's embrace the darkness together! Don't be afraid!
Creak
Creak
Waaaaaaaaah!
That's creepy! If you don't cut it out, I'm going to start crying, too!
Come to Big Brother France! Delicious French cuisine awaits if you choose me!
Shit, what a dirty trick! Hey, do we have anything enticing on our side?
Uh ...
Yeah ...
Didn't think so.
Grind
Grind
Are you okay?
Gr...
Shock
Man, I just got jilted.

Battle for the New World
F**kin' France

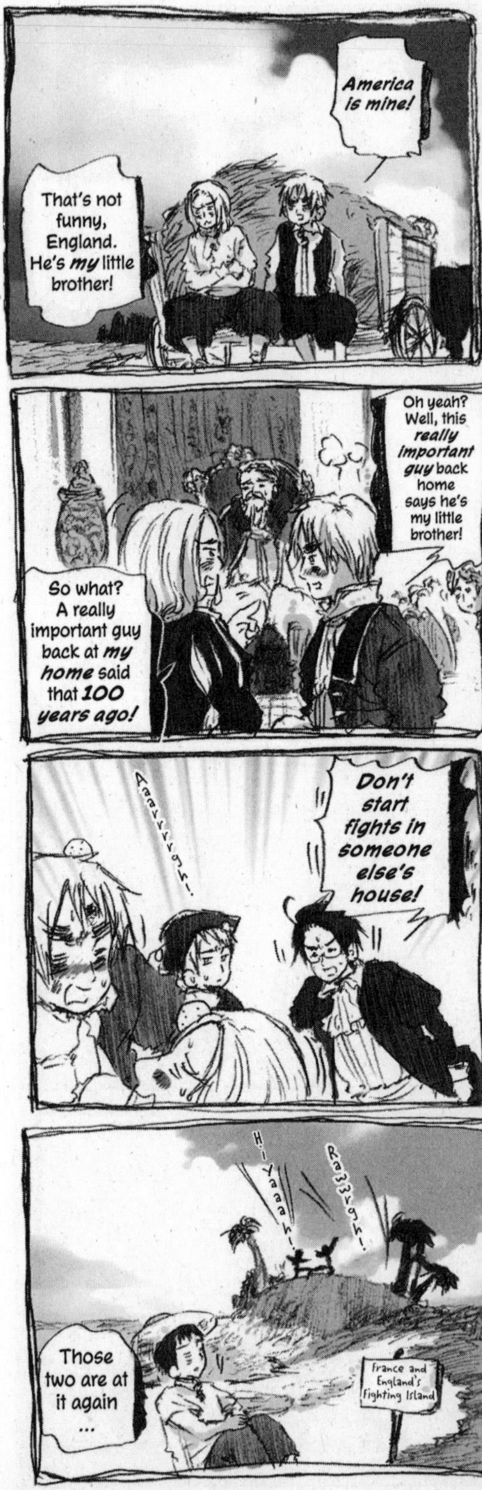
America is mine!
That's not funny, England. He's *my* little brother!
Oh yeah? Well, this *really important guy* back home says he's my little brother!
So what? A really important guy back at *my home* said that *100 years ago!*
Don't start fights in someone else's house!
Aaarrrrgh!
Rawwrgh!
Hi-Yaaah!
France and England's Fighting Island
Those two are at it again ...

[I Don't Care, As Long As I Can Beat Up France]

When England and France were fighting over American territory, the War of the Austrian Succession and Seven Years War were going on at the same time. England just wanted to beat up France so he would side with France's enemies no matter what was at stake.

<War of the Austrian Succession>
France, Prussia, Saxony
VS
Austria and England

<Seven Years War>
France, Austria, Russia
VS
Prussia and England

Battle for the New World
England the Flag Crusher

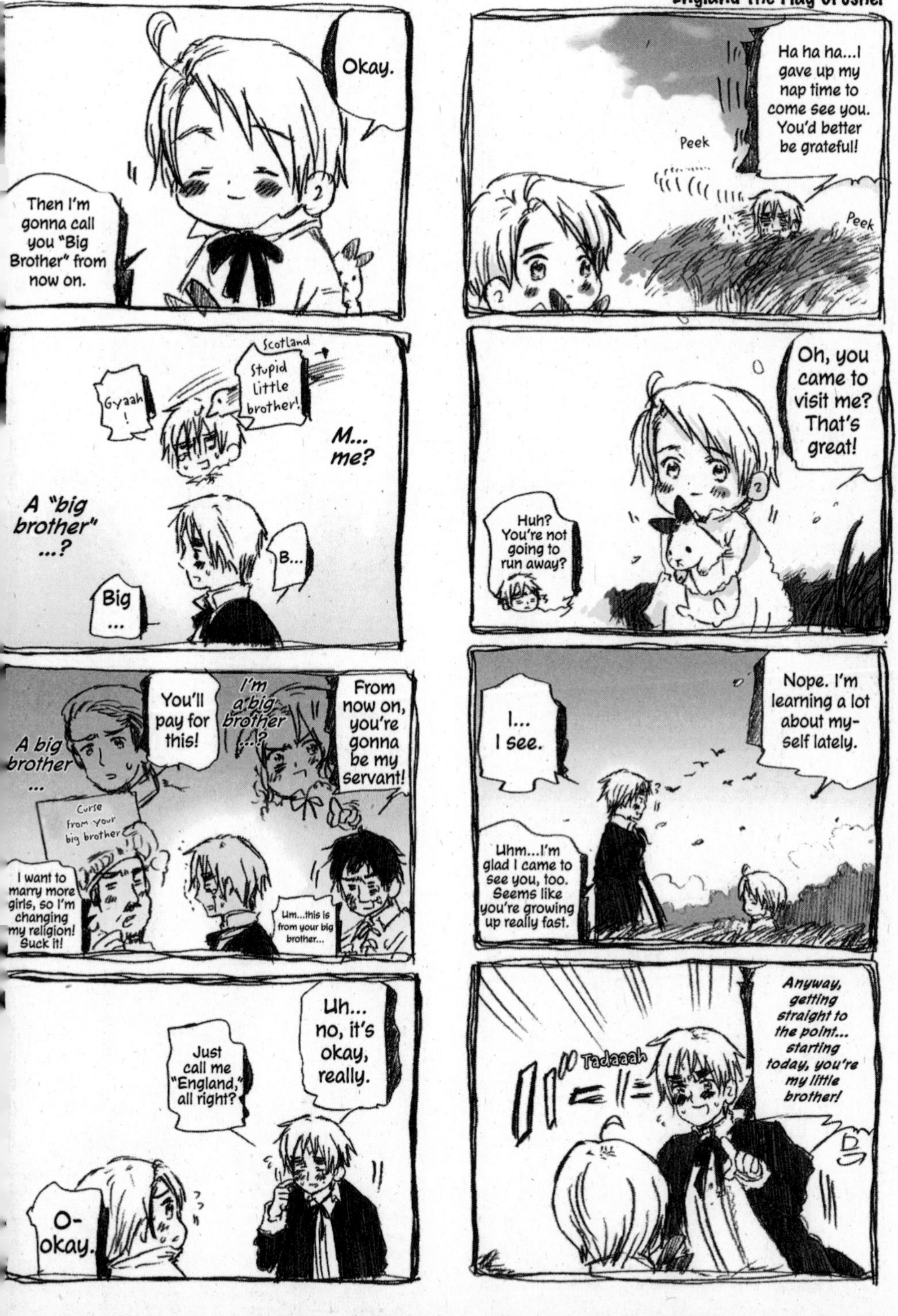

Ha ha ha...I gave up my nap time to come see you. You'd better be grateful!
Peek
Peek
Oh, you came to visit me? That's great!
Huh? You're not going to run away?
Nope. I'm learning a lot about my-self lately.
I... I see.
Uhm...I'm glad I came to see you, too. Seems like you're growing up really fast.
Anyway, getting straight to the point... starting today, you're my little brother!
Tadaaah
Okay.
Then I'm gonna call you "Big Brother" from now on.
Scotland
Stupid little brother!
Gyaah!
M... me?
A "big brother" ...?
B...
Big ...
From now on, you're gonna be my servant!
I'm a big brother ...?
You'll pay for this!
A big brother ...
Curse from your big brother
I want to marry more girls, so I'm changing my religion! Suck it!
Um...this is from your big brother...
Uh... no, it's okay, really.
Just call me "England," all right?
O-okay.

Battle for the New World
Our Little Brother

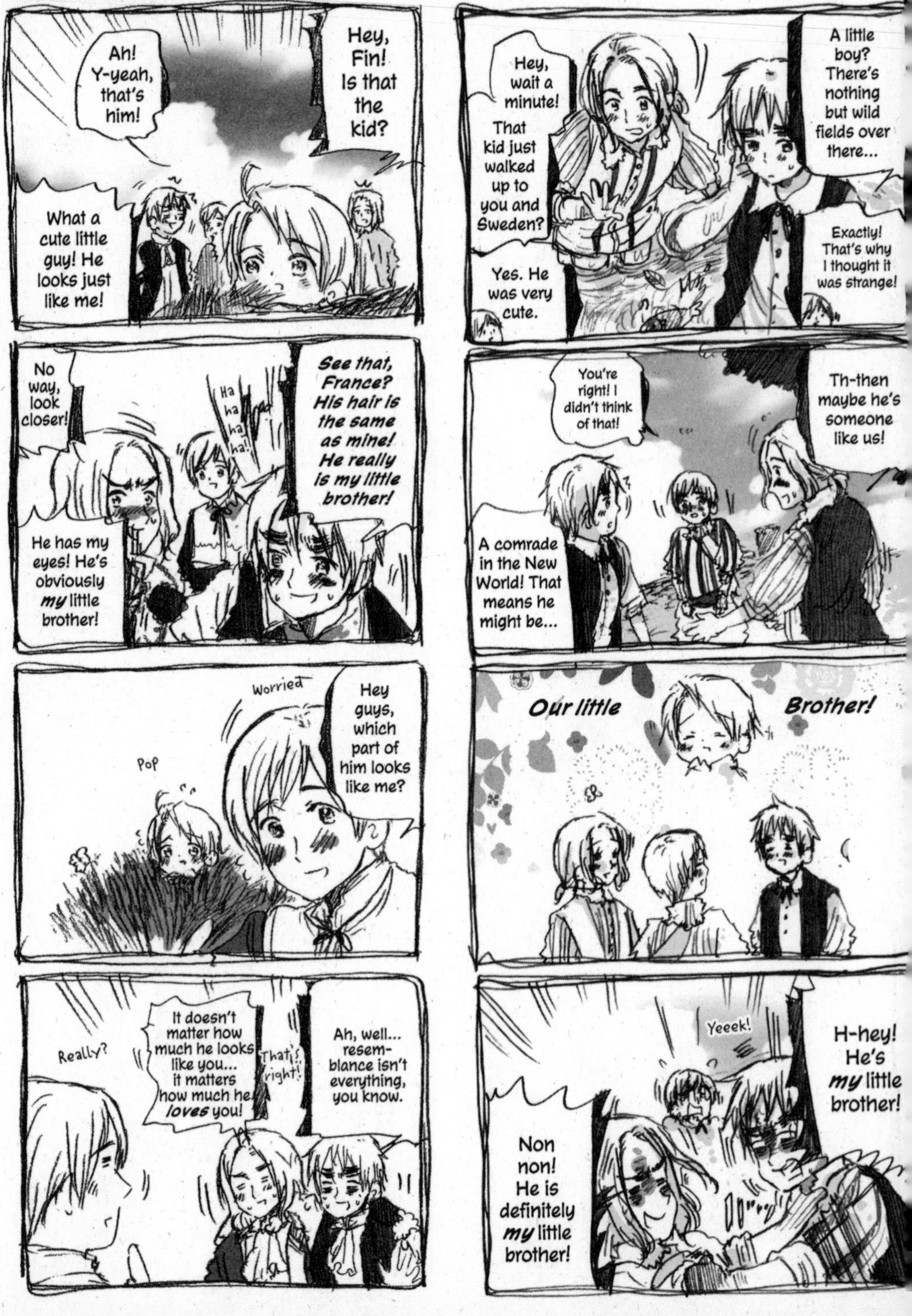
A little boy? There's nothing but wild fields over there...
Hey, wait a minute!
That kid just walked up to you and Sweden?
Exactly! That's why I thought it was strange!
Yes. He was very cute.
Th-then maybe he's someone like us!
You're right! I didn't think of that!
A comrade in the New World! That means he might be...
Our little Brother!
H-hey! He's my little brother!
Yeeek!
Non non! He is definitely my little brother!
Hey, Fin! Is that the kid?
Ah! Y-yeah, that's him!
What a cute little guy! He looks just like me!
See that, France? His hair is the same as mine! He really is my little brother!
Ha ha ha ha!
No way, look closer!
He has my eyes! He's obviously my little brother!
Hey guys, which part of him looks like me?
Worried
Pop
Ah, well... resemblance isn't everything, you know.
That's right!
It doesn't matter how much he looks like you... it matters how much he loves you!
Really?

Battle for the New World

AXIS POWERS HETALIA 2

It is the 17th century.
Sweden was in the process of expanding and developing American colonies with the aid of Finnish and German troops. Ultimately, they created New Sweden (currently Delaware). Unfortunately, they overdid it a bit and meddled into Dutch territory, infuriating the Dutch troops. In the end, the Dutch beat up Sweden and Finland, took over their land and houses and kicked them out of America.

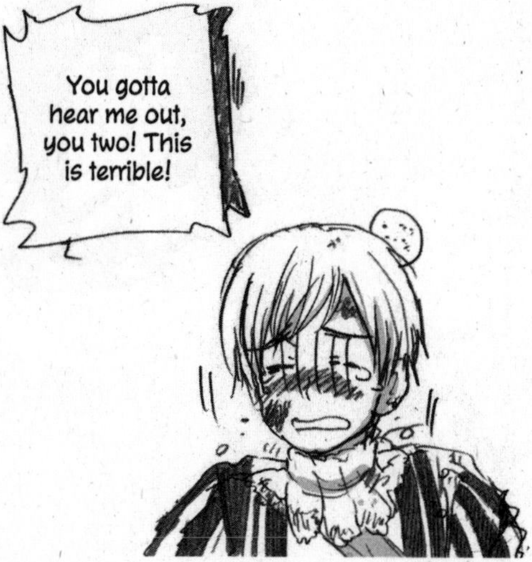
You gotta hear me out, you two! This is terrible!

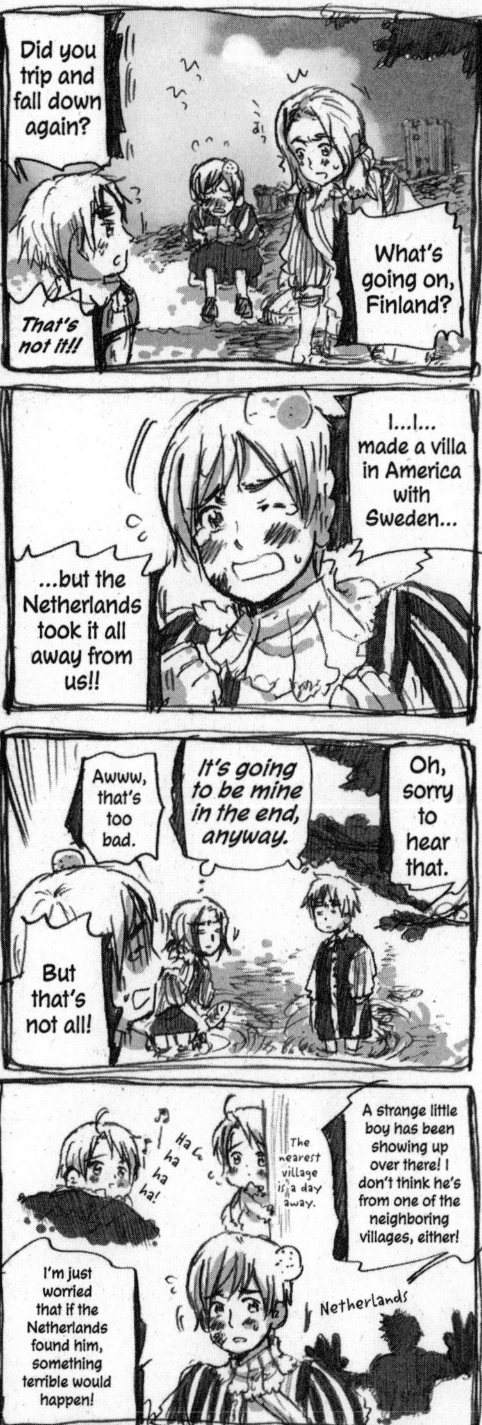
What's going on, Finland?
Did you trip and fall down again?
That's not it!!
I...I... made a villa in America with Sweden...
...but the Netherlands took it all away from us!!
Oh, sorry to hear that.
It's going to be mine in the end, anyway.
Awww, that's too bad.
But that's not all!
A strange little boy has been showing up over there! I don't think he's from one of the neighboring villages, either!
The nearest village is a day away.
Ha ha ha ha!
Netherlands
I'm just worried that if the Netherlands found him, something terrible would happen!

[Strange little boy]
This is the beginning of America. It seems that a unique American culture developed around the East Coast during the 17th century.

Japan-kun and America-kun 6

It's annoying when you receive too many tissue packets*, but it's also sad to be ignored.

AXIS POWERS
HETALIA 2

What a nice lady, giving me free tissues!

Uh... well, actually ...

*Many of these tissue advertisements are stereotypically ads for brothels or host clubs.

Medieval England's Fashion Fiasco
Back to the Drawing Board

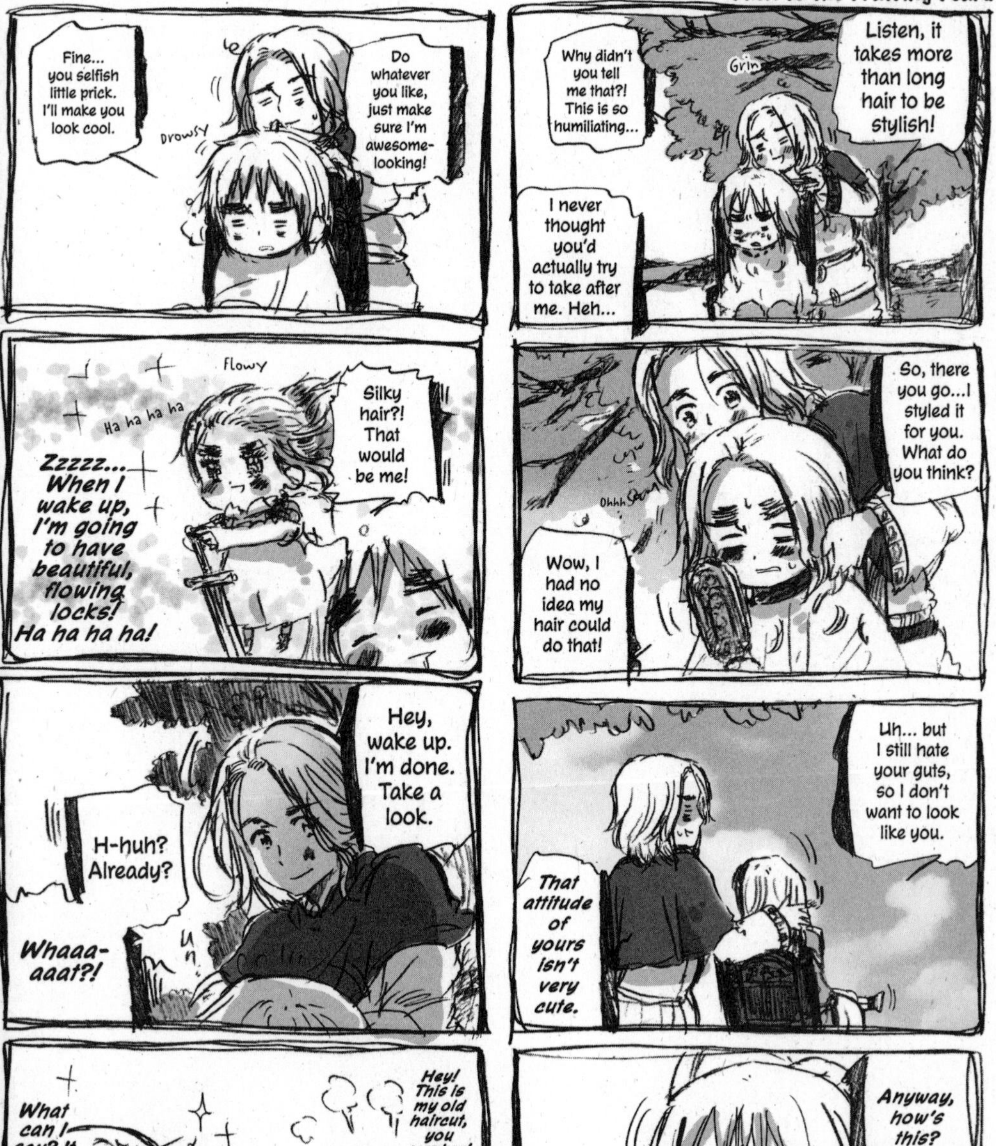

Listen, it takes more than long hair to be stylish!
Grin
Why didn't you tell me that?! This is so humiliating...
I never thought you'd actually try to take after me. Heh...
So, there you go...I styled it for you. What do you think?
Wow, I had no idea my hair could do that!
Uh... but I still hate your guts, so I don't want to look like you.
That attitude of yours isn't very cute.
Anyway, how's this? Better?
Not bad, but I think I saw someone in your neighborhood with the exact same style.
Do whatever you like, just make sure I'm awesome-looking!
Fine... you selfish little prick. I'll make you look cool.
Drowsy
Silky hair?! That would be me!
Flowy
Ha ha ha ha
Zzzzz... When I wake up, I'm going to have beautiful, flowing locks! Ha ha ha ha!
Hey, wake up. I'm done. Take a look.
H-huh? Already?
Un
Whaaa-aaat?!
Hey! This is my old haircut, you wanker!
What can I say? It suits you!

[Mirrors]
Mirrors made out of reflective glass weren't invented until the 14th century, so during this time, shiny metals were buffed to make them reflective. The mirrors of today weren't invented until 19th century. Surprising how recent they are!

Medieval England's Fashion Fiasco
Golden Caterpillar

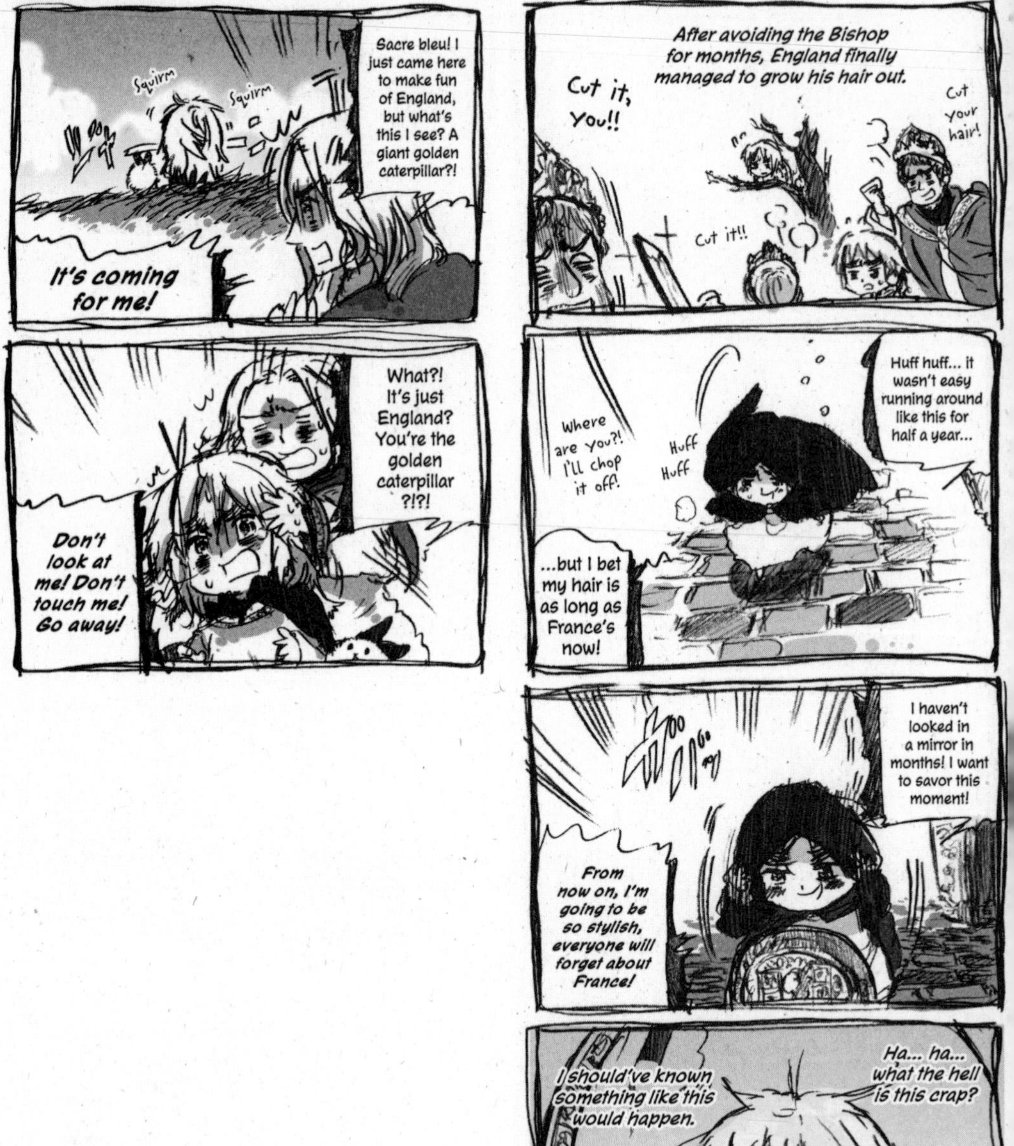
After avoiding the Bishop for months, England finally managed to grow his hair out.
Cut your hair!
Cut it, You!!
Cut it!!
Huff huff... it wasn't easy running around like this for half a year...
Huff Huff
Where are you?! I'll chop it off!
...but I bet my hair is as long as France's now!
I haven't looked in a mirror in months! I want to savor this moment!
From now on, I'm going to be so stylish, everyone will forget about France!
Ha... ha... what the hell is this crap?
I should've known something like this would happen.
Sacre bleu! I just came here to make fun of England, but what's this I see? A giant golden caterpillar?!
Squirm
Squirm
It's coming for me!
What?! It's just England? You're the golden caterpillar ?!?!
Don't look at me! Don't touch me! Go away!

Fk Long Hair**
In England, there was once an extremely anti-French bishop named Wolfstan. Constantly criticizing French-style hair, he encouraged his countrymen to "never forget the British spirit." His hatred towards long hair was so intense, that when his parishioners knelt down, the bishop would grab their hair and cut it himself. Bishop Wolfstan's motto was, "Long hair will send you to hell!"

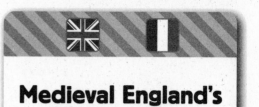

Medieval England's Fashion Fiasco

AXIS POWERS HETALIA 2

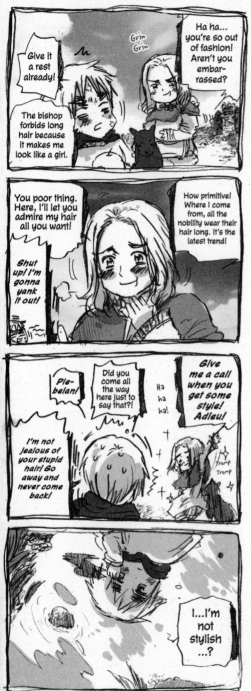

In the 11th century, long and luxurious French-style hair was very popular in England. This is because the King of England was a big fan of French culture.

Hey, England! Why's your hair so short?
Bed Head
Ha ha ha

Ha ha... you're so out of fashion! Aren't you embarrassed?
Grin Grin
Give it a rest already!
The bishop forbids long hair because it makes me look like a girl.
How primitive! Where I come from, all the nobility wear their hair long. It's the latest trend!
You poor thing. Here, I'll let you admire my hair all you want!
Shut up! I'm gonna yank it out!
Give me a call when you get some style! Adieu!
Ha ha ha!
Did you come all the way here just to say that?!
Ple-beian!
Tromp Tromp
I'm not jealous of your stupid hair! Go away and never come back!
I...I'm not stylish ...?

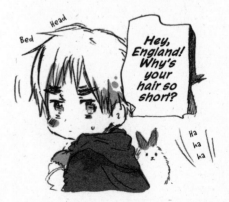

[Not Stylish]

In England, everyone's hair was wild and tangled. On the other hand, the French nobility took great care of their hair, even going so far as to officially endorse certain styles.

Japan-kun and America-kun 5

AXIS POWERS HETALIA 2

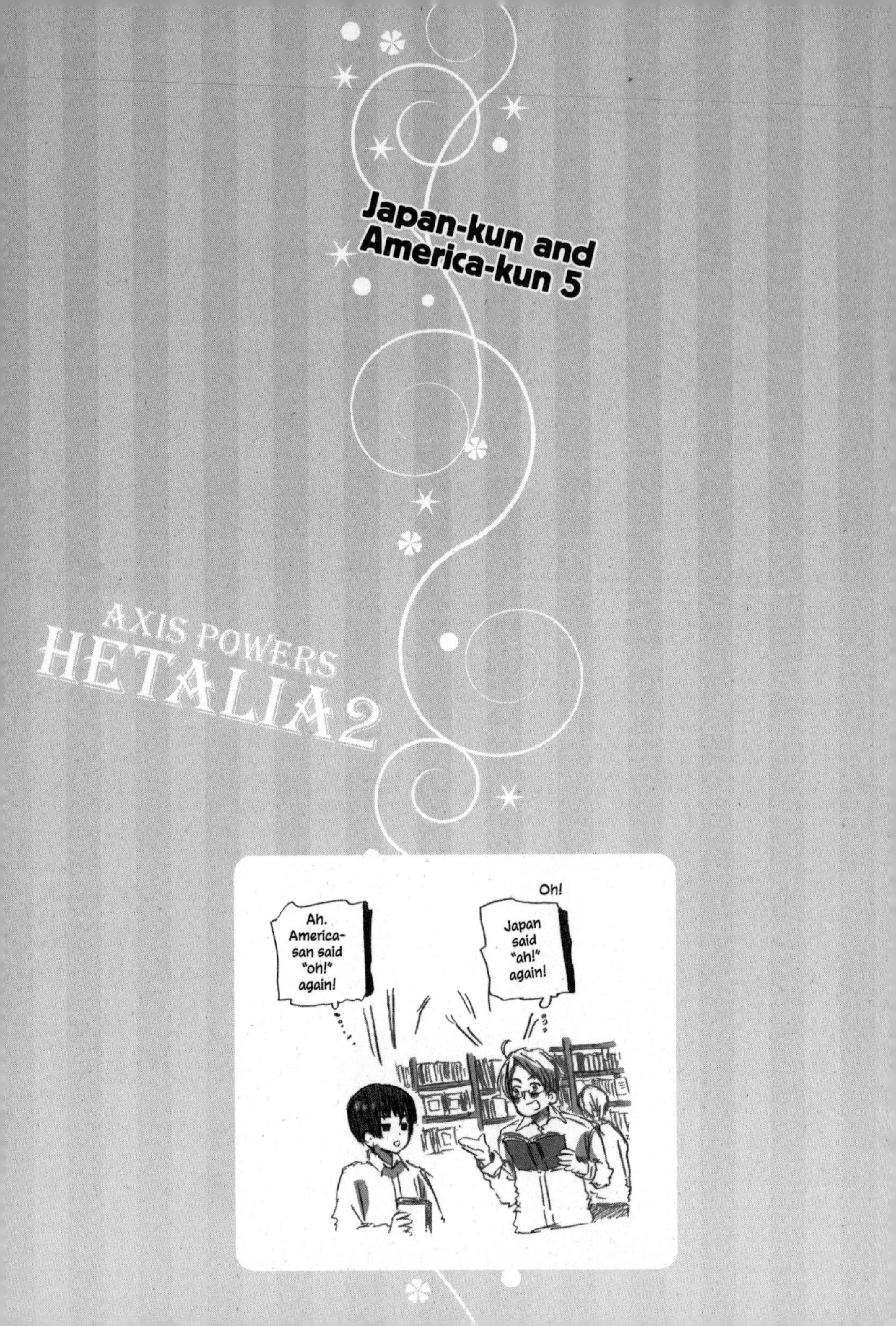
Oh!
Japan said "ah!" again!
Ah. America-san said "oh!" again!

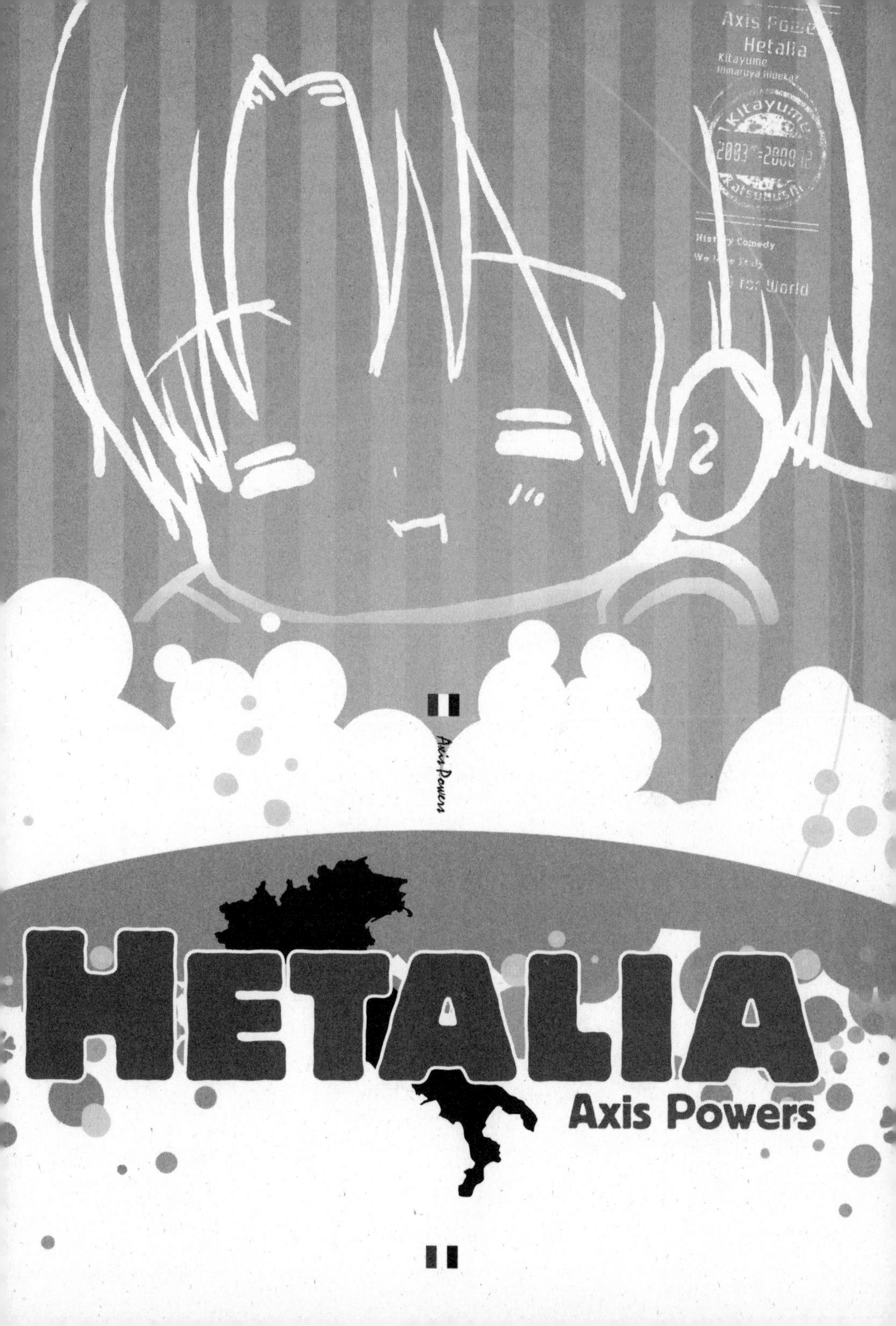
Axis Powers
Hetalia
Kitayume
Himaruya Hidekaz
2003 - 2009
History Comedy
World
Axis Powers
HETALIA
Axis Powers

American Ghosts

23% of the American population have either seen ghosts or believe that they are real. This is no surprise since American ghosts seem to crave attention.

There are so many ghost-related TV shows these days that it's more laughable than scary. It's common to see things like ghosts showing up in photos, walking through surveillance videos or popping into people's houses. The funniest was the case of a ghost standing right in the middle of a big group photo. It didn't even have the typical ghost-like characteristics of transparency.

It seems as if Americans like to be the center of attention even after they're dead.

When I used to live in a dorm, my roommates would always sit around the TV and watch stuff like this. When I heard them all screaming, I had to take a peek. It turns out they were freaking out every time they saw a "haunted photo."

On the other hand, the Chinese guys were cracking up laughing.

Huh?

Man, this is hilarious!

But if they're watching a Japanese movie with some creepy girl or kid standing behind someone, everyone thinks it's hilarious. It defies logic.

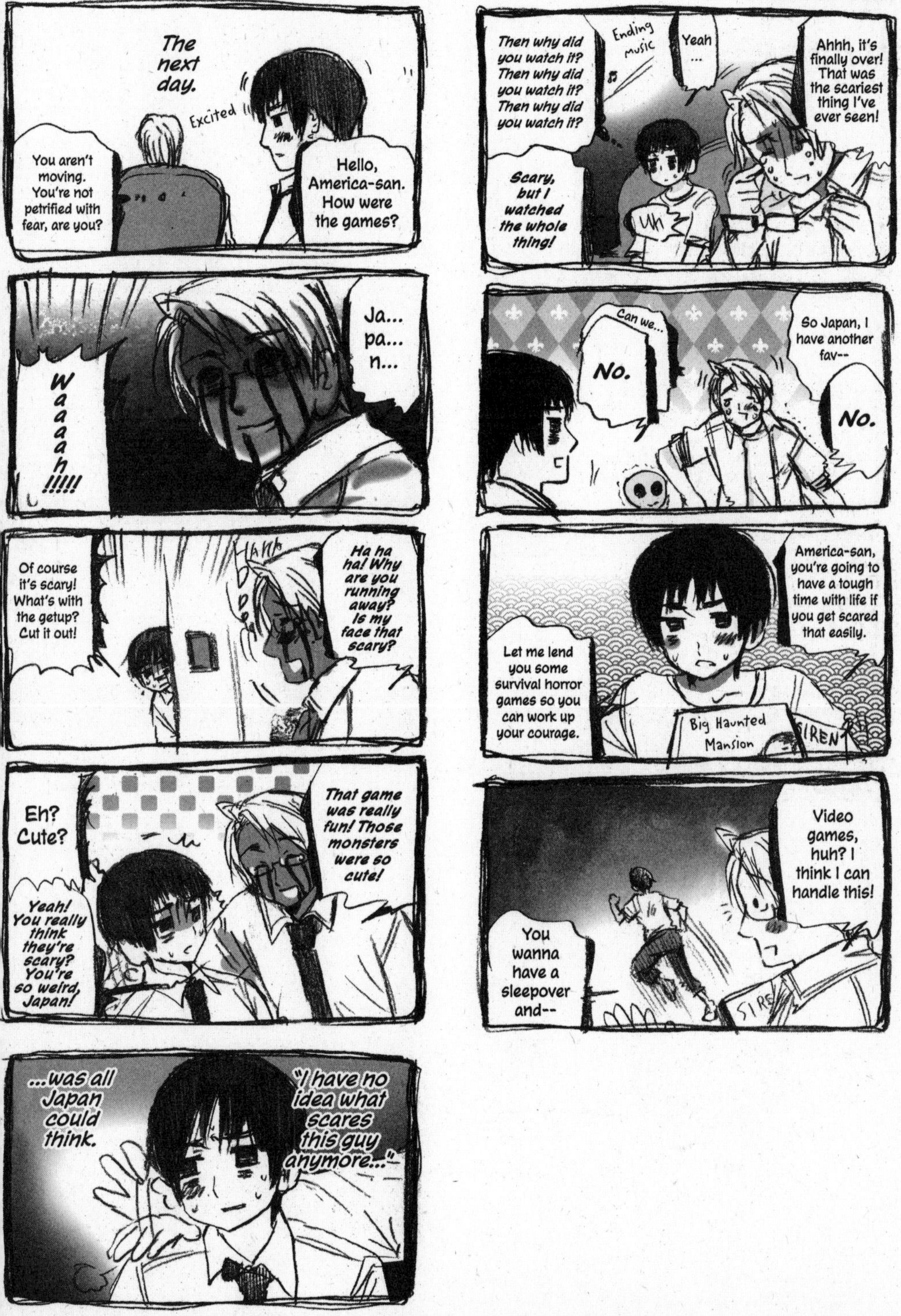
Ahhh, it's finally over! That was the scariest thing I've ever seen!
Yeah ...
Ending music
Then why did you watch it? Then why did you watch it? Then why did you watch it? Then why did you watch it?
Scary, but I watched the whole thing!
Uh
So Japan, I have another fav--
No.
Can we...
No.
America-san, you're going to have a tough time with life if you get scared that easily.
Let me lend you some survival horror games so you can work up your courage.
Big Haunted Mansion
SIREN
Video games, huh? I think I can handle this!
You wanna have a sleepover and--
The next day.
Excited
Hello, America-san. How were the games?
You aren't moving. You're not petrified with fear, are you?
Ja... pa... n...
Waaaaah!!!!!
Ha ha ha! Why are you running away? Is my face that scary?
HAHA
Of course it's scary! What's with the getup? Cut it out!
That game was really fun! Those monsters were so cute!
Eh? Cute?
Yeah! You really think they're scary? You're so weird, Japan!
"I have no idea what scares this guy anymore..."
...was all Japan could think.

American Ghosts

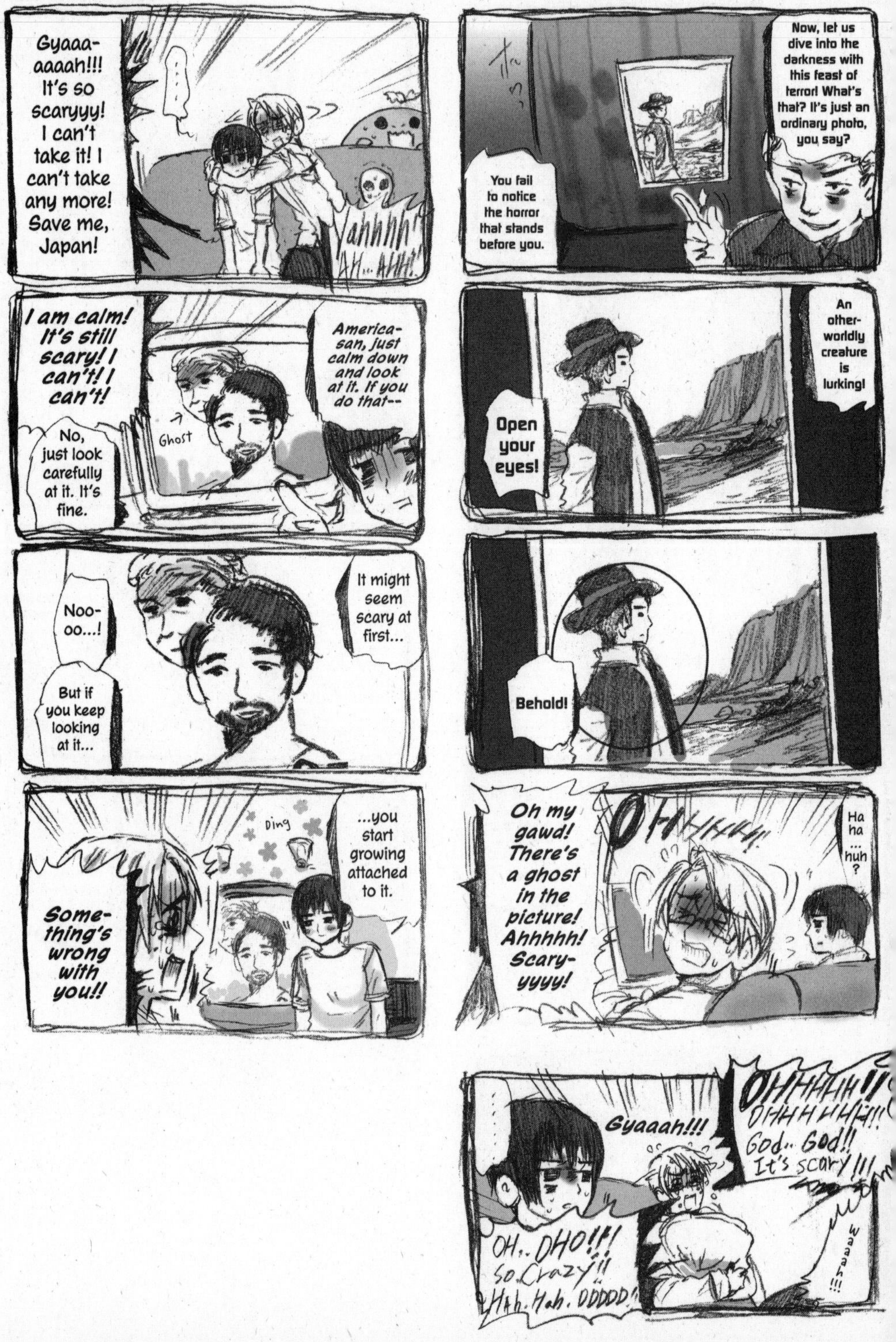
Now, let us dive into the darkness with this feast of terror! What's that? It's just an ordinary photo, you say?
You fail to notice the horror that stands before you.
An other-worldly creature is lurking!
Open your eyes!
Behold!
Ha ha ... huh?
OHHHHHH!!
Oh my gawd! There's a ghost in the picture! Ahhhhh! Scary-yyyy!
OHHHHH!! OHHHHHH!! God.. God!! It's scary!!!
Gyaaah!!!
Waaaah!!!
OH.. OHO!!! So Crazy!! Hah. Hah. OOOOO!
Gyaaa-aaaah!!! It's so scaryyy! I can't take it! I can't take any more! Save me, Japan!
ahhhh AH... AHH.
America-san, just calm down and look at it. If you do that--
I am calm! It's still scary! I can't! I can't!
Ghost
No, just look carefully at it. It's fine.
It might seem scary at first...
Noo-oo...!
But if you keep looking at it...
...you start growing attached to it.
Ding
Something's wrong with you!!

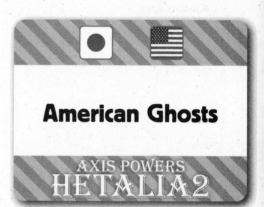

American Ghosts

AXIS POWERS HETALIA 2

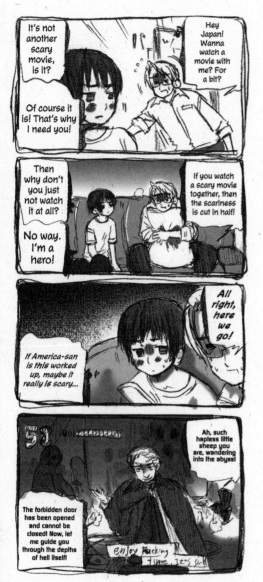

America's Ghost Situation

Hey Japan! Wanna watch a movie with me? For a bit?
It's not another scary movie, is it?
Of course it is! That's why I need you!
If you watch a scary movie together, then the scariness is cut in half!
Then why don't you just not watch it at all?
No way. I'm a hero!
All right, here we go!
If America-san is this worked up, maybe it really is scary...
Ah, such hapless little sheep you are, wandering into the abyss!
The forbidden door has been opened and cannot be closed! Now, let me guide you through the depths of hell itself!
53
enJoy Fucking
time. It's

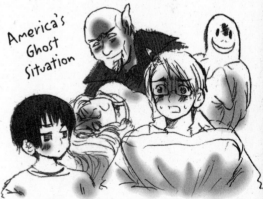

Japan-kun and America-kun 4

America-san likes "buy one get one free" deals too.

AXIS POWERS HETALIA 2

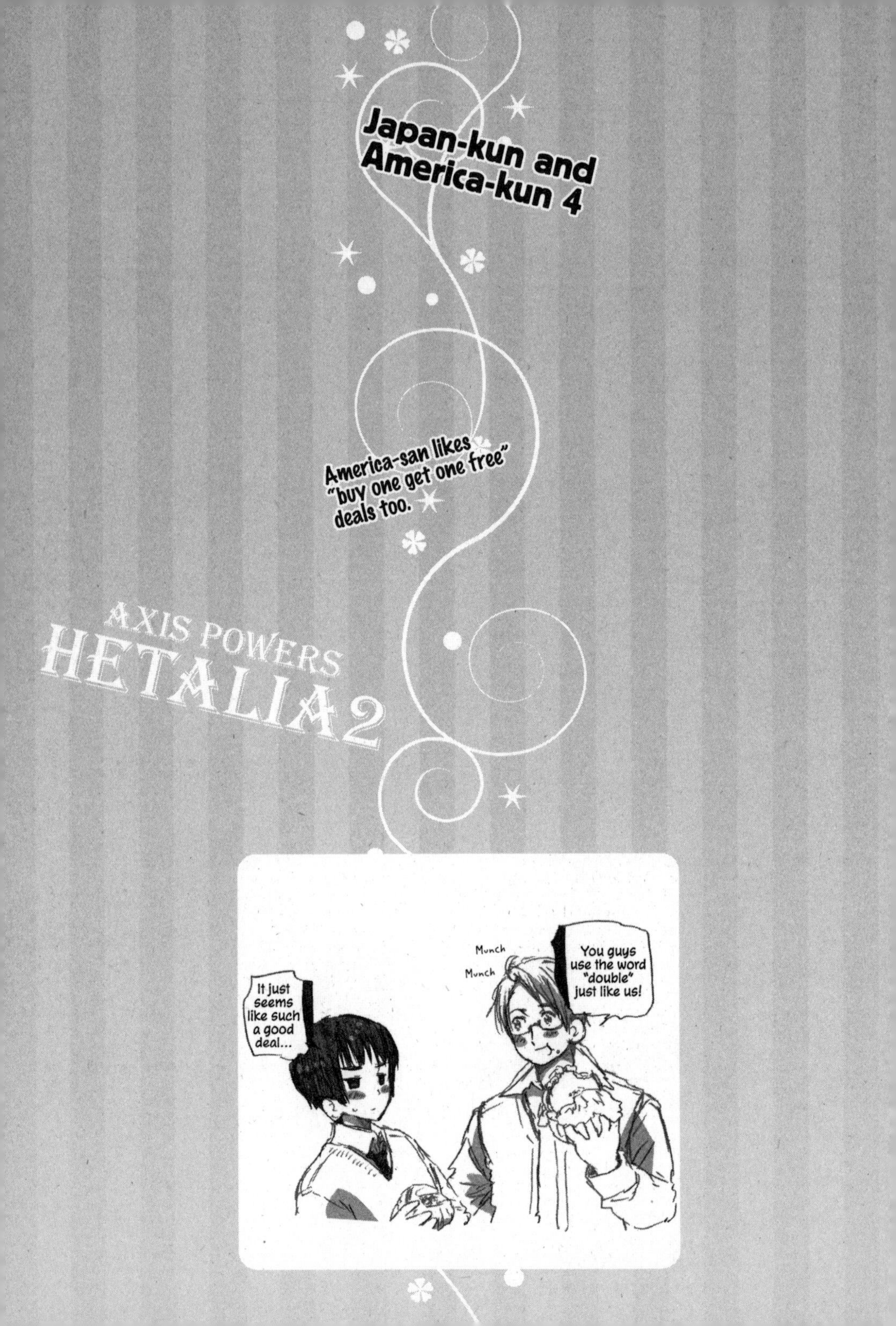
Munch
Munch
You guys use the word "double" just like us!
It just seems like such a good deal...

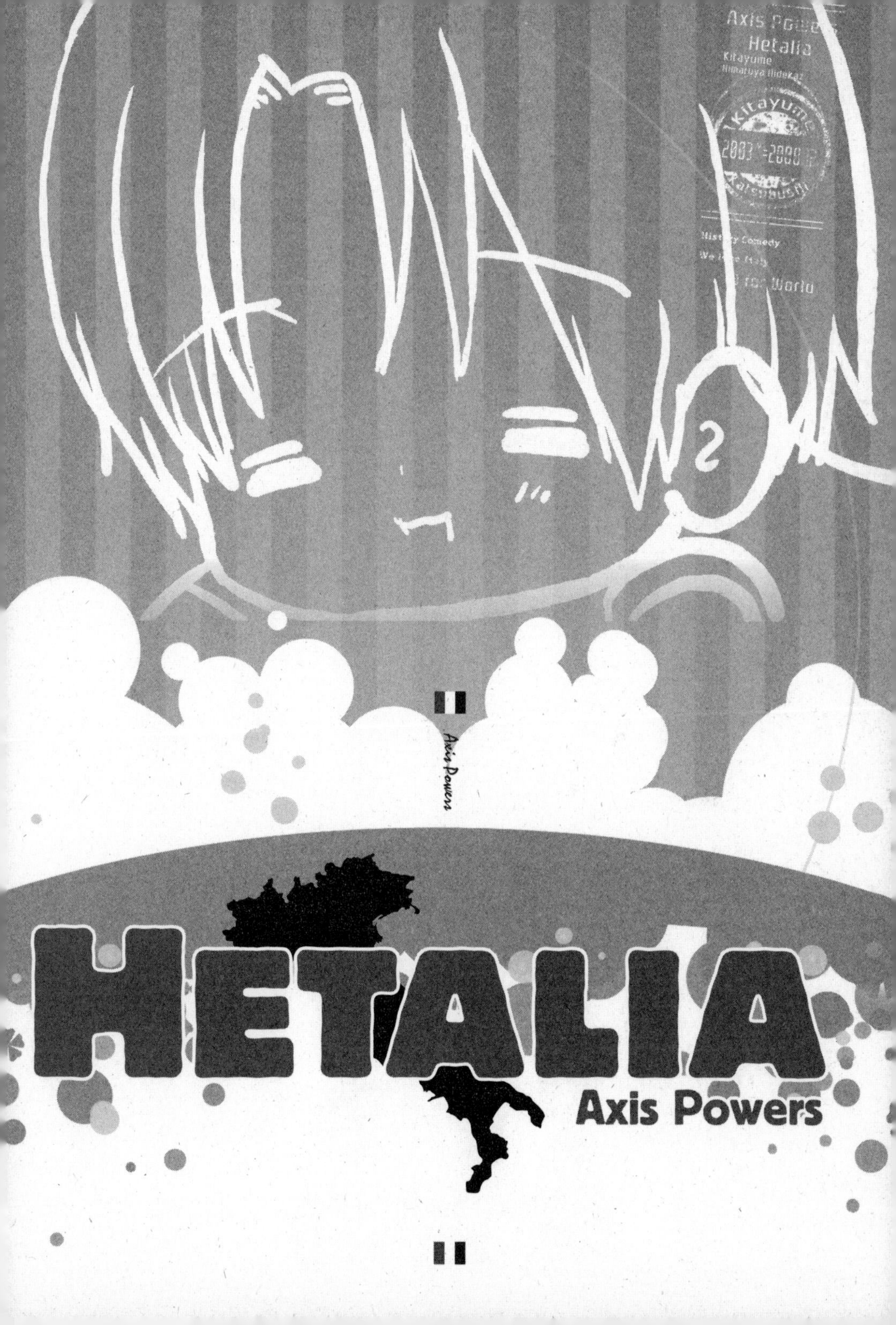
Axis Powers
HETALIA
Axis Powers

Things that Were Popular
Back in the Day

Beer and coffee also became quite common in Japan during this time. Beef hot pot became popular as well. Although it may appear that Japan was compliant to everything, the idea of cutting your hair short was bitterly resisted by the citizens of Japan. At the time, it must have been strange to see long-haired Japanese people wearing Westernized clothes.

AXIS POWERS
HETALIA 2

Japan's Path to Cultural Enlightenment
Final Weapon: Bunnies

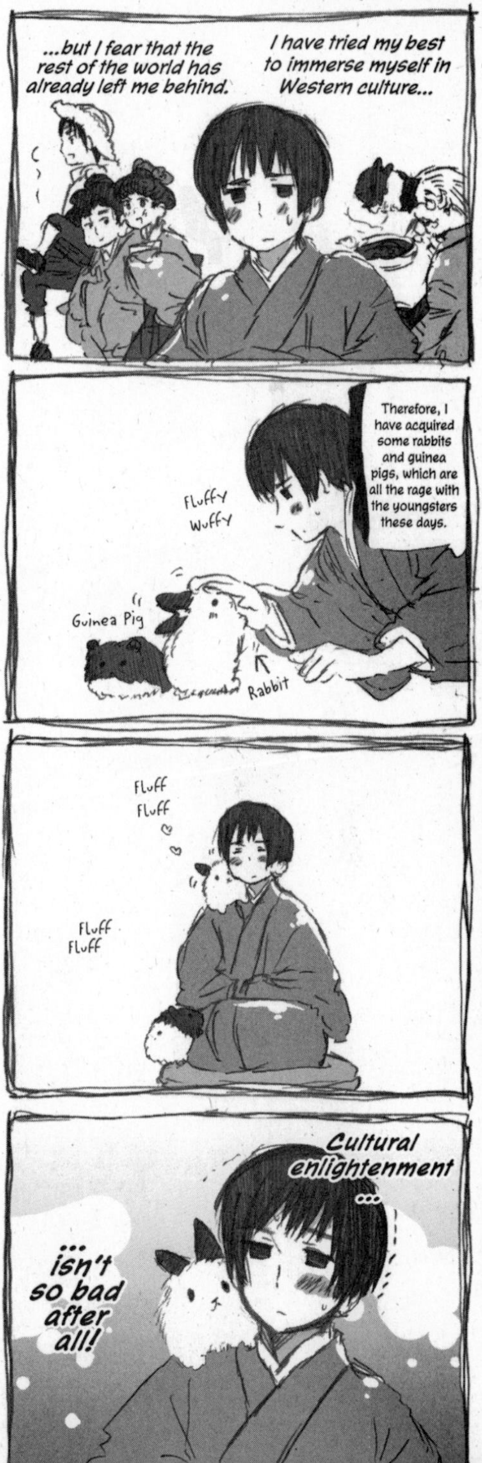
I have tried my best to immerse myself in Western culture...
...but I fear that the rest of the world has already left me behind.
Therefore, I have acquired some rabbits and guinea pigs, which are all the rage with the youngsters these days.
Fluffy Wuffy
Guinea Pig
Rabbit
Fluff Fluff
Fluff Fluff
Cultural enlightenment...
...isn't so bad after all!

Common animals that were
ntroduced during this time]

abbits

veryone (including the uthor) loves rabbits. During he cultural enlightenment eriod, they became popular ets. At that time, they were o expensive, that you could ooner afford a ritzy piece of roperty in Ginza. The rabbit oom got bigger and bigger, ntil the government added tax of one yen per rabbit er month. After that, they vere discarded into the wild n masse. People should take esponsibility for their pets!

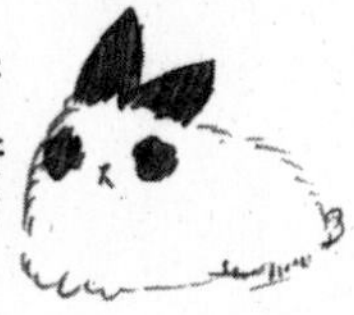

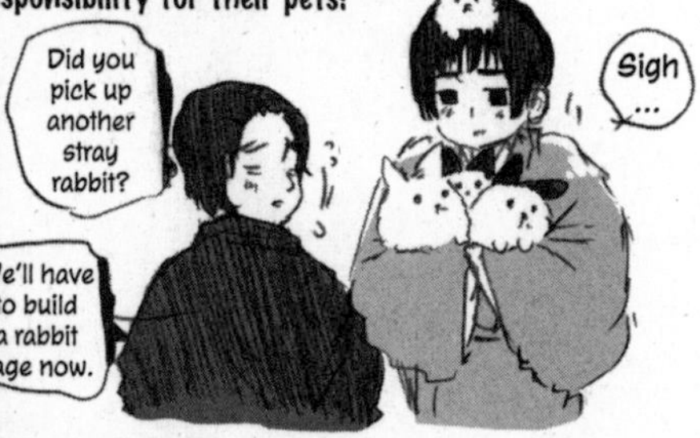
Did you pick up another stray rabbit?
Sigh ...
Ve'll have to build a rabbit age now.

uinea Pigs

uinea pigs were also popular during this time. The rice of a guinea pig was 100 times greater than a olice sergeant's paycheck. The first person to have guinea pig as a pet was the Emperor of Japan. pparently, one of the Italian nobles gave it to him as gift. Who knew they would grow to be so common...

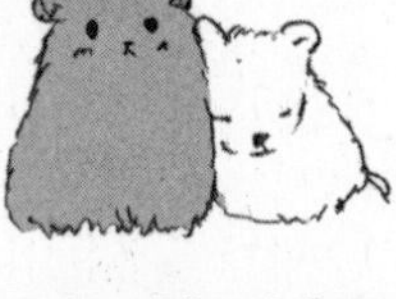

y the way, guinea pigs with curly hair were developed Japan. Some guy crossbred a guinea pig with a ouse and ended up with a curly-haired guinea pig. mazing what difference a little mice can make!

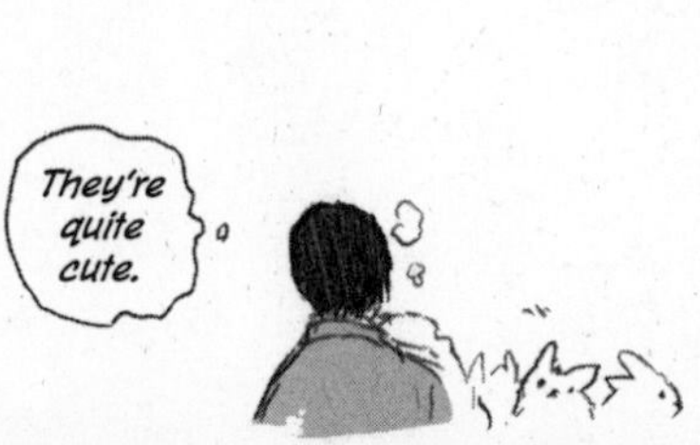
They're quite cute.

Japan's Path to Cultural Enlightenment
I'm Older Than I Look

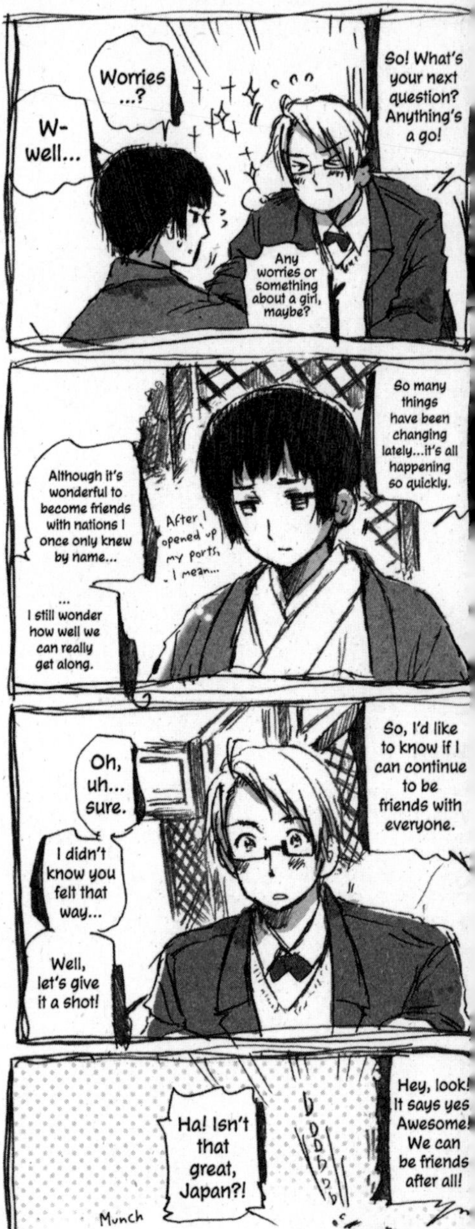
So! What's your next question? Anything's a go!
Worries ...?
W-well...
Any worries or something about a girl, maybe?
So many things have been changing lately...it's all happening so quickly.
Although it's wonderful to become friends with nations I once only knew by name...
After I opened up my ports, I mean...
... I still wonder how well we can really get along.
So, I'd like to know if I can continue to be friends with everyone.
Oh, uh... sure.
I didn't know you felt that way...
Well, let's give it a shot!
Hey, look! It says yes Awesome! We can be friends after all!
Ha! Isn't that great, Japan?!
Munch Munch

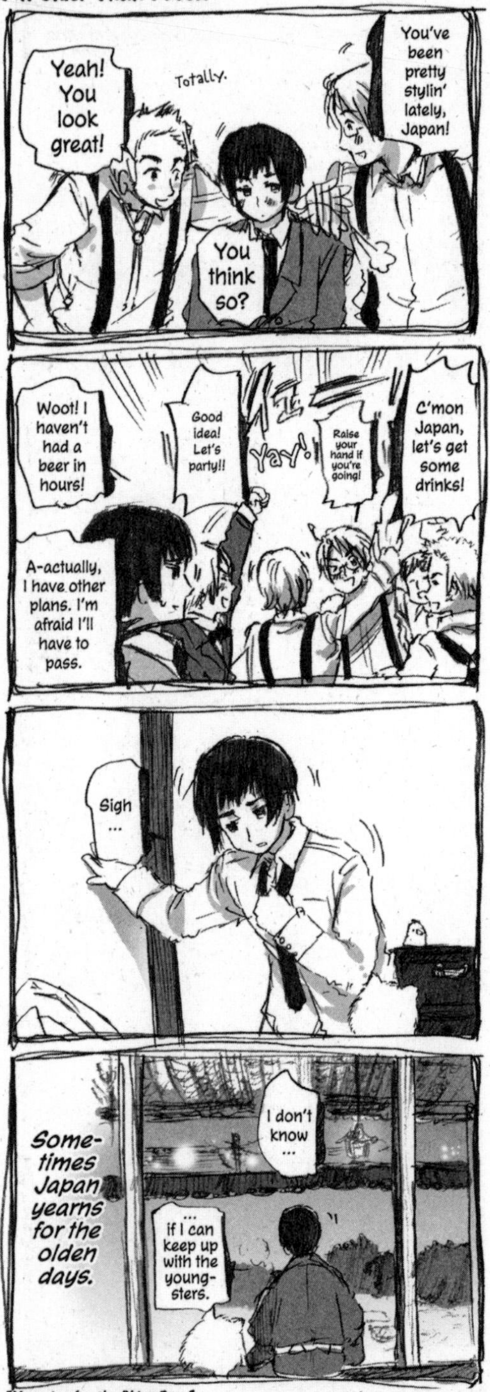
You've been pretty stylin' lately, Japan!
Totally.
Yeah! You look great!
You think so?
C'mon Japan, let's get some drinks!
Raise your hand if you're going!
Yay!
Good idea! Let's party!!
Woot! I haven't had a beer in hours!
A-actually, I have other plans. I'm afraid I'll have to pass.
Sigh ...
I don't know ...
... if I can keep up with the youngsters.
Sometimes Japan yearns for the olden days.

[Yearning for the Olden Days]
Even as Japan was awash in a sea of cultural change, some still believed it would be better for the country to revert back to "the old ways." With all of its noisy visitors, it's only sensible that Japan would be more at peace when surrounded by traditionally Japanese things. I guess that means retro movements have always been popular...

Japan's Path to Cultural Enlightenment
Let's Table Turning!!

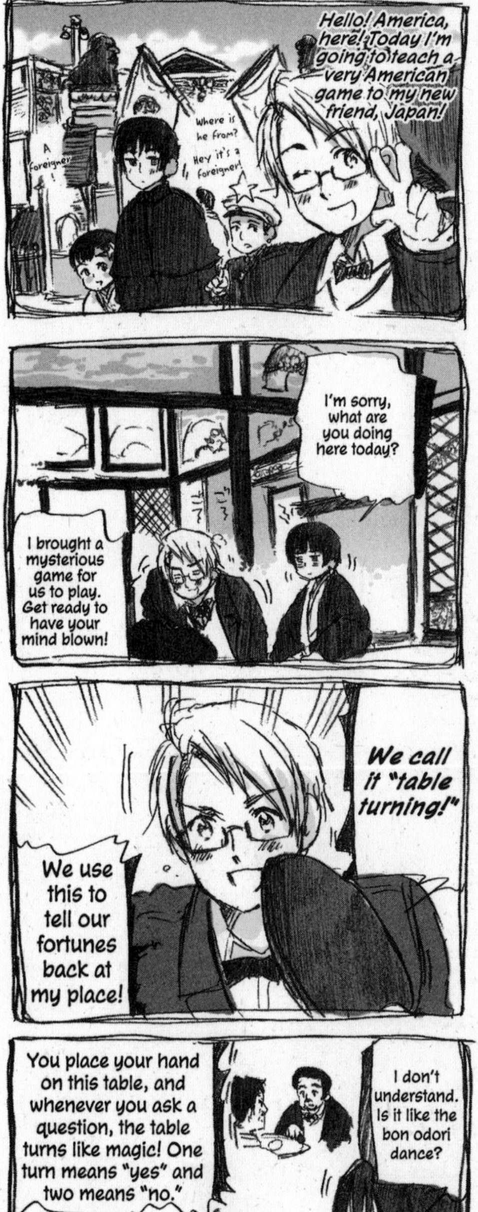
Hello! America, here! Today I'm going to teach a very American game to my new friend, Japan!
Where is he from?
Hey it's a foreigner!
A foreigner
I'm sorry, what are you doing here today?
I brought a mysterious game for us to play. Get ready to have your mind blown!
We call it "table turning!"
We use this to tell our fortunes back at my place!
I don't understand. Is it like the bon odori dance?
You place your hand on this table, and whenever you ask a question, the table turns like magic! One turn means "yes" and two means "no."
Spirits of the dead, huh? I should've guessed...

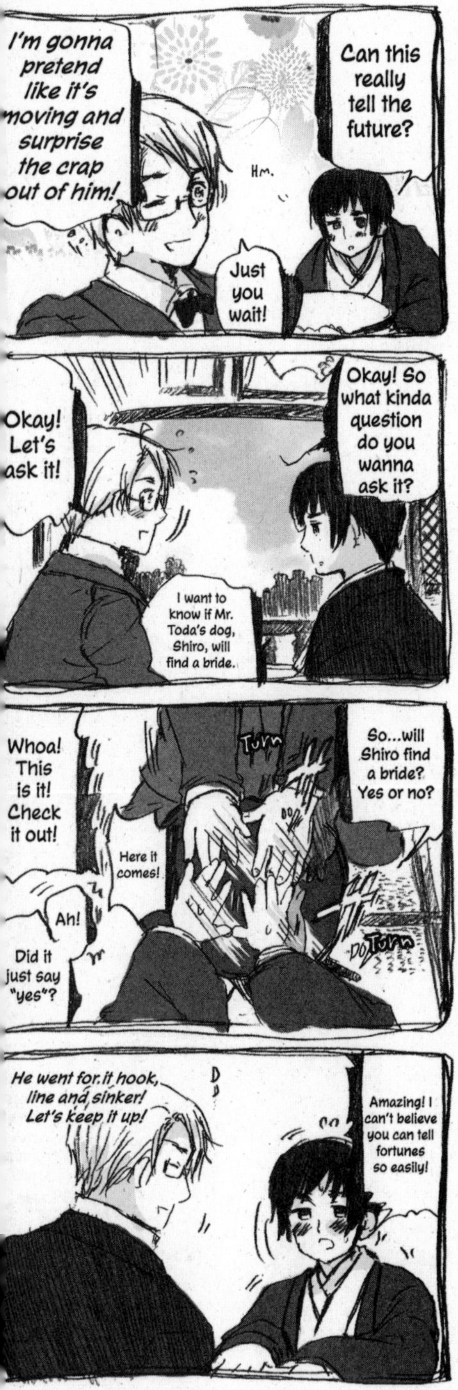
Can this really tell the future?
I'm gonna pretend like it's moving and surprise the crap out of him!
Hm.
Just you wait!
Okay! So what kinda question do you wanna ask it?
Okay! Let's ask it!
I want to know if Mr. Toda's dog, Shiro, will find a bride.
So...will Shiro find a bride? Yes or no?
Turn
Whoa! This is it! Check it out!
Here it comes!
Ah!
Did it just say "yes"?
Turn
Amazing! I can't believe you can tell fortunes so easily!
He went for it hook, line and sinker! Let's keep it up!

[Table Turning]
An American-style séance, using a small, three-legged table. Participants hold hands and ask questions as the table tips and turns in response. The Japanese-style séance, called "Kokkuri-san" supposedly originated from this practice. When the game came into Japan, it was an explosive hit, leading to the opening of a specialized "table turning store" in year 19 of the Meiji era.

Japan's Path to Cultural Enlightenment
"Flexibility" is Also a Talent

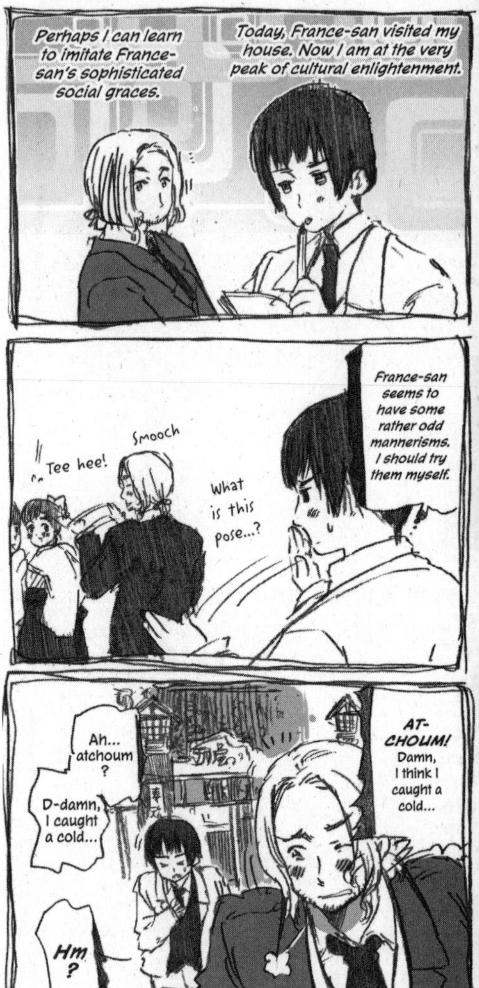
Today, France-san visited my house. Now I am at the very peak of cultural enlightenment.
Perhaps I can learn to imitate France-san's sophisticated social graces.
France-san seems to have some rather odd mannerisms. I should try them myself.
What is this pose...?
Smooch
Tee hee!
AT-CHOUM! Damn, I think I caught a cold...
Ah... atchoum?
D-damn, I caught a cold...
Hm?
Oh my! Big Brother France is so cool, it brings tears to my eyes!
Oh my! Big Brother France is so cool, it--
Hey!

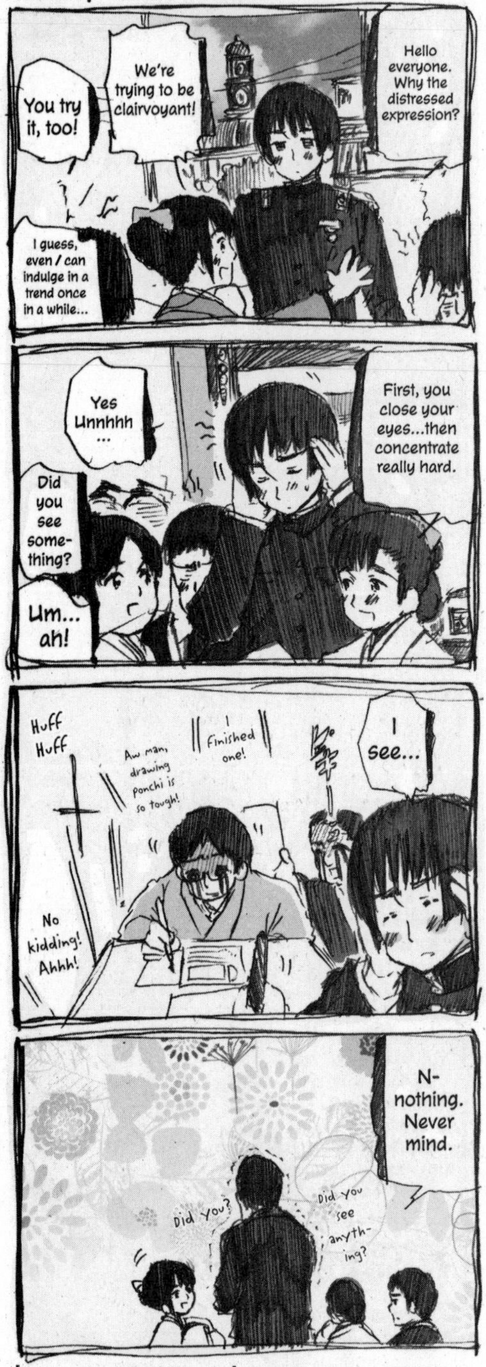
Hello everyone. Why the distressed expression?
We're trying to be clairvoyant!
You try it, too!
I guess, even I can indulge in a trend once in a while...
First, you close your eyes...then concentrate really hard.
Yes Unnhhh ...
Did you see something?
Um... ah!
I see...
I finished one!
Aw man, drawing ponchi is so tough!
Huff Huff
No kidding! Ahhh!
N-nothing. Never mind.
Did you see anything?
Did you?

[Clairvoyance and Ponchi drawings]
Back in the day, it was quite popular to explore the supernatural power of clairvoyance. The vision that Japan saw was the terrifying world of ponchi art. In the past, manga artists were known as "ponchi artists." Although the name has changed, it looks like they always had it rough.

[Sneezing in France]
In France, you say "atchoum" instead of "achoo" in English or "Hackshon" in Japanese. When you hear someone else sneeze, the correct response is, "A vos(tes) souhaits" meaning, "to your wishes."

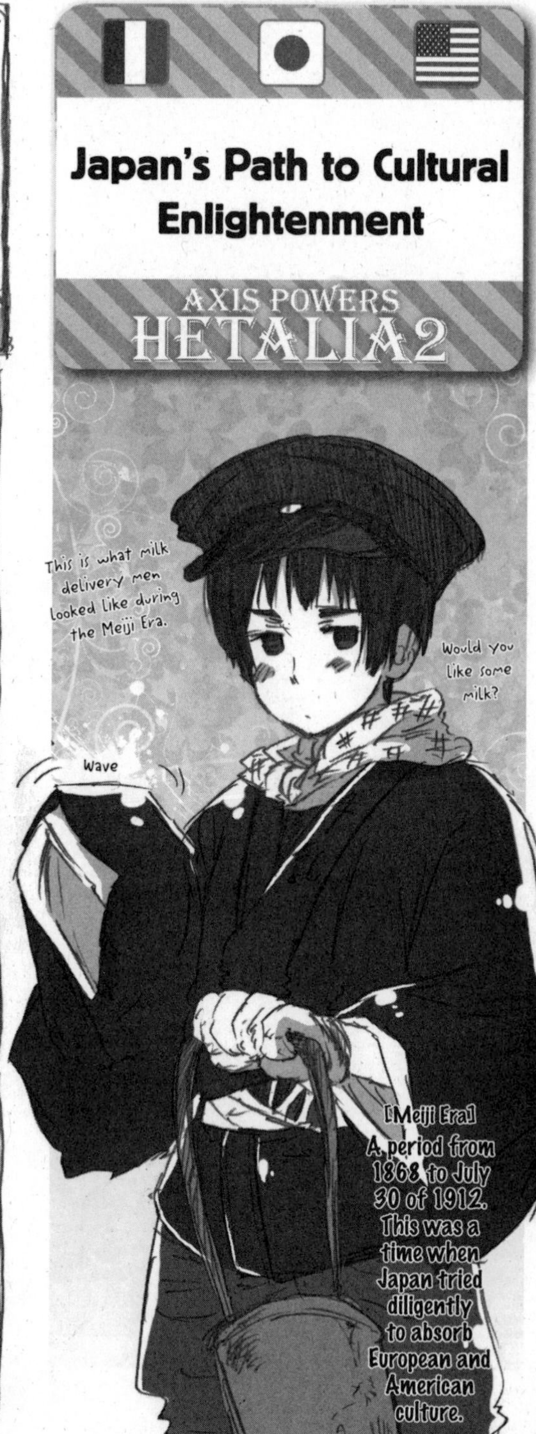
Japan's Path to Cultural Enlightenment
AXIS POWERS
HETALIA2
This is what milk delivery men looked like during the Meiji Era.
Would you like some milk?
Wave
[Meiji Era]
A period from 1868 to July 30 of 1912. This was a time when Japan tried diligently to absorb European and American culture.

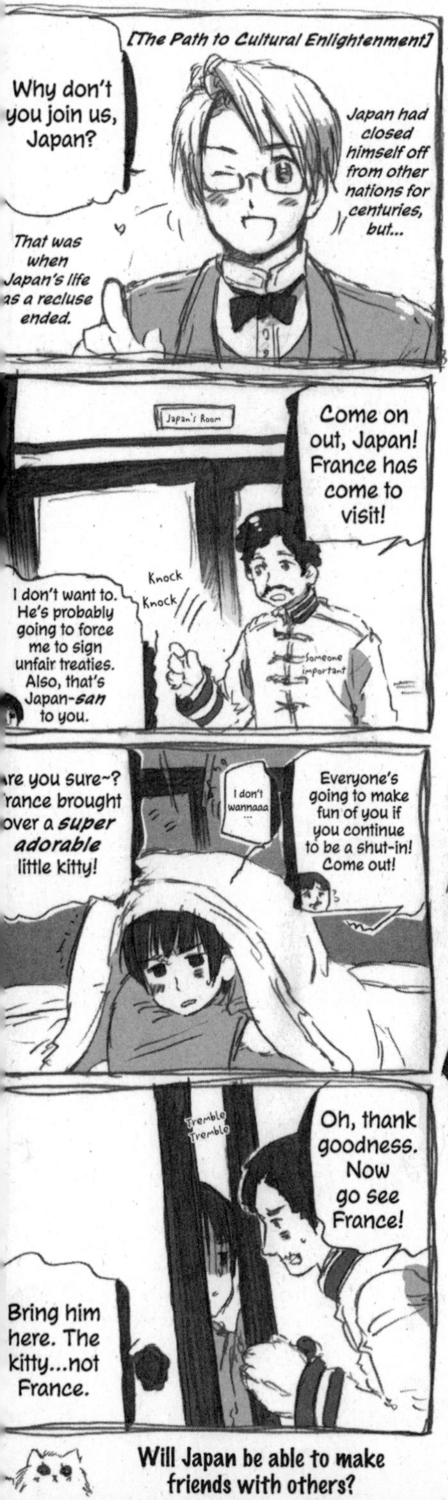
[The Path to Cultural Enlightenment]
Japan had closed himself off from other nations for centuries, but...
Why don't you join us, Japan?
That was when Japan's life as a recluse ended.
Japan's Room
Come on out, Japan! France has come to visit!
Knock Knock
Someone important
I don't want to. He's probably going to force me to sign unfair treaties. Also, that's Japan-*san* to you.
Everyone's going to make fun of you if you continue to be a shut-in! Come out!
I don't wannaaa...
re you sure~? rance brought over a *super adorable* little kitty!
Tremble Tremble
Oh, thank goodness. Now go see France!
Bring him here. The kitty...not France.
Will Japan be able to make friends with others?

Japan-kun and America-kun 3

Sightseeing is so exciting!

Temple

Shinjuku nightlife

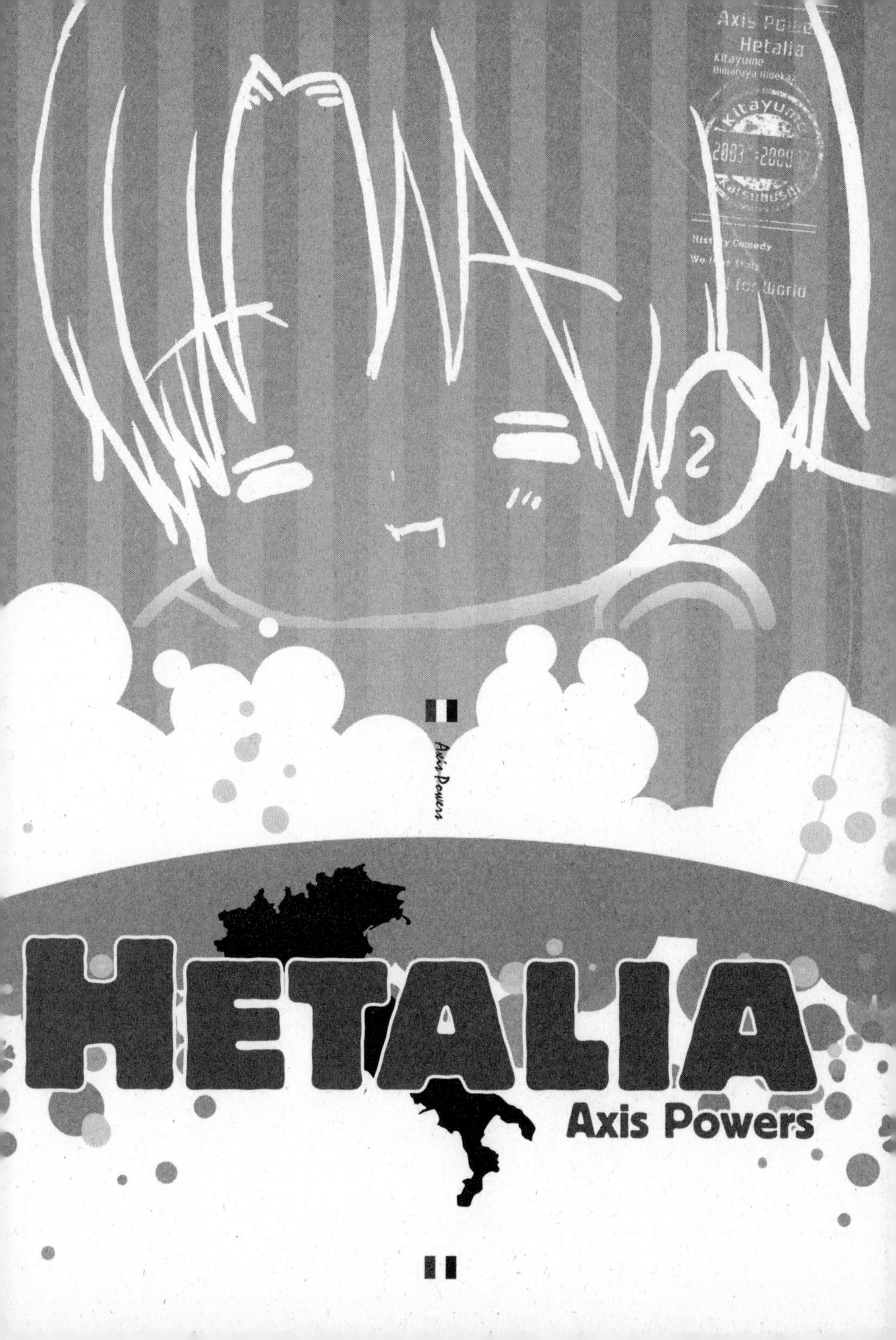
Hetalia
Kitayume
Axis Powers
HETALIA
Axis Powers

Big Brother France's Olympian Love

Here's an interesting story about the Ancient Olympics. It's a well-known fact that the Olympics were done in the nude, but Nero, the Roman Emperor who was famous for being a tyrant, supposedly participated in the Olympics as well.

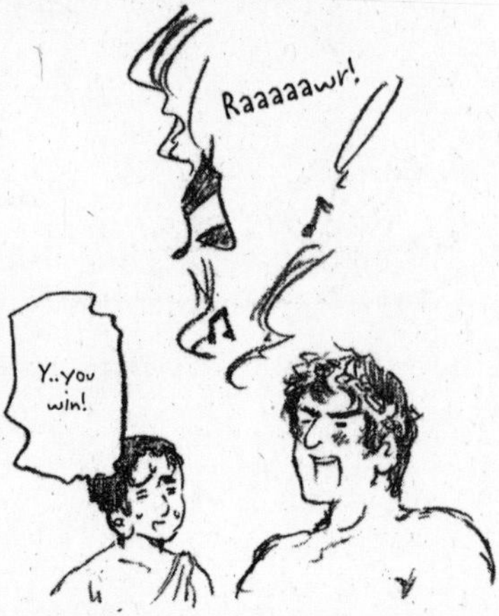

Raaaaawr!
Y..you win!

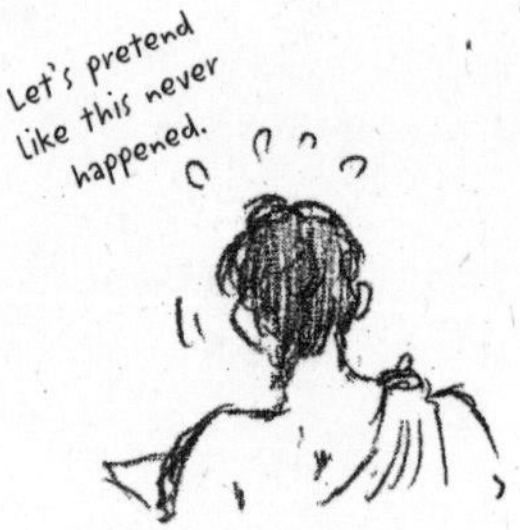

Let's pretend like this never happened.

The Emperor won in seven different competitions only because all the contestants were afraid to beat him. He even won in the singing contest, despite the fact that he couldn't hold a note to save his life. After Nero's death, his winning records were buried and forgotten.

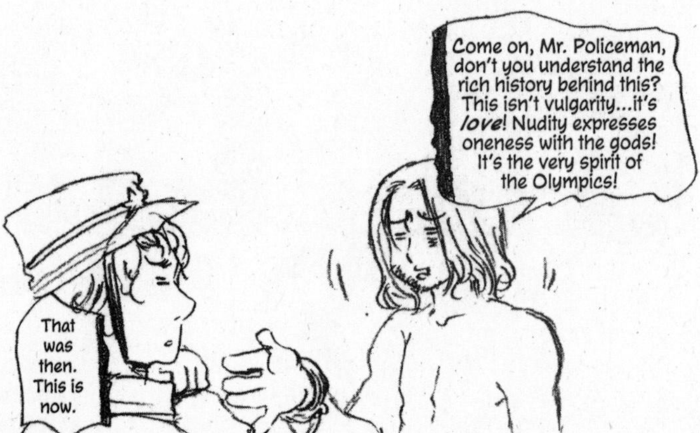

Come on, Mr. Policeman, don't you understand the rich history behind this? This isn't vulgarity...it's *love*! Nudity expresses oneness with the gods! It's the very spirit of the Olympics!
That was then. This is now.

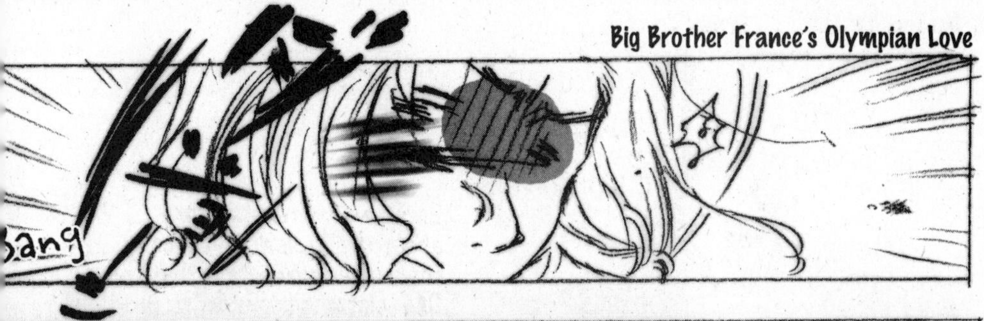
Bang

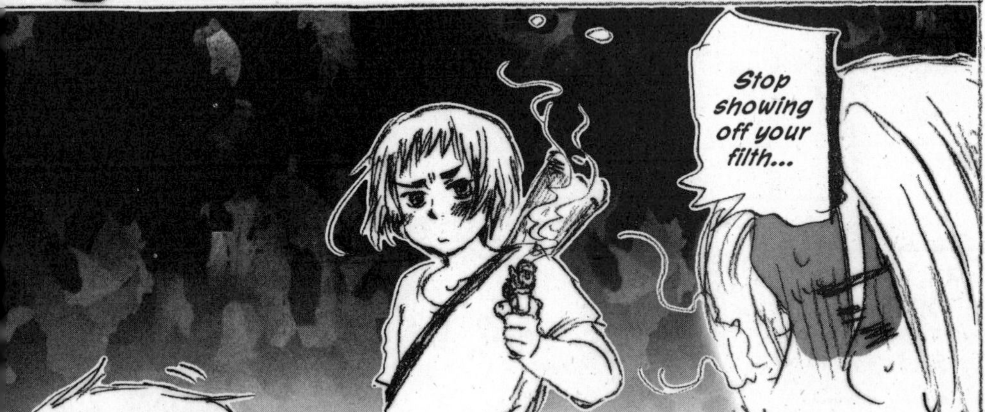
Stop showing off your filth...

In the Ancient Olympic Games, everyone was naked. However, this was mainly to prevent cheating (or female entrants disguised as men). Either way, the ancient Greeks revered the naked male figure.

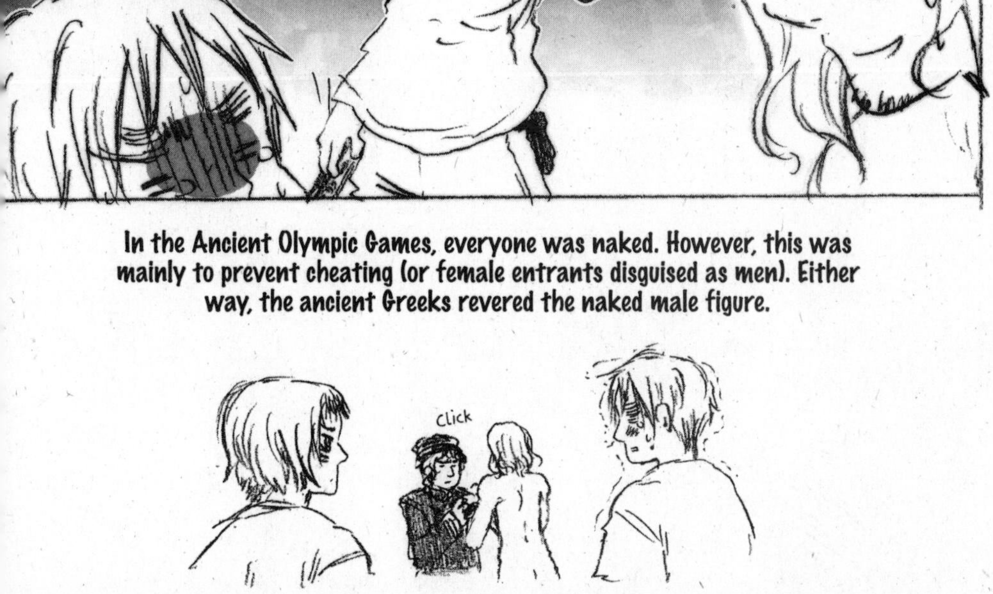
Click

In fact, they liked it so much that all statues and paintings of men (or gods) were naked. Hercules, Zeus and all their buddies were all butt naked. If a heroic soldier was memorialized, he would be naked too. It's kind of embarrassing to think that your junk would be put on display for centuries. Ironically, people in Ancient Greece were actually shy about showing off their bodies in public. If someone showed up naked outside of the Olympic Games, they would be arrested.

Big Brother France's Olympian Love

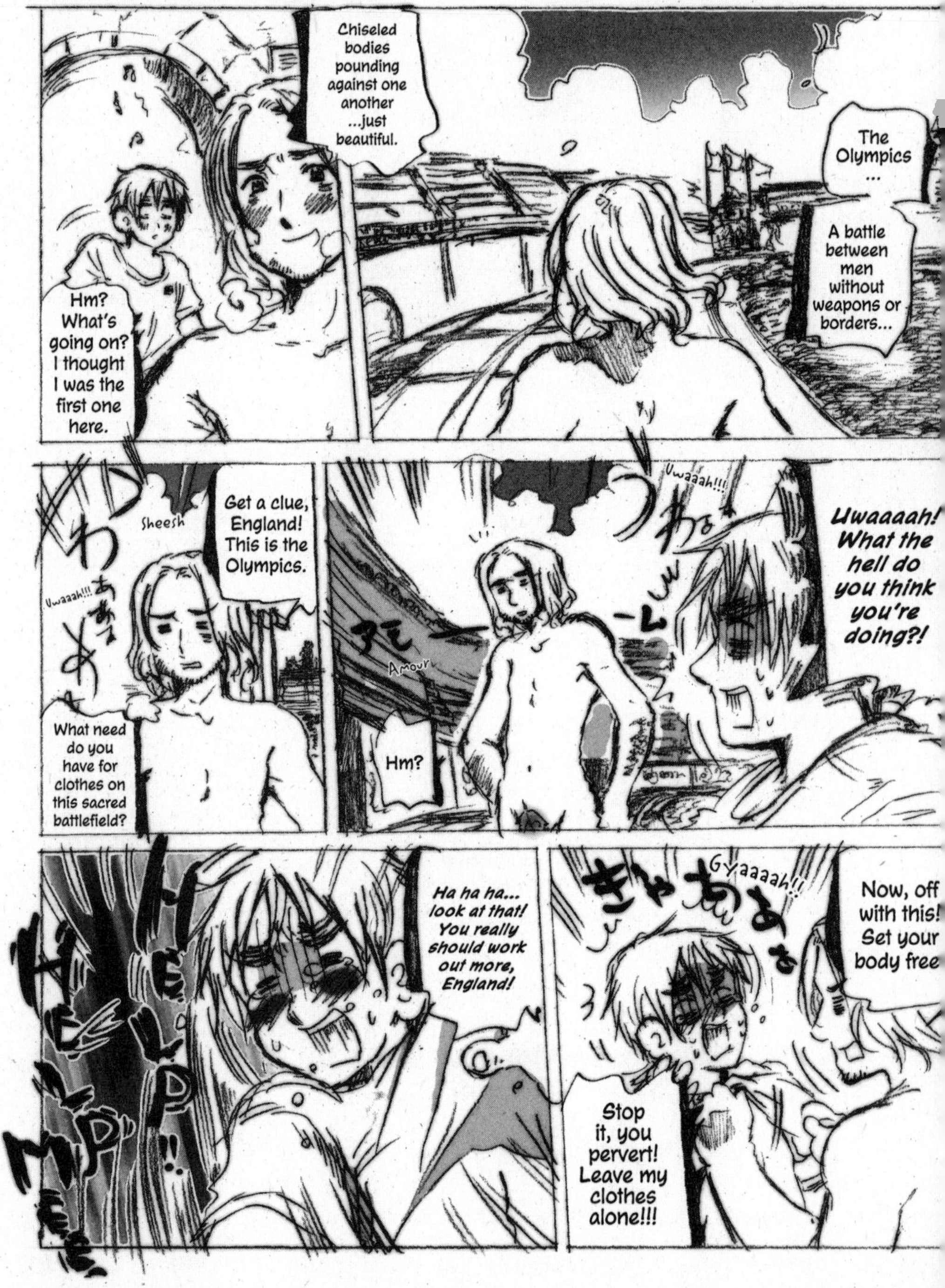
The Olympics ...
A battle between men without weapons or borders...
Chiseled bodies pounding against one another ...just beautiful.
Hm? What's going on? I thought I was the first one here.
Uwaaaah! What the hell do you think you're doing?!
Uwaaah!!!
Amour
Hm?
Get a clue, England! This is the Olympics.
Sheesh
Uwaaah!!!
What need do you have for clothes on this sacred battlefield?
Now, off with this! Set your body free
Gyaaaah!!
Stop it, you pervert! Leave my clothes alone!!!
Ha ha ha... look at that! You really should work out more, England!

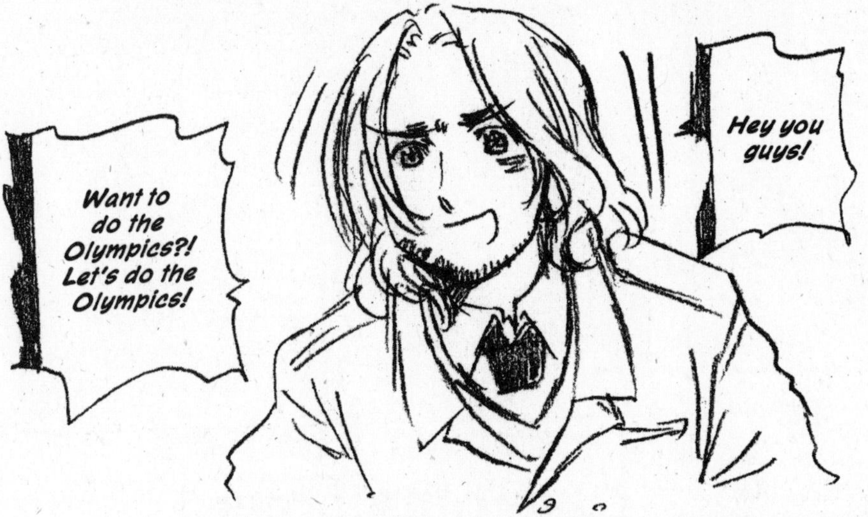
Hey you guys!
Want to do the Olympics?! Let's do the Olympics!

And so, thanks to France's insistence, the Olympic Games were held in an attempt to "unify the hearts of every young man from the different countries around the world."

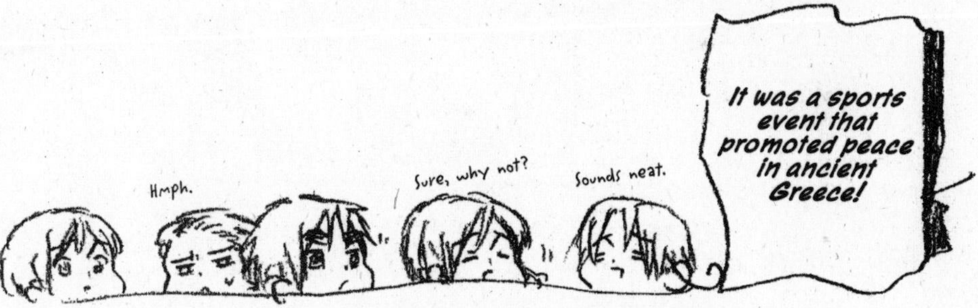
It was a sports event that promoted peace in ancient Greece!
Sounds neat.
Sure, why not?
Hmph.

The proposal was supported by numerous nations, and on April 6, 1896, the first modern Olympic Games were held in Athens.

At that time, there were only 13 nations that participated: France, America, England, Germany, Austria, Hungary, Switzerland, Denmark, Sweden, Australia, and a few others.

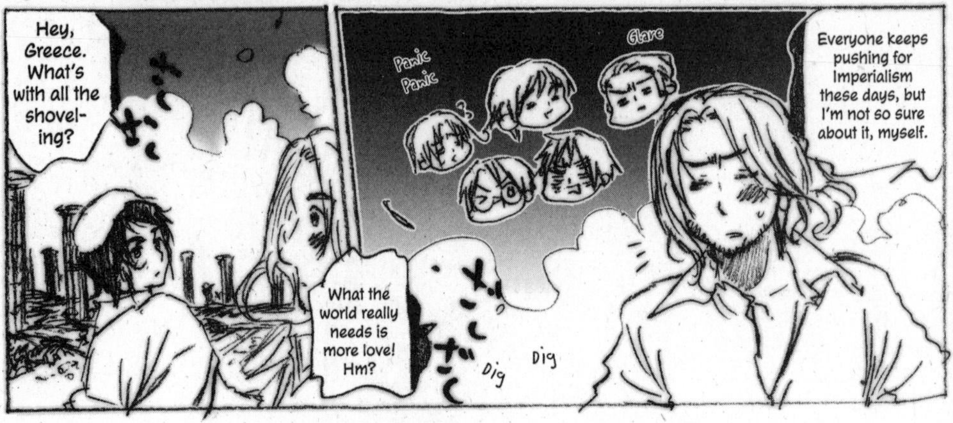

Everyone keeps pushing for Imperialism these days, but I'm not so sure about it, myself.
Glare
Panic Panic
What the world really needs is more love! Hm?
Dig
Dig
Hey, Greece. What's with all the shovel-ing?

Big Brother France's Olympian Love

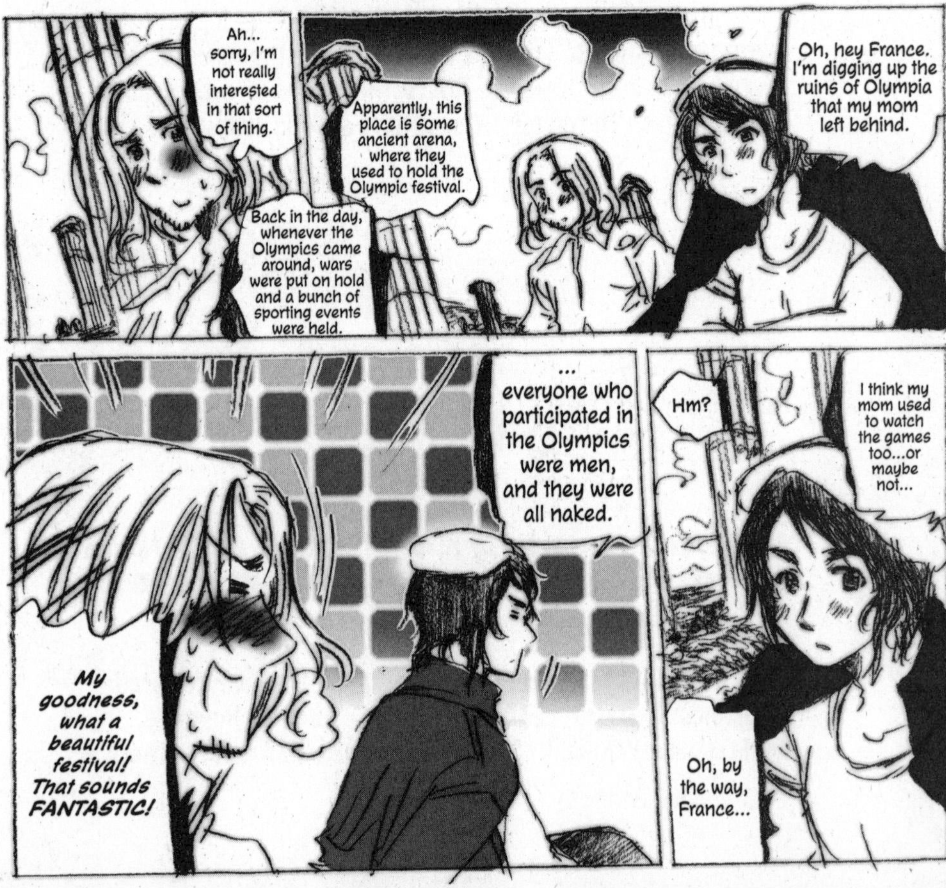

Oh, hey France. I'm digging up the ruins of Olympia that my mom left behind.
Apparently, this place is some ancient arena, where they used to hold the Olympic festival.
Back in the day, whenever the Olympics came around, wars were put on hold and a bunch of sporting events were held.
Ah... sorry, I'm not really interested in that sort of thing.
I think my mom used to watch the games too...or maybe not...
Hm?
Oh, by the way, France...
... everyone who participated in the Olympics were men, and they were all naked.
My goodness, what a beautiful festival! That sounds FANTASTIC!

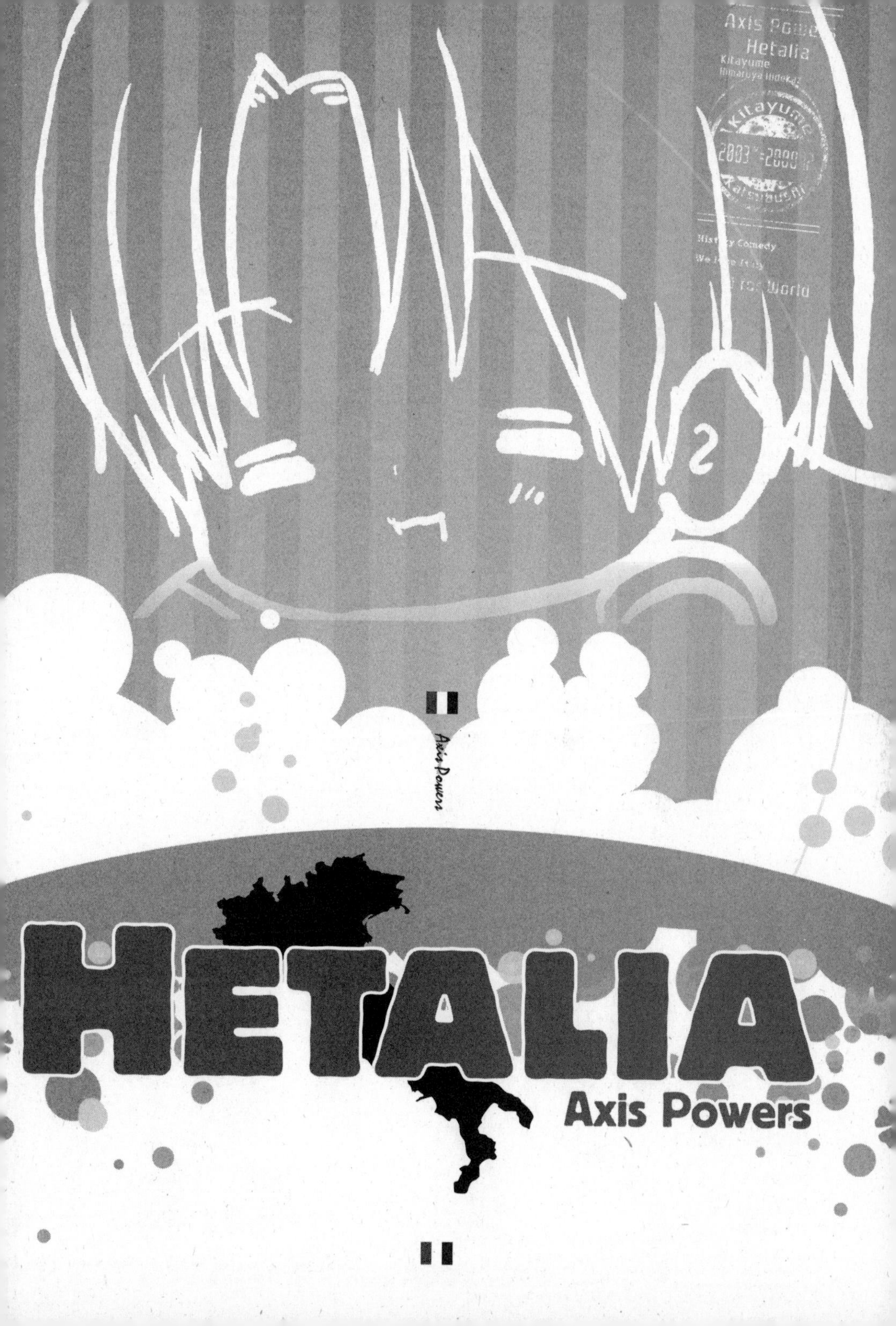
Axis Powers
Hetalia
Kitayume
History Comedy
Axis Powers
HETALIA
Axis Powers

Hello World! Hello Italy!
I Can't Eat at This Café Part 2

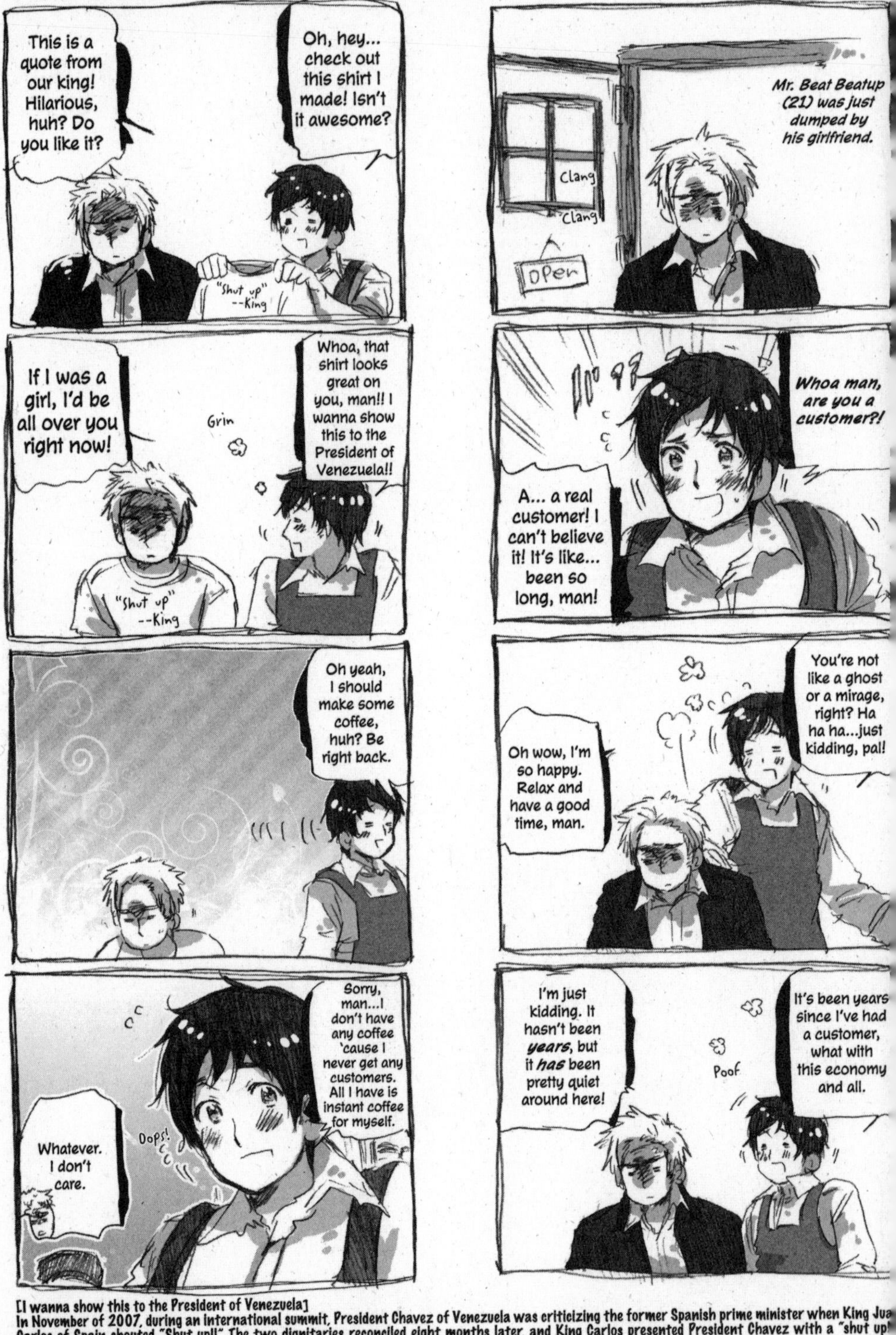
Mr. Beat Beatup (21) was just dumped by his girlfriend.
Clang
Clang
OPen
Whoa man, are you a customer?!
A... a real customer! I can't believe it! It's like... been so long, man!
You're not like a ghost or a mirage, right? Ha ha ha...just kidding, pal!
Oh wow, I'm so happy. Relax and have a good time, man.
It's been years since I've had a customer, what with this economy and all.
Poof
I'm just kidding. It hasn't been *years*, but it *has* been pretty quiet around here!
Oh, hey... check out this shirt I made! Isn't it awesome?
This is a quote from our king! Hilarious, huh? Do you like it?
"Shut up" --King
Whoa, that shirt looks great on you, man!! I wanna show this to the President of Venezuela!!
Grin
If I was a girl, I'd be all over you right now!
"Shut up" --King
Oh yeah, I should make some coffee, huh? Be right back.
Sorry, man...I don't have any coffee 'cause I never get any customers. All I have is instant coffee for myself.
Oops!
Whatever. I don't care.

[I wanna show this to the President of Venezuela]
In November of 2007, during an international summit, President Chavez of Venezuela was criticizing the former Spanish prime minister when King Jua Carlos of Spain shouted "Shut up!!" The two dignitaries reconciled eight months later, and King Carlos presented President Chavez with a "shut up T-shirt. Reprints of the same shirt became a big seller in Spain.

Hello World! Hello Italy!
I Can't Eat at This Café Part 1

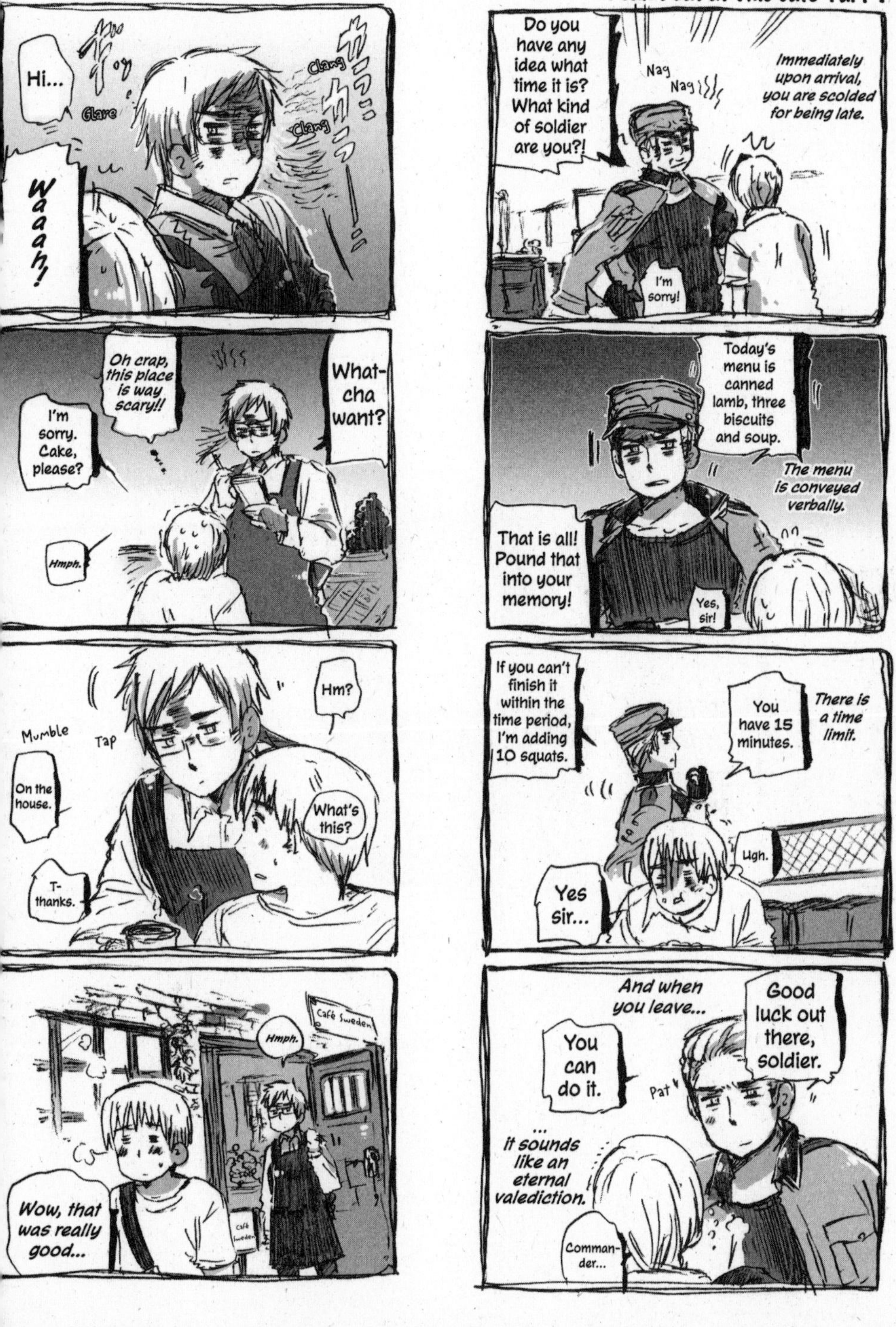
Immediately upon arrival, you are scolded for being late.
Do you have any idea what time it is? What kind of soldier are you?!
Nag
Nag
I'm sorry!
Today's menu is canned lamb, three biscuits and soup.
The menu is conveyed verbally.
That is all! Pound that into your memory!
Yes, sir!
There is a time limit.
You have 15 minutes.
If you can't finish it within the time period, I'm adding 10 squats.
Ugh.
Yes sir...
Good luck out there, soldier.
And when you leave...
You can do it.
Pat
... it sounds like an eternal valediction.
Commander...
Clang
Clang
Hi...
Glare
Waaaah!
What-cha want?
Oh crap, this place is way scary!!
I'm sorry. Cake, please?
Hmph.
Hm?
Mumble
Tap
On the house.
What's this?
T-thanks.
Café Sweden
Hmph.
Café Sweden
Wow, that was really good...

Hello World! Hello Italy!
4,000 Years of History

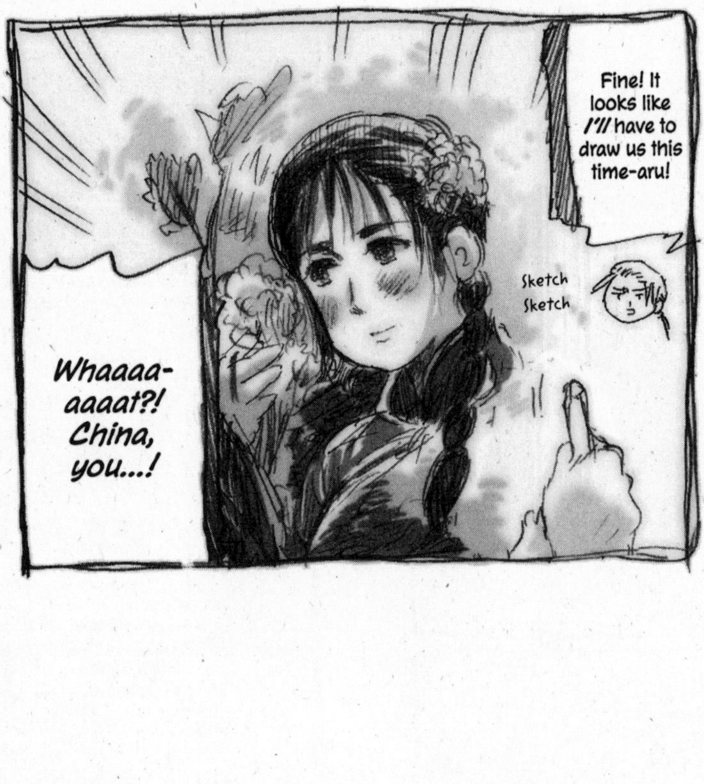
Fine! It looks like I'll have to draw us this time-aru!
Sketch Sketch
Whaaaa-aaaat?! China, you...!

Hello World! Hello Italy!
Do As I Say, Not As I Do

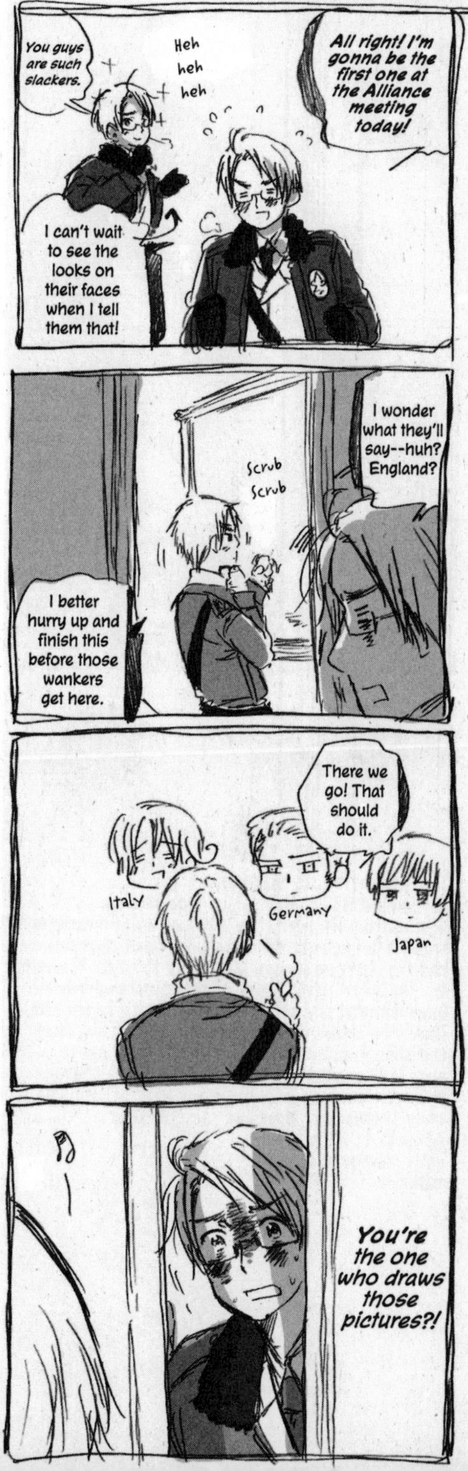
All right! I'm gonna be the first one at the Alliance meeting today!
Heh heh heh
You guys are such slackers.
I can't wait to see the looks on their faces when I tell them that!
I wonder what they'll say--huh? England?
Scrub Scrub
I better hurry up and finish this before those wankers get here.
There we go! That should do it.
Italy
Germany
Japan
You're the one who draws those pictures?!

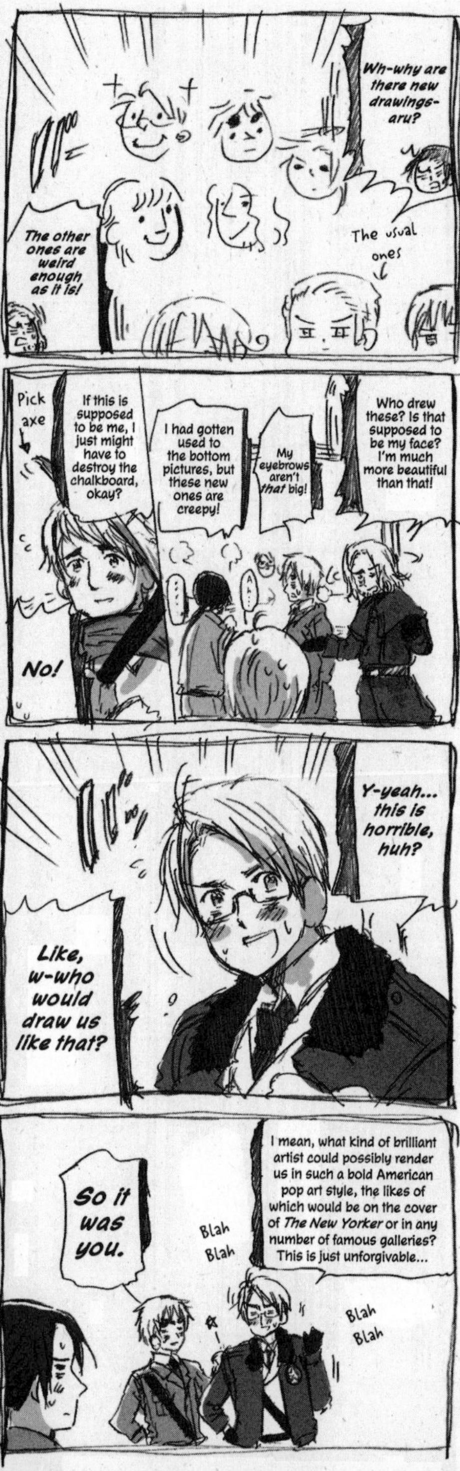
Wh-why are there new drawings-aru?
The usual ones
The other ones are weird enough as it is!
Who drew these? Is that supposed to be my face? I'm much more beautiful than that!
My eyebrows aren't *that* big!
I had gotten used to the bottom pictures, but these new ones are creepy!
If this is supposed to be me, I just might have to destroy the chalkboard, okay?
Pick axe
No!
Y-yeah... this is horrible, huh?
Like, w-who would draw us like that?
I mean, what kind of brilliant artist could possibly render us in such a bold American pop art style, the likes of which would be on the cover of *The New Yorker* or in any number of famous galleries? This is just unforgivable...
Blah Blah
Blah Blah
So it was you.

Hello World! Hello Italy!
It Came From England

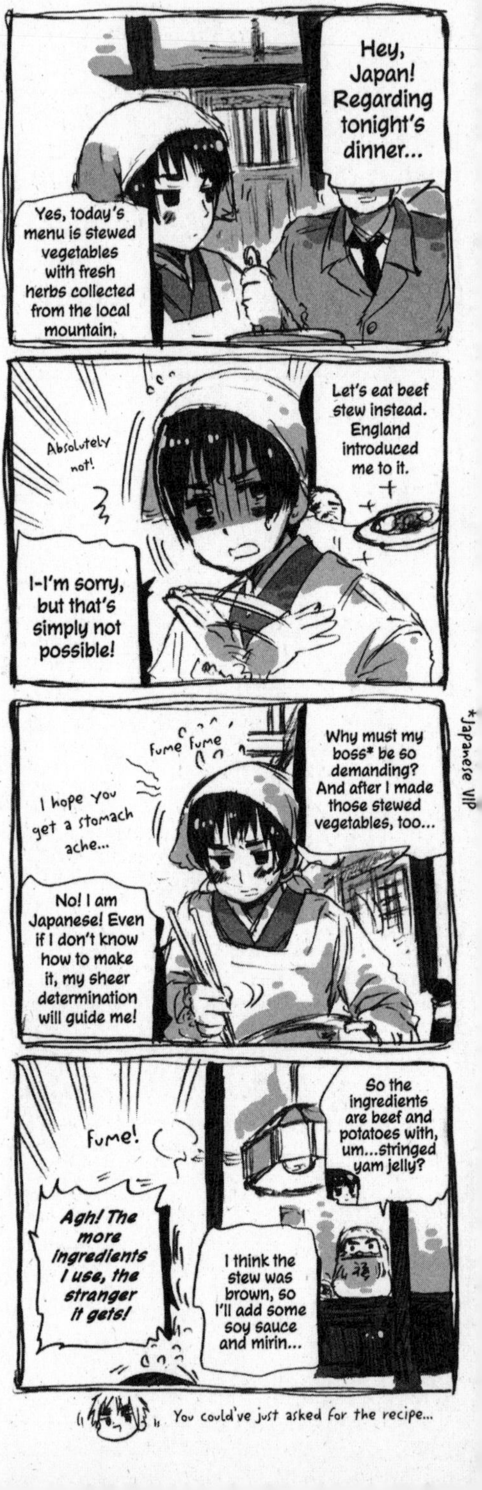
Hey, Japan! Regarding tonight's dinner...
Yes, today's menu is stewed vegetables with fresh herbs collected from the local mountain.
Let's eat beef stew instead. England introduced me to it.
Absolutely not!
I-I'm sorry, but that's simply not possible!
Why must my boss* be so demanding? And after I made those stewed vegetables, too...
Fume fume
I hope you get a stomach ache...
No! I am Japanese! Even if I don't know how to make it, my sheer determination will guide me!
So the ingredients are beef and potatoes with, um...stringed yam jelly?
Fume!
I think the stew was brown, so I'll add some soy sauce and mirin...
Agh! The more ingredients I use, the stranger it gets!
*Japanese VIP
You could've just asked for the recipe...

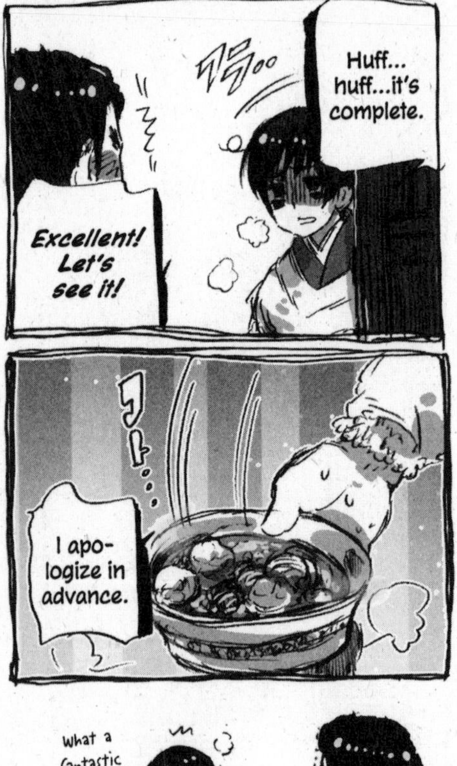
Huff... huff...it's complete.
Excellent! Let's see it!
I apo-logize in advance.

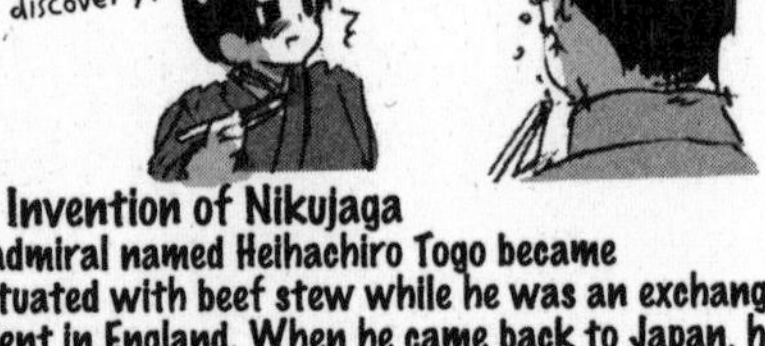
What a fantastic discovery!

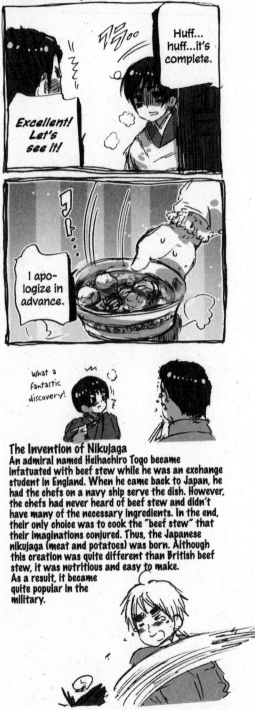

The Invention of Nikujaga
An admiral named Heihachiro Togo became infatuated with beef stew while he was an exchange student in England. When he came back to Japan, he had the chefs on a navy ship serve the dish. However, the chefs had never heard of beef stew and didn't have many of the necessary ingredients. In the end, their only choice was to cook the "beef stew" that their imaginations conjured. Thus, the Japanese nikujaga (meat and potatoes) was born. Although this creation was quite different than British beef stew, it was nutritious and easy to make. As a result, it became quite popular in the military.

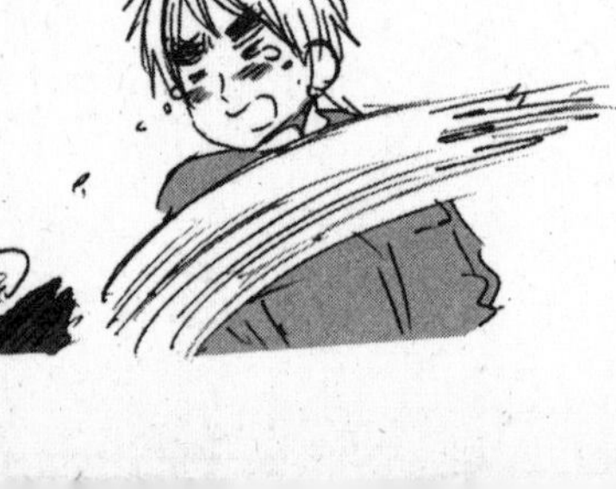

Hello World! Hello Italy!
Pampering, German Style

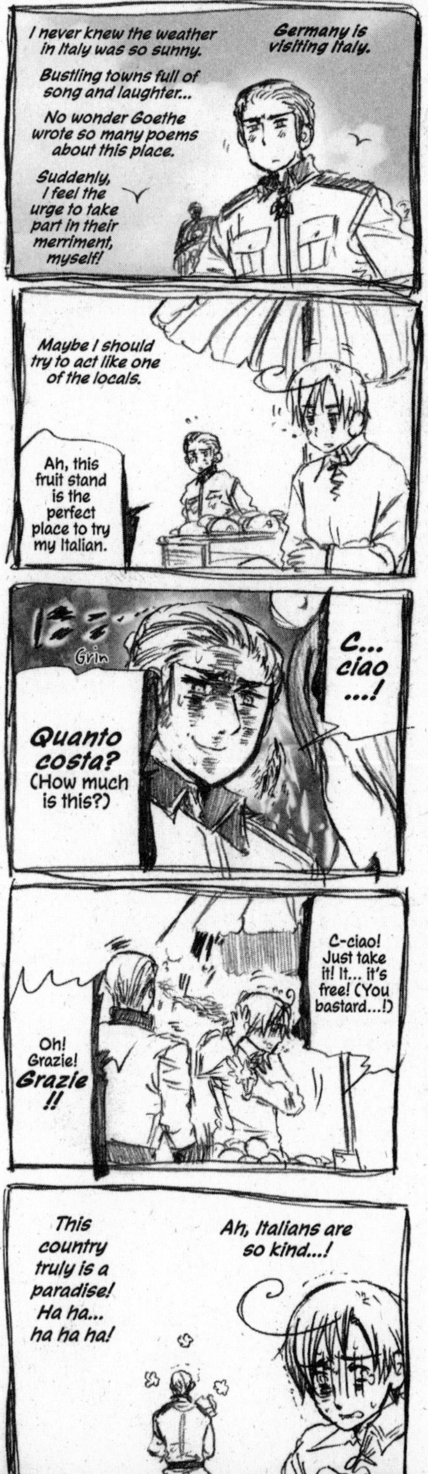
Germany is visiting Italy.
I never knew the weather in Italy was so sunny.
Bustling towns full of song and laughter...
No wonder Goethe wrote so many poems about this place.
Suddenly, I feel the urge to take part in their merriment, myself!
Maybe I should try to act like one of the locals.
Ah, this fruit stand is the perfect place to try my Italian.
C... ciao ...!
Grin
Quanto costa? (How much is this?)
C-ciao! Just take it! It... it's free! (You bastard...!)
Oh! Grazie! Grazie !!
Ah, Italians are so kind...!
This country truly is a paradise! Ha ha... ha ha ha!

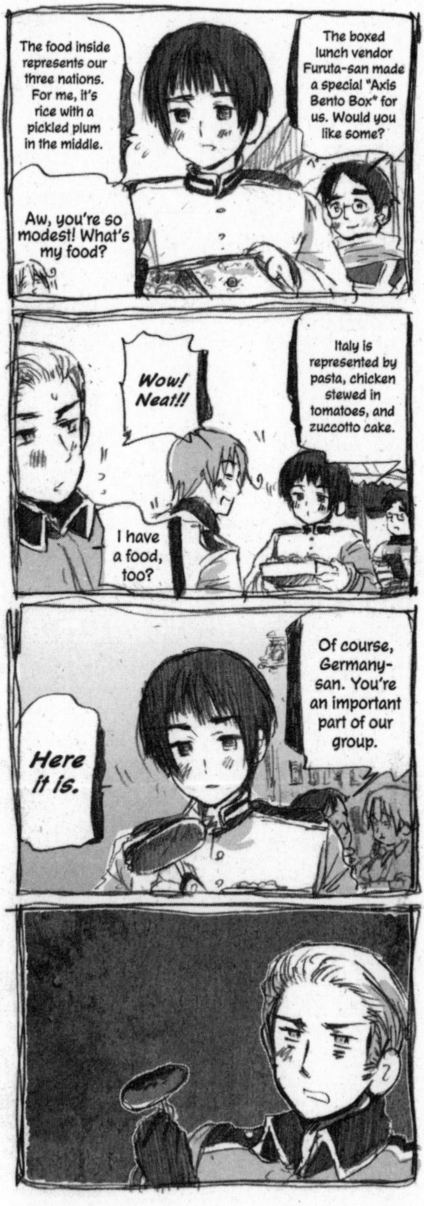
The boxed lunch vendor Furuta-san made a special "Axis Bento Box" for us. Would you like some?
The food inside represents our three nations. For me, it's rice with a pickled plum in the middle.
Aw, you're so modest! What's my food?
Italy is represented by pasta, chicken stewed in tomatoes, and zuccotto cake.
Wow! Neat!!
I have a food, too?
Of course, Germany-san. You're an important part of our group.
Here it is.

Hello World! Hello Italy!

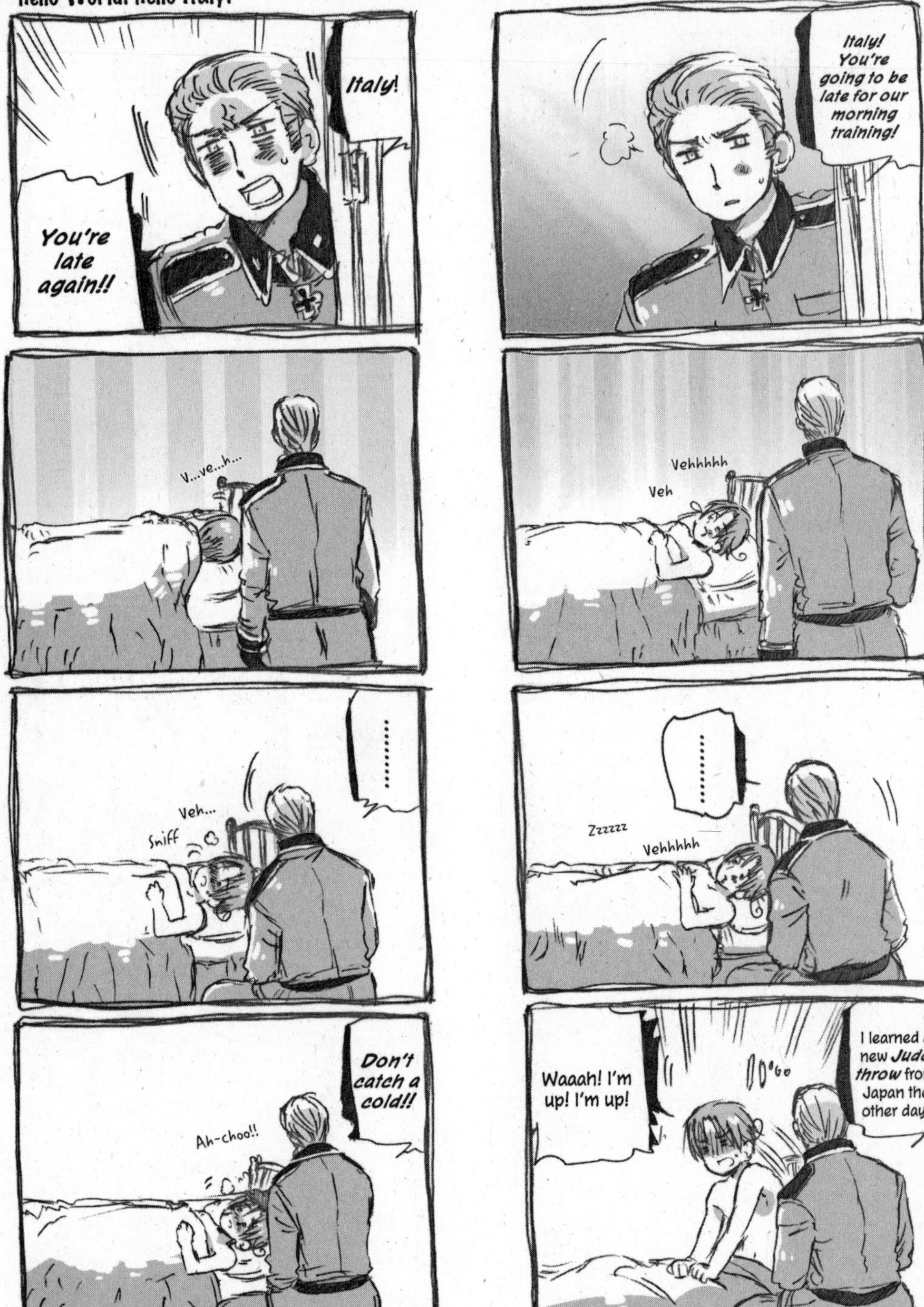
Italy! You're going to be late for our morning training!
Vehhhhh
Veh
....
Zzzzzz
Vehhhhh
I learned a new Judo throw from Japan the other day.
Waaah! I'm up! I'm up!
Italy!
You're late again!!
V...ve...h...
....
Veh...
Sniff
Don't catch a cold!!
Ah-choo!!

Hello World! Hello Italy!

AXIS POWERS HETALIA 2

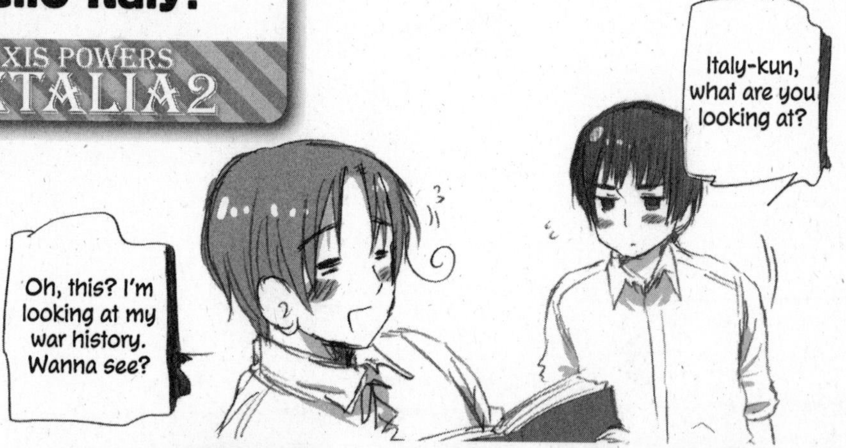
Italy-kun, what are you looking at?
Oh, this? I'm looking at my war history. Wanna see?

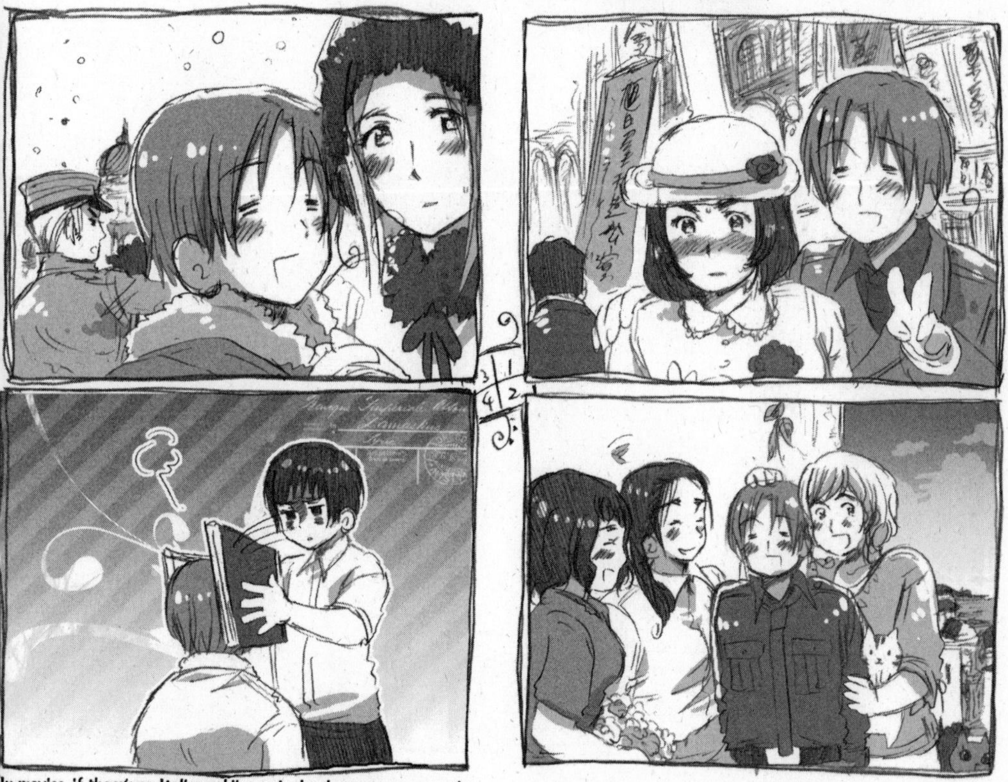

In movies, if there's an Italian soldier and a local woman appears, the soldier and the woman will inevitably fall in love.

Japan-kun and America-kun 2

In America, some desserts are colored so brightly they don't even look edible. Other foods have the word "devil" nonchalantly labeled on the packaging.

AXIS POWERS HETALIA 2

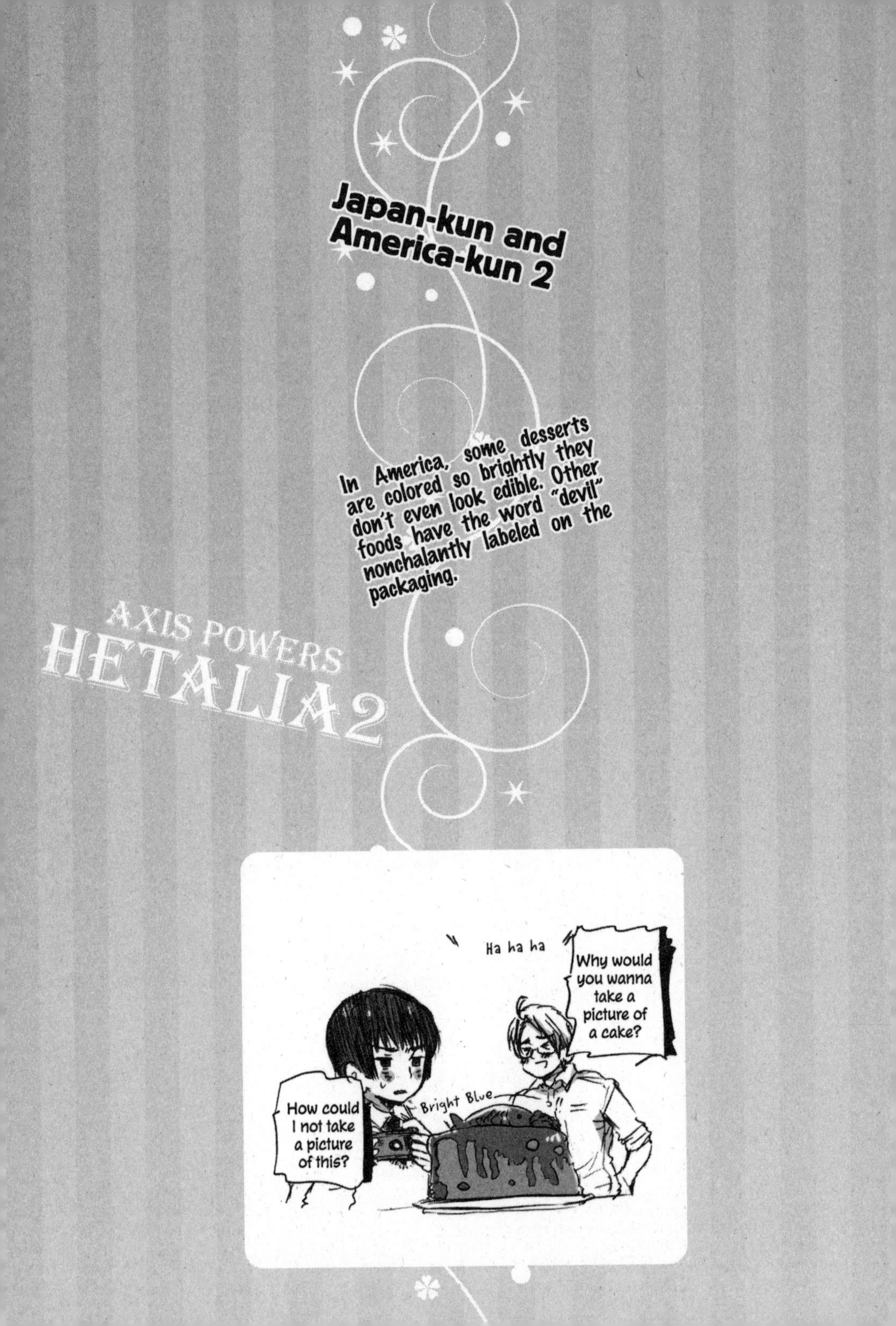
Why would you wanna take a picture of a cake?
Ha ha ha
Bright Blue
How could I not take a picture of this?

Russia's Sisters
Memories Were Too Beautiful

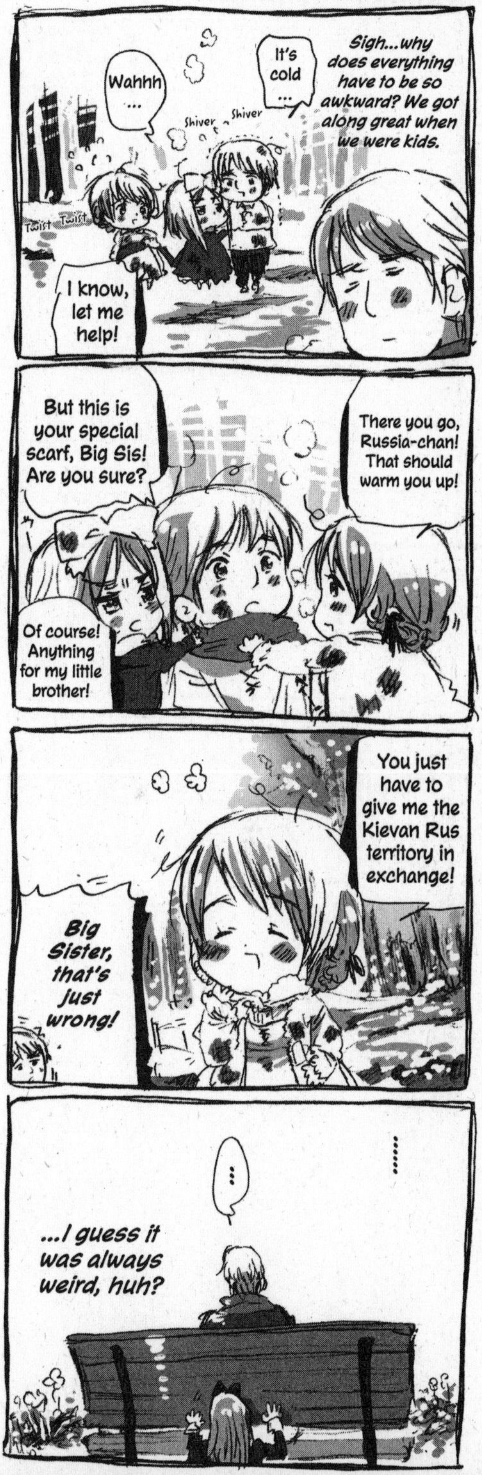
Sigh...why does everything have to be so awkward? We got along great when we were kids.
It's cold ...
Wahhh ...
Shiver
Shiver
Twist Twist
I know, let me help!
There you go, Russia-chan! That should warm you up!
But this is your special scarf, Big Sis! Are you sure?
Of course! Anything for my little brother!
You just have to give me the Kievan Rus territory in exchange!
Big Sister, that's just wrong!
......
...
...I guess it was always weird, huh?

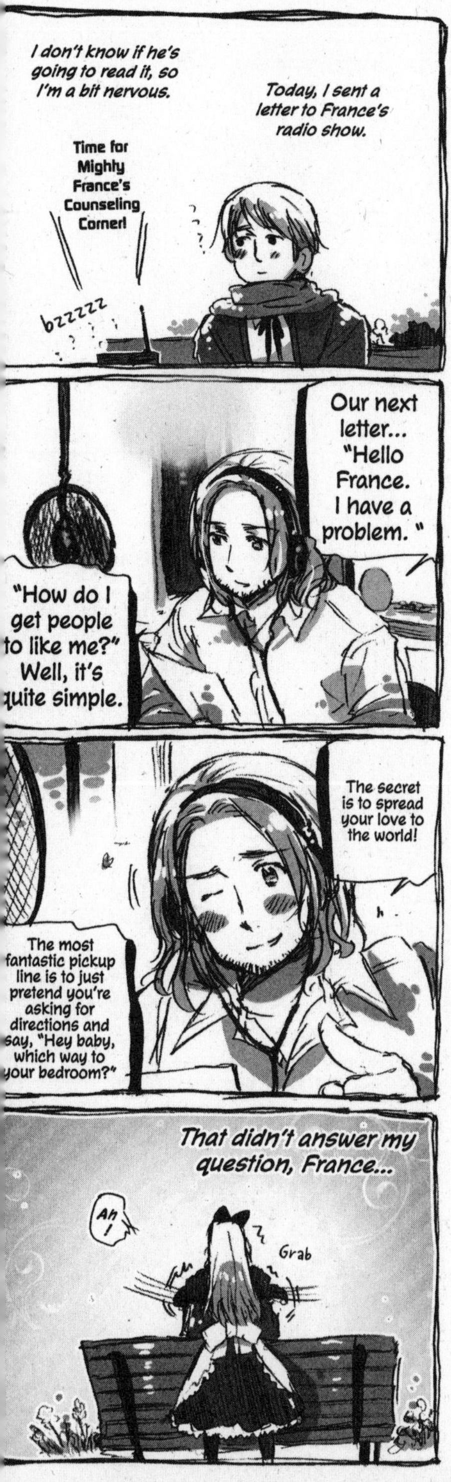
Today, I sent a letter to France's radio show.
I don't know if he's going to read it, so I'm a bit nervous.
Time for Mighty France's Counseling Corner!
bzzzzz
Our next letter... "Hello France. I have a problem. "
"How do I get people to like me?" Well, it's quite simple.
The secret is to spread your love to the world!
The most fantastic pickup line is to just pretend you're asking for directions and say, "Hey baby, which way to your bedroom?"
That didn't answer my question, France...
Ah!
Grab

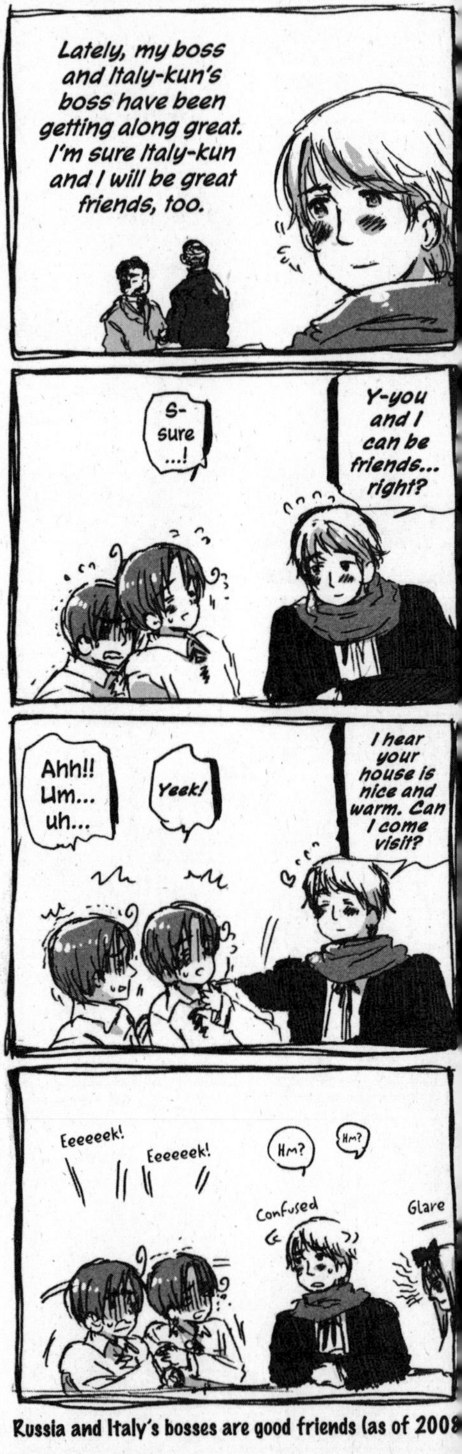
Lately, my boss and Italy-kun's boss have been getting along great. I'm sure Italy-kun and I will be great friends, too.
Y-you and I can be friends... right?
S-sure ...!
I hear your house is nice and warm. Can I come visit?
Yeek!
Ahh!! Um... uh...
Hm?
Hm?
Eeeeeek!
Eeeeeek!
Glare
Confused

Russia and Italy's bosses are good friends (as of 2008

Russia's Sisters Don't Think Too Much Into It

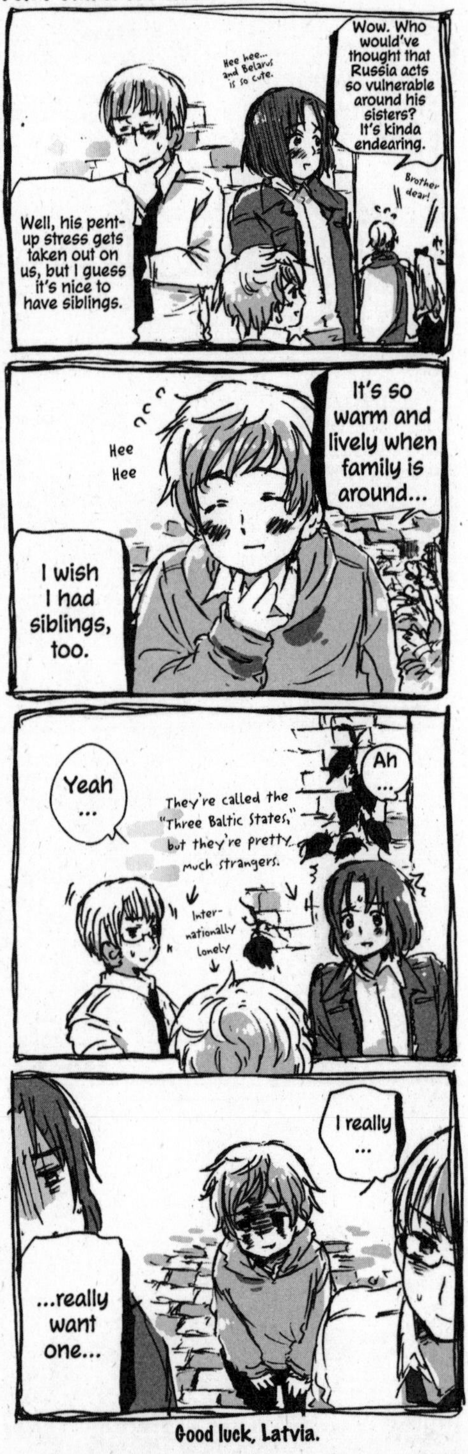
Wow. Who would've thought that Russia acts so vulnerable around his sisters? It's kinda endearing.
Brother dear!
Hee hee... and Belarus is so cute.
Well, his pent-up stress gets taken out on us, but I guess it's nice to have siblings.
It's so warm and lively when family is around...
Hee Hee
I wish I had siblings, too.
Ah ...
They're called the "Three Baltic States," but they're pretty much strangers.
Inter-nationally lonely
Yeah ...
I really ...
...really want one...

Good luck, Latvia.

Russia's Sisters
Unrequited Love

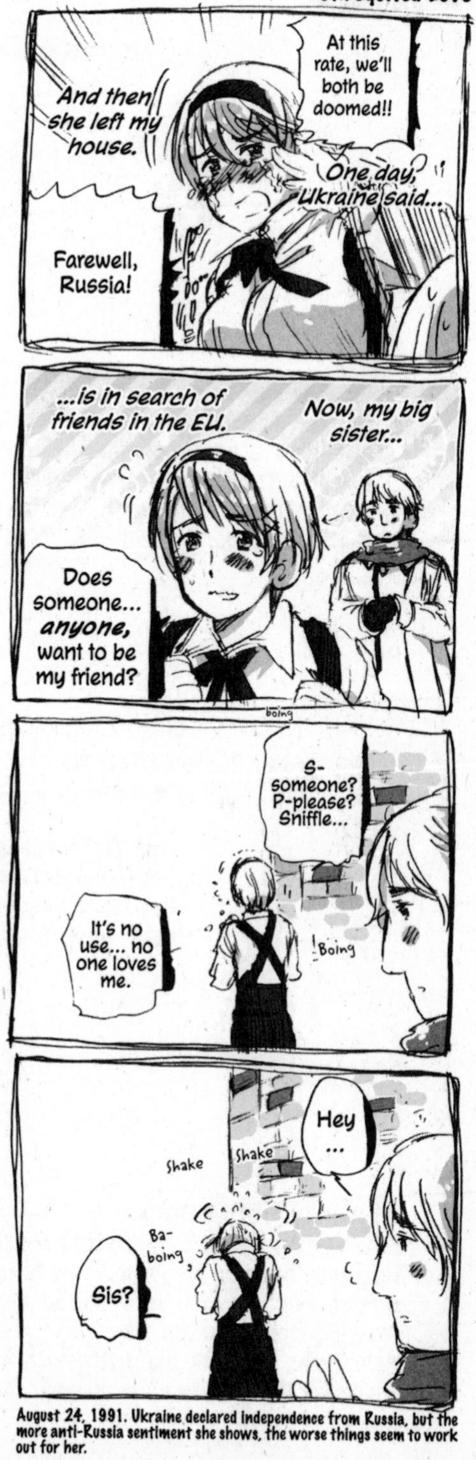
One day, Ukraine said...
At this rate, we'll both be doomed!!
And then she left my house.
Farewell, Russia!
Now, my big sister...
...is in search of friends in the EU.
Does someone... ***anyone,*** want to be my friend?
boing
S-someone? P-please? Sniffle...
Boing
It's no use... no one loves me.
Hey...
Shake
Shake
Ba-boing
Sis?

August 24, 1991. Ukraine declared independence from Russia, but the more anti-Russia sentiment she shows, the worse things seem to work out for her.

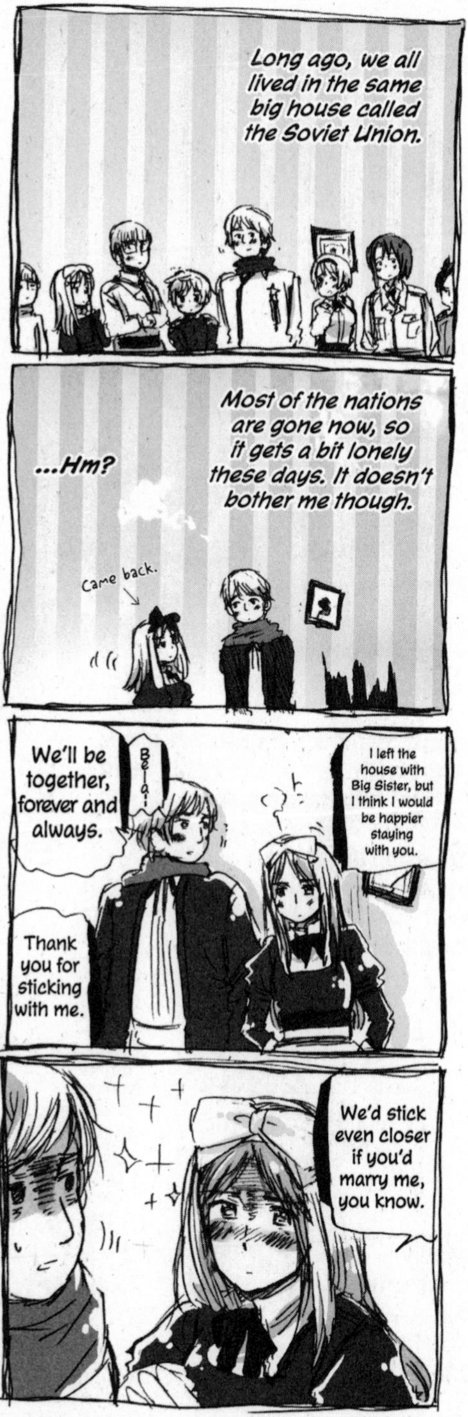
Long ago, we all lived in the same big house called the Soviet Union.
Most of the nations are gone now, so it gets a bit lonely these days. It doesn't bother me though.
...Hm?
came back.
I left the house with Big Sister, but I think I would be happier staying with you.
Bela-
We'll be together, forever and always.
Thank you for sticking with me.
We'd stick even closer if you'd marry me, you know.

[Russia's older and younger sisters]

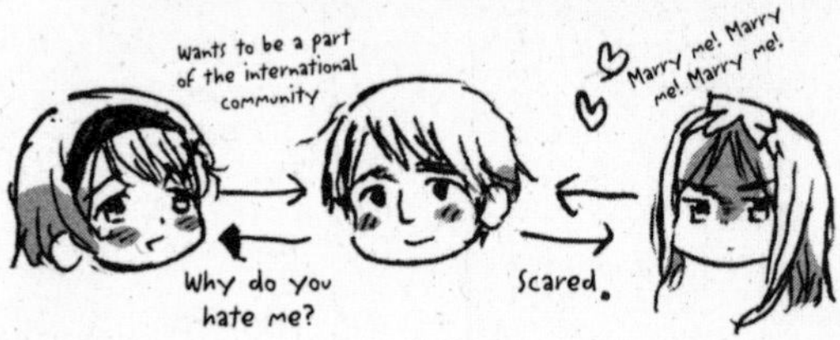
Wants to be a part of the international community
Marry me! Marry me! Marry me!
Why do you hate me?
Scared.

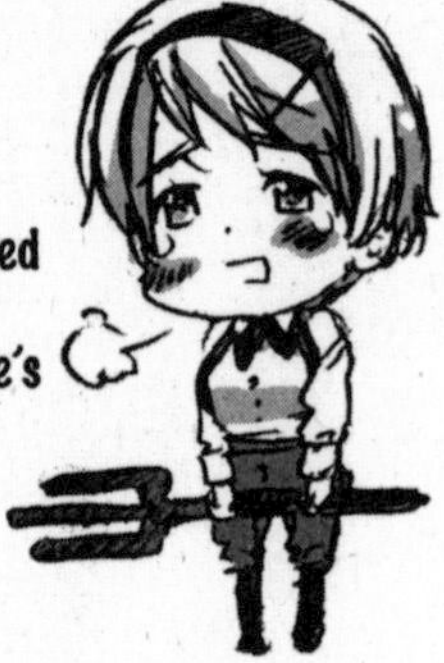

Ukraine-san
Russia's older sister who has a long history of getting dragged into messes. After becoming independent in 1991, Ukraine has been trying to distance herself from her big brother. She's been getting friendly with America and Europe lately but is still quite poor and is forced to slave away in the fields.

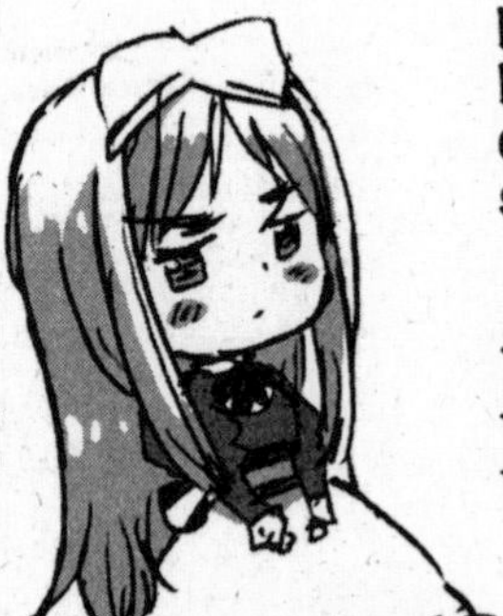

Belarus-san
Russia's intimidating younger sister is a tremendous source of stress for him. An expert with "carrot and stick" tactics, she is known as Europe's final totalitarian nation.

<The Worst Economic Situation in Europe>
Though Belarus' economy is in terrible shape, she believes that everything is all right "as long as there is food on the table." As a result, she's quite devoted to agriculture.

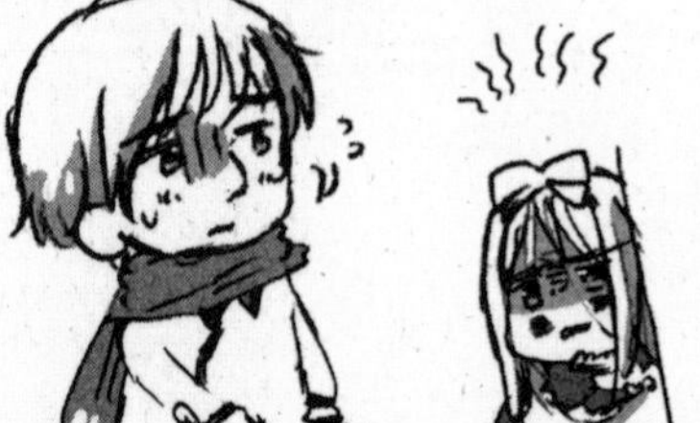

<I Love My Brother Dear>
Belarus loves Russia so much that she's practically forgotten her own language. From Russia's perspective, getting together with her would be more trouble than it's worth. On the other hand, if he completely ignores her, then she might side with America and make things even more difficult for him.

Russia's Sisters
To My Dear Older Brother

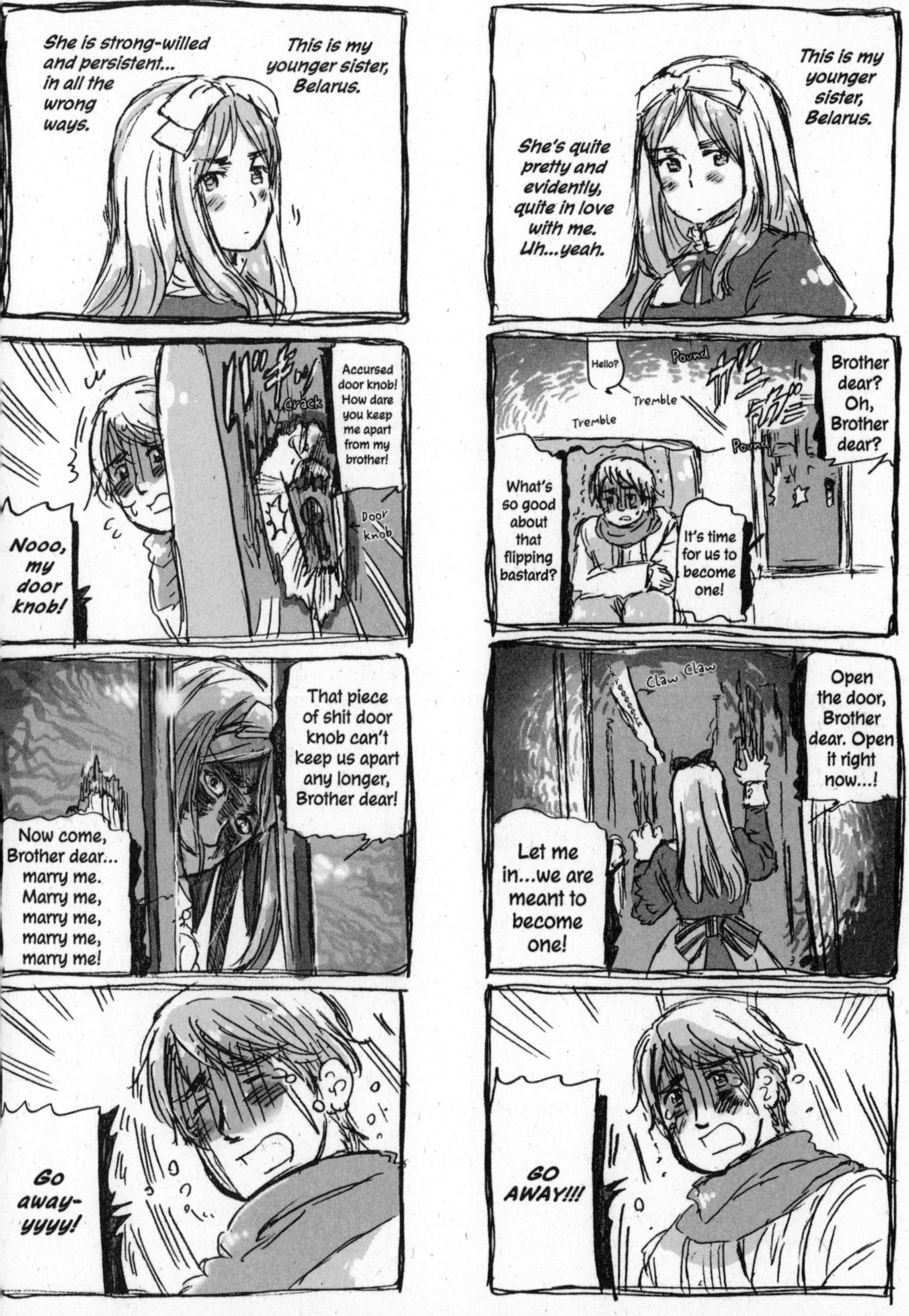
This is my younger sister, Belarus.
She's quite pretty and evidently, quite in love with me. Uh...yeah.
Brother dear? Oh, Brother dear?
Pound
Hello?
Tremble
Tremble
Pound
It's time for us to become one!
What's so good about that flipping bastard?
Open the door, Brother dear. Open it right now...!
Claw Claw
Let me in...we are meant to become one!
GO AWAY!!!
This is my younger sister, Belarus.
She is strong-willed and persistent... in all the wrong ways.
Accursed door knob! How dare you keep me apart from my brother!
Crack
Door knob
Nooo, my door knob!
That piece of shit door knob can't keep us apart any longer, Brother dear!
Now come, Brother dear... marry me. Marry me, marry me, marry me, marry me!
Go away-yyyy!

Russia's Sisters
I Hate My Big Boobs!

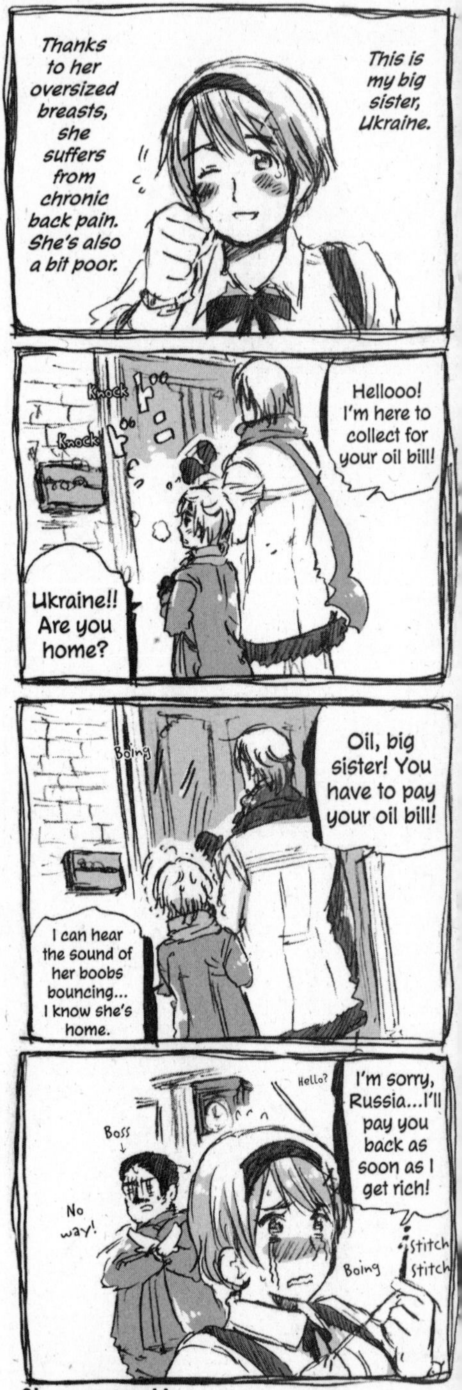

This is my big sister, Ukraine.
Thanks to her oversized breasts, she suffers from chronic back pain. She's also a bit poor.
Hellooo! I'm here to collect for your oil bill!
Knock
Knock
Ukraine!! Are you home?
Oil, big sister! You have to pay your oil bill!
Boing
I can hear the sound of her boobs bouncing... I know she's home.
I'm sorry, Russia...I'll pay you back as soon as I get rich!
Hello?
Boss
No way!
Stitch
Stitch
Boing

She never paid.

As an added note, Ukraine's natural gas supply was once shut of

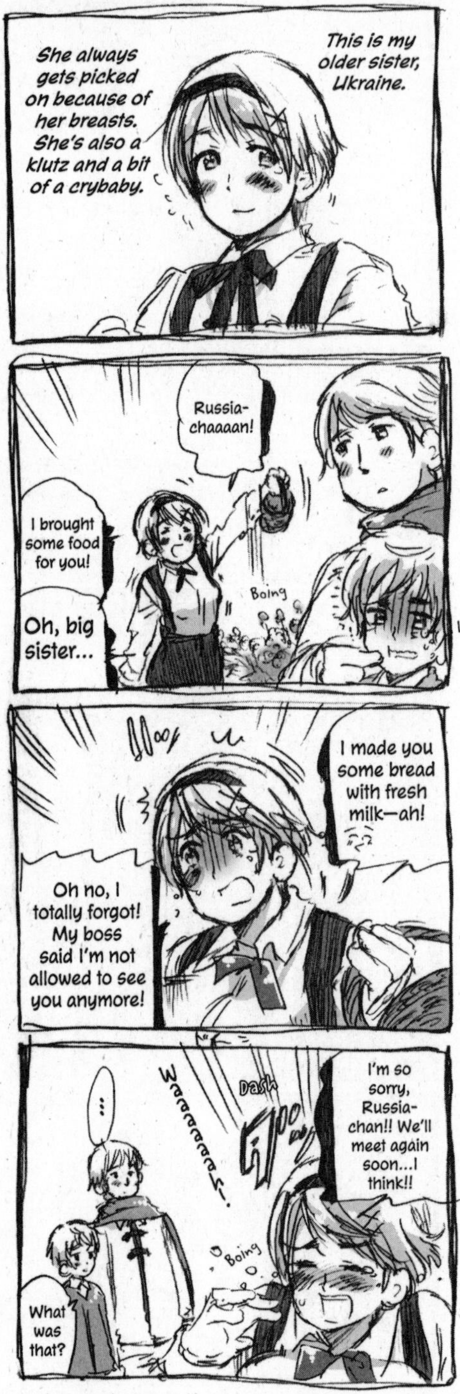

This is my older sister, Ukraine.
She always gets picked on because of her breasts. She's also a klutz and a bit of a crybaby.
Russia-chaaaan!
I brought some food for you!
Boing
Oh, big sister...
Latvia
I made you some bread with fresh milk—ah!
Oh no, I totally forgot! My boss said I'm not allowed to see you anymore!
I'm so sorry, Russia-chan!! We'll meet again soon...I think!!
Dash
Waaaaaaaah!
...
Boing
What was that?

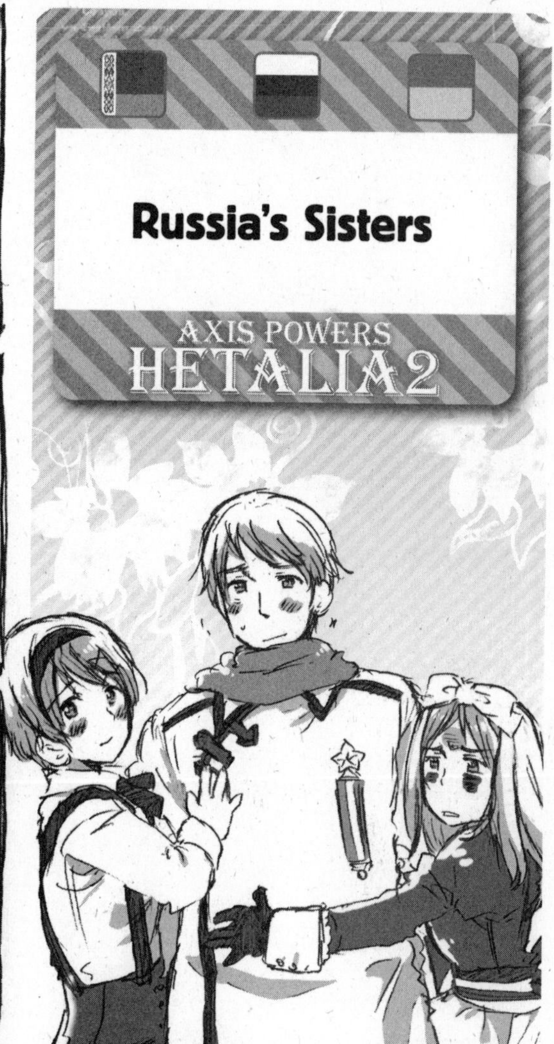
Russia's Sisters
AXIS POWERS
HETALIA 2

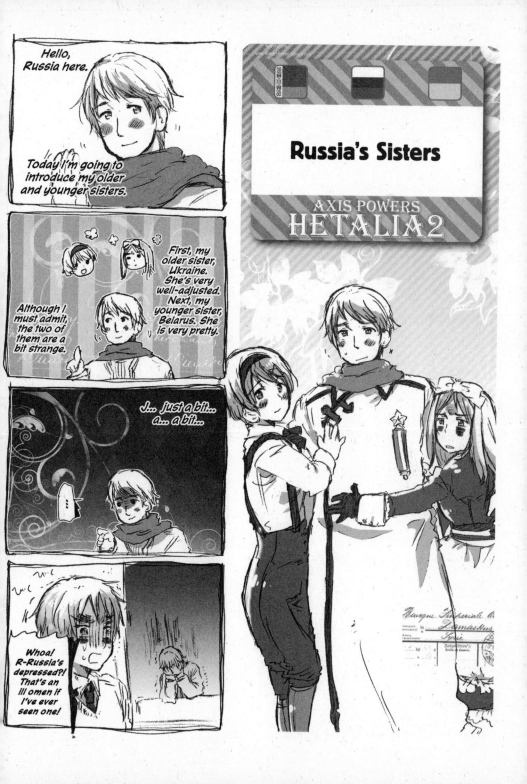

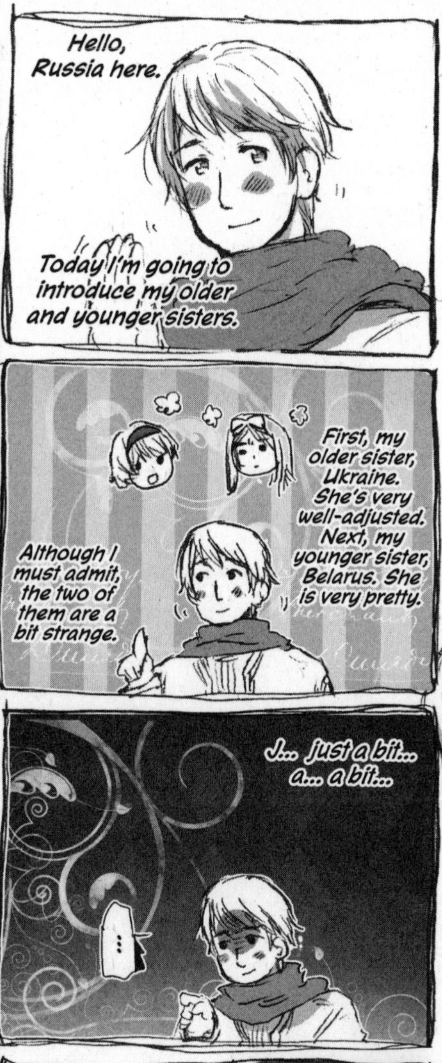
Hello, Russia here.
Today I'm going to introduce my older and younger sisters.
First, my older sister, Ukraine. She's very well-adjusted. Next, my younger sister, Belarus. She is very pretty.
Although I must admit, the two of them are a bit strange.
J... just a bit... a... a bit...
...
Whoa! R-Russia's depressed?! That's an ill omen if I've ever seen one!

Japan-kun and America-kun 1

In order to expand their knowledge and deepen their relationship, Japan and America started to visit each other's houses.

AXIS POWERS
HETALIA 2

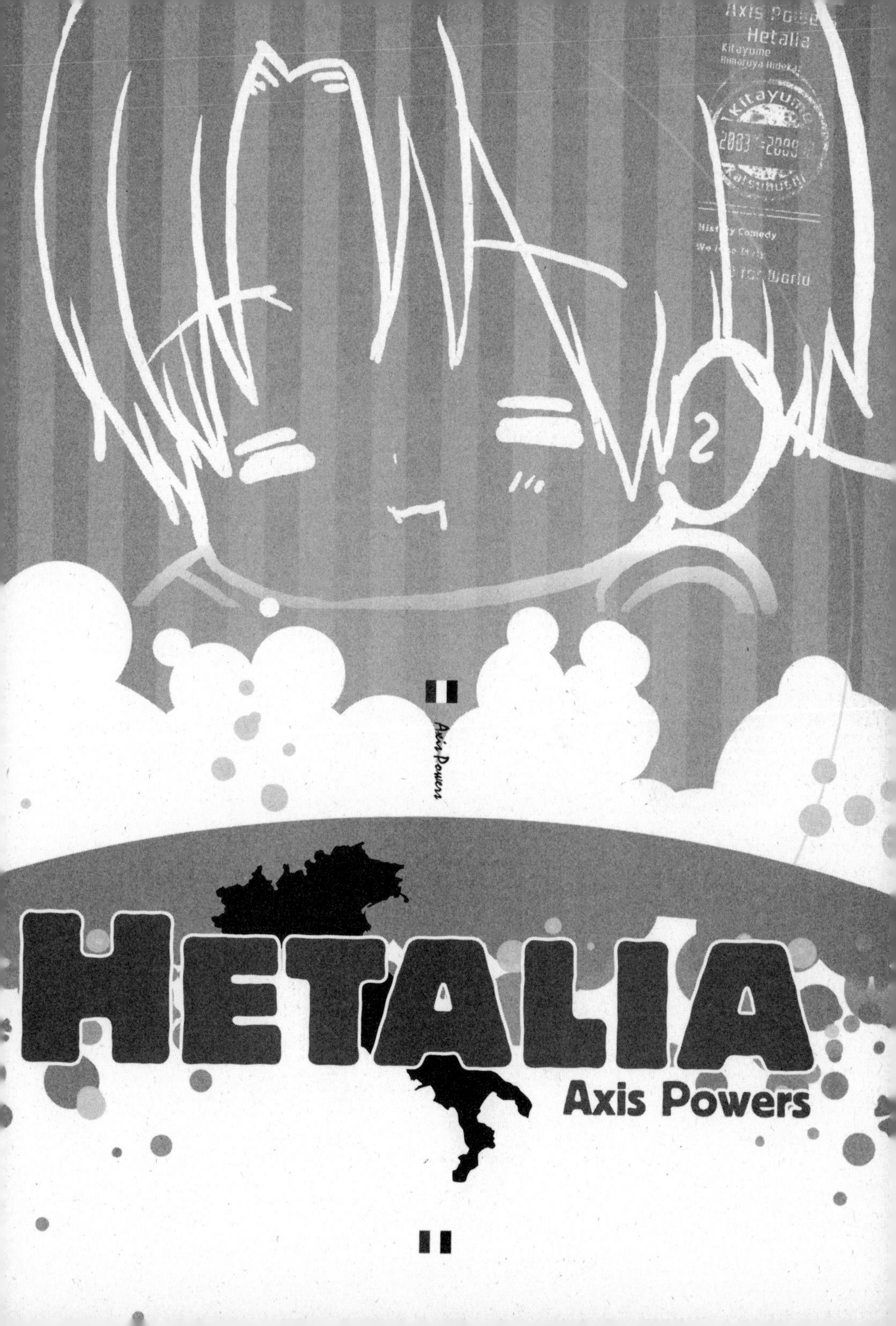
Hetalia
Kitayume
Axis Powers
HETALIA
Axis Powers

Liechtenstein's Doting Brother Diaries 2

At the end of World War 1, Liechtenstein, which was not even involved in the war itself, was tossed into economic turmoil and major food shortages. Luckily for them, Switzerland reached out to save them in their darkest hour. Apparently, helping this tiny neighboring nation with a population of less than 10,000 was done from the notion of "Solidarität" or "Solidarity." Switzerland did not expect anything in return.

AXIS POWERS
HETALIA 2

Liechtenstein's Doting Brother Diaries
Liechtenstein vs England

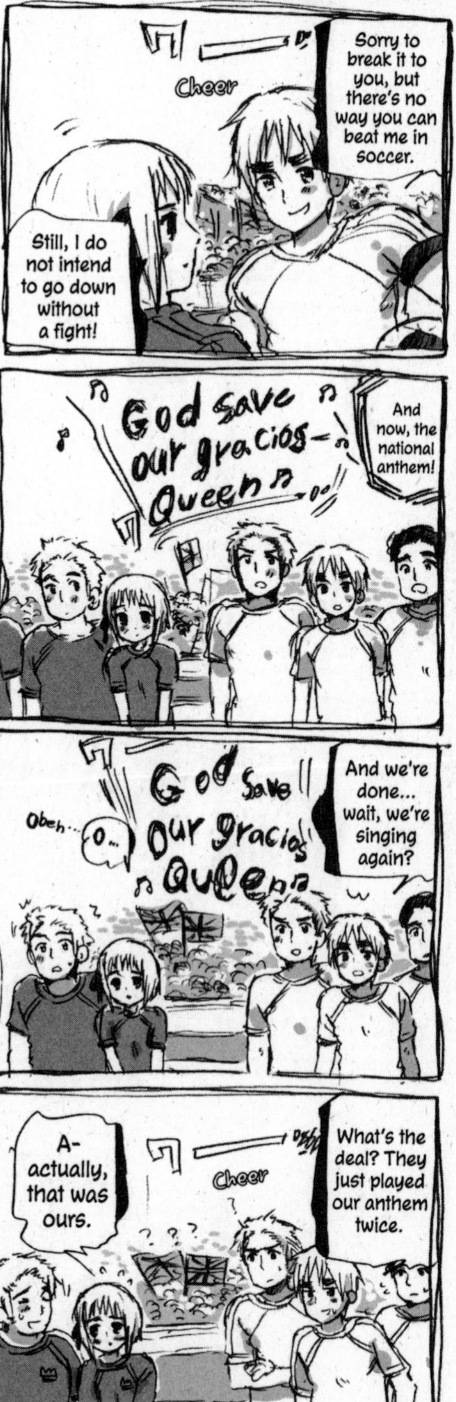
Sorry to break it to you, but there's no way you can beat me in soccer.
Cheer
Still, I do not intend to go down without a fight!
And now, the national anthem!
God Save our gracios Queen
And we're done... wait, we're singing again?
God Save our gracios Queen
Obeh... O...
What's the deal? They just played our anthem twice.
Cheer
A-actually, that was ours.

March 29, 2003.
Although Liechtenstein is the fourth smallest nation in the world, the EURO 2004 soccer preliminaries were held at their stadium.

An interesting incident occurred during the match between Liechtenstein and England.

Liechtenstein and England's national anthems have the same melody.

So when both countries' anthems were played before the match, the English proudly sang "God Save the Queen" twice, even though many thought it was a bit odd.

Liechtenstein is always the underdog in the group, but they were able to score one point during their EURO match with Macedonia. Liechtenstein's defense was also quite solid during the England match.

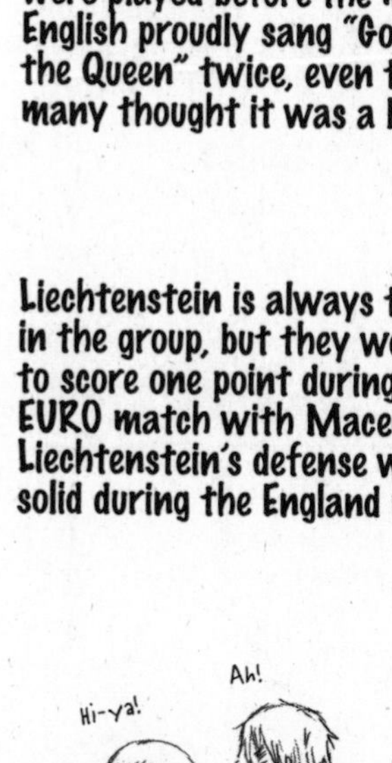
Ah!
Hi-ya!

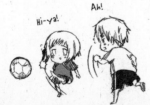

Liechtenstein's Doting Brother Diaries
Agape

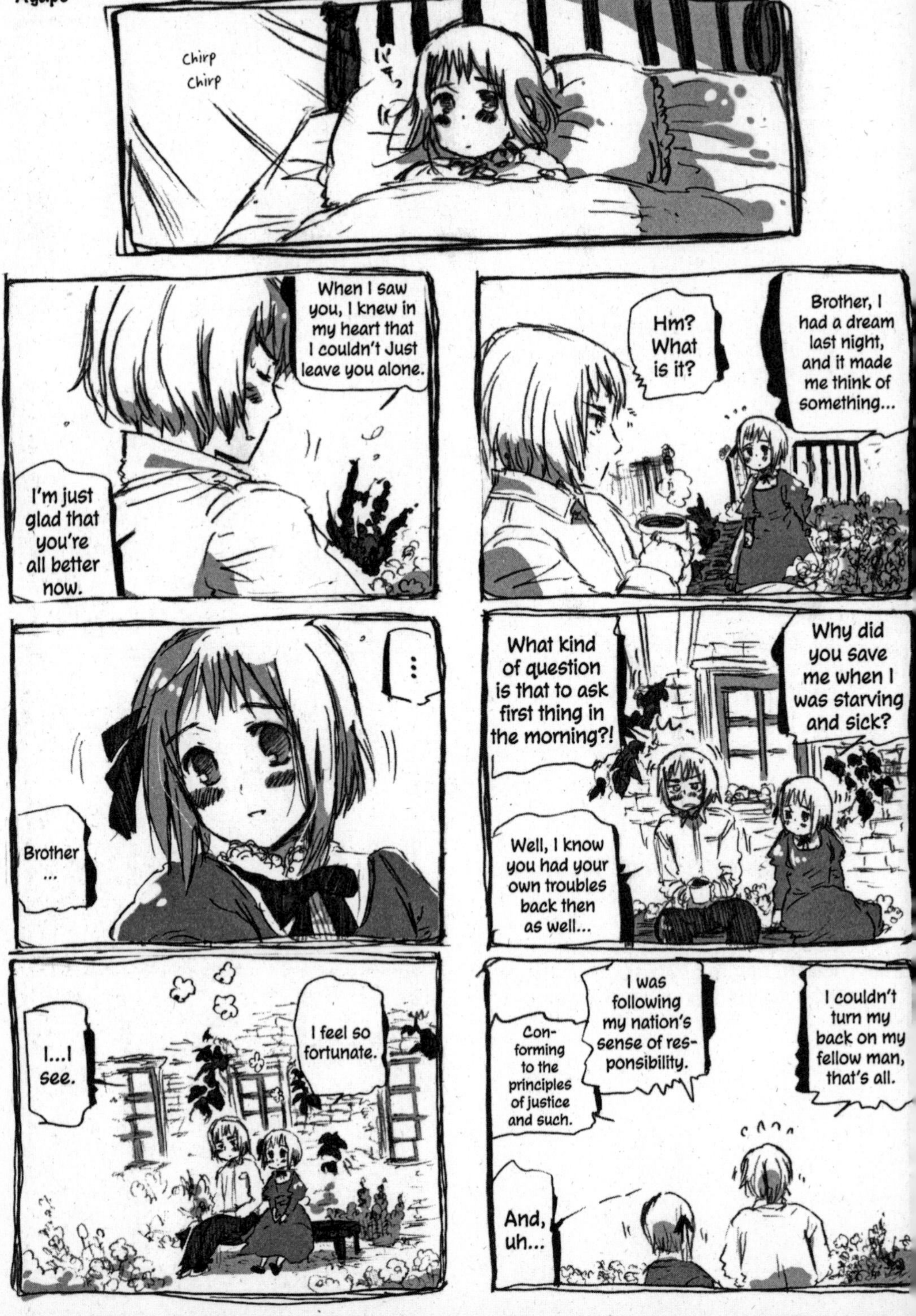
Chirp
Chirp
Brother, I had a dream last night, and it made me think of something...
Hm? What is it?
When I saw you, I knew in my heart that I couldn't Just leave you alone.
I'm just glad that you're all better now.
Why did you save me when I was starving and sick?
What kind of question is that to ask first thing in the morning?!
Well, I know you had your own troubles back then as well...
...
Brother ...
I couldn't turn my back on my fellow man, that's all.
I was following my nation's sense of res-ponsibility.
Con-forming to the principles of justice and such.
And, uh...
I feel so fortunate.
I...I see.

Liechtenstein's Doting Brother Diaries
We Can Meet in Our Dreams

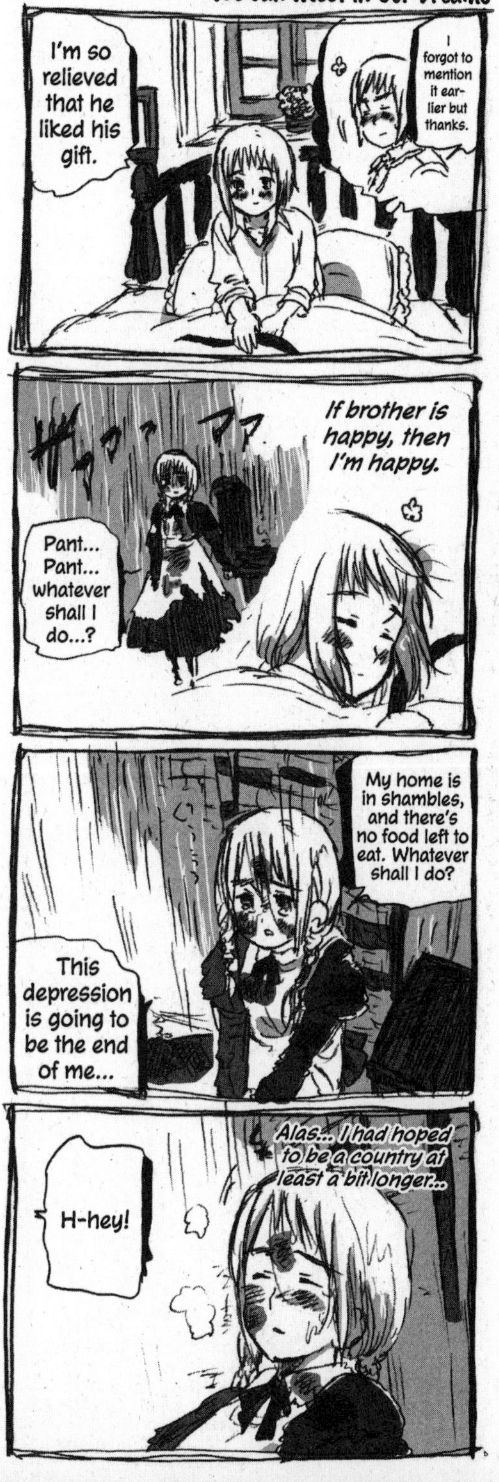
I forgot to mention it earlier but thanks.
I'm so relieved that he liked his gift.
If brother is happy, then I'm happy.
Pant... Pant... whatever shall I do...?
My home is in shambles, and there's no food left to eat. Whatever shall I do?
This depression is going to be the end of me...
Alas... I had hoped to be a country at least a bit longer...
H-hey!

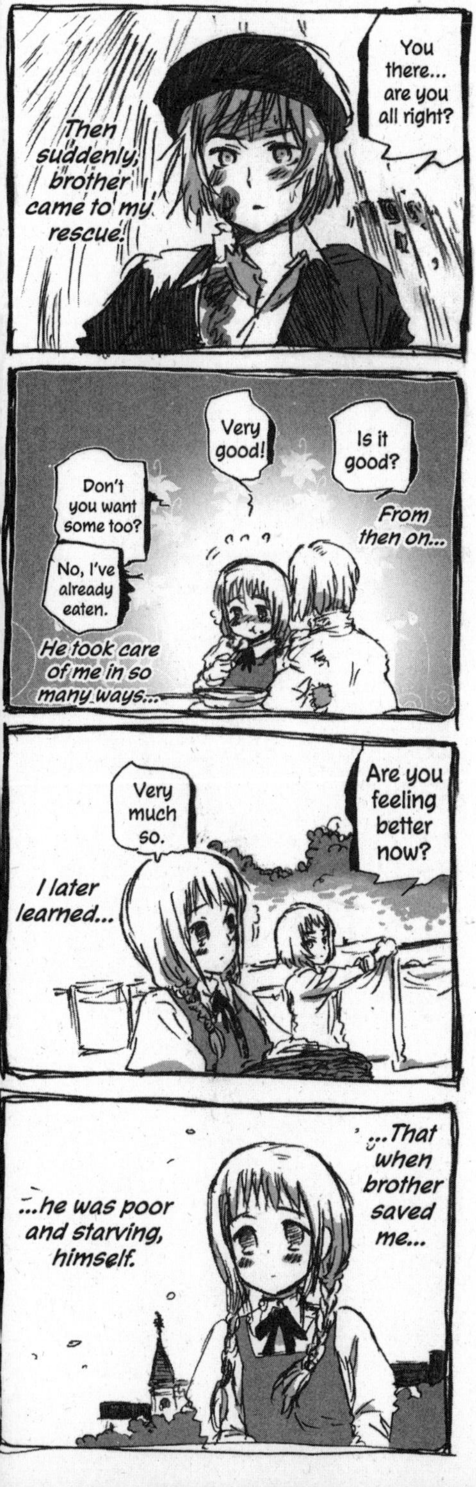
You there... are you all right?
Then suddenly, brother came to my rescue.
Is it good?
Very good!
From then on...
Don't you want some too?
No, I've already eaten.
He took care of me in so many ways...
Are you feeling better now?
Very much so.
I later learned...
...That when brother saved me...
...he was poor and starving, himself.

Liechtenstein's Doting Brother Diaries
To My Dear Brother...

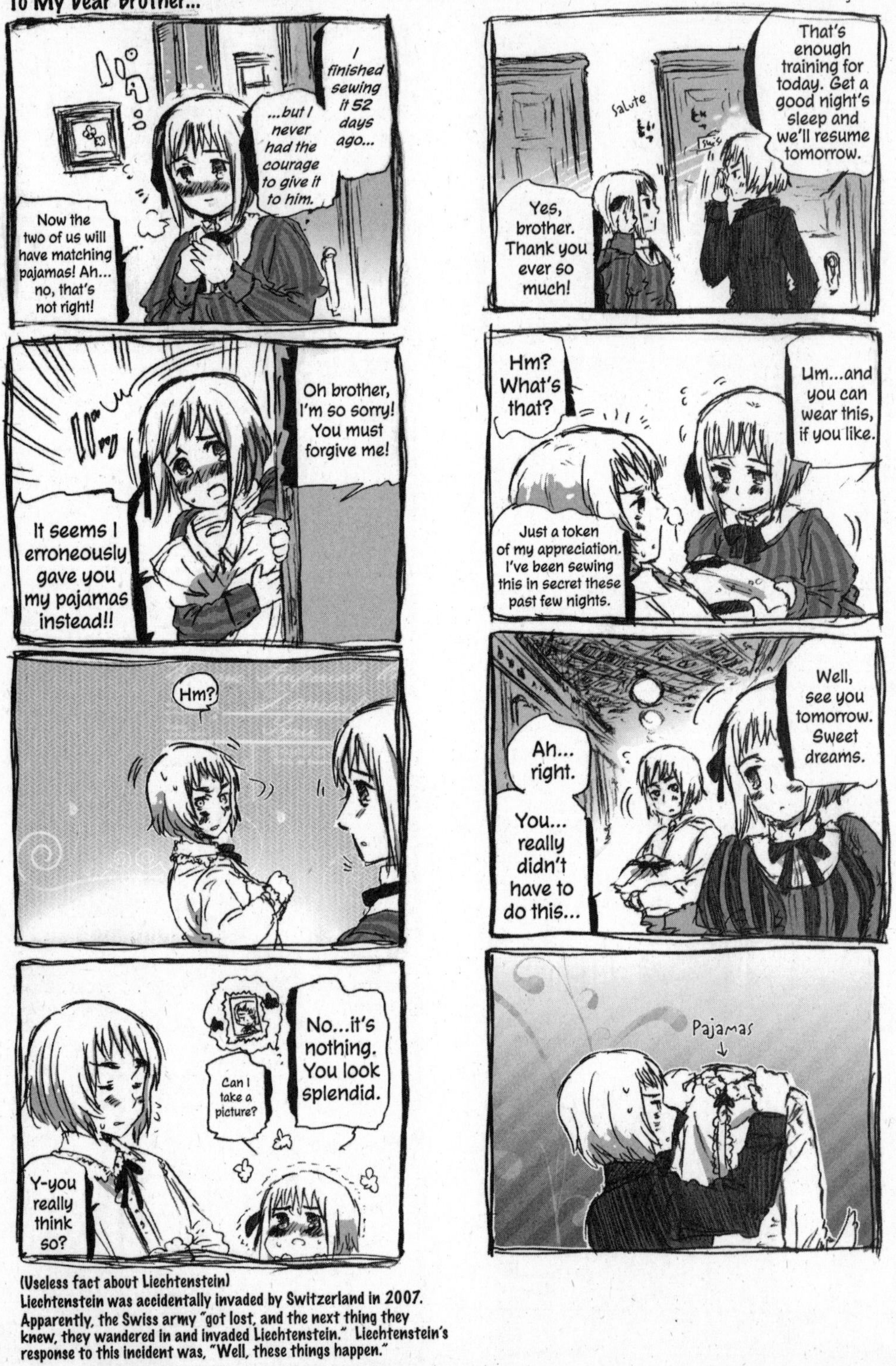

That night...
That's enough training for today. Get a good night's sleep and we'll resume tomorrow.
Salute
Yes, brother. Thank you ever so much!
Um...and you can wear this, if you like.
Hm? What's that?
Just a token of my appreciation. I've been sewing this in secret these past few nights.
Well, see you tomorrow. Sweet dreams.
Ah... right.
You... really didn't have to do this...
Pajamas
I finished sewing it 52 days ago...
...but I never had the courage to give it to him.
Now the two of us will have matching pajamas! Ah... no, that's not right!
Oh brother, I'm so sorry! You must forgive me!
It seems I erroneously gave you my pajamas instead!!
Hm?
No...it's nothing. You look splendid.
Can I take a picture?
Y-you really think so?

(Useless fact about Liechtenstein)
Liechtenstein was accidentally invaded by Switzerland in 2007. Apparently, the Swiss army "got lost, and the next thing they knew, they wandered in and invaded Liechtenstein." Liechtenstein's response to this incident was, "Well, these things happen."

Liechtenstein's Doting Brother Diaries
Bunnies Can Die from Loneliness

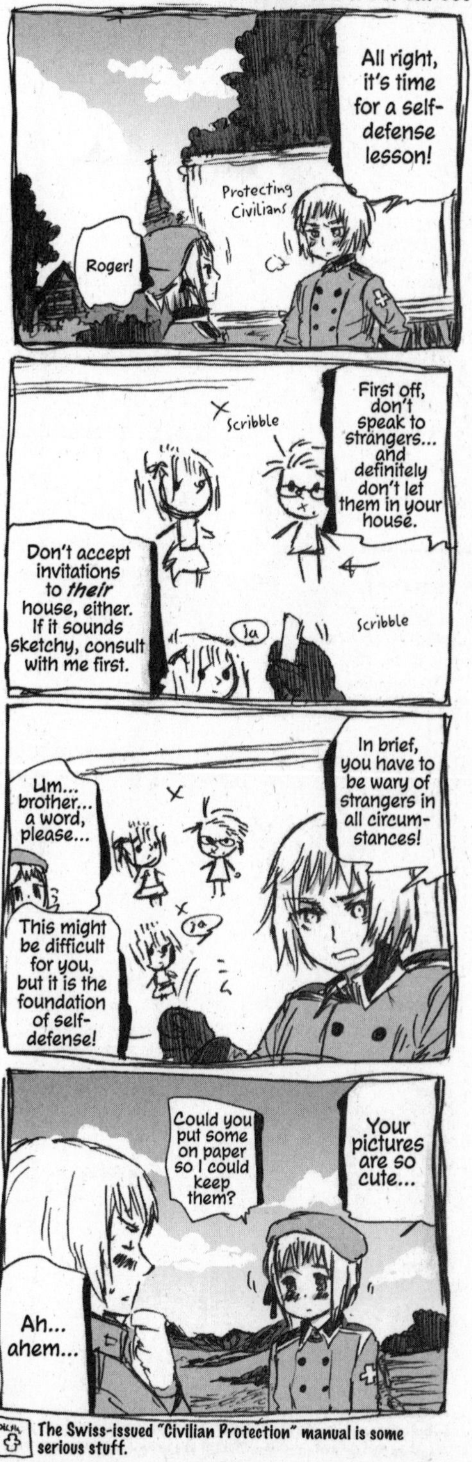
All right, it's time for a self-defense lesson!
Protecting Civilians
Roger!
First off, don't speak to strangers... and definitely don't let them in your house.
Scribble
Don't accept invitations to *their* house, either. If it sounds sketchy, consult with me first.
Ja
Scribble
In brief, you have to be wary of strangers in all circumstances!
Um... brother... a word, please...
Ja
This might be difficult for you, but it is the foundation of self-defense!
Your pictures are so cute...
Could you put some on paper so I could keep them?
Ah... ahem...

The Swiss-issued "Civilian Protection" manual is some serious stuff.

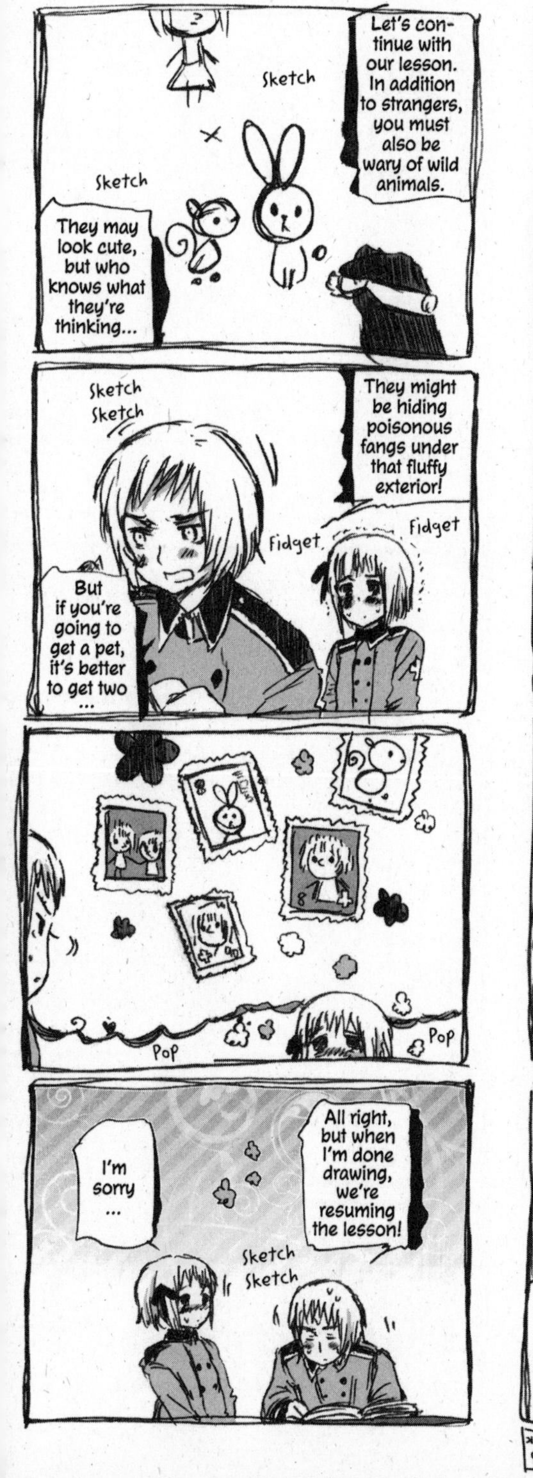
Let's continue with our lesson. In addition to strangers, you must also be wary of wild animals.
Sketch
Sketch
They may look cute, but who knows what they're thinking...
They might be hiding poisonous fangs under that fluffy exterior!
Sketch Sketch
Fidget
Fidget
But if you're going to get a pet, it's better to get two ...
Pop
Pop
All right, but when I'm done drawing, we're resuming the lesson!
I'm sorry ...
Sketch Sketch

Liechtenstein's Doting Brother Diaries
Don't Worry About it

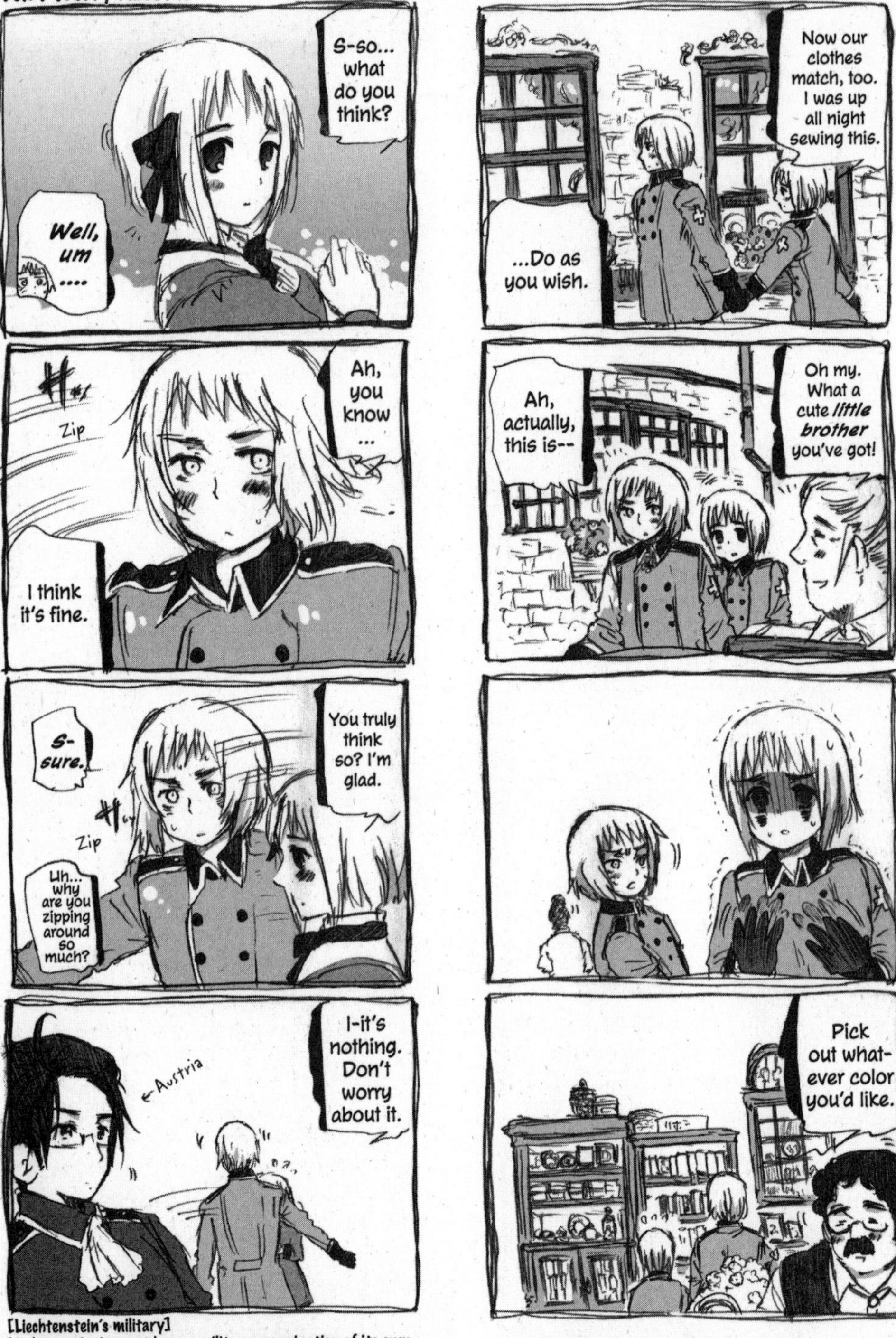

Now our clothes match, too. I was up all night sewing this.
...Do as you wish.
Oh my. What a cute *little brother* you've got!
Ah, actually, this is--
Pick out whatever color you'd like.
S-so... what do you think?
Well, um ....
Ah, you know ...
Zip
I think it's fine.
You truly think so? I'm glad.
S-sure.
Zip
Uh... why are you zipping around so much?
I-it's nothing. Don't worry about it.
←Austria

[Liechtenstein's military]
Liechtenstein does not have a military organization of its own, and their entire police force only consists of about 70 officers. As a result, they are reliant on the watchful protection of Switzerland.

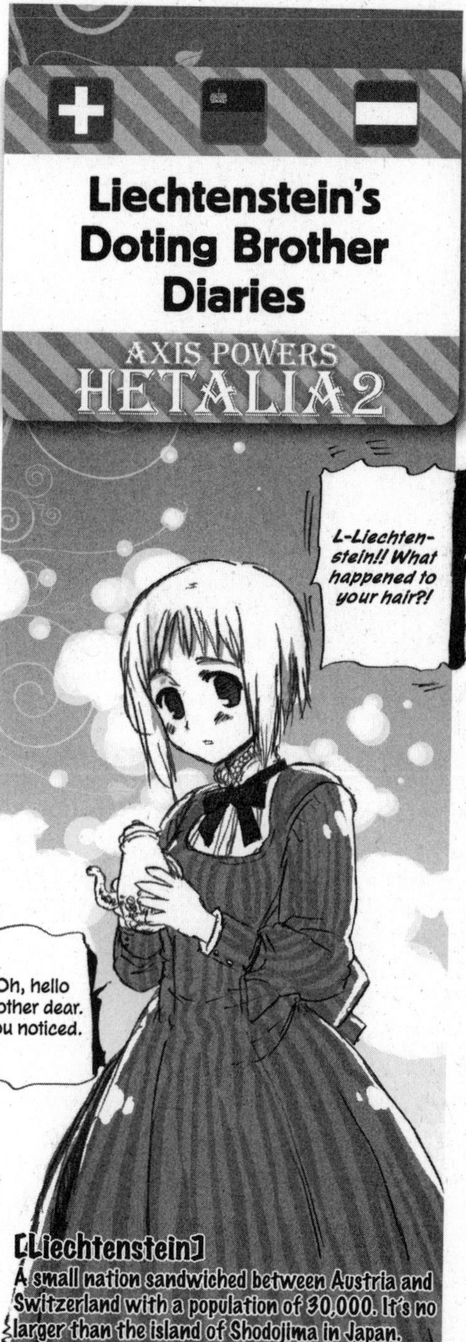
Liechtenstein's Doting Brother Diaries
AXIS POWERS HETALIA 2
L-Liechtenstein!! What happened to your hair?!
Oh, hello brother dear. You noticed.

[Liechtenstein]
A small nation sandwiched between Austria and Switzerland with a population of 30,000. It's no larger than the island of Shodojima in Japan.

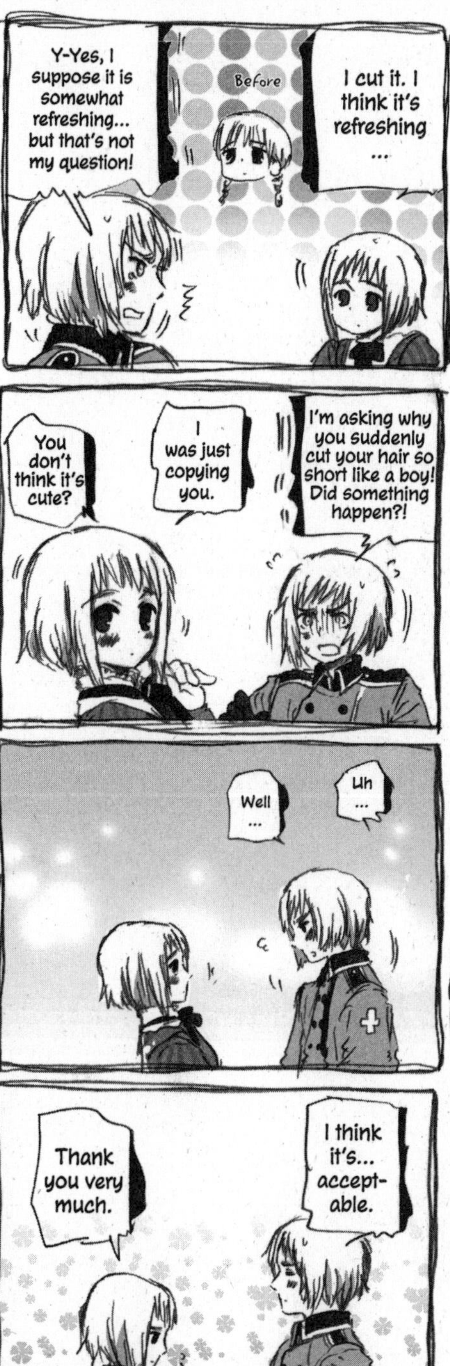
I cut it. I think it's refreshing ...
Before
Y-Yes, I suppose it is somewhat refreshing... but that's not my question!
I'm asking why you suddenly cut your hair so short like a boy! Did something happen?!
I was just copying you.
You don't think it's cute?
Uh ...
Well ...
I think it's... accept-able.
Thank you very much.

Liechtenstein's Doting Brother Diaries 1

Since Liechtenstein and Switzerland have a customs agreement, travelers are free to go back and forth between the two nations. In addition, if someone tries to get into Liechtenstein from the Austrian border, they will have to go through Swiss customs--not Liechtenstein customs. In other words, because Liechtenstein is not in charge of its own customs inspections, there is no customs stamp. However, tourists who enter Liechtenstein can receive a commemorative stamp with a crown decal if they like.

AXIS POWERS HETALIA 2

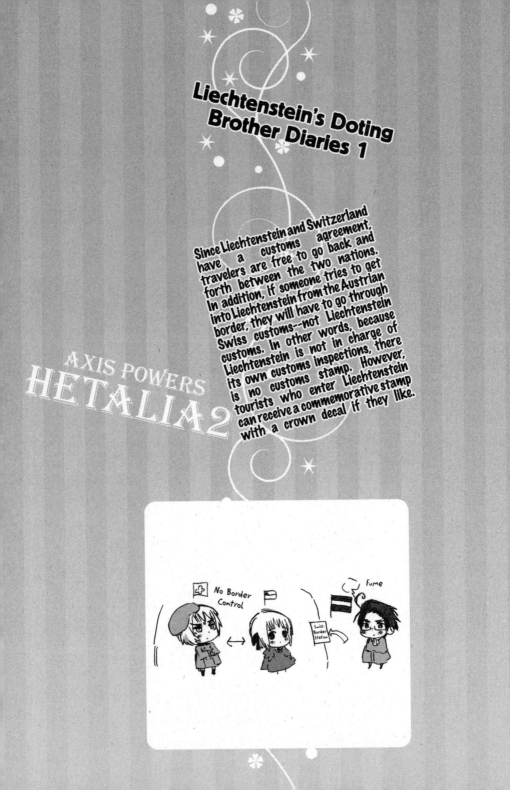

No Border Control
Fume
Swiss Border Station

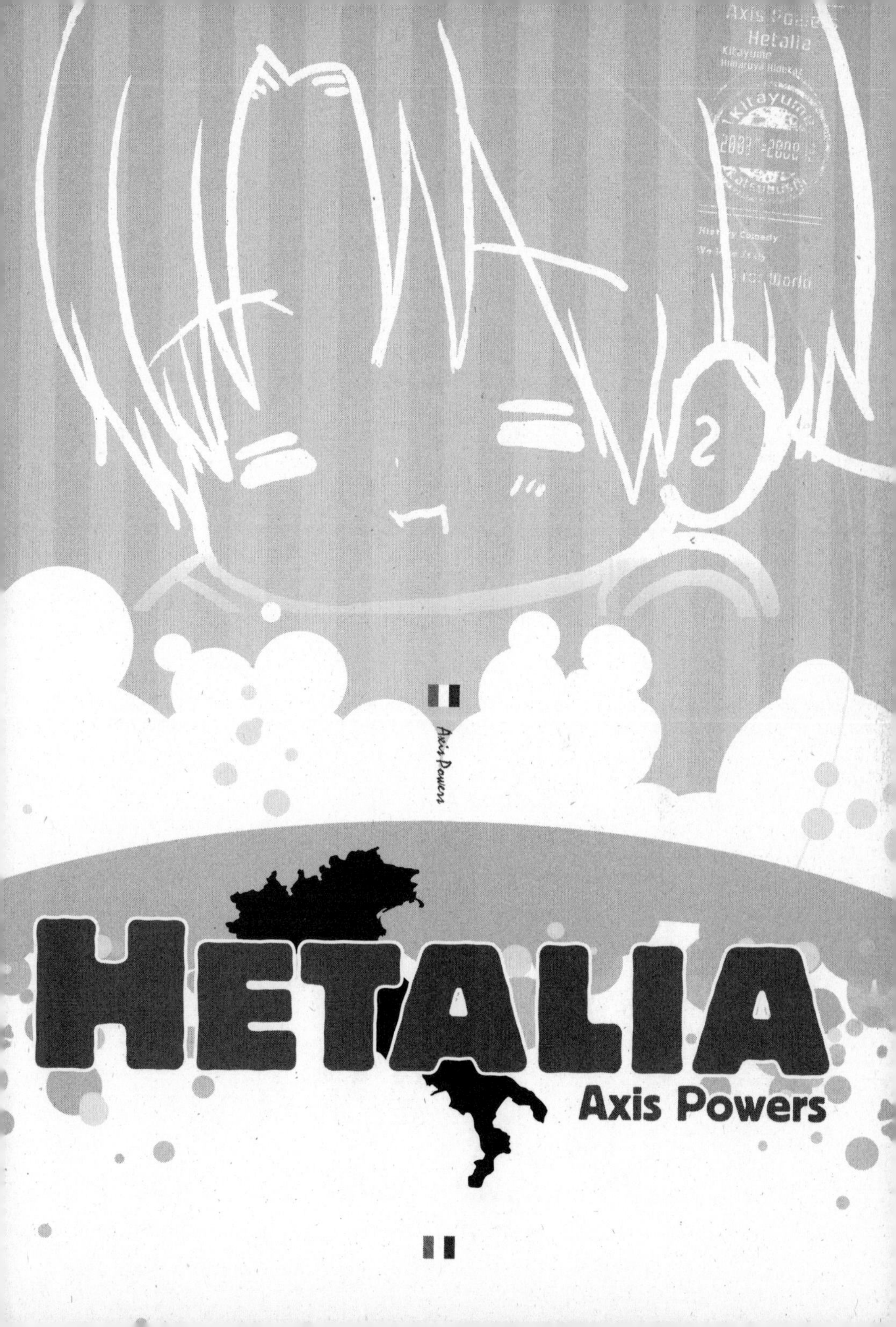
Hetalia
Kitayume
Axis Powers
HETALIA
Axis Powers

Greek Mythology is Totally Hardcore

The stories in Greek Mythology are way more interesting than the soap operas we have today. One minute Zeus is battling his own father to become the king of the gods, and the next minute he transforms himself into a bull so he can cheat on his wife! But at the end of the day, even the mighty Zeus cowers before Hera, making him the kind of endearing rascal that we all love to root for.

AXIS POWERS
HETALIA 2

It's not like I want to be mad all the time!

Yeeeek!

Greece and Japan's Easygoing Relationship
Never Forget Your Training

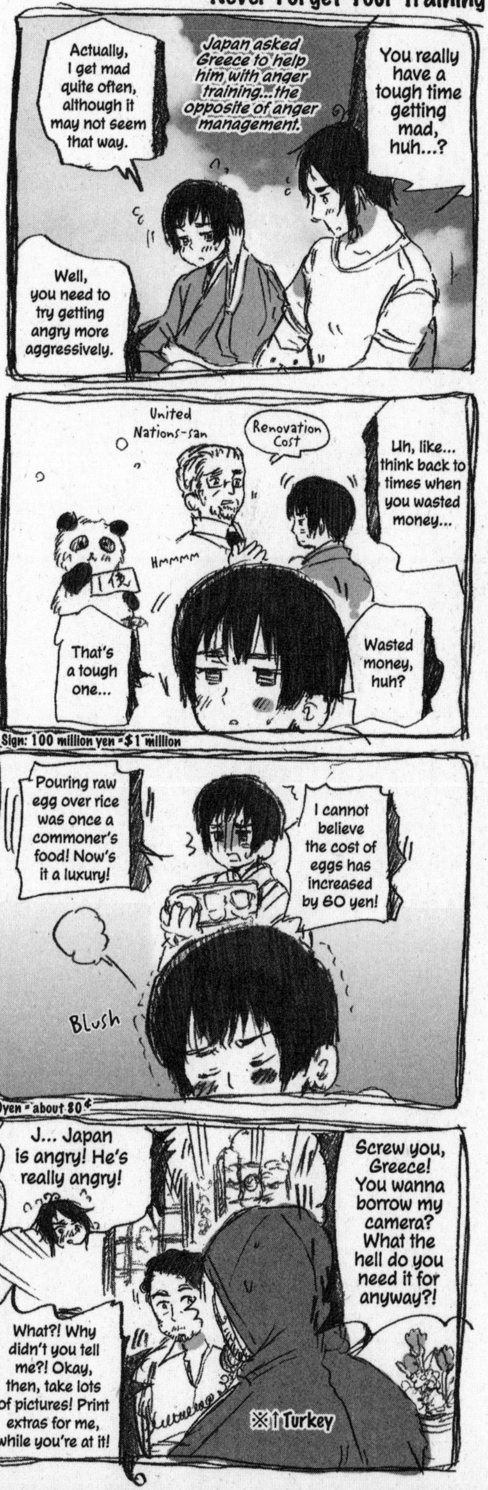
You really have a tough time getting mad, huh...?
Japan asked Greece to help him with anger training...the opposite of anger management.
Actually, I get mad quite often, although it may not seem that way.
Well, you need to try getting angry more aggressively.
Uh, like... think back to times when you wasted money...
Renovation Cost
United Nations-san
Hmmmm
Wasted money, huh?
That's a tough one...
Sign: 100 million yen = $1 million
I cannot believe the cost of eggs has increased by 60 yen!
Pouring raw egg over rice was once a commoner's food! Now's it a luxury!
Blush
60yen = about 80¢
Screw you, Greece! You wanna borrow my camera? What the hell do you need it for anyway?!
J... Japan is angry! He's really angry!
※↑Turkey
What?! Why didn't you tell me?! Okay, then, take lots of pictures! Print extras for me, while you're at it!

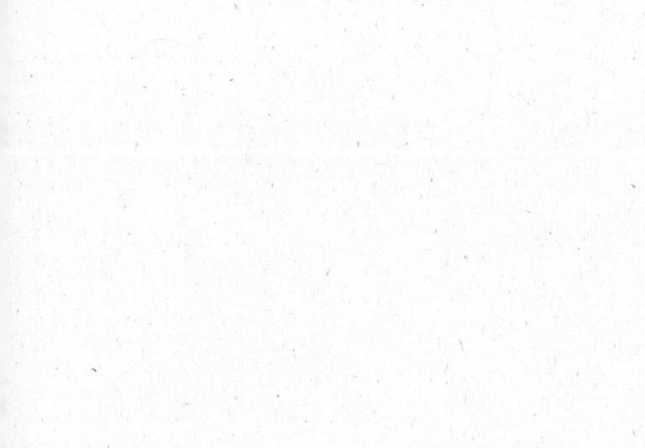
T is for tangerine.
I don't get it.

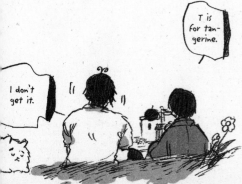

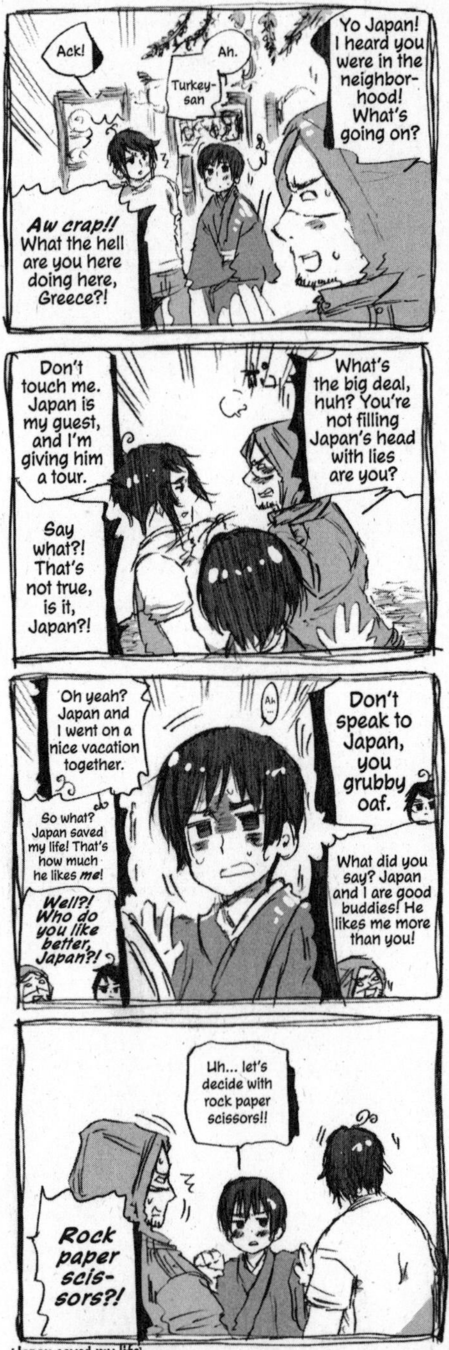
Yo Japan! I heard you were in the neighbor-hood! What's going on?
Ah.
Turkey-san
Ack!
Aw crap!! What the hell are you here doing here, Greece?!
What's the big deal, huh? You're not filling Japan's head with lies are you?
Don't touch me. Japan is my guest, and I'm giving him a tour.
Say what?! That's not true, is it, Japan?!
Don't speak to Japan, you grubby oaf.
Ah...
Oh yeah? Japan and I went on a nice vacation together.
What did you say? Japan and I are good buddies! He likes me more than you!
So what? Japan saved my life! That's how much he likes *me*!
Well?! Who do you like better, Japan?!
Uh... let's decide with rock paper scissors!!
Rock paper scis-sors?!

[Japan saved my life]
In 1890, a Turkish navy vessel named the Ertuğrul crashed on the shor of Japan's Wakayama Prefecture. During that time, the Japanese village diligently worked to rescue the survivors. When Japanese citizens we stranded in Iran during the Iran-Iraq War in 1985, Turkish voluntee risked their lives and sent a commercial plane to rescue the Japanese. Th was supposedly done in part because of Japan's actions in 1890.

Greece and Japan's Easygoing Relationship
Breaking the Ice is my Specialty

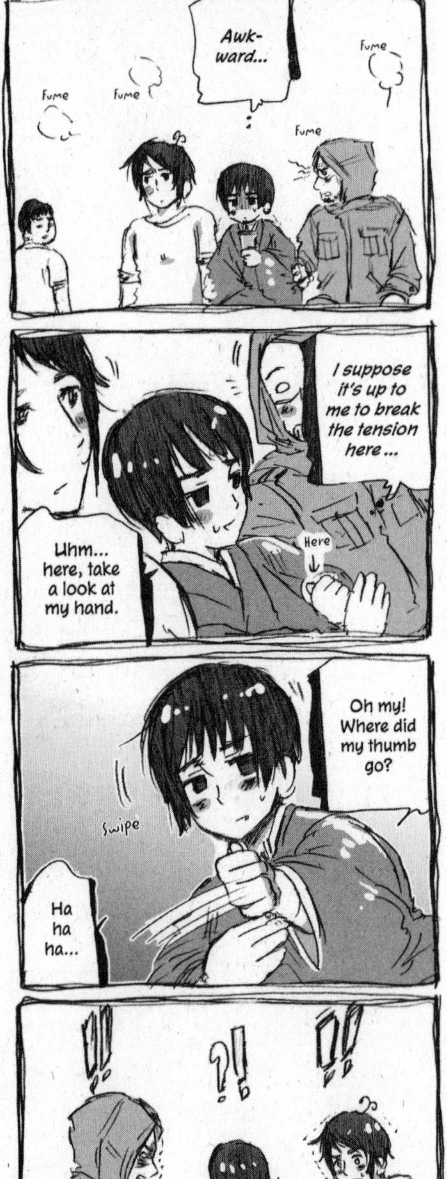
Awk-ward...
Fume
Fume
Fume
Fume
I suppose it's up to me to break the tension here...
Here
Uhm... here, take a look at my hand.
Oh my! Where did my thumb go?
Swipe
Ha ha ha...
!!
?!
!!

Try it yourself! It's guaranteed to please.

Greece and Japan's Easygoing Relationship Rocking it in the BC

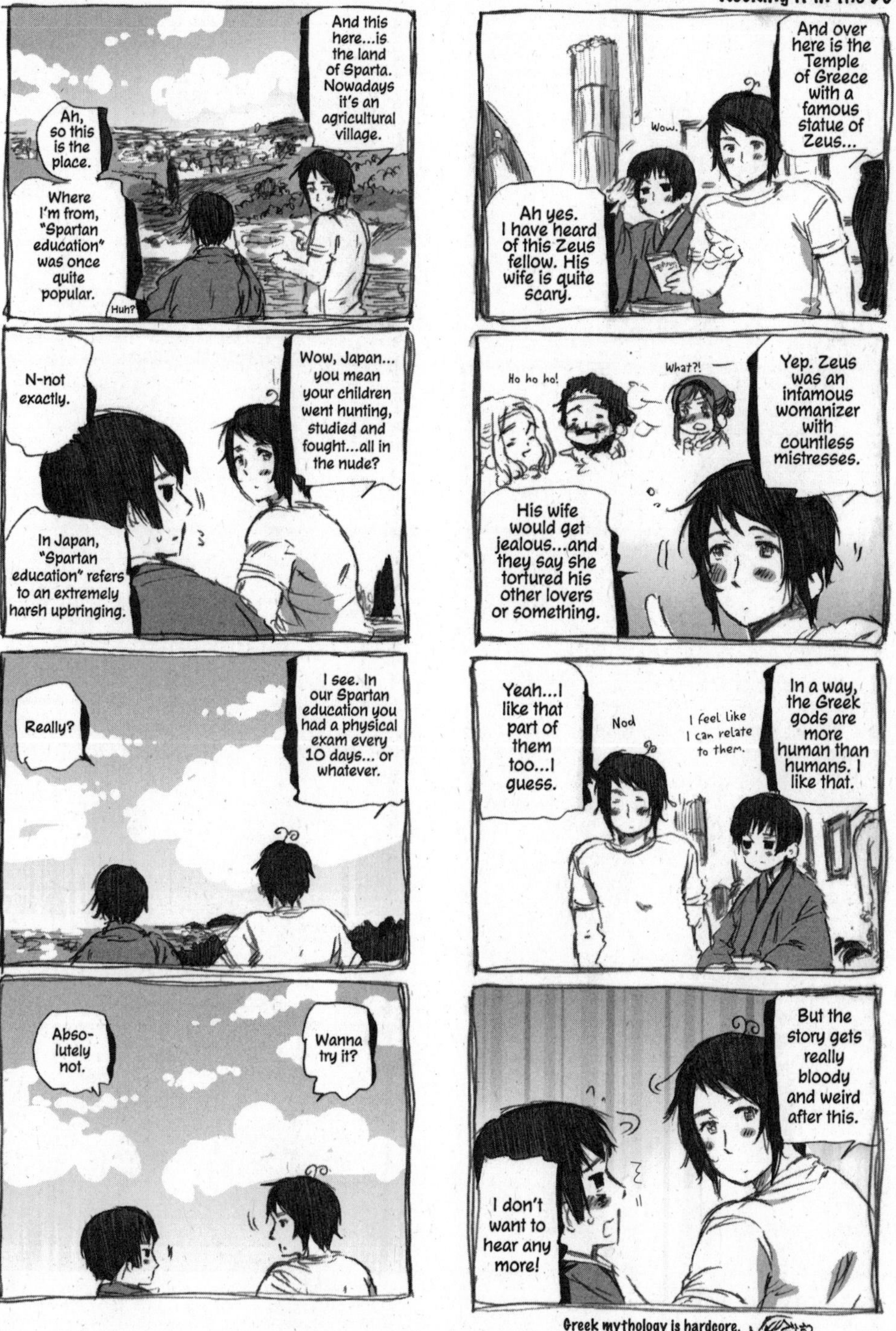
And over here is the Temple of Greece with a famous statue of Zeus...
Wow.
Ah yes. I have heard of this Zeus fellow. His wife is quite scary.
Yep. Zeus was an infamous womanizer with countless mistresses.
What?!
Ho ho ho!
His wife would get jealous...and they say she tortured his other lovers or something.
In a way, the Greek gods are more human than humans. I like that.
I feel like I can relate to them.
Yeah...I like that part of them too...I guess.
Nod
But the story gets really bloody and weird after this.
I don't want to hear any more!
And this here...is the land of Sparta. Nowadays it's an agricultural village.
Ah, so this is the place.
Where I'm from, "Spartan education" was once quite popular.
Huh?
Wow, Japan... you mean your children went hunting, studied and fought...all in the nude?
N-not exactly.
In Japan, "Spartan education" refers to an extremely harsh upbringing.
I see. In our Spartan education you had a physical exam every 10 days... or whatever.
Really?
Wanna try it?
Absolutely not.

Greek mythology is hardcore.

Greece and Japan's Easygoing Relationship
Neko Crazy

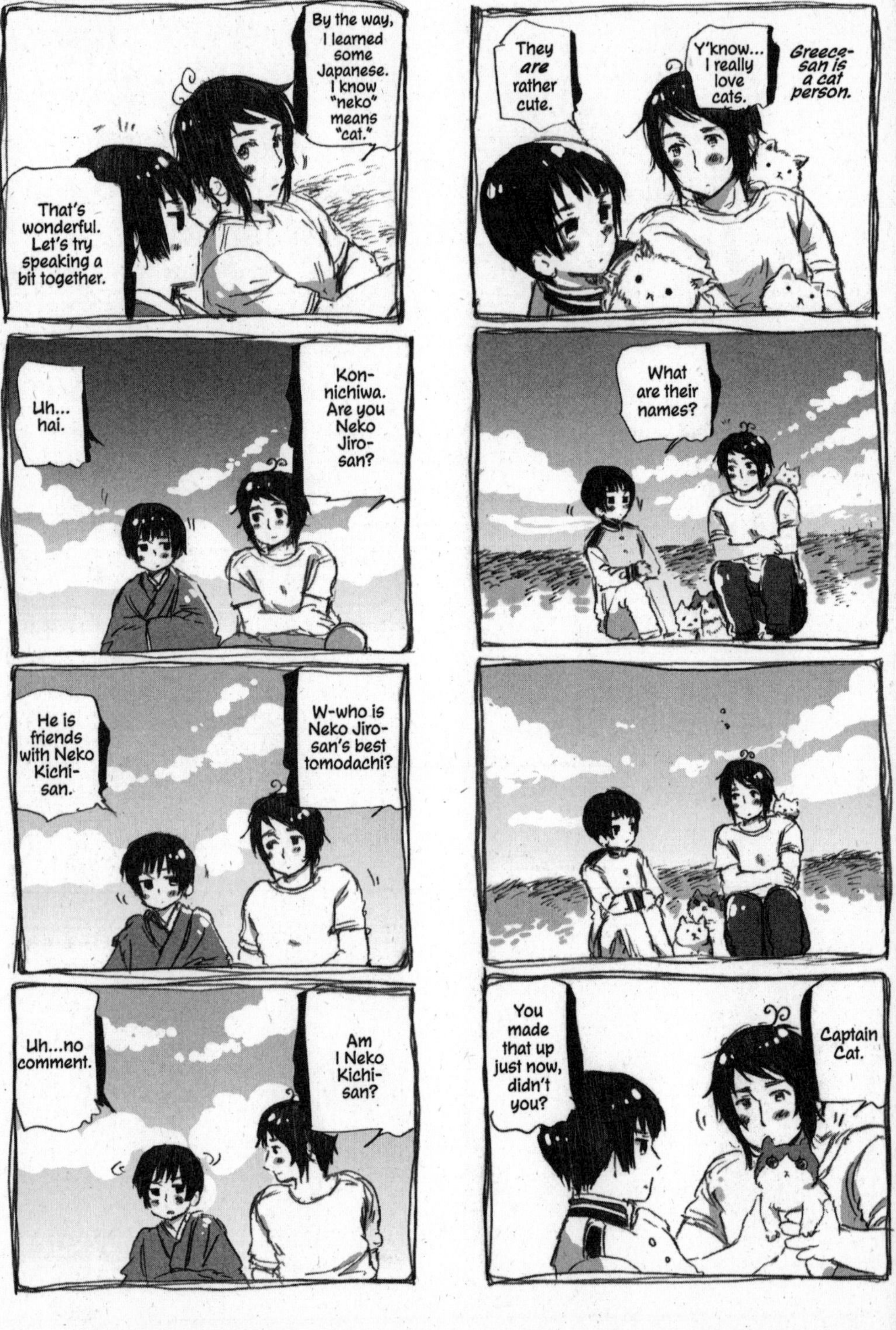

Greece-san is a cat person.
Y'know... I really love cats.
They *are* rather cute.
What are their names?
Captain Cat.
You made that up just now, didn't you?
By the way, I learned some Japanese. I know "neko" means "cat."
That's wonderful. Let's try speaking a bit together.
Kon-nichiwa. Are you Neko Jiro-san?
Uh... hai.
W-who is Neko Jiro-san's best tomodachi?
He is friends with Neko Kichi-san.
Am I Neko Kichi-san?
Uh...no comment.

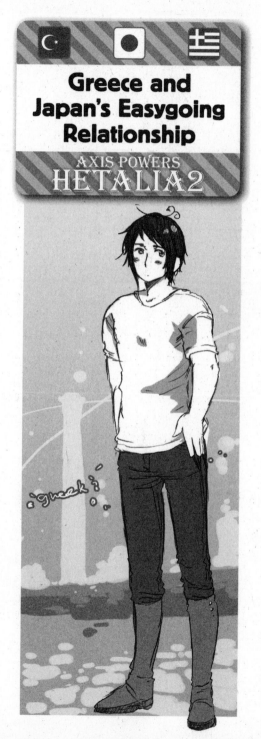

Greece and Japan's Easygoing Relationship

AXIS POWERS HETALIA2

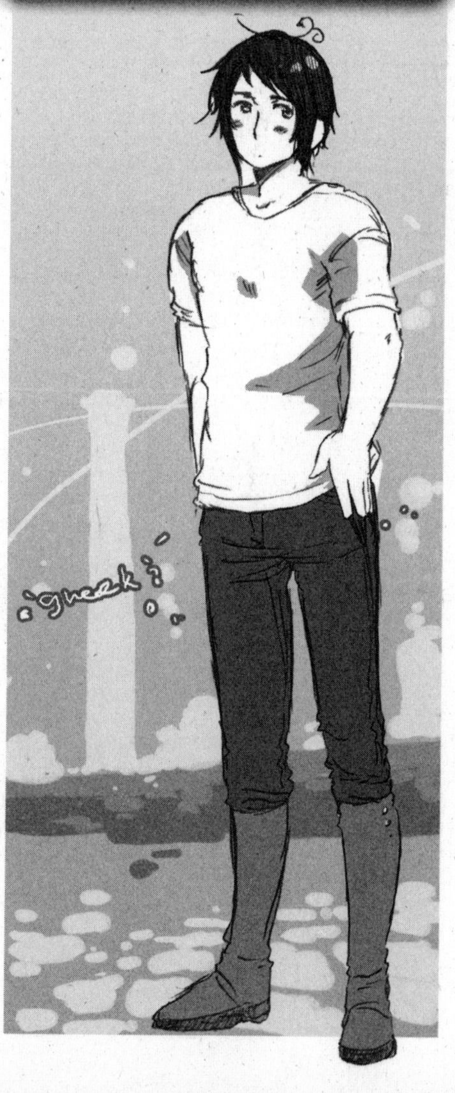
greek

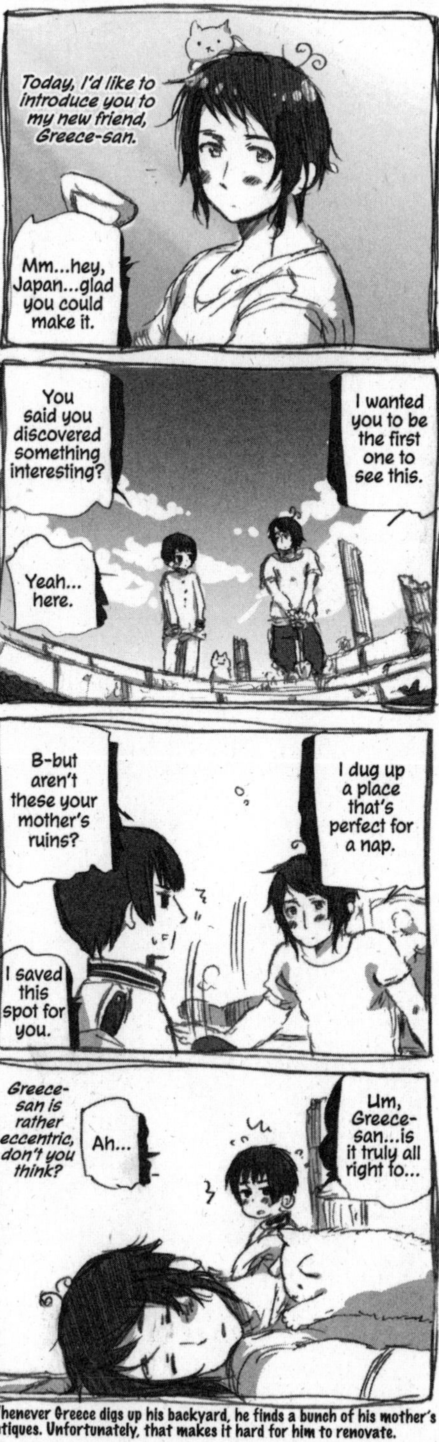
Today, I'd like to introduce you to my new friend, Greece-san.
Mm...hey, Japan...glad you could make it.
I wanted you to be the first one to see this.
You said you discovered something interesting?
Yeah... here.
I dug up a place that's perfect for a nap.
B-but aren't these your mother's ruins?
I saved this spot for you.
Um, Greece-san...is it truly all right to...
Ah...
Greece-san is rather eccentric, don't you think?

Whenever Greece digs up his backyard, he finds a bunch of his mother's antiques. Unfortunately, that makes it hard for him to renovate.

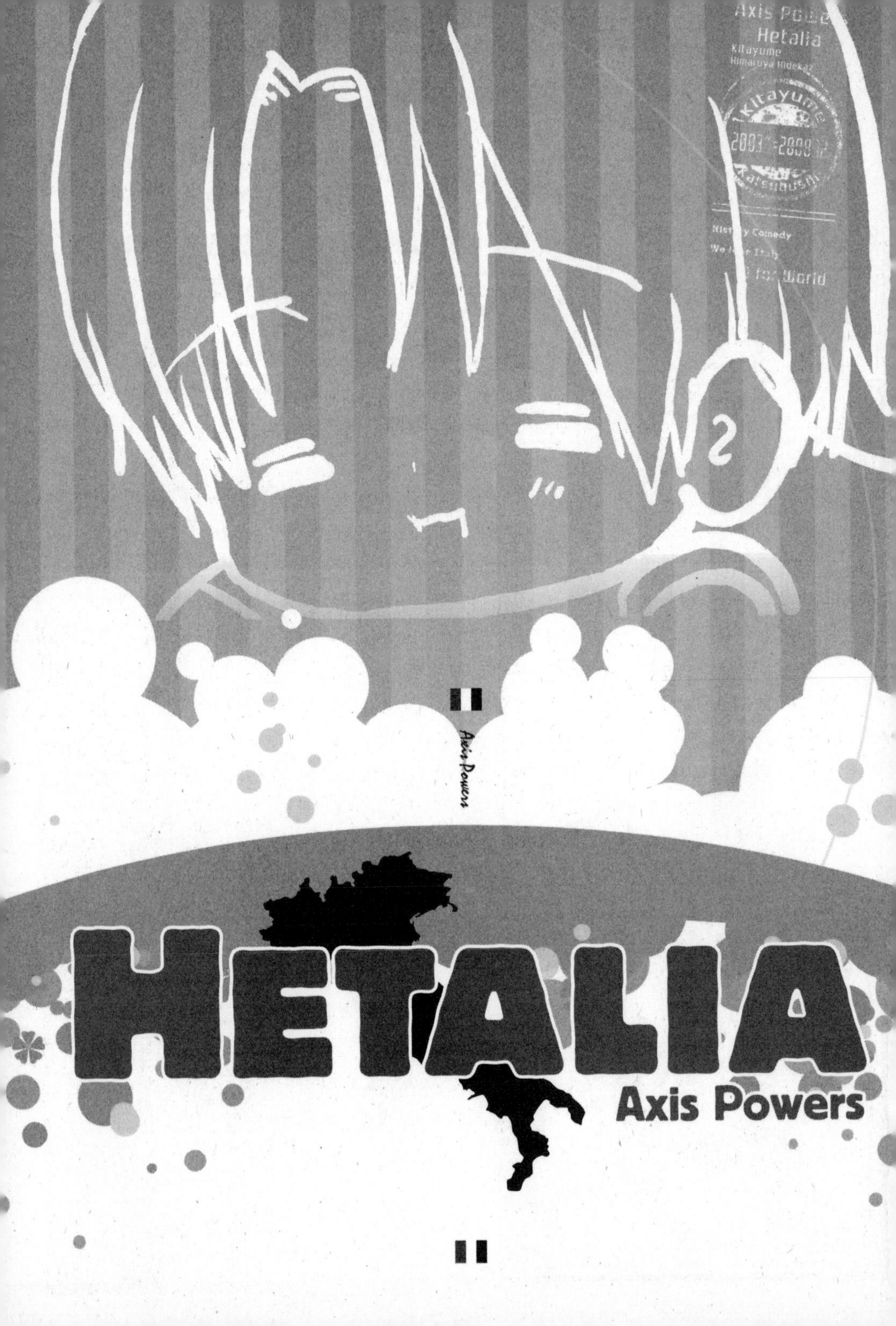
Hetalia
II
Axis Powers
HETALIA
Axis Powers
II

Grandpa Rome Pays a Visit
Grandpa Rome and Germania

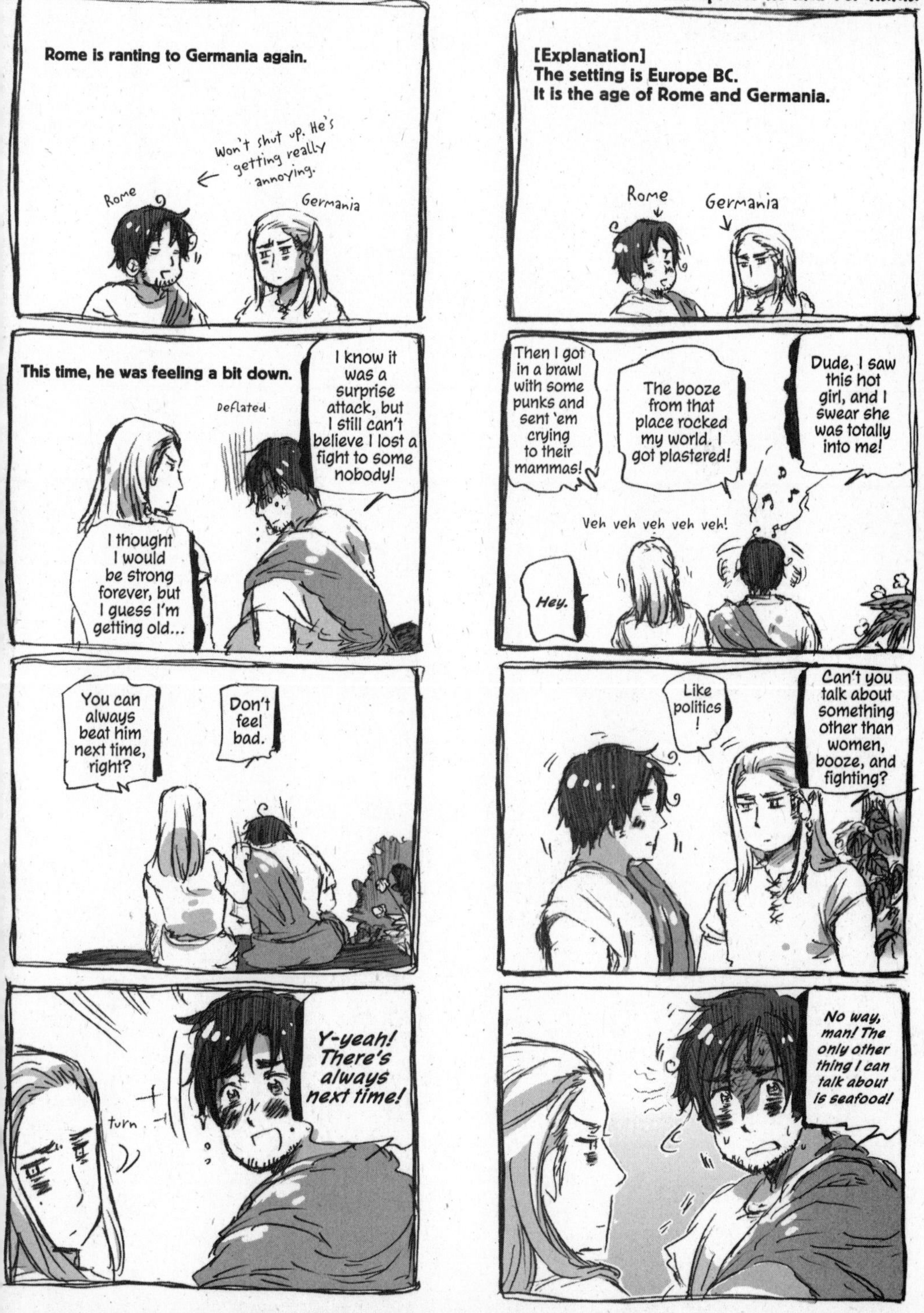
[Explanation]
The setting is Europe BC.
It is the age of Rome and Germania.
Rome
Germania
Dude, I saw this hot girl, and I swear she was totally into me!
The booze from that place rocked my world. I got plastered!
Then I got in a brawl with some punks and sent 'em crying to their mammas!
Veh veh veh veh veh!
Hey.
Can't you talk about something other than women, booze, and fighting?
Like politics!
No way, man! The only other thing I can talk about is seafood!
Rome is ranting to Germania again.
Won't shut up. He's getting really annoying.
Rome
Germania
I know it was a surprise attack, but I still can't believe I lost a fight to some nobody!
Deflated
This time, he was feeling a bit down.
I thought I would be strong forever, but I guess I'm getting old...
Don't feel bad.
You can always beat him next time, right?
Y-yeah! There's always next time!
turn

Grandpa Rome Pays a Visit
Together with Grandpa

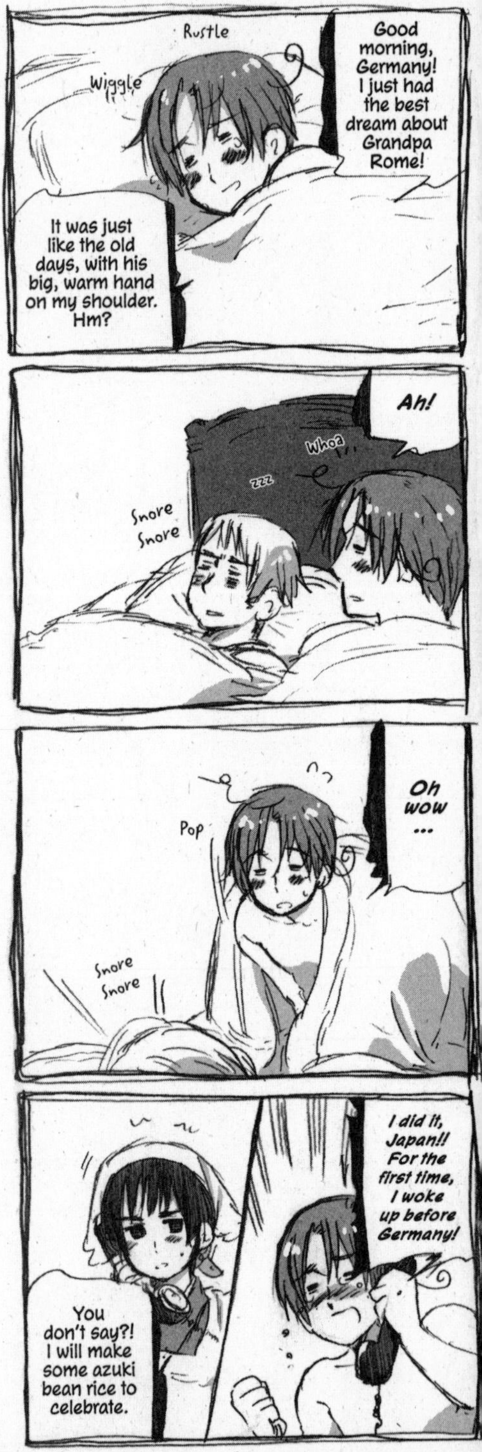
Good morning, Germany! I just had the best dream about Grandpa Rome!
Rustle
Wiggle
It was just like the old days, with his big, warm hand on my shoulder. Hm?
Ah!
Whoa
zzz
Snore Snore
Oh wow ...
Pop
Snore Snore
I did it, Japan!! For the first time, I woke up before Germany!
You don't say?! I will make some azuki bean rice to celebrate.

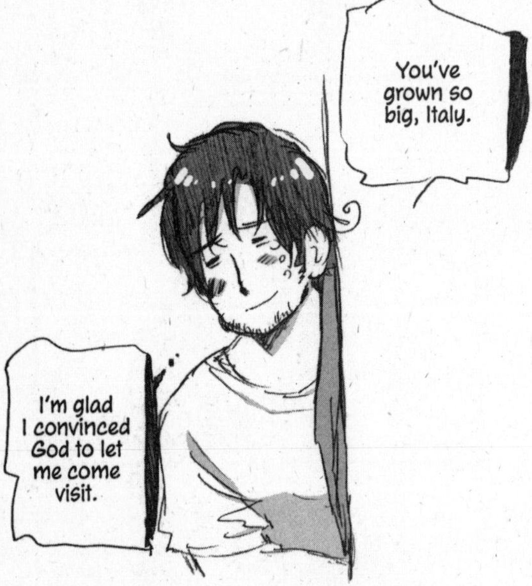
You've grown so big, Italy.
I'm glad I convinced God to let me come visit.

Grandpa Rome Pays a Visit
Rome the Fallen

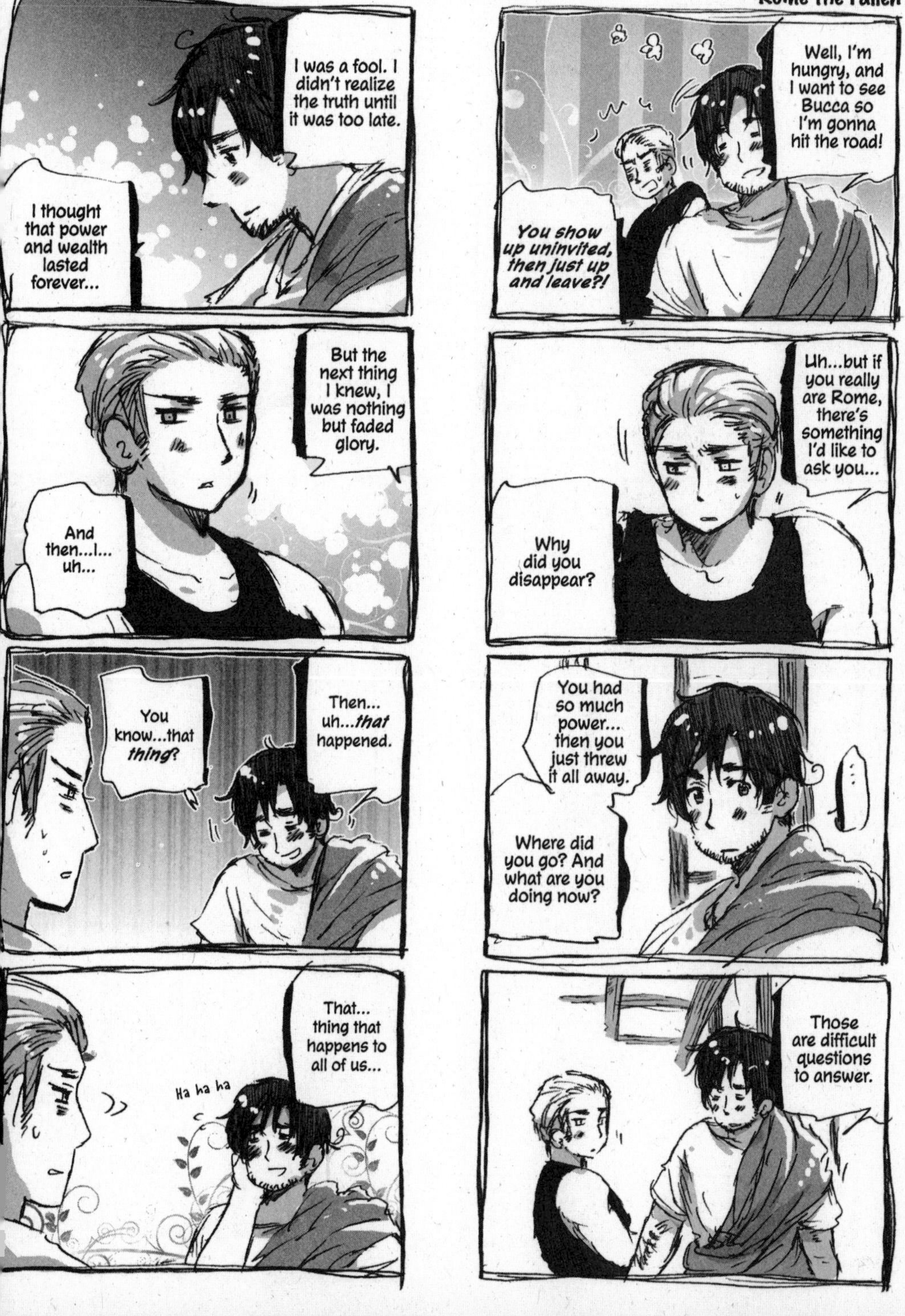

Well, I'm hungry, and I want to see Bucca so I'm gonna hit the road!
You show up uninvited, then just up and leave?!
Uh...but if you really are Rome, there's something I'd like to ask you...
Why did you disappear?
You had so much power... then you just threw it all away.
...
Where did you go? And what are you doing now?
Those are difficult questions to answer.
I was a fool. I didn't realize the truth until it was too late.
I thought that power and wealth lasted forever...
But the next thing I knew, I was nothing but faded glory.
And then...I... uh...
Then... uh...*that* happened.
You know...that *thing*?
That... thing that happens to all of us...
Ha ha ha

Grandpa Rome Pays a Visit
Rome the Chef

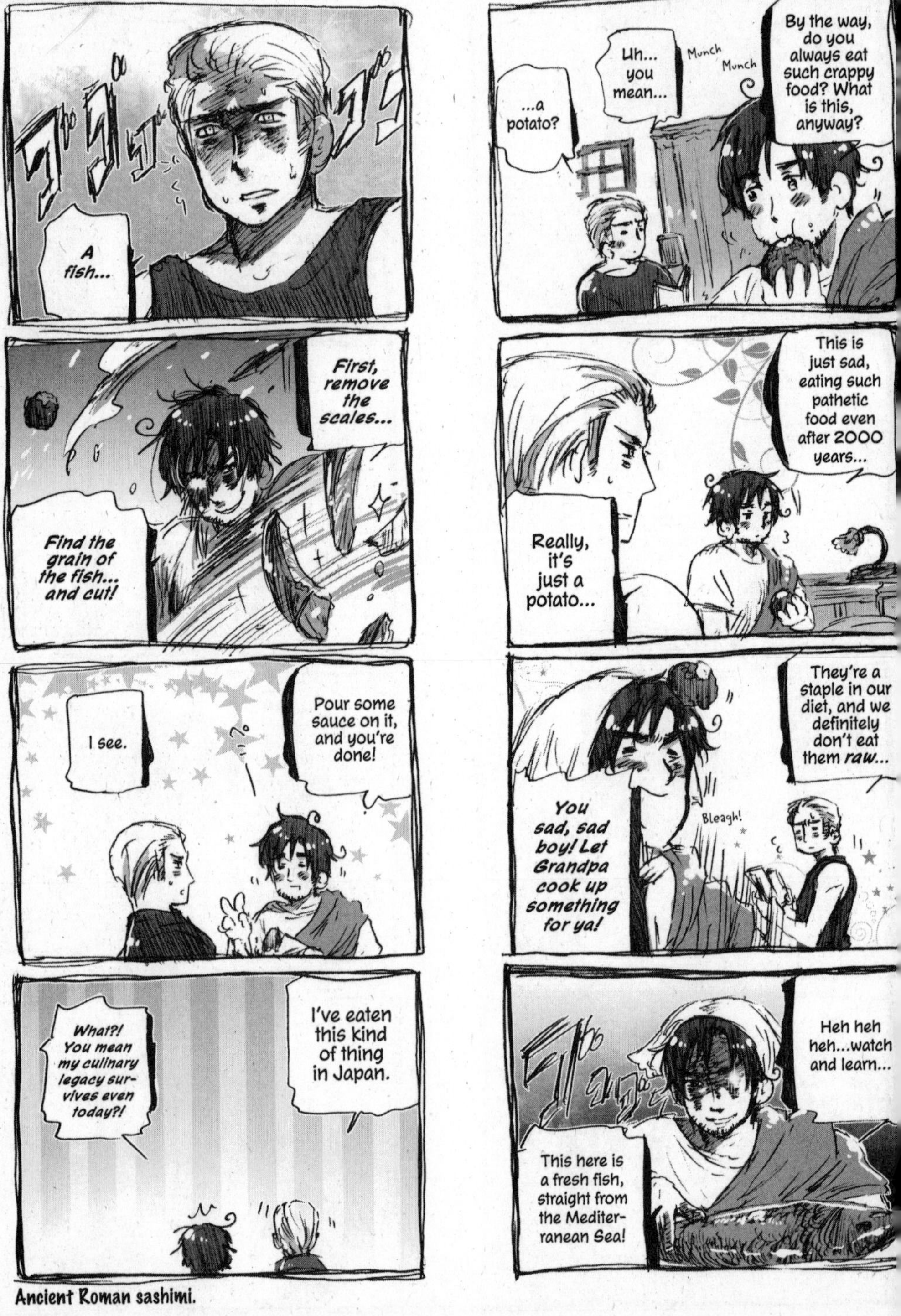

By the way, do you always eat such crappy food? What is this, anyway?
Munch Munch
Uh... you mean...
...a potato?
This is just sad, eating such pathetic food even after 2000 years...
Really, it's just a potato...
They're a staple in our diet, and we definitely don't eat them *raw*...
Bleagh!
You sad, sad boy! Let Grandpa cook up something for ya!
Heh heh heh...watch and learn...
This here is a fresh fish, straight from the Mediter-ranean Sea!
A fish...
First, remove the scales...
Find the grain of the fish... and cut!
Pour some sauce on it, and you're done!
I see.
I've eaten this kind of thing in Japan.
What?! You mean my culinary legacy sur-vives even today?!

Ancient Roman sashimi.

Grandpa Rome Pays a Visit
Rome the Teacher

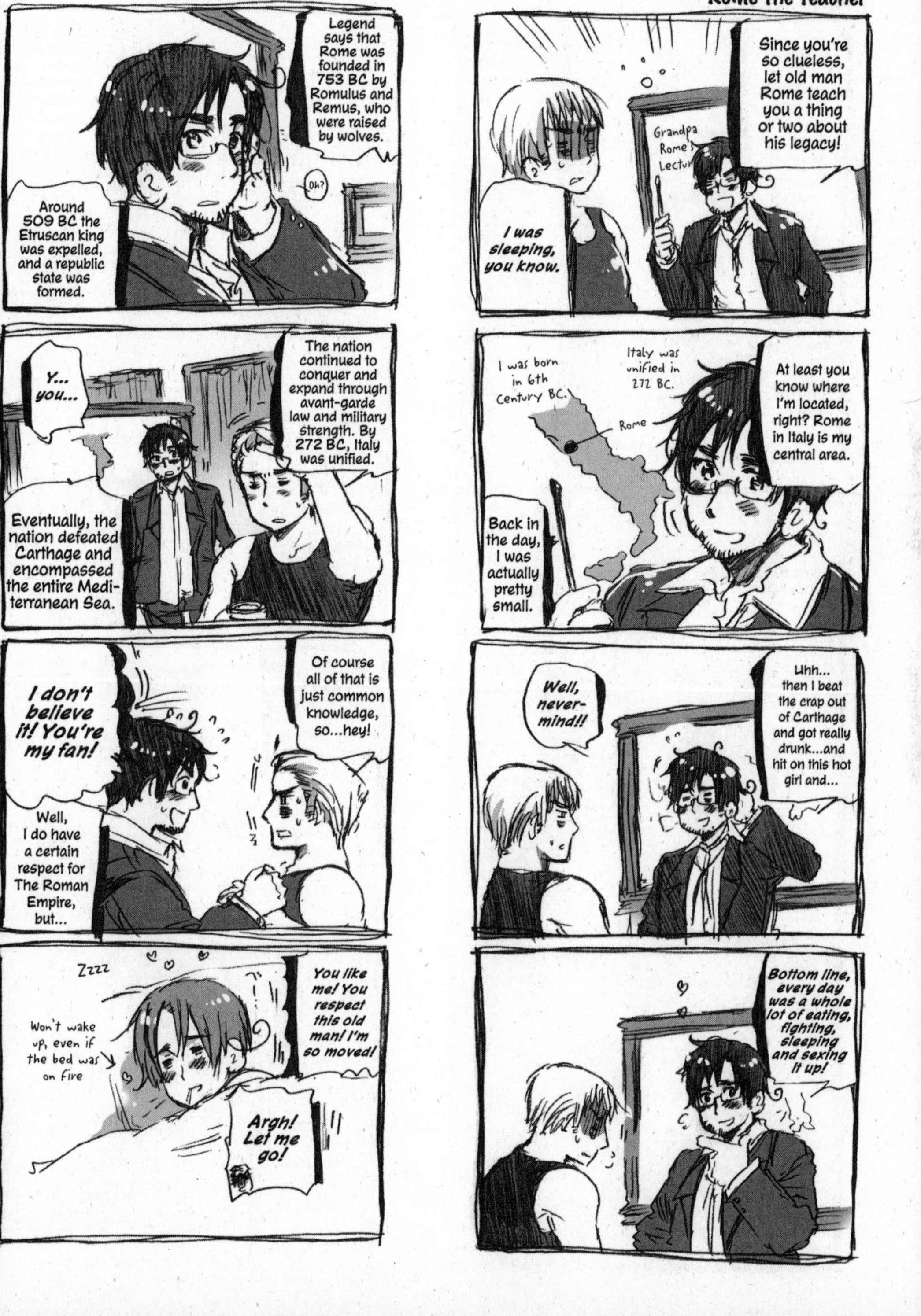
Since you're so clueless, let old man Rome teach you a thing or two about his legacy!
Grandpa Rome's Lectu
I was sleeping, you know.
At least you know where I'm located, right? Rome in Italy is my central area.
Italy was unified in 272 BC.
I was born in 6th Century BC.
Rome
Back in the day, I was actually pretty small.
Uhh... then I beat the crap out of Carthage and got really drunk...and hit on this hot girl and...
Well, never-mind!!
Bottom line, every day was a whole lot of eating, fighting, sleeping and sexing it up!
Legend says that Rome was founded in 753 BC by Romulus and Remus, who were raised by wolves.
Oh?
Around 509 BC the Etruscan king was expelled, and a republic state was formed.
The nation continued to conquer and expand through avant-garde law and military strength. By 272 BC, Italy was unified.
Y... you...
Eventually, the nation defeated Carthage and encompassed the entire Medi-terranean Sea.
Of course all of that is just common knowledge, so...hey!
I don't believe it! You're my fan!
Well, I do have a certain respect for The Roman Empire, but...
You like me! You respect this old man! I'm so moved!
Zzzz
Won't wake up, even if the bed was on fire
Argh! Let me go!

Grandpa Rome Pays a Visit
Rome the Pervert

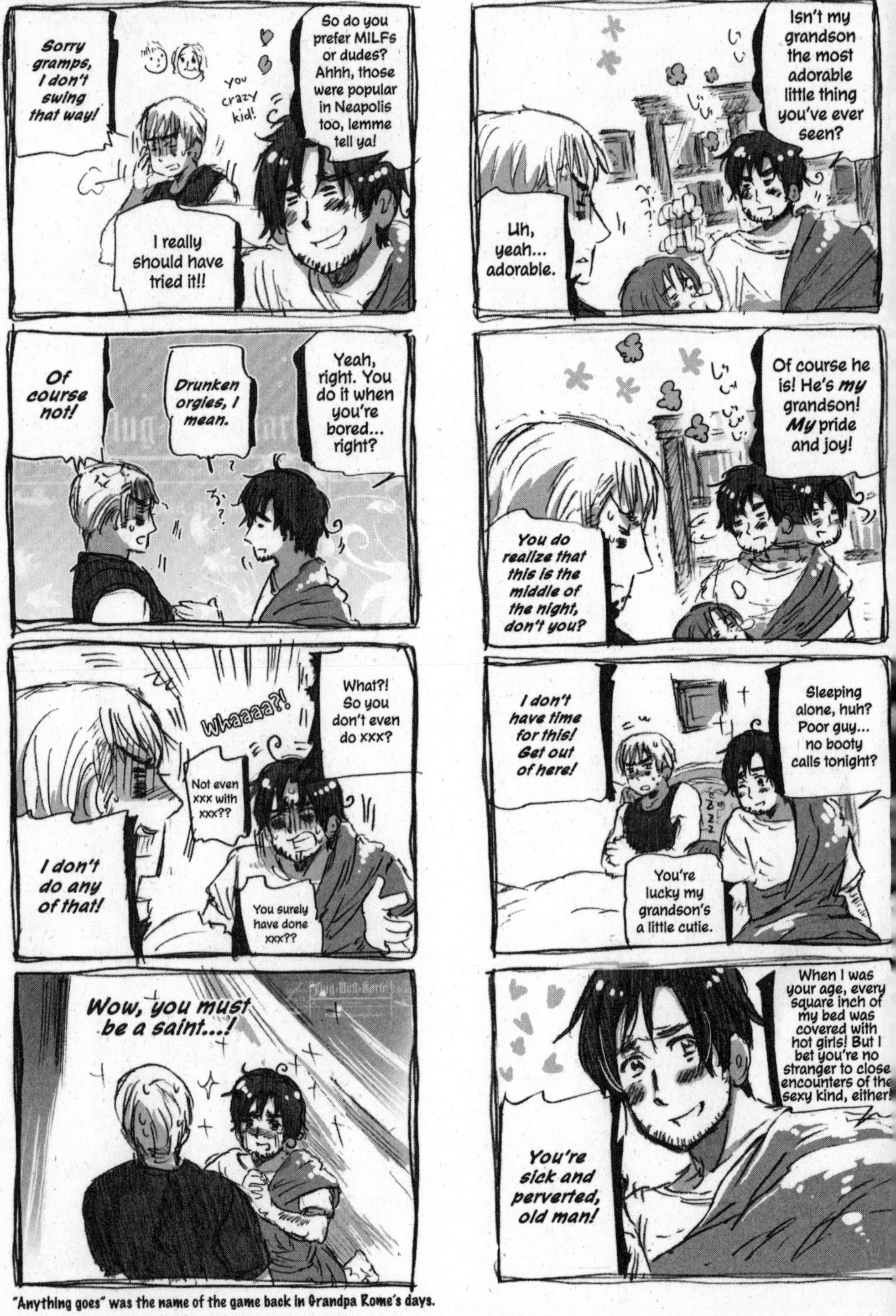
Isn't my grandson the most adorable little thing you've ever seen?
Uh, yeah... adorable.
Of course he is! He's *my* grandson! *My* pride and joy!
You do realize that this is the middle of the night, don't you?
Sleeping alone, huh? Poor guy... no booty calls tonight?
I don't have time for this! Get out of here!
You're lucky my grandson's a little cutie.
When I was your age, every square inch of my bed was covered with hot girls! But I bet you're no stranger to close encounters of the sexy kind, either!
You're sick and perverted, old man!
So do you prefer MILFs or dudes? Ahhh, those were popular in Neapolis too, lemme tell ya!
You crazy kid!
Sorry gramps, I don't swing that way!
I really should have tried it!!
Yeah, right. You do it when you're bored... right?
Drunken orgies, I mean.
Of course not!
What?! So you don't even do xxx?
Whaaaa?!
Not even xxx with xxx??
I don't do any of that!
You surely have done xxx??
Wow, you must be a saint...!

"Anything goes" was the name of the game back in Grandpa Rome's days.

Grandpa Rome Pays a Visit
Rome the Trespasser

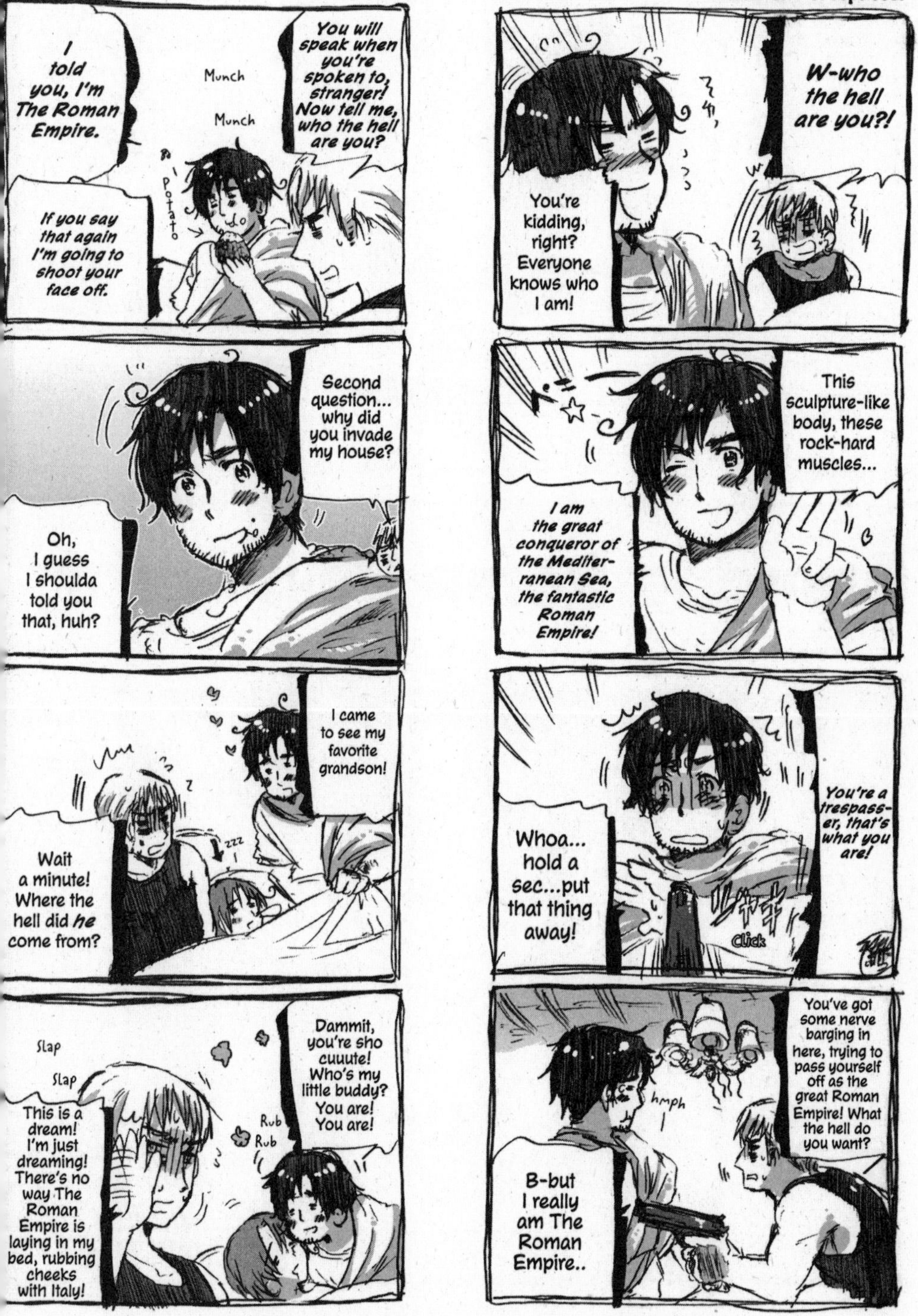
W-who the hell are you?!
You're kidding, right? Everyone knows who I am!
This sculpture-like body, these rock-hard muscles...
I am the great conqueror of the Mediter-ranean Sea, the fantastic Roman Empire!
You're a trespass-er, that's what you are!
Whoa... hold a sec...put that thing away!
Click
You've got some nerve barging in here, trying to pass yourself off as the great Roman Empire! What the hell do you want?
hmph
B-but I really am The Roman Empire..
You will speak when you're spoken to, stranger! Now tell me, who the hell are you?
Munch
Munch
I told you, I'm The Roman Empire.
Potato
If you say that again I'm going to shoot your face off.
Second question... why did you invade my house?
Oh, I guess I shoulda told you that, huh?
I came to see my favorite grandson!
zzz
Wait a minute! Where the hell did *he* come from?
Dammit, you're sho cuuute! Who's my little buddy? You are! You are!
Rub
Rub
Slap
Slap
This is a dream! I'm just dreaming! There's no way The Roman Empire is laying in my bed, rubbing cheeks with Italy!

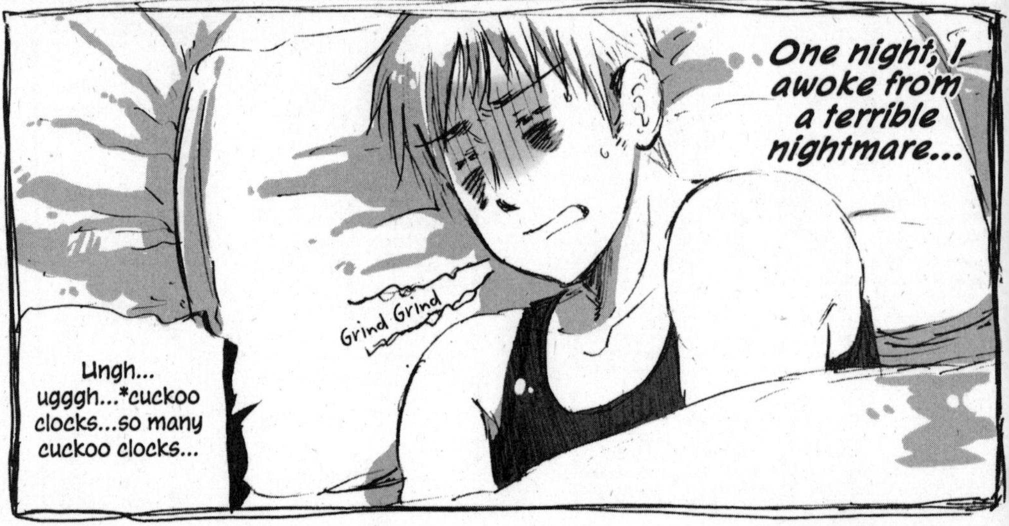
One night, I awoke from a terrible nightmare...
Grind Grind
Ungh... ugggh...*cuckoo clocks...so many cuckoo clocks...

*See page 26 in volume 1.

Grandpa Rome Pays a Visit

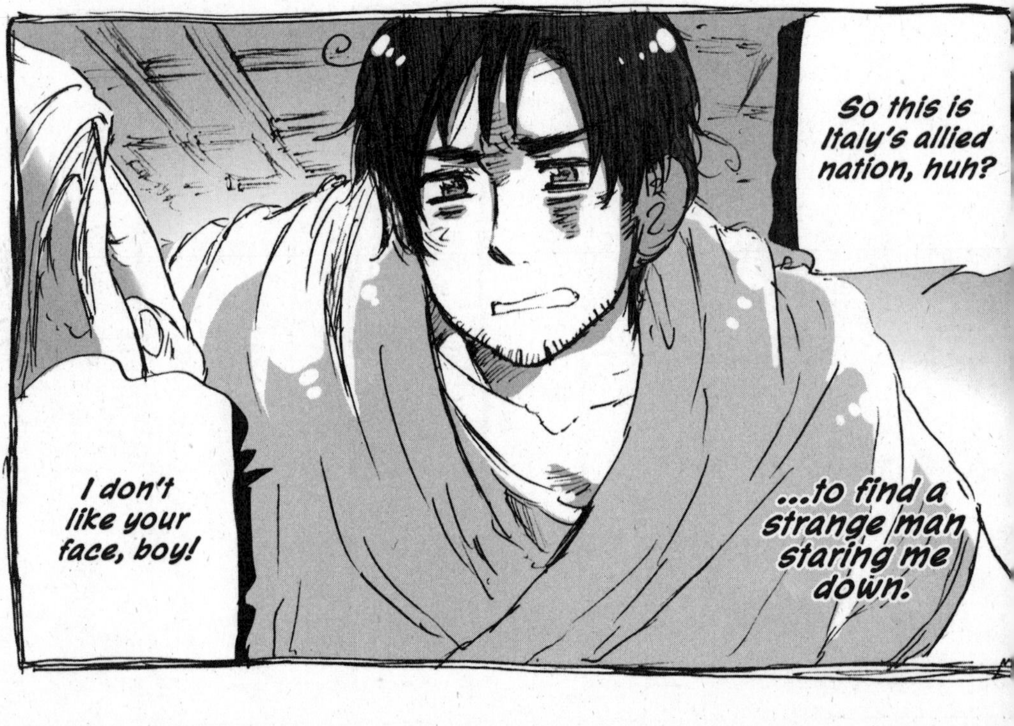
So this is Italy's allied nation, huh?
...to find a strange man staring me down.
I don't like your face, boy!

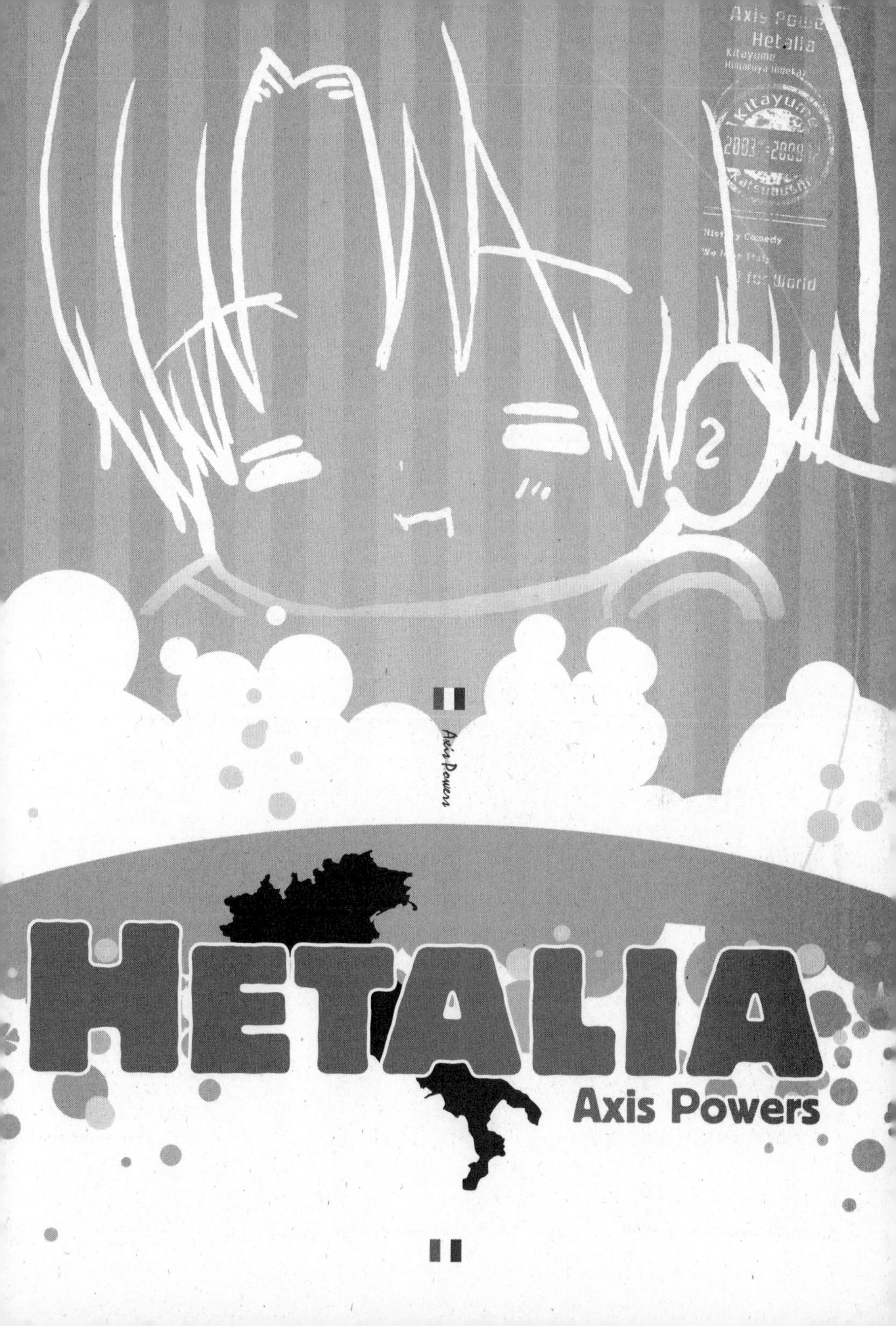
Axis Powers
Hetalia
Kitayume
Axis Powers
HETALIA
Axis Powers
II

HETALIA AND HIS MERRY FRIENDS

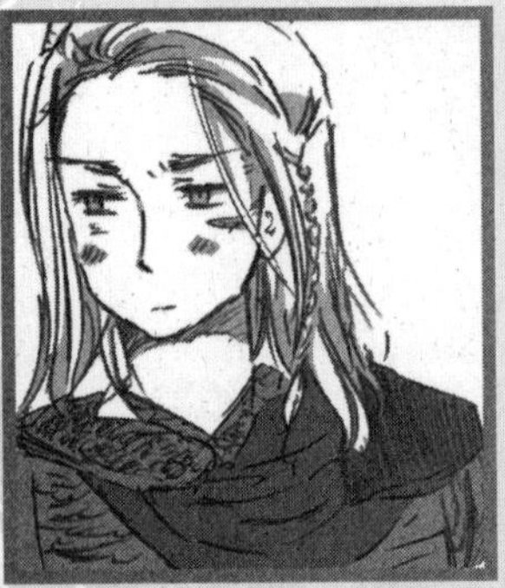

Germania

A fierce man of few words, Germania is the grandfather of Holy Rome. Once a guard for (Grandpa) Rome, his hatred toward his former leader runs deep. It is believed that Germania was responsible for Rome's death, but the truth remains shrouded in darkness.

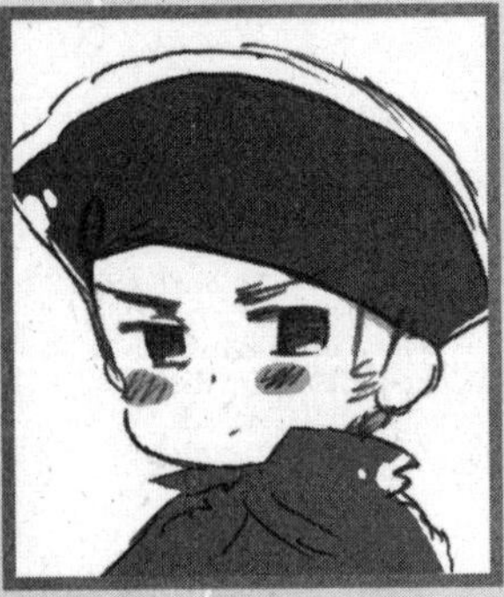

Holy Rome

[Official Name] Heiliges Romisches Reich
A descendent of Germania, Holy Rome may look strong, but he is actually quite frail. Prone to obsession, if he is interested in someone, he will chase them down for hundreds of years if necessary. His feelings for Italy were so strong, that he was happy to be by his side, even as his house crumbled. Although Holy Rome was able to hold on for a while thanks to Austria's boss, numerous wars and hardships eventually caused him to collapse.

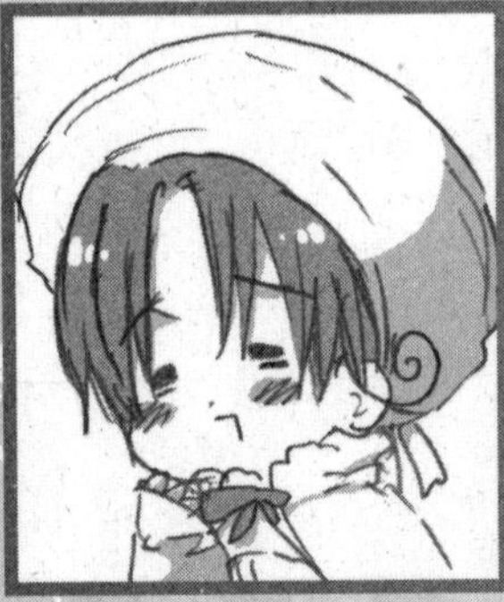

Chibitalia

Grandpa Rome's favorite grandson, Italy was once known as "Chibitalia." Thanks to his charming culture and fertile lands he was the target of many nations who wanted him for their own. By the time Austria had taken him in, Chibitalia had already become the lazy glutton that we all know and love.

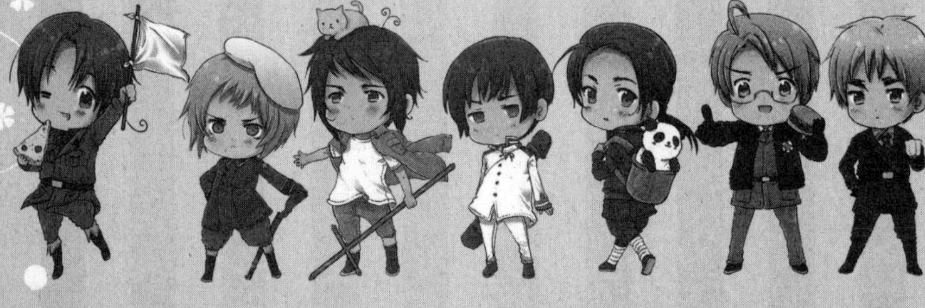

HETALIA AND HIS MERRY FRIENDS

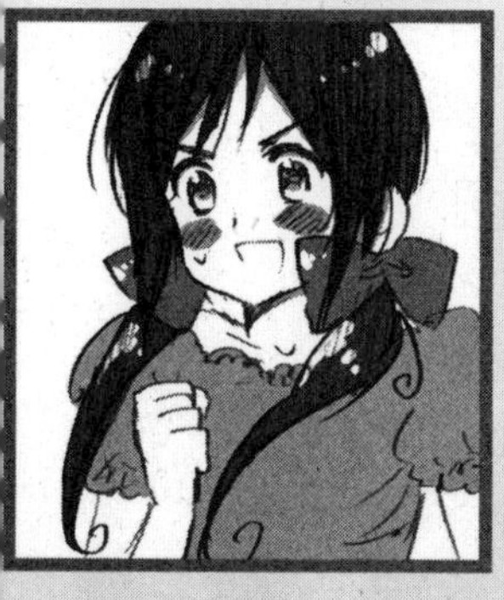

Seychelles

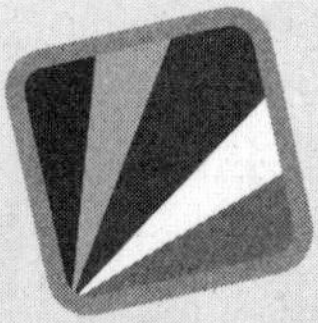

[Official Name] Republic of Seychelles
[Capital] Victoria
[Official Language] Seychellois Creole
[Birthday] June 29

A paradise in the Indian Ocean, Seychelles is a strange girl who speaks a mix of French and English. Laid-back and messy, she has a nice tan and raven hair. 0% self-sufficient, she always complains about the high cost of living. Regardless, she is able to keep up her lavish lifestyle thanks to frequent visits from Britain and France.

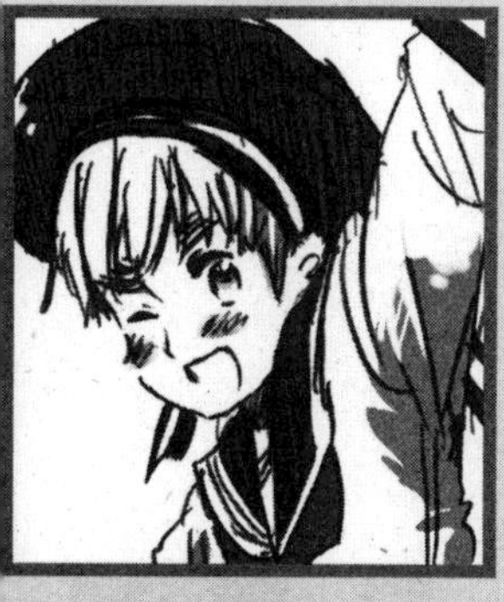

Sealand

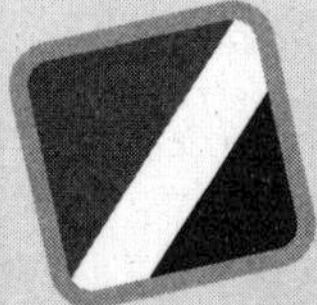

[Official Name] Principality of Sealand
[Capital] The entire region
[Birthday] September 2

The smallest (unofficial) nation in the world, Sealand made his appearance on the global stage after Britain left him at sea and forgot about him. Sealand may be small, but he is made completely of metal and claims that he can do a powerful rocket punch as a result (although he's probably lying). He has been doing surprisingly well lately, thanks to America and Japan buying titles in his registry of nobles. Unfortunately, he is in danger of being sold off by his Prince. His hobby is playing on his high-speed internet.

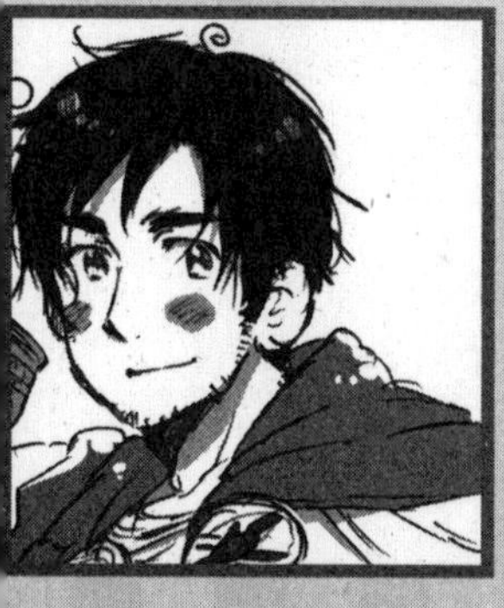

Grandpa Rome

[Official Name] Imperium Romanum
[Capital] Rome

A kind-hearted man, Rome was once the ruler of the Mediterranean Sea. He is an extremely doting grandfather and a great patron of the arts. He loves paintings, sculptures, music, cute girls and delicious food. He is thrilled at the sight of powerful nations, be they friend or foe. He has had many loves in his life, the greatest being Greece and Egypt's mothers.

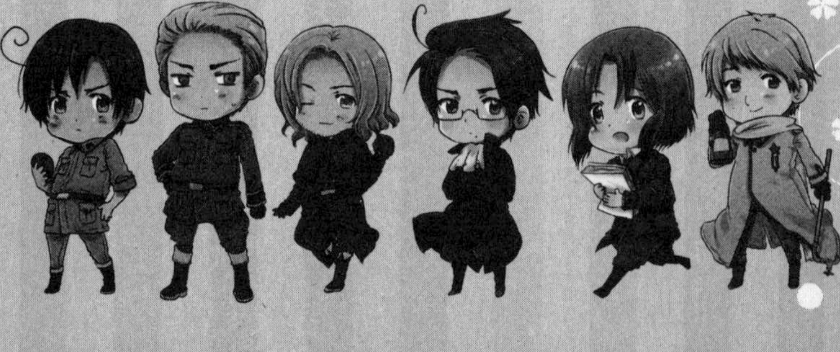

HETALIA AND HIS MERRY FRIENDS

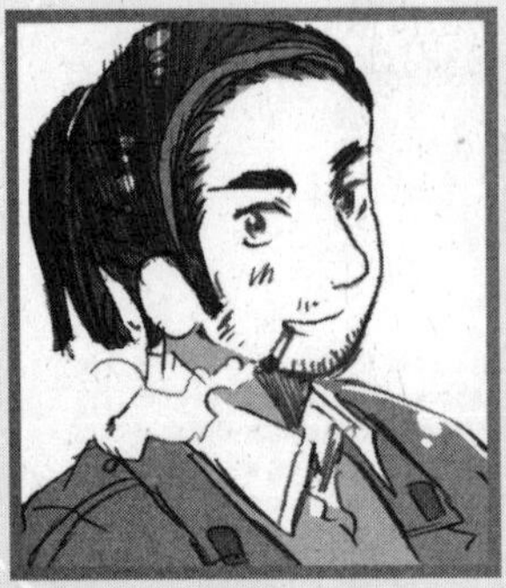

Cuba

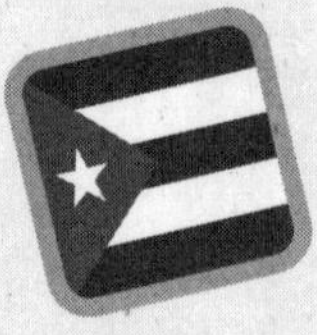

[Official Name] Republic of Cuba
[Capital] Havana
[Official Language] Spanish
[Birthday] May 20
[National Flower] Mariposa

Unpretentious, loyal and crazy about ice cream, Cuba is a true bro. He may not get along very well with America, but he and Canada are good pals.

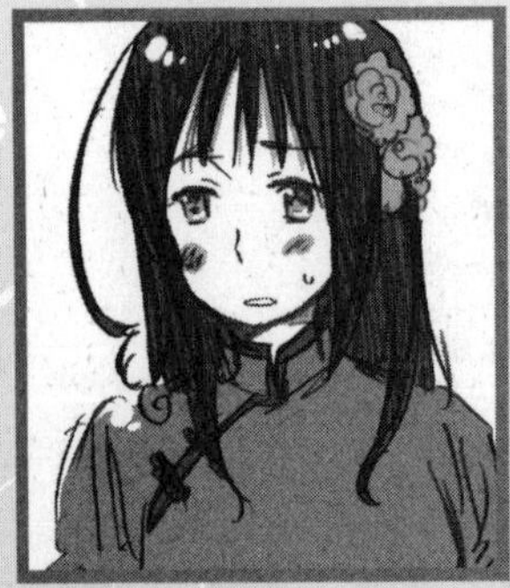

Taiwan

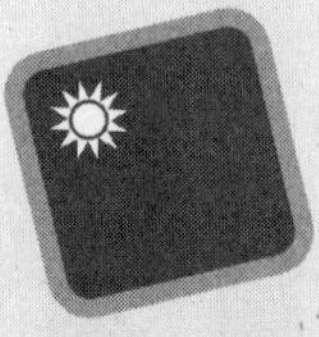

[Official Name] Republic of China
[Capital] Taipei
[Official Language] Mandarin
[Birthday] October 25
[National Flower] Plum Blossom

A strong-minded and stylish girl. She's been really stressed out lately...

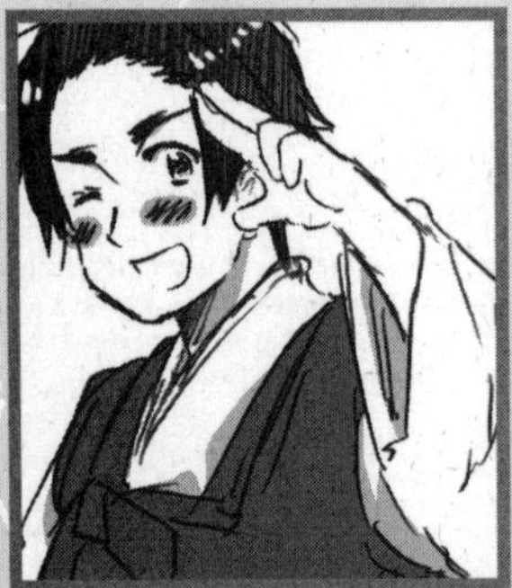

South Korea

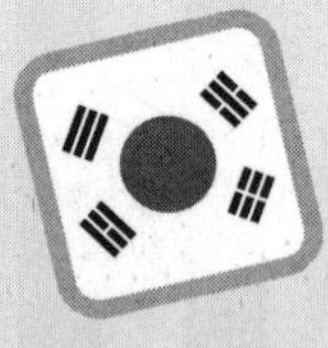

[Official Name] Republic of Korea
[Capital] Seoul
[Official Language] Korean
[Birthday] August 15
[National Flower] Rose of Sharon

A wild and free-spirited man, South Korea's favorite hobby is claiming that he invented everything. Although he usually has a hip way of speaking, he sometimes tones it down to show respect to his elders. South Korea loves Canada, studying abroad, watching heart-wrenching dramas, the Internet and video games.

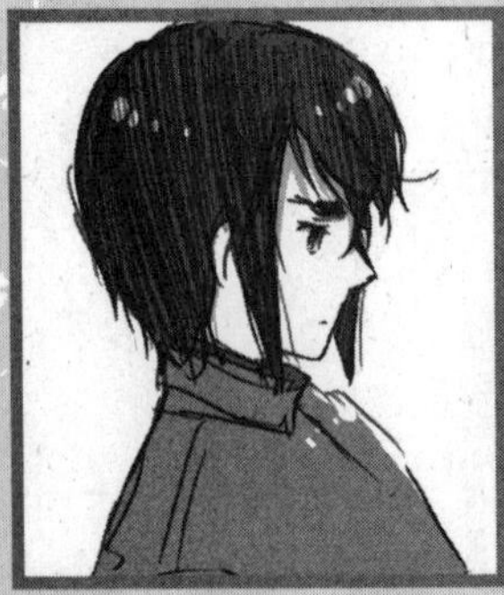

Hong Kong

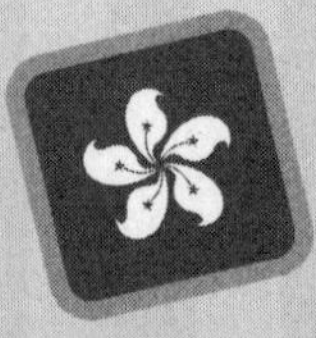

[Official Name] Hong Kong Special Administrative Region of the People's Republic of China
[Capital]
[Official Language] Chinese, English
[Birthday]
[National Flower] Bauhinia Blakeana

A former nation that was recently under British rule. It is difficult to figure out what Hong Kong is thinking, and his strange accent makes him difficult to understand as well. He was once scolded by England for making too much noise with firecrackers.

HETALIA AND HIS MERRY FRIENDS

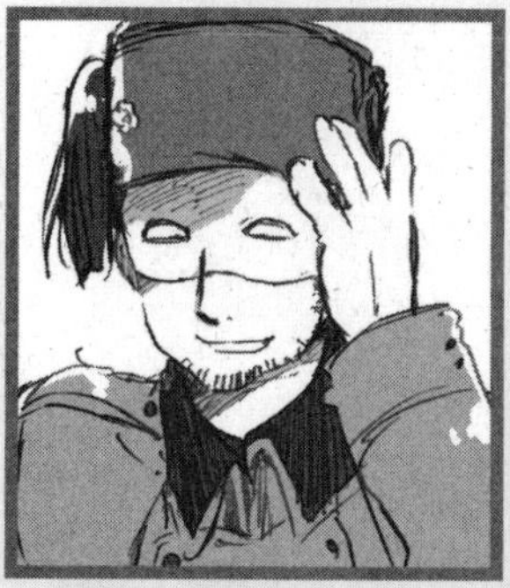

Turkey

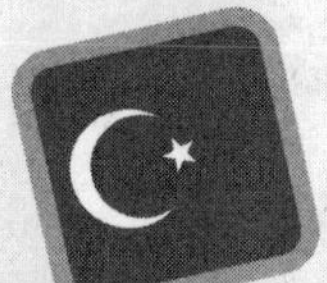

[Official Name] Republic of Turkey
[Capital] Ankara
[Official Language] Turkish
[Birthday] October 29
[National Flower] Tulip

A masked old guy who has a dynamic personality and speaks in an old-fashioned dialect. Turkey is unnecessarily passionate and uncomfortably friendly. However, despite his jovial personality, Turkey can be stubborn about trivial things. He loves sweets, baths and entertaining tourists. A fan of war and an enemy of Greece, he can be extremely competitive at times.

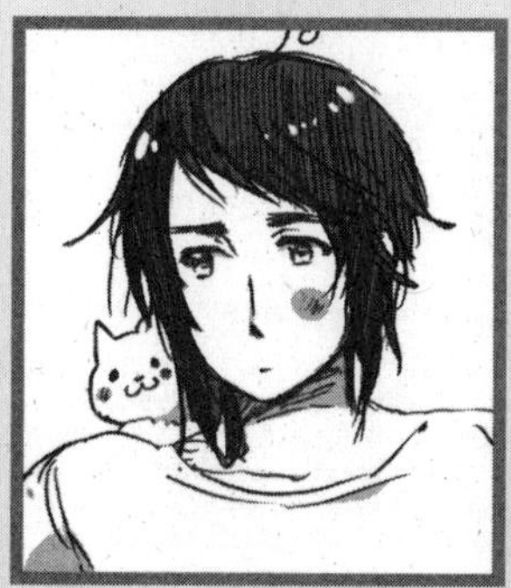

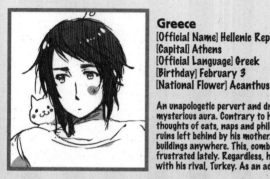

Greece

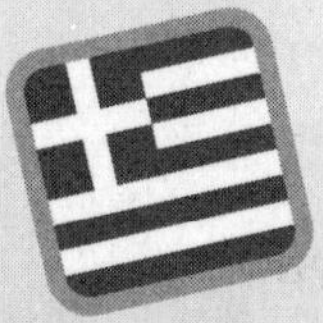

[Official Name] Hellenic Republic
[Capital] Athens
[Official Language] Greek
[Birthday] February 3
[National Flower] Acanthus

An unapologetic pervert and dreamer at heart, Greece is a man with an undeniably mysterious aura. Contrary to his carefree appearance, his mind is always running with thoughts of cats, naps and philosophy. Whenever Greece digs up his back yard, he finds ruins left behind by his mother. As a result, he is unable to build subways or metropolitan buildings anywhere. This, combined with an Albanian invasion, has left him quite frustrated lately. Regardless, he tends to pick fights even in times of peace, especially with his rival, Turkey. As an added note, his national anthem is the longest in the world.

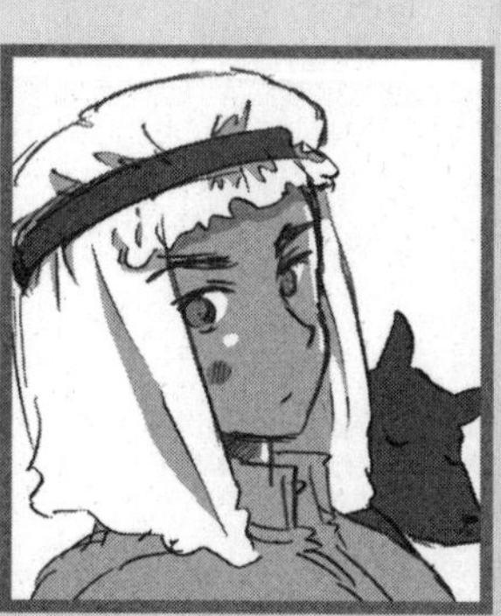

Egypt

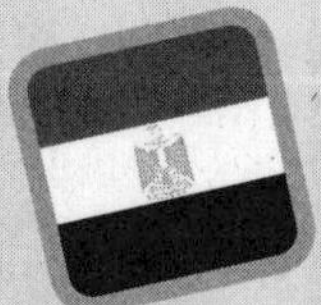

[Official Name] Arab Republic of Egypt
[Capital] Cairo
[Official Language] Arabic
[Birthday] February 28
[National Flower] Water Lily

A unique and carefree man, Egypt is tough, but friendly to others. Like Greece, he is unable to modernize himself because his mother's mementos are buried all around the place. However, he has a great love for his family and doesn't seem to mind. Oddly enough, it is rare for others to catch Egypt talking.

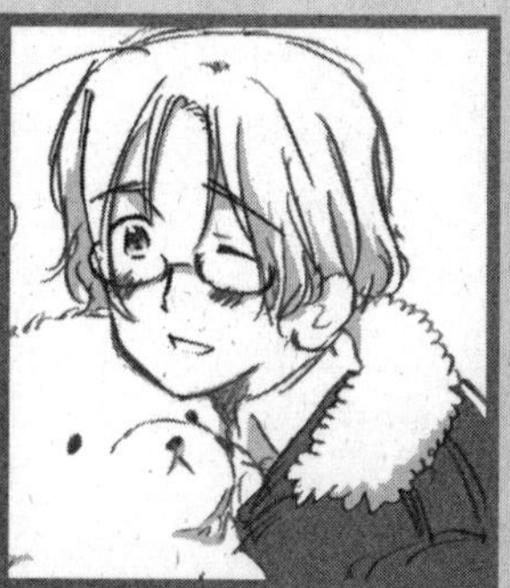

Canada

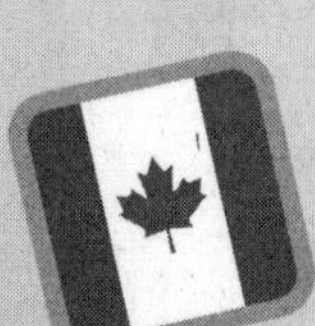

[Official Name] Canada
[Capital] Ottawa
[Official Languages] English, French
[Birthday] July 1
[National Flower] Sugar Maple

A good-natured and soft-spoken man, Canada has a gentle personality. Even though he always hangs out with the polar bear Kumajiro, the two don't even know each other's names. Canada doesn't like being mistaken for America, so he struggles in vain to promote his individuality. He likes to stay out of trouble, but thanks to his neighbor to the south, it's unlikely that he'll ever find peace.

HETALIA AND HIS MERRY FRIENDS

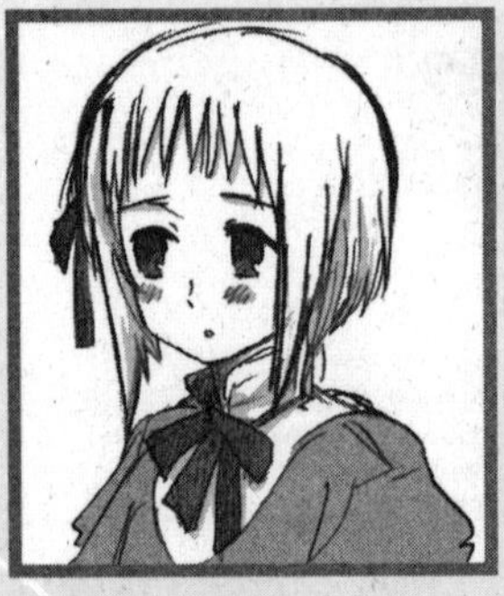

Liechtenstein

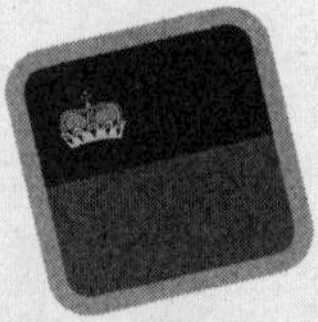

[Official Name] Principality of Liechtenstein
[Capital] Vaduz
[Official Language] German
[Birthday] July 12
[National Flower] Lily

Although Liechtenstein is under the protection of Switzerland, she is very mature and intelligent. She appears quite graceful and docile, but speaks her mind freely. She is surprisingly high-tech.

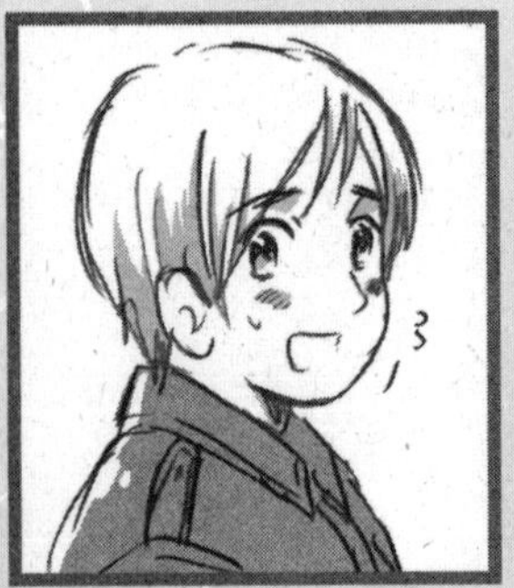

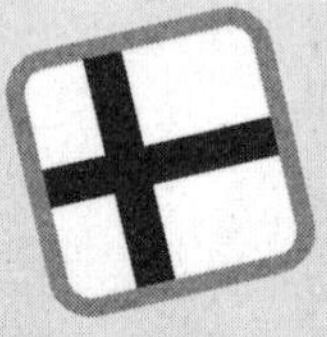

Finland

[Official Name] Republic of Finland
[Capital] Helsinki
[Official Language] Finnish, Swedish
[Birthday] December 6
[National Flower] Lily of the Valley

Moi moi! A warm-hearted and simple-minded young man who works hard at everything he does. He may seem soft-spoken, but once he starts talking it can be difficult to shut him up. Finland loves saunas and is unusually resilient to cold. During times of emergencies he displays superhuman strength, making him quite frightening to anyone who gets on his bad side. Finland enjoys holding strange festivals where Estonia ends up winning all the prizes.

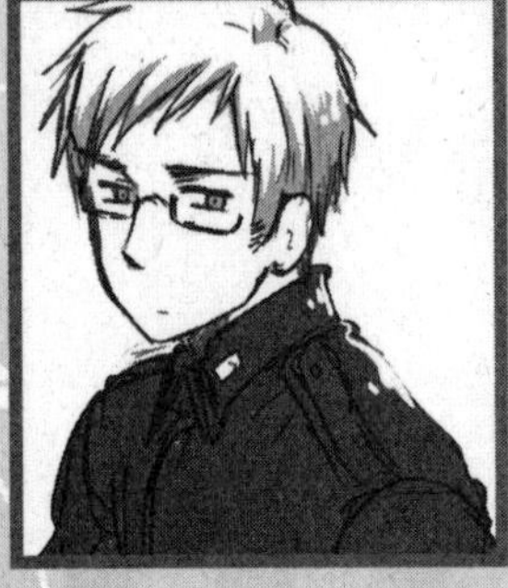

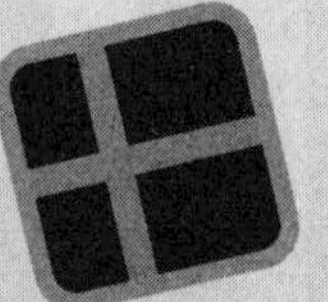

Sweden

[Official Name] Kingdom of Sweden
[Capital] Stockholm
[Official Language] Swedish
[Birthday] June 6 (National Day)
[National Flower] German Lily of the Valley

Tall and intimidating, Sweden's quiet nature makes it difficult to figure out what he is thinking. Although he comes across as quite terrifying, in truth, he has a playful and mischievous personality. Sweden was once known as the conqueror of Northern Europe, but lately he has calmed down and focused on public welfare instead. His hobbies include carpentry, interior design and participating in debates.

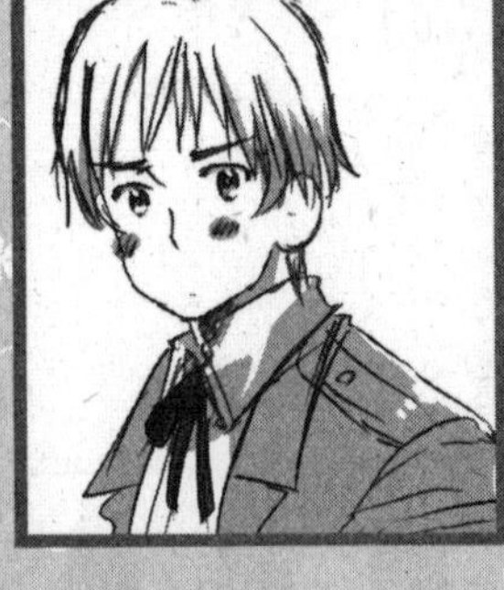

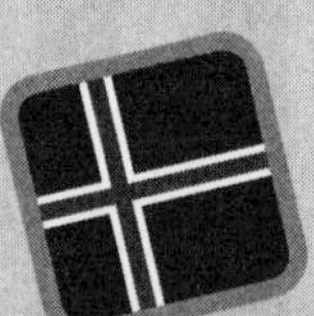

Iceland

[Official Name] Republic of Iceland
[Capital] Reykjavik
[Official Language] Icelandic
[Birthday] June 17
[National Flower] White Dryas

Cold on the outside, hot on the inside, Iceland is one of the strangest nations in Europe. Recently he caught a terrible cold and has become suspicious of Russia's unusually kind treatment. Until his fever subsides, he'll grudgingly accept Russia's care, but after that, anything is game.

HETALIA AND HIS MERRY FRIENDS

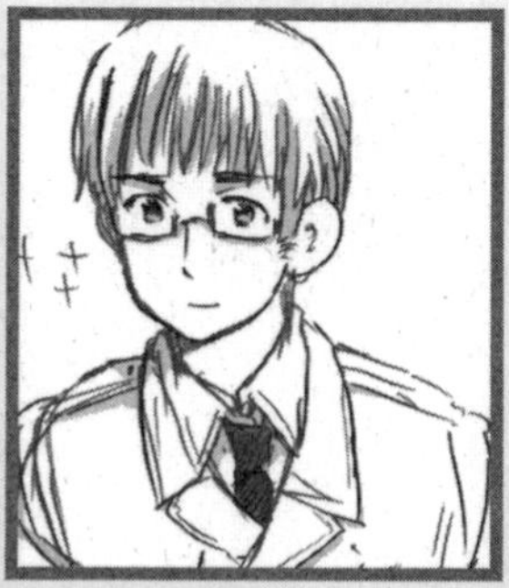

Estonia

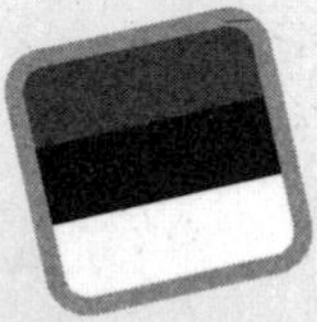

[Official Name] Eesti Vabariik
[Capital] Tallinn
[Official Language] Estonian
[Birthday] February 24
[National Bird] Swallow

The honor student of the Baltic States, Estonia often escapes hairy situations with his wit. Estonia acts like a calm and composed businessman around others but is quite laid back in his private life. Compared to the other Baltic States, he is not very reliant on Russia. He is excellent with IT and enjoys visiting strange festivals with Finland (perhaps a bit too much).

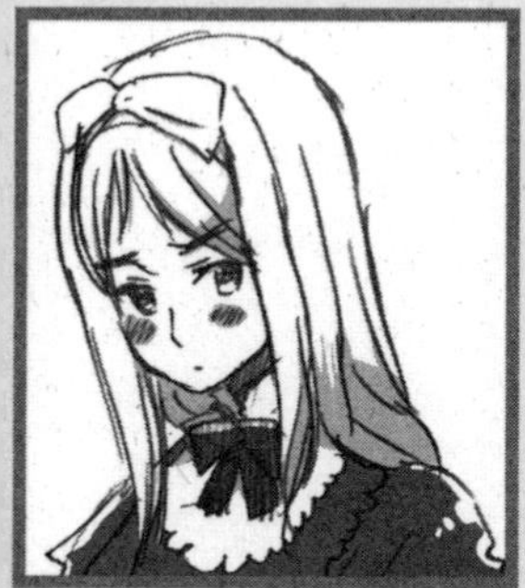

Belarus

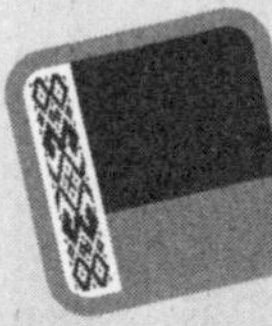

[Official Name] Republic of Belarus
[Capital] Minsk
[Official Language] Belarusian, Russian
[Birthday] August 25

Russia's intimidating younger sister. Although she aggressively professes her love to Russia, her efforts are never rewarded.

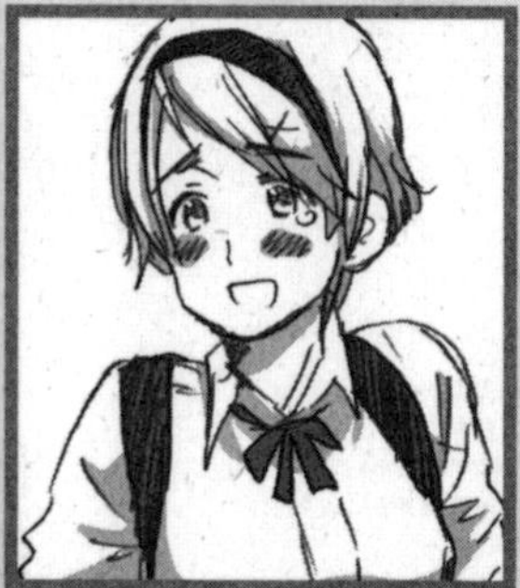

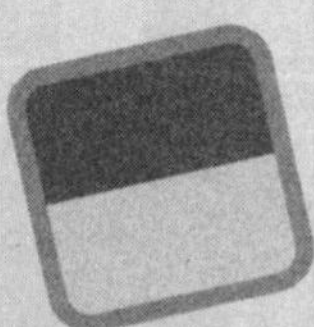

Ukraine

[Official Name] Ukraine
[Capital] Kiev
[Official Language] Ukrainian
[Birthday] August 24

Russia's older sister who can't seem to stay out of trouble, despite her best intentions. You can hear her coming by the sound of her bouncing boobs.

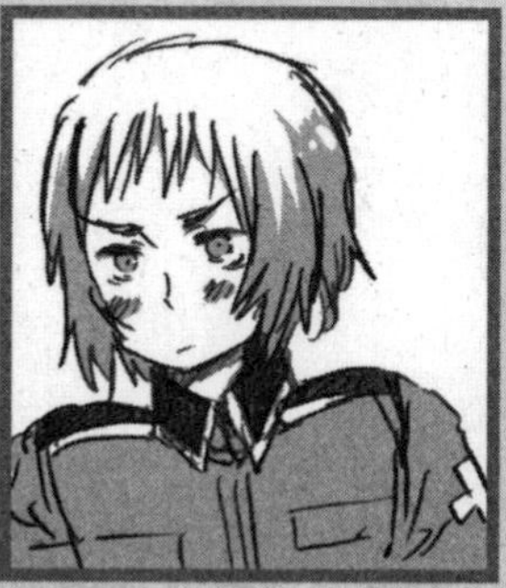

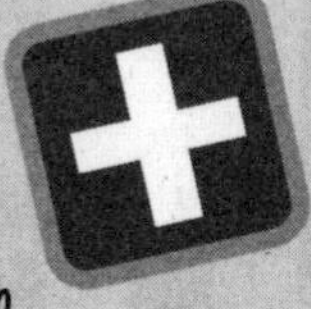

Switzerland

[Official Name] Schweizerische Eidgenossenchaft
[Capital] Bern
[Official Language] German, French, Italian, Romanish
[Birthday] August 1
[National Flower] Edelweiss

Surrounded by mountains and constantly invaded by neighbors, Switzerland's long history of suffering has made him wary of others. He may come across as tough and composed, but he is often pushed around by Germany and Italy. He is extremely protective of Liechtenstein.

HETALIA AND HIS MERRY FRIENDS

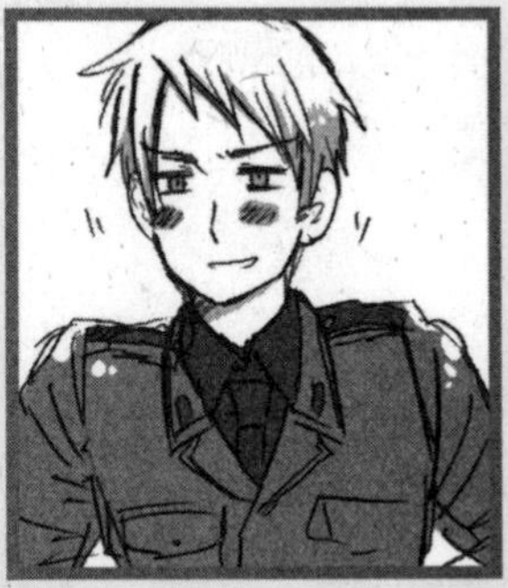

Prussia

Committed to being the strongest at any price, Prussia was born to fight. Unlike Austria who continuously married other nations for his benefit, Prussia simply fought his way through life. He has a rough personality but is very loyal to his boss, "Uncle Fritz." He hates Russia, but affectionately refers to Germany as "West."

*How Prussia was formed:

Saint Maria Religious Order → German Teutonic Knights → (a bunch of crazy stuff happened) → Prussia

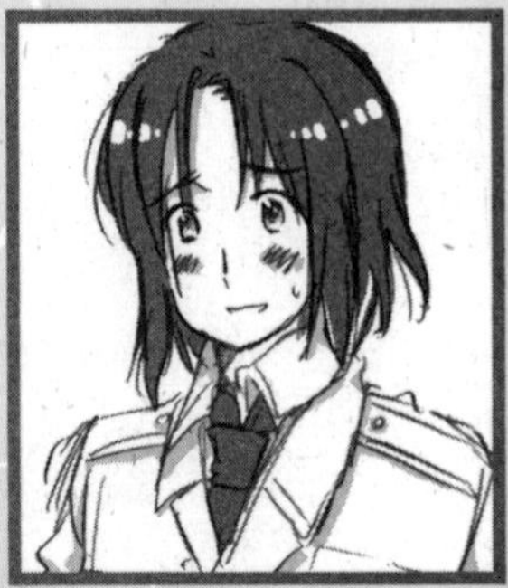

Lithuania

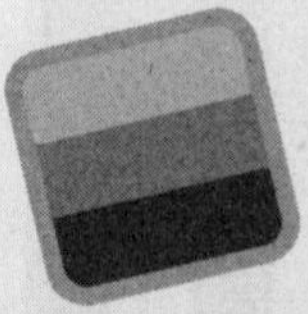

[Official Name] Lietuvos Respublika
[Capital] Vilnius
[Official Language] Lithuanian
[National Foundation Day] February 16
[National Flower] Common Rue

Serious and patient, Lithuania tends to overthink things and give himself a stomach ache. Although he is good friends with Poland, he always seems to get the short end of the stick in their relationship. Perhaps due to some trauma from his days in the Soviet Union, Lithuania enjoys making bizarre theme parks. Currently both Lithuania and Poland are in rehab, trying to clear up their dependence on Russia.

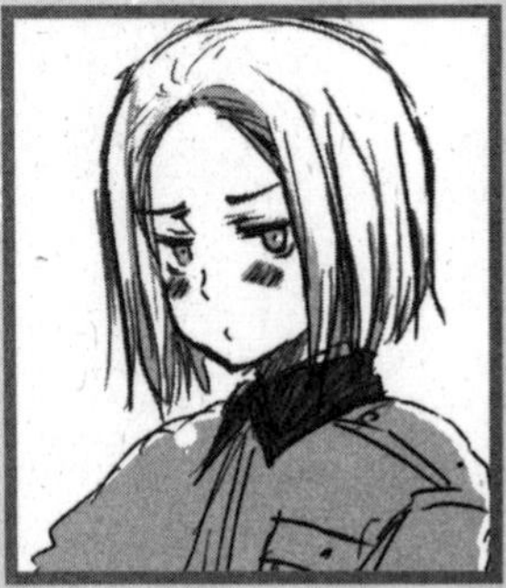

Poland

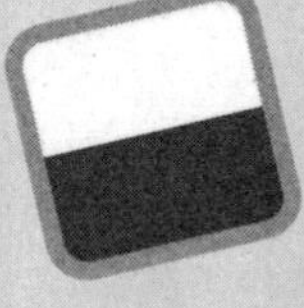

[Official Name] Rzeczpospolita Polska
[Capital] Warsaw
[Official Language] Polish
[Birthday] November 11
[National Flower] Pansy

A good friend to Lithuania, Poland's deep thoughts are hidden behind his spacey-looking exterior. He is extremely shy around strangers and warms up to people slowly, but he also tends to be both clingy and quite blunt when he finally opens up to someone.

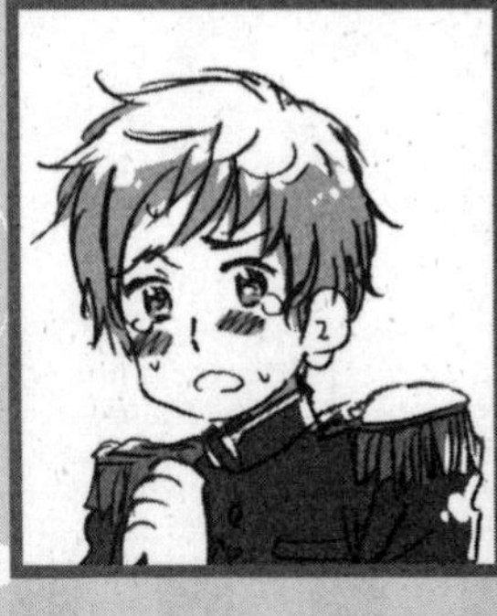

Latvia

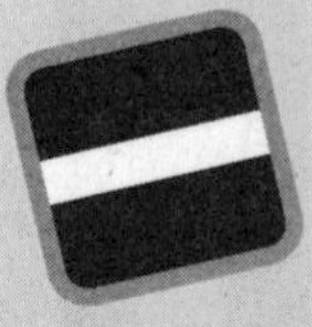

[Official Name] Latvijas Respublika
[Capital] Riga
[Official Language] Latvian
[National Foundation Day] November 18
[National Flower] Margaret

Latvia is an introverted, shy crybaby. He has an unfortunate tendency to get sucked into things against his will. Highly dependent on Russia, he always fails at cutting ties with him no matter how many times he tries. He is currently in search of a best friend. Contrary to his appearance, he is a heavy drinker.

HETALIA AND HIS MERRY FRIENDS

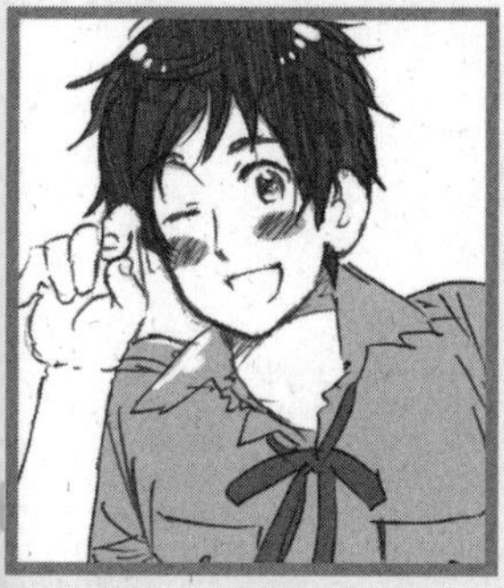

Spain

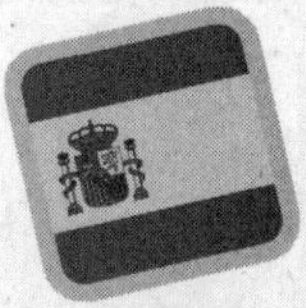

[Official Name] España
[Capital] Madrid
[Official Language] Spanish
[Birthday] February 12
[National Flower] Carnation

Once known as the country of passion where the sun never sets, Spain is optimistic, laid back, and a bit insensitive. He is both easily enthused and easily sidetracked. Despite his cheery disposition, he is quite frightening when angry. For whatever reason, he has an unusually big spot in his heart for Romano.

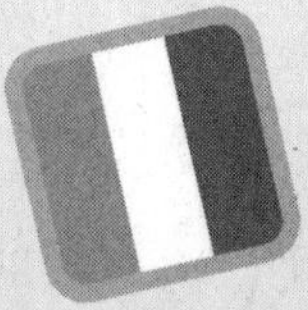

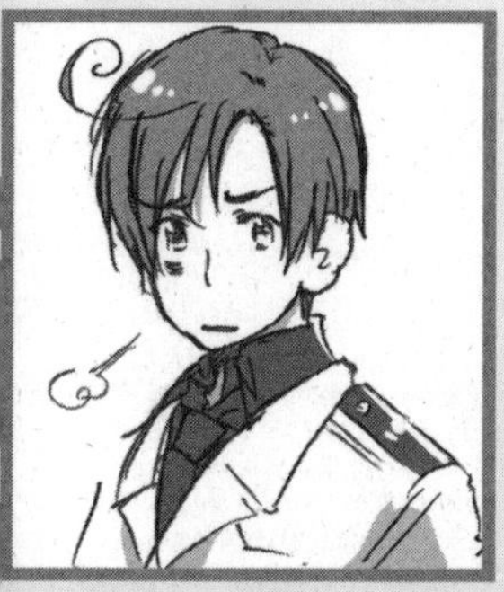

South Italy (Romano)

[Official Name] Repubblica Italiana
[Capital] Rome
[Official Language] Italian
[Birthday] March 17th, 1861 (Italy unified)
[National Flower] Daisy

Italy's ineffectual older brother. Although the two brothers do not get along especially well, they share a love for girls and pasta. Romano may act tough and aggressive towards Germany, but in truth, he is a coward, an idiot and a crybaby. Romano has spent most of his life with Spain, and as a result tends to follow Spanish customs and religious views. Persecuted by the Mafia all his life, he has a jaded view of the world. Kind to girls and terrible to men, he flies into a rage if you pull on his curly hair.

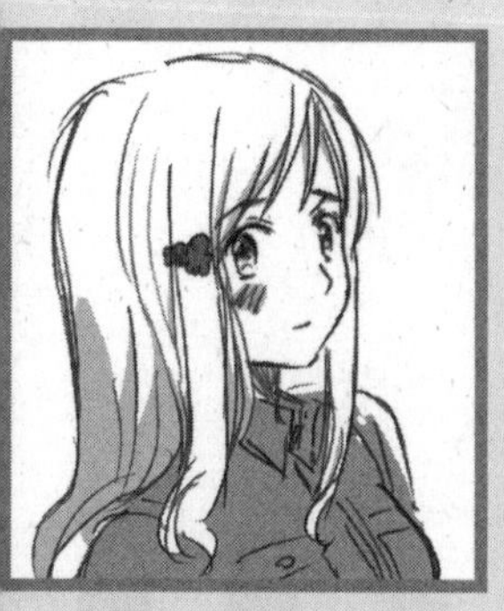

Hungary

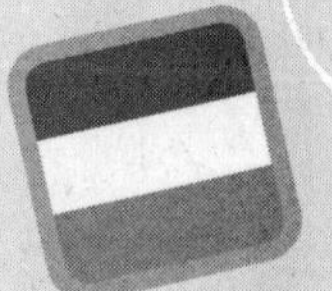

[Official Name] Magyar Köztársaság
[Capital] Budapest
[Official Language] Hungarian
[Marriage Anniversary] June 8, 1867
[National Flower] Pelargonium, Tulip

Contrary to her cute exterior, Hungary has the blood of a wild nomad running through her veins. She is a reliable friend and a fearsome enemy. Don't let her lady-like manners and beautiful singing voice fool you...she is probably the manliest character in the manga. Hungary often collaborates with Austria but has a cat-and-dog relationship with Romania.

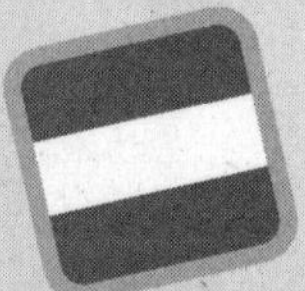

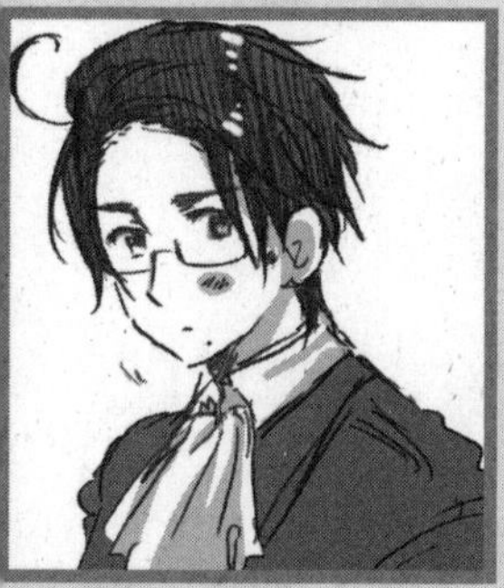

Austria

[Official Name] Republik Osterreich
[Capital] Vienna
[Official Language] German
[Birthday] October 26, 976
[National Flower] Edelweiss

A pampered man who loves music and cake. He has a pompous demeanor and never shows his true feelings. Austria may seem to be all glitz and glam, but in truth, he is extremely frugal. His glasses are supposed to accent his "musical" style, but he looks pretty plain if he takes them off. The curly piece of hair on his head represents Mariazell and changes from time to time. For example, it stood straight up at the pinnacle of his Holy Roman days but has become more limp and relaxed recently. Austria has suffered through many troublesome marriages and has an awful sense of direction.

HETALIA AND HIS MERRY FRIENDS

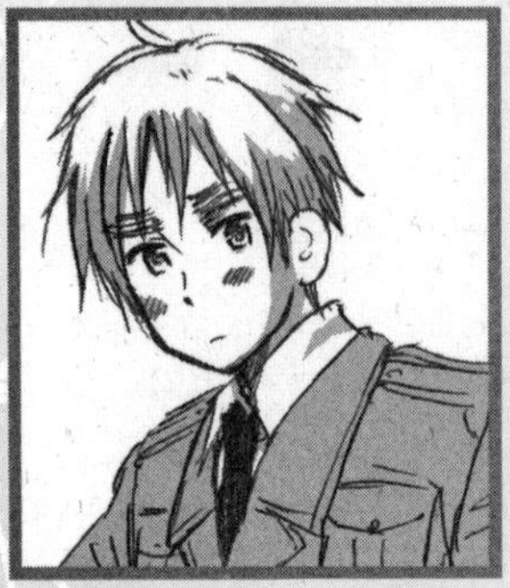

England

[Official Name] The United Kingdom of Great Britain and Northern Ireland
[Capital] London
[Official Language] English
[Birthday] Unknown
[National Flower] Rose

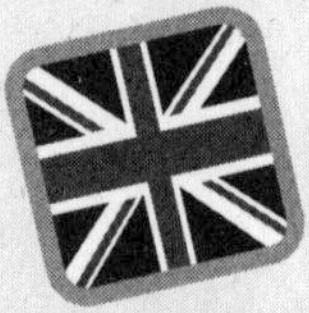

A former delinquent with a stubborn and cynical personality. Although he enjoys cooking, his food is notoriously awful. No stranger to the occult, England makes friends with fairies and ghosts when he isn't busy summoning demons to thwart his enemies. His hobbies include embroidery, drinking tea and getting horribly drunk. As a side note, England is the one who draws the caricatures of the Axis Nations on the blackboard in the war room. Despite his constant bickering with France, the two seem to have an underlying respect for one another.

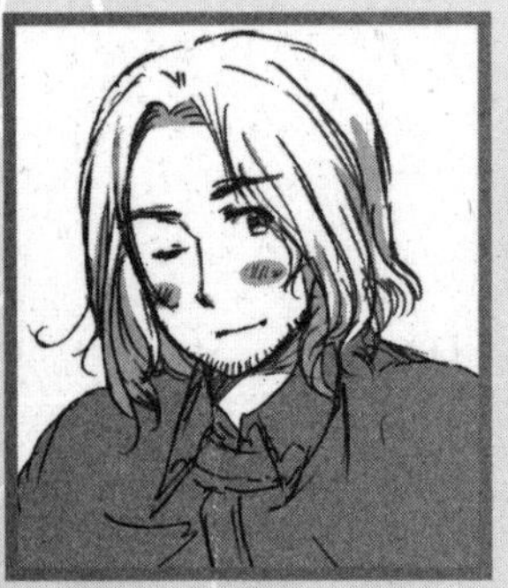

France

[Official Name] République française
[Capital] Paris
[Official Language] French
[Birthday] July 14
[National Flower] Iris

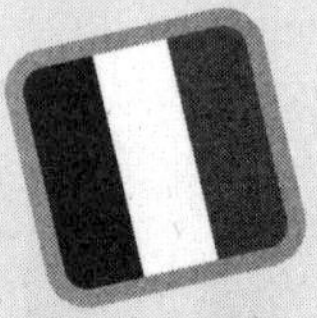

A pretentious and romantic man who does everything at his own pace. He is quick to remind everyone that French is the language of love. Although he claims to be a gourmand, some of the food he eats is more disgusting than sophisticated. An advocate of art and culture, France loves anything or anyone beautiful. This love for beauty does not discriminate between gender, race, age or even species. Despite his disagreements with England, France believes he would be quite tolerable if he could learn to shut his mouth. On a side note, he is so self-centered that he refuses to learn English himself.

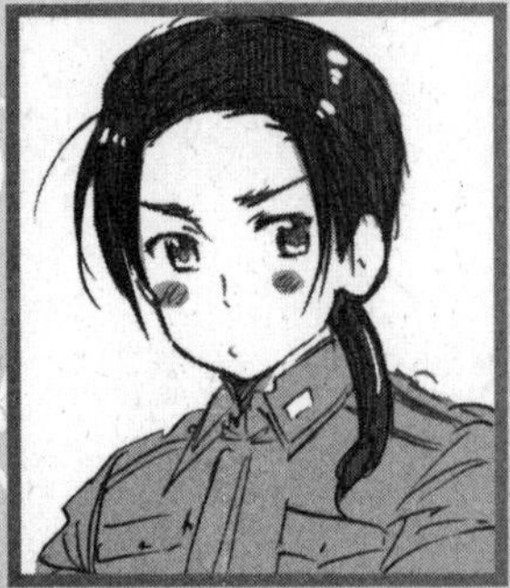

China

[Official Name] People's Republic of China
[Capital] Beijing
[Official Language] Mandarin
[Birthday] Unknown
[National Flower] Peony

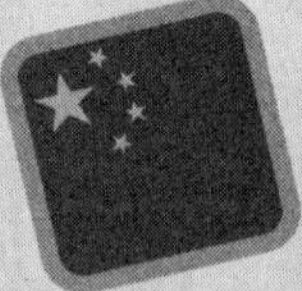

Despite his appearance, China is a very old man, perhaps even immortal. He tries to act as an older brother to the others but is never treated as one. China is good at cooking and martial arts. However, due to his old age, he's not quite as strong as he used to be. China owns villas in almost every major city in the world (but abandoned the ones in Korea) making cheap Chinese food available to everyone. He is very good at drawing human portraits, but when he draws animal mascots, they tend to look suspiciously familiar.

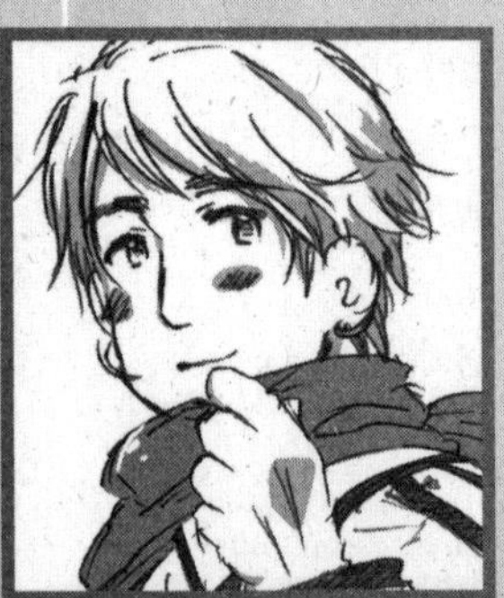

Russia

[Official Name] Rossiyskaya Federatsiya
[Capital] Moscow
[Official Language] Russian
[Birthday] December 30
[National Flower] Sunflower

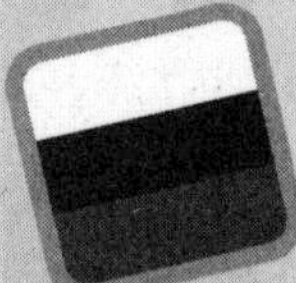

A massive northern nation, Russia is both naïve and childishly cruel. Despite his seemingly easygoing disposition, he is quite intimidating. His hobbies include drinking vodka, yanking water pipes out of walls and eating sweets stuffed with bizarre ingredients. He has always dreamed of living in a warm place, surrounded by sunflowers, but it seems unlikely that this dream will ever be fulfilled.

HETALIA AND HIS MERRY FRIENDS

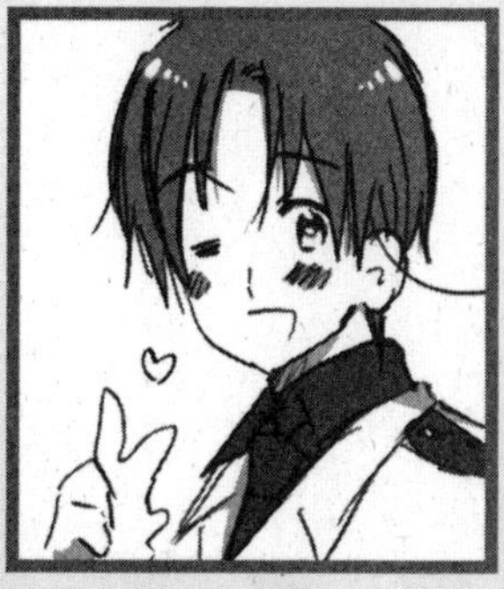

North Italy (Veneziano)

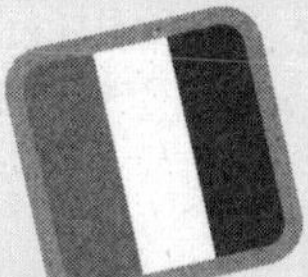

[Official Name] Repubblica Italiana
[Capital] Rome
[Official Language] Italian
[Birthday] March 17th, 1861 (Italy unified)
[National Flower] Daisy

Throughout this series, Italy is sometimes called Veneziano to distinguish him from his older brother Romano. Italy is a cheerful crybaby, with a love for girls and pasta. Inheriting his grandfather Rome's artistic talent, he loves to draw, sing and design clothes. Although Italy always relies on Germany, he never listens to his orders. To make matters worse for Germany, Italy also has a tendency to remodel German cars. The wild call of "veh" that escapes his mouth is an unexplained physiological phenomenon.

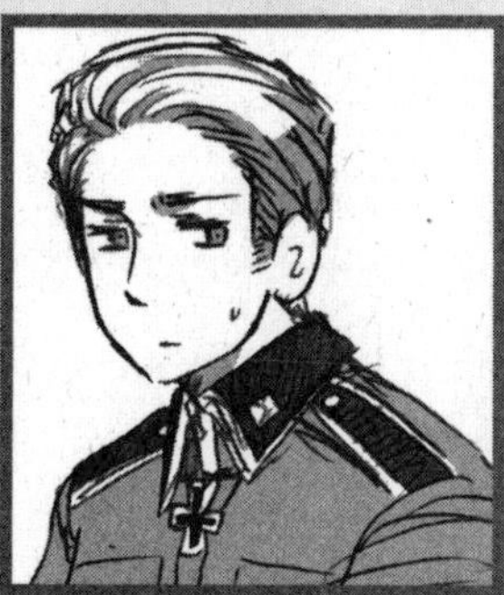

Germany

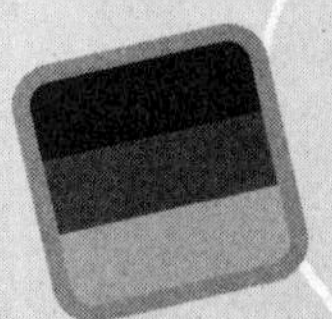

[Official Name] Bundesrepublik Deutschland
[Capital] Berlin
[Official Language] German
[Birthday] Unknown
[National Flower] Blue Cornflower

A serious man who has lived a life of hardship. His hobbies include reading, making sweets and walking his dogs. He relies heavily on manuals and rules and can be quite inflexible as a result. A notorious clean freak, he's obsessed with recycling. All three of his dogs are as manly as he is. Although he tends to complain about Italy, he always takes good care of him.

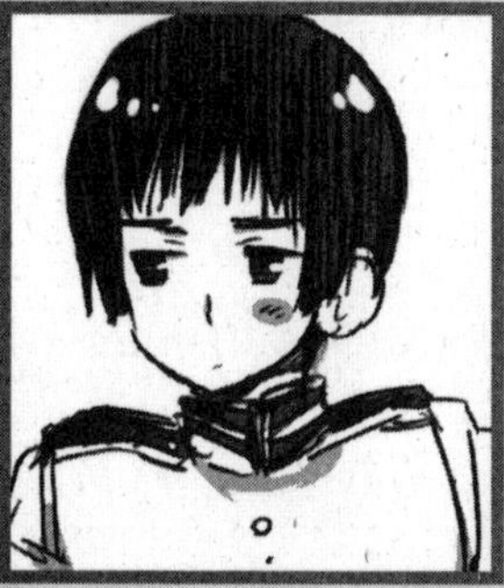

Japan

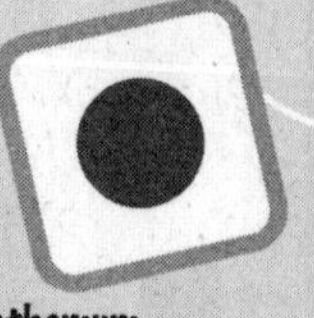

[Official Name] Nihon-koku
[Capital] Tokyo
[Official Language] Japanese
[Birthday] February 11
[National Flower] Cherry Blossoms, Chrysanthemum

A bushido nation in the East, Japan is soft-spoken, serious and slightly prudish. Thanks to his quiet nature, he is often bullied by other nations. Talented in technology and the arts, he loves to watch the changing of seasons. Secluded from the rest of the world for years, Japan has developed a very unique culture and personality. Anything Japan thinks of as "normal" is probably bizarre to everyone else.

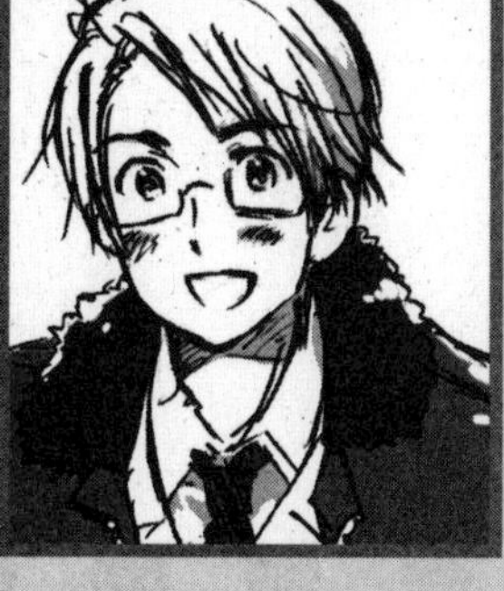

America

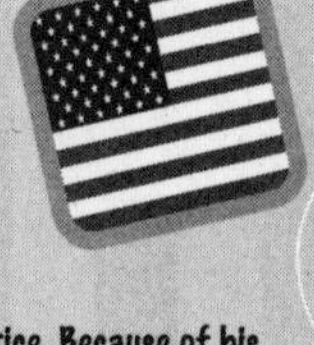

[Official Name] United States of America
[Capital] Washington D.C.
[Official Language] English
[Birthday] July 4, 1776
[National Flower] Rose

America is youthful, energetic and obsessed with justice. Because of his impulsive nature, the only people who can tolerate him are England and Japan. Despite the fact that he is personal friends with space aliens, he is unable to see things like unicorns and fairies. America's hobbies include archeology, sketching and making movies. Since he inherited his sense of taste from England, he tends to enjoy strangely-colored snacks. Lately, America has been obsessed with strange diets and weight-loss machines.

HETALIA2 WORLD MAP

Hetalia and his Merry Friends 16

≪ Single Columns & Single Manga ≫

Greek Mythology is Totally Hardcore 41

Liechtenstein's Doting Brother Diaries 1 43

Liechtenstein's Doting Brother Diaries 2 51

Japan-kun and America-kun 1 53

Japan-kun and America-kun 2 61

Japan-kun and America-kun 3 77

Things that were Popular Back in the day 83

Japan-kun and America-kun 4 85

Japan-kun and America-kun 5 91

Japan-kun and America-kun 6 95

Japan-kun and America-kun 7 103

Japan-kun and America-kun 8 115

Japan-kun and America-kun 9 121

America's Convenience Stores 127

Japan-kun and America-kun 10 129

Specialty = Cute Occupation = Cute 134

12

Hetalia 2

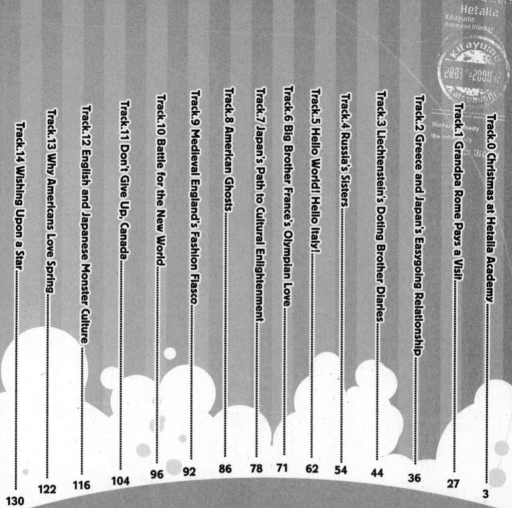

Axis Powers
Hetalia
Kitayume
Himaruya Hidekaz

Kitayume
2003 -2008 12

matsumen

History Comedy
We introduce...
Check it!!

Track.14 Wishing Upon a Star 130

Track.13 Why Americans Love Spring 122

Track.12 English and Japanese Monster Culture 116

Track.11 Don't Give Up, Canada 104

Track.10 Battle for the New World 96

Track.9 Medieval England's Fashion Fiasco 92

Track.8 American Ghosts 86

Track.7 Japan's Path to Cultural Enlightenment 78

Track.6 Big Brother France's Olympian Love 71

Track.5 Hello World! Hello Italy! 62

Track.4 Russia's Sisters 54

Track.3 Liechtenstein's Doting Brother Diaries 44

Track.2 Greece and Japan's Easygoing Relationship ... 36

Track.1 Grandpa Rome Pays a Visit 27

Track.0 Christmas at Hetalia Academy 3

C O N T E N T S

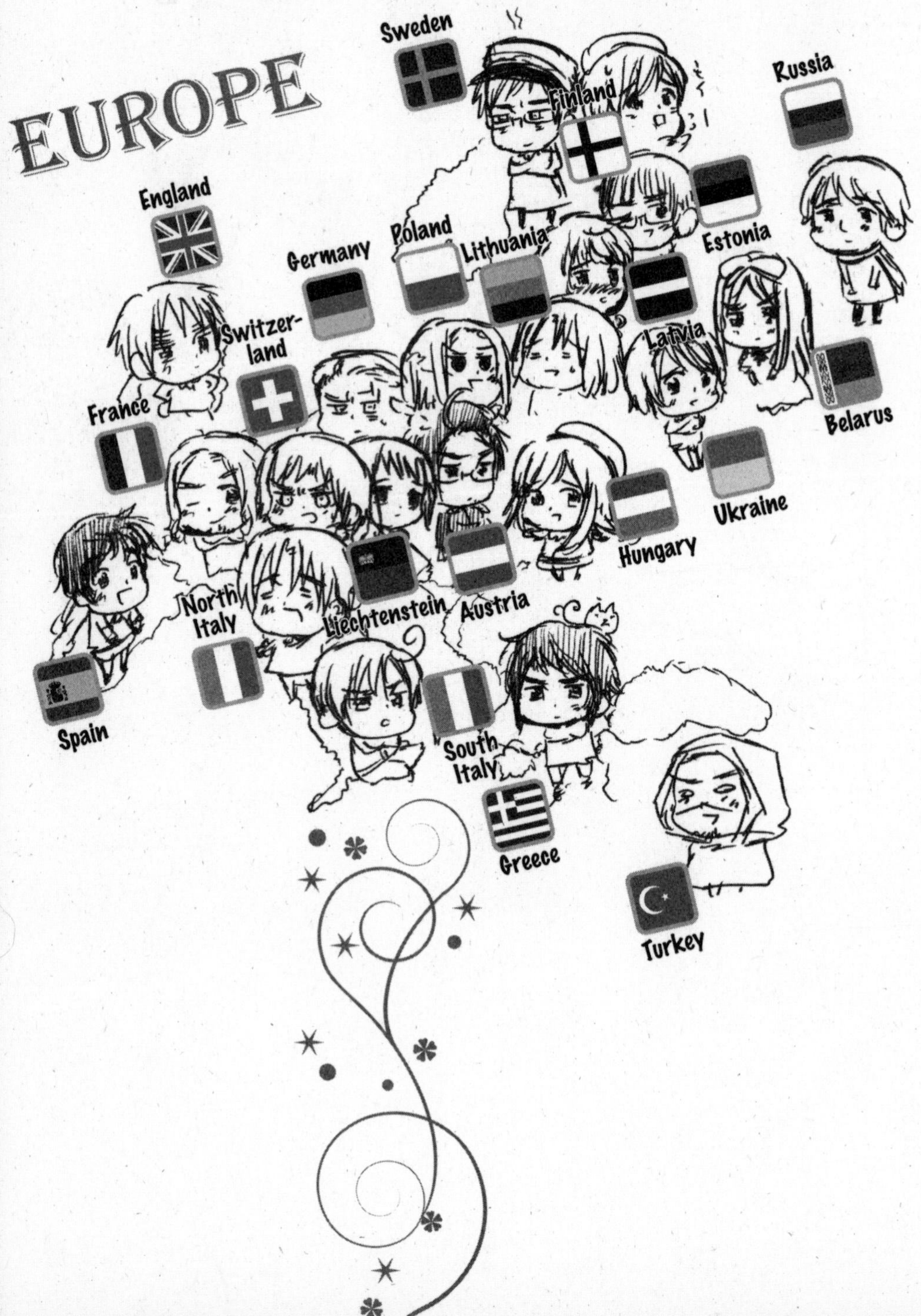
EUROPE
Sweden
Finland
Russia
England
Estonia
Poland
Lithuania
Germany
Switzer-
land
Latvia
France
Belarus
Ukraine
Hungary
North
Italy
Liechtenstein
Austria
Spain
South
Italy
Greece
Turkey

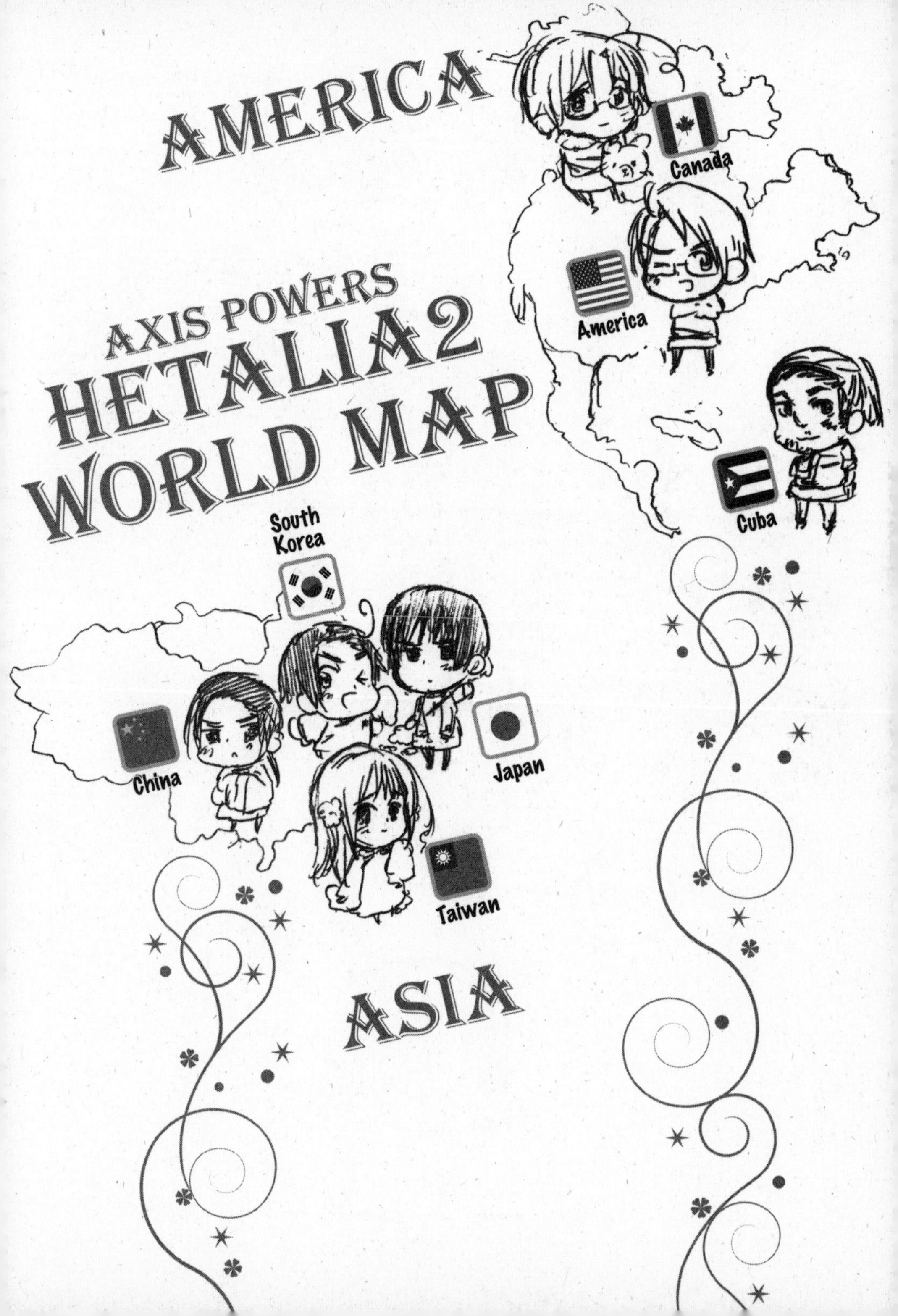
AMERICA
AXIS POWERS
HETALIA 2
WORLD MAP
Canada
America
Cuba
South Korea
China
Japan
Taiwan
ASIA

AXIS POWERS
HETALIA 2

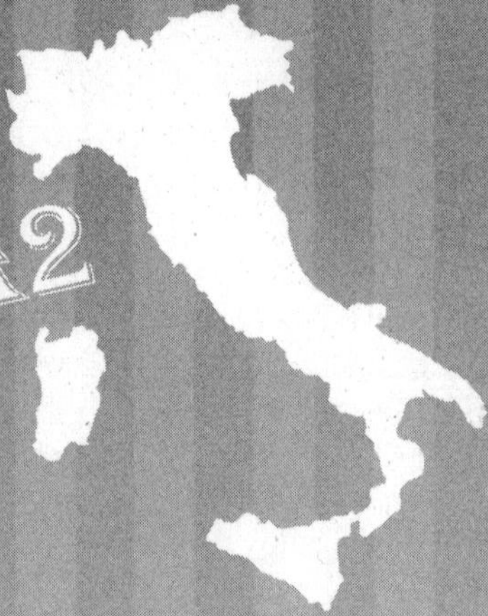

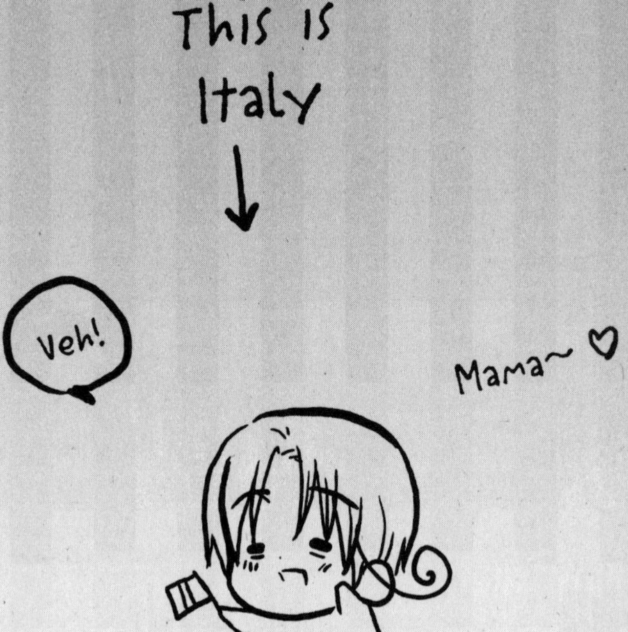
This is Italy
Veh!
Mama~ ♡

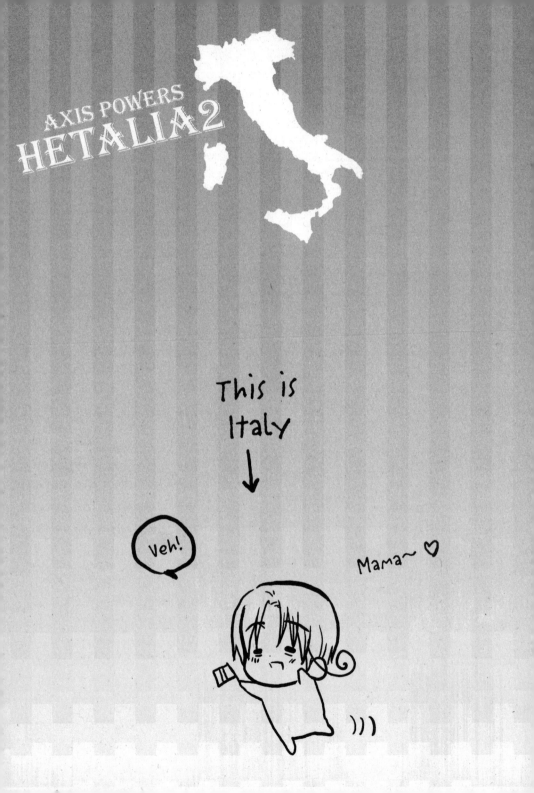

Hetalia Axis Powers 02
Created by Hidekaz Himaruya

Translation - Monica Seya Chin
English Adaptation - Clint Bickham
Script Editor - Daniella Orihuela-Gruber
Copy Editor - Jan Suzukawa & Jill Bentley
Retouch and Lettering - Star Print Brokers
Layout and Production Artist - Michael Paolilli & Rui Kyo
Graphic Designer - Louis Csontos

Editor - Cindy Suzuki
Print Production Manager - Lucas Rivera
Managing Editor - Vy Nguyen
Senior Designer - Louis Csontos
Art Director - Al-Insan Lashley
Director of Sales and Manufacturing - Allyson De Simone
Associate Publisher - Marco F. Pavia
President and C.O.O. - John Parker
C.E.O. and Chief Creative Officer - Stu Levy

A **TOKYOPOP** Manga

TOKYOPOP and 🐾 are trademarks or registered trademarks of TOKYOPOP Inc.

TOKYOPOP Inc.
5900 Wilshire Blvd. Suite 2000
Los Angeles, CA 90036

E-mail: info@TOKYOPOP.com
Come visit us online at www.TOKYOPOP.com

ISBN: 978-1-4278-1887-4

First TOKYOPOP printing: January 2011
10 9 8 7 6 5 4 3 2 1
Printed in the USA

HETALIA
Axis Powers

Created by
HIDEKAZ HIMARUYA

HAMBURG // LONDON // LOS ANGELES // TOKYO

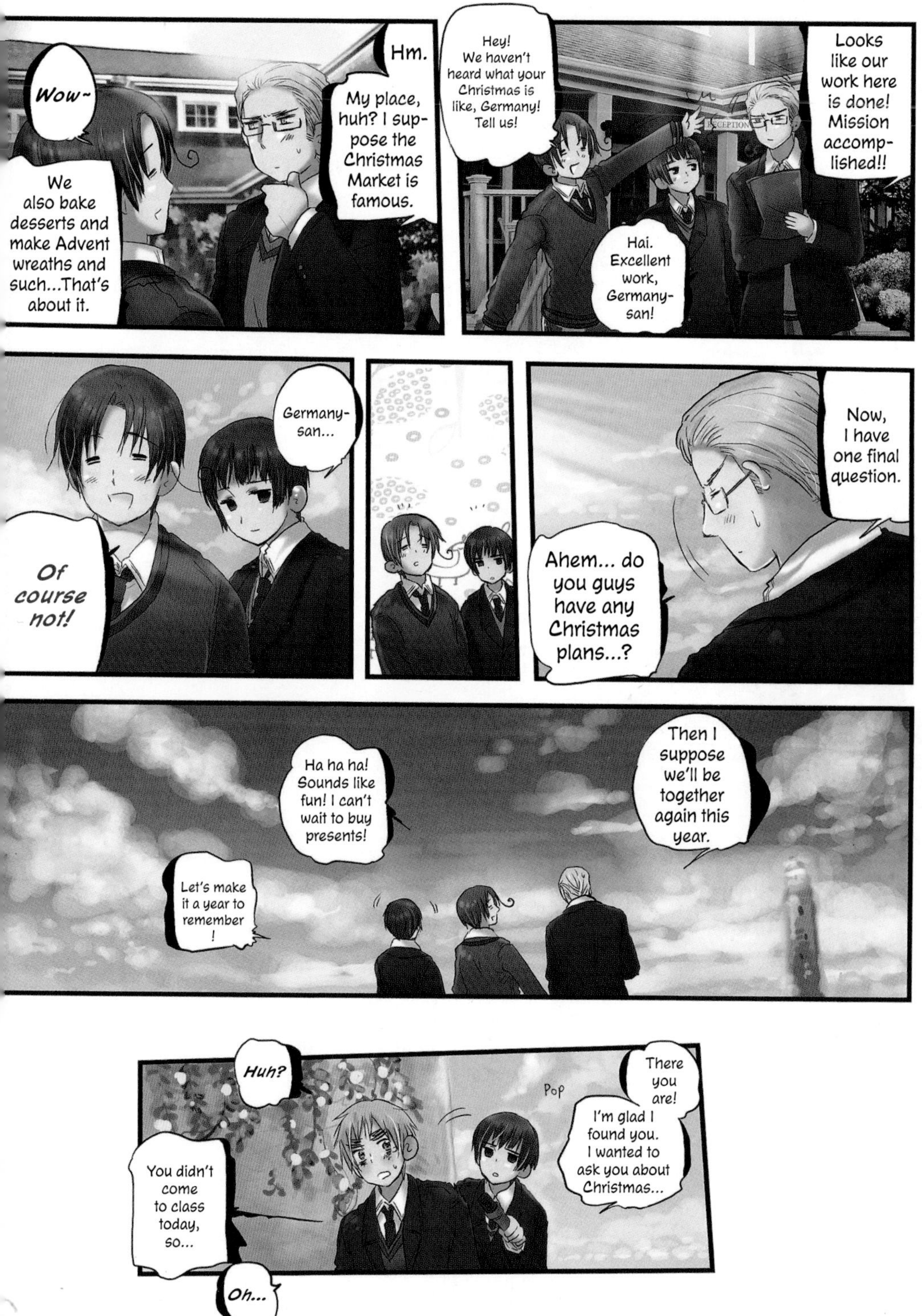
Looks like our work here is done! Mission accomplished!!
Hey! We haven't heard what your Christmas is like, Germany! Tell us!
Hai. Excellent work, Germany-san!
Hm.
My place, huh? I suppose the Christmas Market is famous.
Wow~
We also bake desserts and make Advent wreaths and such...That's about it.
Now, I have one final question.
Ahem... do you guys have any Christmas plans...?
Germany-san...
Of course not!
Then I suppose we'll be together again this year.
Ha ha ha! Sounds like fun! I can't wait to buy presents!
Let's make it a year to remember!
There you are!
Pop
I'm glad I found you. I wanted to ask you about Christmas...
Huh?
You didn't come to class today, so...
Oh...

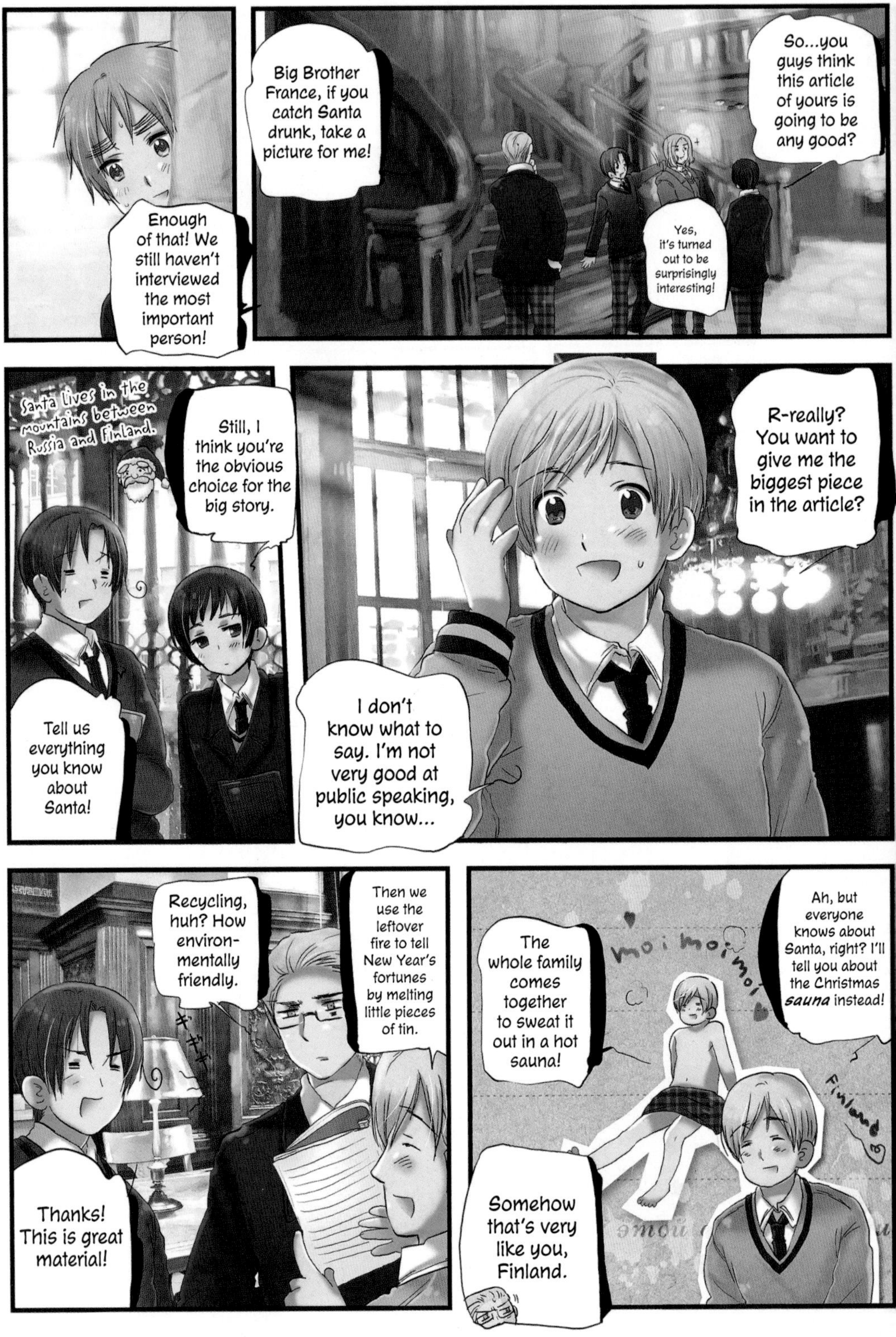
So...you guys think this article of yours is going to be any good?
Big Brother France, if you catch Santa drunk, take a picture for me!
Yes, it's turned out to be surprisingly interesting!
Enough of that! We still haven't interviewed the most important person!
R-really? You want to give me the biggest piece in the article?
I don't know what to say. I'm not very good at public speaking, you know...
Still, I think you're the obvious choice for the big story.
Santa lives in the mountains between Russia and Finland.
Tell us everything you know about Santa!
Ah, but everyone knows about Santa, right? I'll tell you about the Christmas *sauna* instead!
The whole family comes together to sweat it out in a hot sauna!
moi moi moi
Finland
Somehow that's very like you, Finland.
Then we use the leftover fire to tell New Year's fortunes by melting little pieces of tin.
Recycling, huh? How environmentally friendly.
Thanks! This is great material!

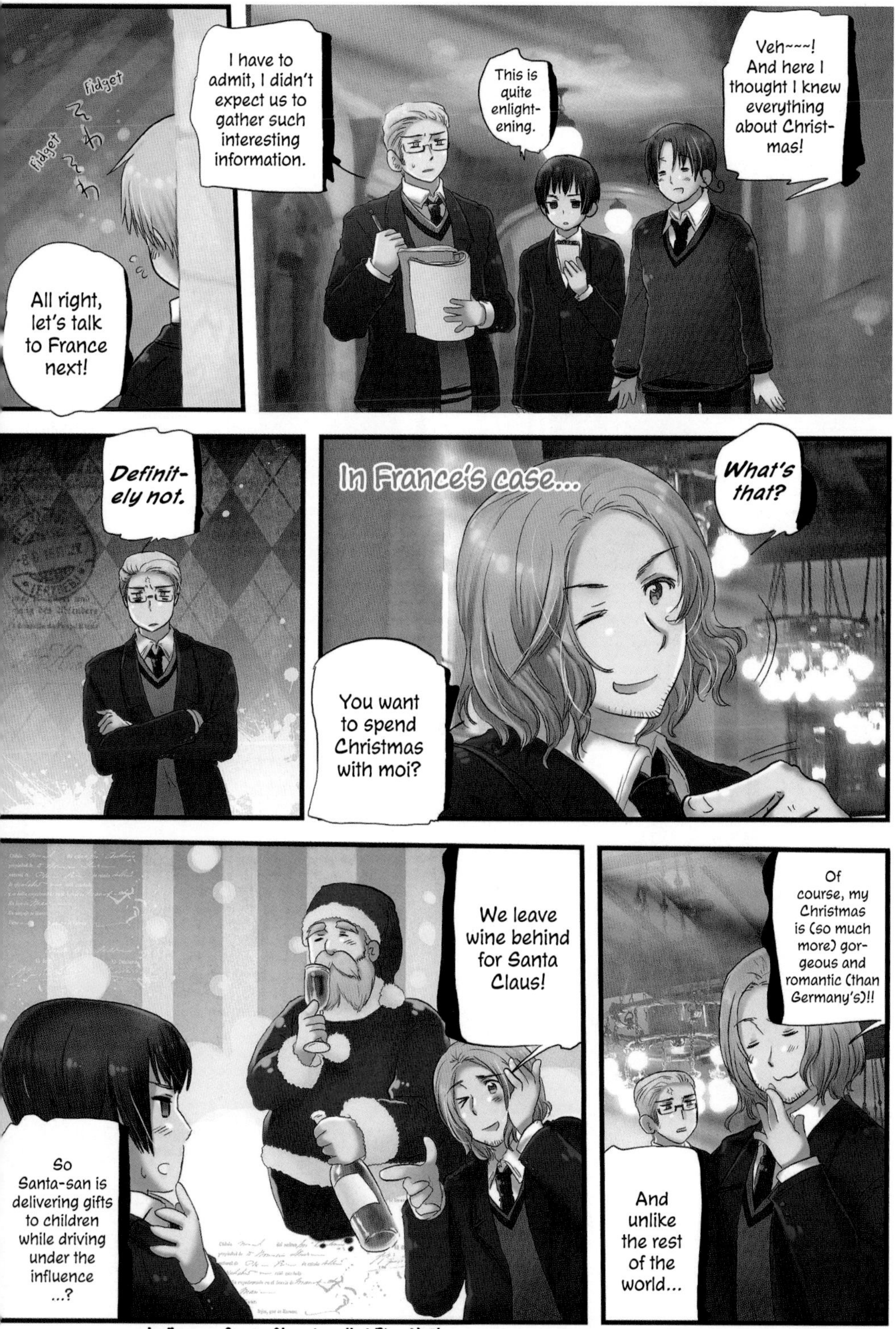
Veh~~~! And here I thought I knew everything about Christmas!
This is quite enlight-ening.
I have to admit, I didn't expect us to gather such interesting information.
fidget fidget
All right, let's talk to France next!
What's that?
In France's case...
You want to spend Christmas with moi?
Definit-ely not.
Of course, my Christmas is (so much more) gor-geous and romantic (than Germany's)!!
And unlike the rest of the world...
We leave wine behind for Santa Claus!
So Santa-san is delivering gifts to children while driving under the influence ...?

In France, Santa Claus is called Père Noël.

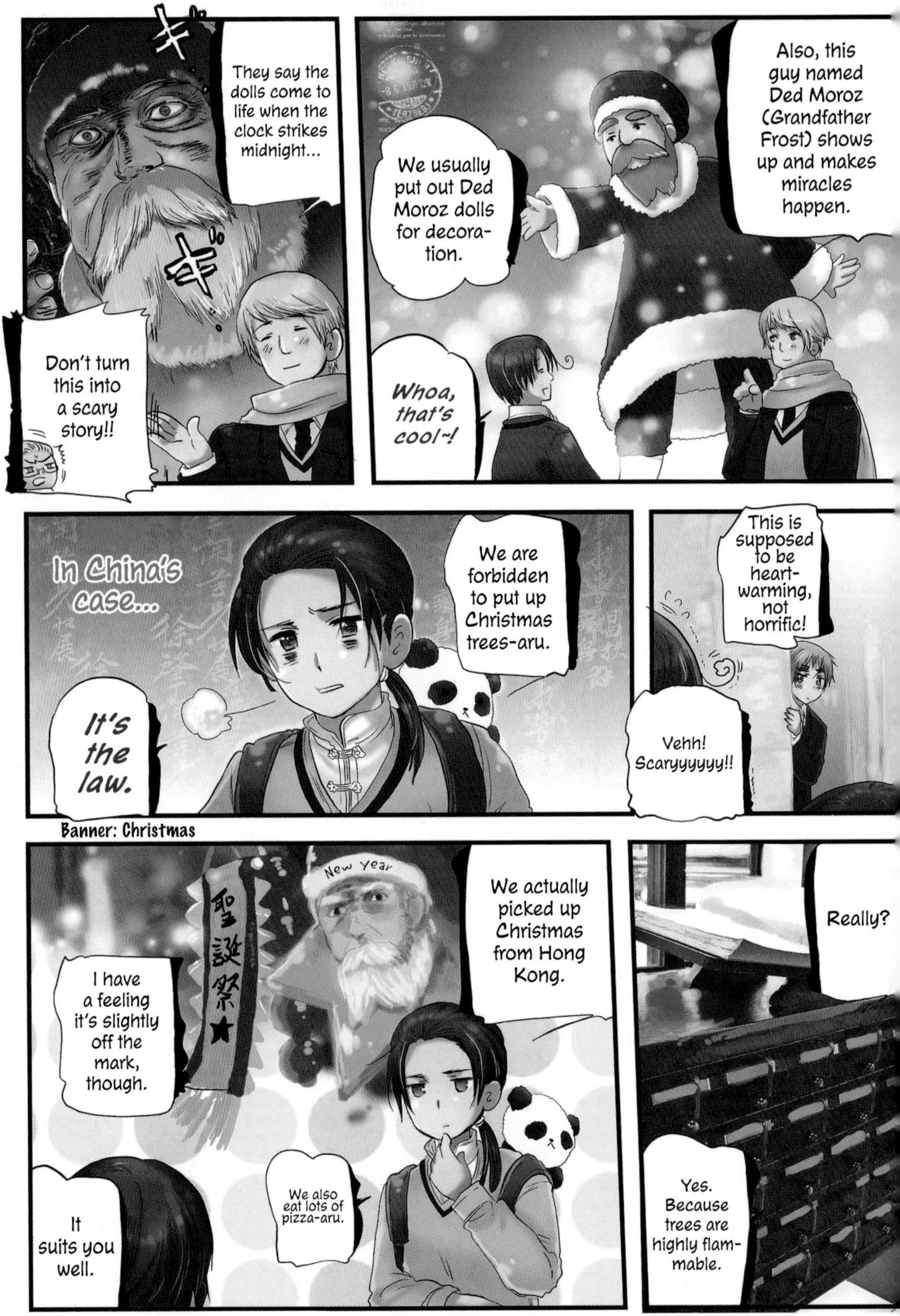
Also, this guy named Ded Moroz (Grandfather Frost) shows up and makes miracles happen.
We usually put out Ded Moroz dolls for decoration.
Whoa, that's cool~!
They say the dolls come to life when the clock strikes midnight...
Don't turn this into a scary story!!
This is supposed to be heart-warming, not horrific!
Vehh! Scaryyyyyy!!
In China's case...
We are forbidden to put up Christmas trees-aru.
It's the law.
Banner: Christmas
Really?
Yes. Because trees are highly flammable.
We actually picked up Christmas from Hong Kong.
New Year
聖誕祭★
I have a feeling it's slightly off the mark, though.
We also eat lots of pizza-aru.
It suits you well.

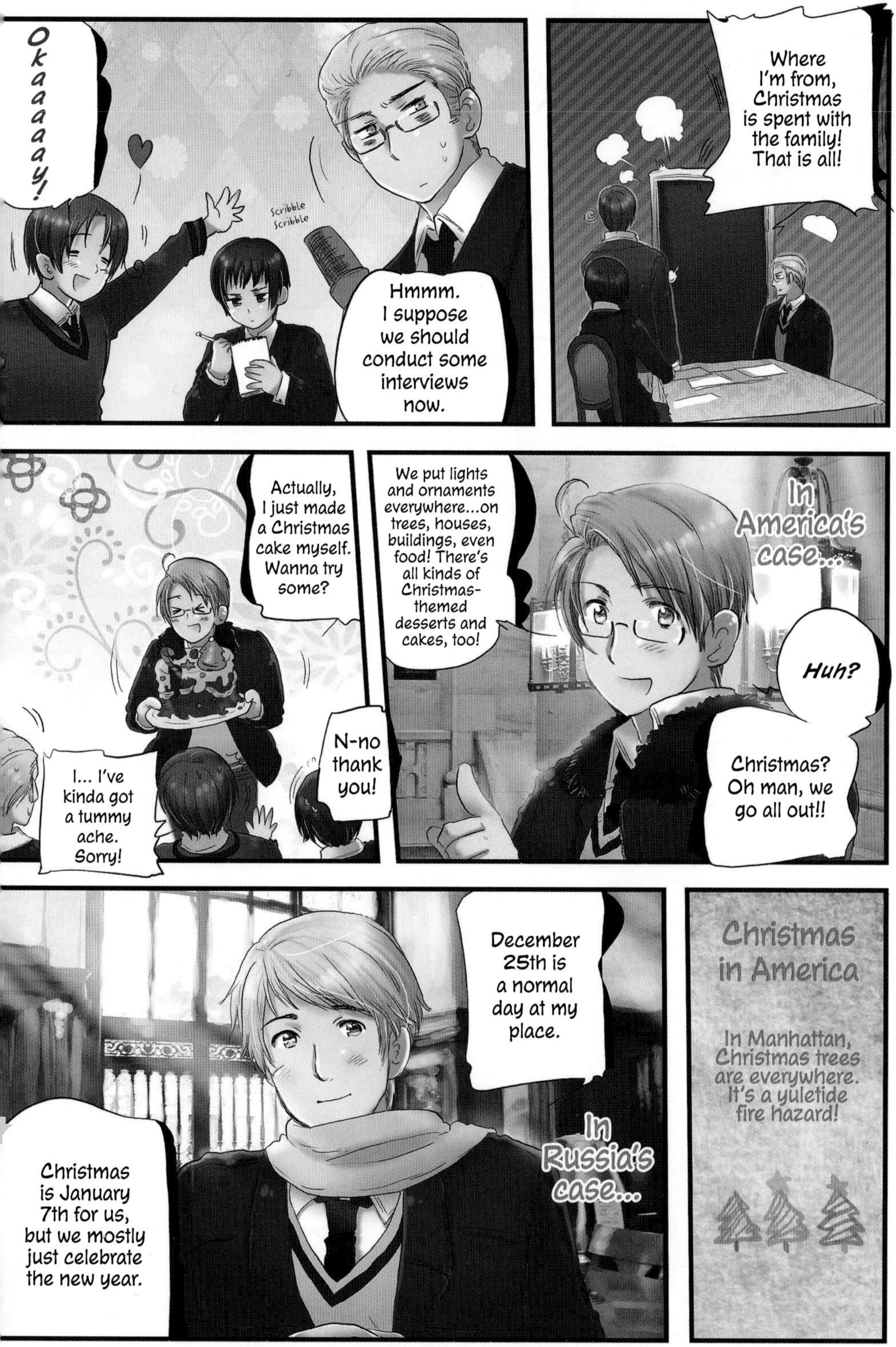
Where I'm from, Christmas is spent with the family! That is all!
Hmmm. I suppose we should conduct some interviews now.
Scribble Scribble
Okaaaaaay!
In America's case...
Huh?
Christmas? Oh man, we go all out!!
We put lights and ornaments everywhere...on trees, houses, buildings, even food! There's all kinds of Christmas-themed desserts and cakes, too!
Actually, I just made a Christmas cake myself. Wanna try some?
N-no thank you!
I... I've kinda got a tummy ache. Sorry!
Christmas in America
In Manhattan, Christmas trees are everywhere. It's a yuletide fire hazard!
In Russia's case...
December 25th is a normal day at my place.
Christmas is January 7th for us, but we mostly just celebrate the new year.

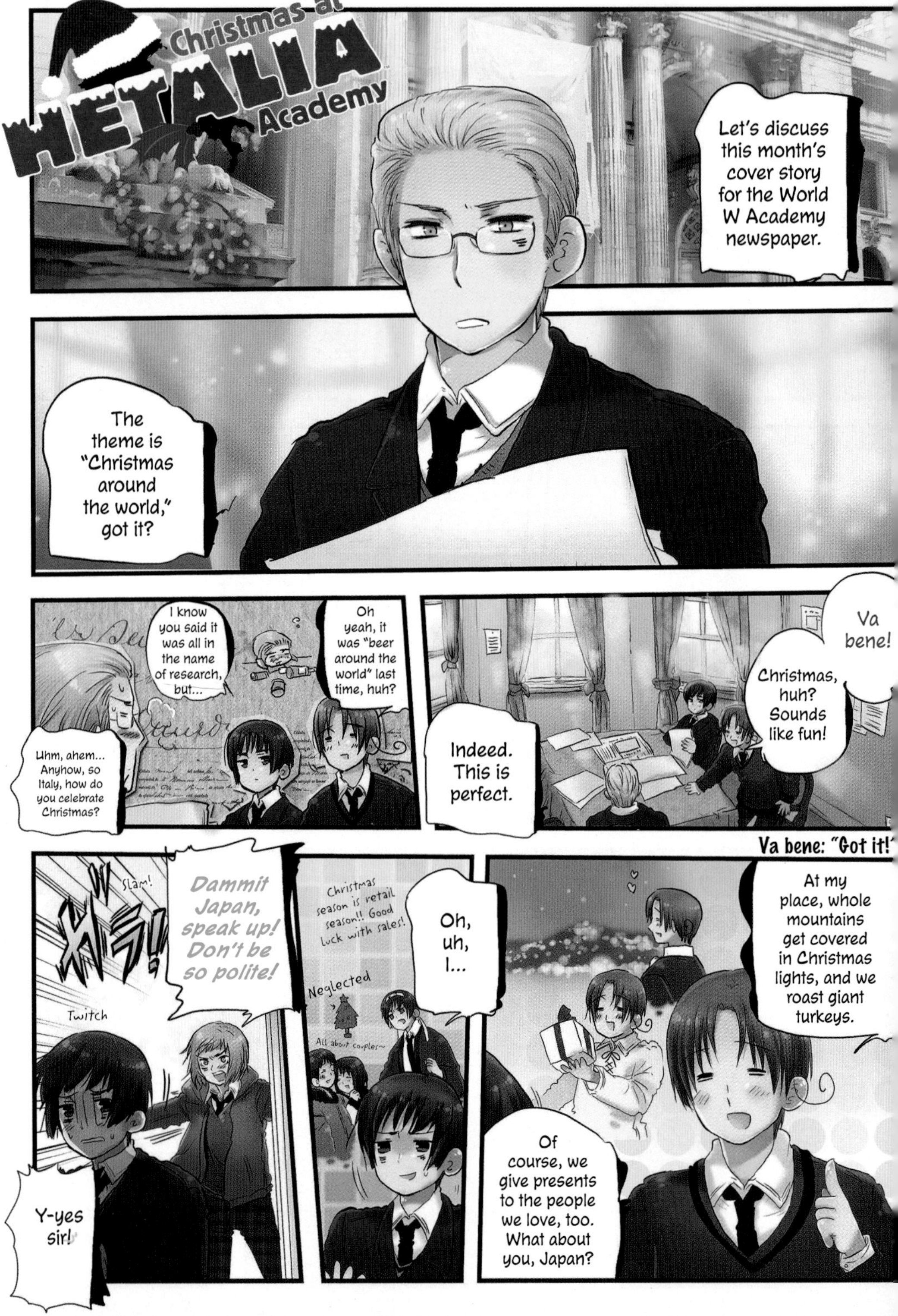
Christmas at
HETALIA
Academy
Let's discuss this month's cover story for the World W Academy newspaper.
The theme is "Christmas around the world," got it?
Va bene!
Christmas, huh? Sounds like fun!
Indeed. This is perfect.
Oh yeah, it was "beer around the world" last time, huh?
I know you said it was all in the name of research, but...
Uhm, ahem... Anyhow, so Italy, how do you celebrate Christmas?
Va bene: "Got it!"
At my place, whole mountains get covered in Christmas lights, and we roast giant turkeys.
Of course, we give presents to the people we love, too. What about you, Japan?
Oh, uh, I...
Christmas season is retail season!! Good luck with sales!
Neglected
All about couples~
Dammit Japan, speak up! Don't be so polite!
Slam!
Twitch
Y-yes sir!

In this world...

It's **heaven** when:

The French are chefs
The British are police
The Germans are engineers
The Swiss are bankers
And the Italians are lovers

It's **hell** when:

The English are chefs
The Germans are police
The French are engineers
The Swiss are lovers
And the Italians are bankers

HETALIA
Axis Powers

AUTHOR
HIDEKAZ HIMARUYA

Axis Powers
Hetalia
Kitayume
Himaruya Hidekaz

Kitayume
2003 - 2009
Himaruya

History Comedy
We Joke You
J for World

AXIS POWERS
HETALIA 2

This is a work of fiction. Any similarity or likeness to any people, historical events or countries in the world is purely coincidental...seriously!